History of Pedlars in

FOR ISABELLE, CAMILLE AND CAROLINE

History of Pedlars in Europe

Laurence Fontaine

Translated by Vicki Whittaker

1996
Duke University Press, Durham

First published 1996.

Published with the assistance of the French Ministry of Foreign Affairs

Published in the United States by
Duke University Press
Durham, North Carolina
and in Great Britain by
Polity Press
Cambridge, UK

ISBN 0–8223–1786–9
ISBN 0–8223–1794–X

Library of Congress Cataloging-in-Publication Data

Fontaine, Laurence.
    [Histoire du colporteur en Europe. English]
    History of pedlars in Europe/Laurence Fontaine; translated by
Vicki Whittaker.
        p. cm.
    Translation of: Histoire du colporteur en Europe.
    Includes bibliographical references and index.
    ISBN 0–8223–1786–9 (cloth : alk. paper). — ISBN 0–8223–1794–X
(pbk. : alk. paper)
    1. Peddlers and peddling—Europe—History. I. Title.
HF5459.E85F66   1996
381'.1—dc20   95–45528
                                                            CIP

Typeset in 10 on 11.5 pt. Sabon
by Graphicraft Typesetters Ltd., Hong Kong
Printed in Great Britain by TJ Press Ltd., Padstow, Cornwall

This book is printed on acid-free paper.

Contents

Introduction

In modern times, the ways in which the educated classes have defined the pedlar, as well as the names by which he is popularly known, express the difficulty of fitting the occupation of pedlar into straight-forward categories and the ambiguity with which he is perceived by the settled population. In France, the word was first used to mean one who traversed the town selling pictures and loose printed sheets. Secondly, by some linguistic twist, it was applied to the itinerant rural tradesman who had been known up until then as *petit mercier* (petty trader), *porte-balle* (packman), *marcelot* or *mercelot* (wandering trader). The first meaning refers to a recognized trade – albeit an unimportant one – whereas the second meaning of the word is nothing more than another way of saying 'tramp' or 'trickster'.[1] Drawing a parallel with England, the *Encyclopédie* asserts that 'historically, they were tricksters who wandered from town to town, buying and selling copper and pewter crockery and other similar merchandise which should normally only be sold in the open marketplace.... In France, such people are called *porte-balle* (packman), *coureurs* (itinerants), *mercelots* (wandering traders) or *brocanteurs* (second-hand dealers).'[2]

It was only from the second half of the eighteenth century that rural peddling acquired the status of a trade; in the 1762 *Dictionnaire de l'Académie* it appeared as *mercier* rather than just *petit mercier*. None the less the pedlar remained a disturbing figure who was on the fringes of society and someone to be guarded against. The encyclopedias all give an account of the repressive legislation levelled against the pedlars, up to and including Franklin who, in his *Dictionaire historique des Arts, métiers et professions exercées dans Paris depuis le XVIIIe siècle*, at the end of the nineteenth century, adopts the same classifications and the same reservations when he states that 'the guilds always viewed them suspiciously', worried that 'they sought, in this manner, to sell off defective merchandise of suspicious origin'.[3]

In England, the word developed in the opposite direction. 'Chapman' (cheapman) was originally a generic term for anyone who bought and sold merchandise (dealers). Often the term was modified by the addition of the adjective 'petty' which denoted the beginnings of a hierarchy between the well-off merchants of Manchester and Yorkshire, who rode all over the country to deliver their merchandise to shopkeepers, and the lowliest pedlars who, pack on back, travelled cross-country to far-flung villages. In the seventeenth century and the first half of the eighteenth century the 'petty chapmen' were described as those who 'buy up commodities of those that sell by wholesale and sell them off dearer by retail, and parcel them out'. As shops became established in the towns and villages, 'chapman' came to mean little more than a man who took his merchandise from fair to fair and from door to door – a synonym for pedlar or hawker.[4] This term had an equally pejorative connotation: 'Hawking... has its derivation from the spying, thievish habits of the bird and man. They also acquired a reputation for ruffianism and brigandage.'[5]

In Spain the pedlar was known as *Gabacho*, the coarse man from the mountains of the North.[6] In Italy he was the *merciajuolo* or *merciajo*[7] and in the Ticino region he is variously recorded in legal records as *mercante, girovagho, trafficante, pertegante, cromero*.[8] In Germany, each town had its own name for him; as well as the more general term of *Hauserier*, he was also known by the fashion in which he plied his trade – hence, *Gänger*, he who walks; *Ausrufer*, he who shouts in the street; and *Hockerer*, he who squats down. In the Münster region, there are references to the pedlar who carried his pack on his back – *Kiepenkerle*. Some pedlars were associated with small luxuries, with the unnecessary items that they sold, and were thus called *Tändler*; or they were known quite simply as charlatans, as *Gaukler*.[9]

Right up to the end of the nineteenth century the pedlar was depicted in literature as a rogue, or trickster, half merchant and half thief. He was someone who belonged to another world, who sold both the stuff of everyday life and the stuff of dreams. He came from far away, possessed some secret knowledge and his misdeeds were compensated for by his clever trickery. Shakespeare describes the English version thus: 'My traffic is sheets... My father named me Autolycus; who being, as I am, littered under Mercury, was likewise a snapper-up of unconsidered trifles... and my revenue is the silly cheat.'[10] The role of Autolycus is primarily that of a rogue and not of a pedlar.

In France, in *La Vie généreuse des mercelots gueux et bohémiens*, published in Lyon in 1596, the pedlar was characterized, in all his disturbing difference, in three ways: he used a secret language to conceal his practices, which the book reveals to a certain extent; he was a dishonest trader – 'In other words we would have tricked the gentlemen, young men and women, village women and peasants by giving them our merchandise'; and he was a thief through and through – the oath that had to be sworn to gain entry to their ranks was 'j'attrime au passeligourt'; in other words, 'I will steal at any opportunity'.[11]

Spanish Golden Age literature is no exception when it comes to the contempt that pedlars inspired wherever they went. Francisco de Quevedo described them as ants, as leeches and as lice, whose sense of profit and saving was offensive to any man of honour, and whenever such a man encountered a pedlar, the tale never had a happy ending.[12]

'Three Frenchmen were crossing the Biscay mountains into Spain. One of them had around his neck a scissor and knife-sharpener's pannier, the second had two bundles – one of bellows and one of mouse-traps – and the third a tray of combs and hairpins. At the steepest part of the climb they met a Spaniard who was travelling to France on foot, his cloak over his shoulder. All four sat down to rest in the shade of a copse and fell into conversation. . . . The Spaniard expressed some astonishment at seeing them go to such pains to bring their wares from France and, in a strange land, cross such harsh and mountainous terrain where they ran the risk of falling into the hands of bandits. The knife-grinder, who spoke the least mongrel version of Castilian, answered: "I've made three trips to Spain, with this pannier and this simple mill and I've squandered a fortune there in pistoles or what you call doubloons. . . . You ought to see knife-grinders as a terrestrial fleet come to sharpen and hone your gold ingots instead of your blades . . .".' This last remark got him thrown to the bottom of the ravine.[13]

This theme is taken up again and again. Gracián compared the be-haviour of the French towards the Spanish to that of the conquistadors towards the Indians, whom they tricked with the same cheap rubbish. 'And what better Indies for France than Spain herself? (And all that) without the cost of maintaining a fleet, without firing any bullets, with-out shedding a single drop of blood, without sinking any mines, with-out boring into any abysses, without depopulating France's kingdoms, without crossing the sea. . . . The Spanish are your Red Indians, freer even, because with their fleets they can bring home to you refined and beaten silver, whilst they find themselves left with ingots of mixed alloys – in other words, fleeced.'[14] In a parallel development, the pedlar be-came a comic figure, whose outfit was donned to disguise one's own identity,[15] who provided farce and satire with more than enough fodder for theatrical interludes: characters were called Gabacho, Pierre, Juan Francés, Gascón – references to the mountains, and to France from whence they came.[16]

In the nineteenth century, when the profession was dying out, the literary representation of the pedlar underwent a radical transforma-tion. In Britain, in the eyes of the educated Victorians, he ceased to play his traditionally ambiguous and disturbing role and became instead a national hero, embodying the morality of the conservative countryside as opposed to the corruption of the city.[17] In France, religious literature used him in two diametrically opposed fashions; he was either a figure of Evil, an embodiment of temptations to be repudiated, or, because of his freedom, humility and wisdom, he represented the Christ figure.[18]

The historiography of peddling has found itself dependent on these rough sketches, largely written from an urban perspective, and on the sources which we have just examined. What Fernand Braudel wrote about the mountain could equally well be applied to the pedlar: 'It has no history. . . . As soon as one leaves the mountain and its historical obscurity, one reaches the plains and the cities and the domain of classified archives. Whether this is his first time there or whether he is a second offender, the mountain dweller will always find someone down below who will provide particulars identifying him, a rather amused thumb-nail sketch.'[19] In fact, the double constraint of the history of peddling lies therein: in the multitude of roles which the mountain dwellers and the pedlars have assumed in the eyes of the city dweller and in the written records which the city archives have kept on them. Until now, three types of sources set out to monitor the pedlars: government surveys which sought vainly to record their numbers; correspondence between towns and complaints from sedentary merchants anxious to get rid of them; and, finally, the records of the courts or of the police who occasionally caught one in their net.

To overcome the purely urban viewpoint, one must leave the town behind, discard the concept of itinerancy and concentrate instead upon establishing settled roots, however tenuous – after all, these men-from-nowhere had to be born somewhere. My aim was to rediscover the origins of these men who were marginalized by the settled population, in order to understand the paths which led to exclusion and marginalization. And, behind these humble trades, from the north to the south of Europe, the mountains loomed large. My gamble lay in believing that these 'factories of men', so dear to Fernand Braudel, had a history of their own to be discovered, and that only by studying the villages from which the migrants originally came would we be able to understand why, for several centuries, these villages had produced men whom they subsequently sent forth into the countryside bearing goods from the city. I therefore went back to the sources of merchant migration, to the mountain villages, in order to link individual departures to the social and human framework to which they belonged. The history of peddling then revealed itself as being twofold; indivisible from that of the homeland, of the mountain, and of the marginalized regions from which it developed.

Hence the structure of this book which takes as its starting point the increasing importance and growing population of the mountain regions and then describes the initial model for peddling (chapter 1); traces the different ways in which it developed during the eighteenth century (chapters 2 and 3); describes its flexible typology (chapter 4); returns to the village to understand the unique qualities of a society constructed around merchant migration and chains of credit which forged links between men beyond the confines of their everyday movements; and analyses how these chains were broken (chapters 5 and 6); out of which came a radically different peddling structure (chapter 7). Finally, through the movement of men and goods, the toing and froing between different places and cultures, the ambiguous encounters – anticipated, yet conflictual – between travelling salesmen, sedentary buyers and goods for sale, men created particular cultures and identities (chapter 8); and eventually changed the cultural practices of the communities they visited.

The limits of this overall schema ought to be pointed out from the outset. On the one hand, work done in this area on migratory movements is fragmentary: the organization of the peddling economy has never held historians' attention. On the other hand, that these men should take to the road was seen as being a breaking-away – as was, moreover, the migration from mountain villages as a whole. This was perceived as a system to regulate overpopulation – its bottle of oxygen – and meant a contraction of the community. Consequently, historians have written two juxtaposed accounts of the mountain villages: the noble story of those who stayed, and the other, more shameful story, of those who left. The perspective that I have adopted, which believes that this dichotomy cannot be taken as read but remains to be constructed, therefore comes up against a lack of research into the integral role of migration in the organization of village community life. In other words, in view of the current state of research, a comparative history of the movements of pedlars within Europe would be an impossible undertaking. Nevertheless it seemed time to breathe life into such a history by suggesting a model for the development of the profession, using the Dauphiné alps as a starting point and outlining a comparison with other sites. This allows us to question the specificities of the model proposed by considering developments which were out of step with one another; or departures which, depending on where the pedlars had gone and where they came from, reveal important discrepancies. In so doing, it is to be hoped that these initial comparisons will encourage others to attempt a genuinely comparative study of the communities of migrant merchants in Europe.

Such as it is, this book attempts to make sense of a phenomenon – hitherto studied in a fragmentary fashion – on a European scale and over a long period of time. It is a bold and hazardous venture. In seeking to discover the mechanisms and dynamics at work within peddling, my research has shown that the profession and the men who practised it did not at all correspond to the traditionally accepted picture of economic and social marginalization. But the problems raised and the methodologies brought into play go beyond questions of itinerant trade alone and engage with questions asked by economic, social and cultural historians.

Thus, the essential role played by the migration of merchants in European business until the mid-nineteenth century, as much in the development of sedentary business as in the widespread distribution of new products such as tobacco or books, is a part of the wider concerns of the history of the formation of consumer societies. The ritual exchanges surrounding the act of selling were also cultural encounters. Through their travels, the pedlars brought three cultural forces face to face: men from marginalized regions, they travelled into the countryside to circulate the newest articles from the town. How did they make use of the established cultures to commercial ends? How, through the goods for sale, did they have an effect on the changing morals and cultural practices of the families they met? And how, in return, did the activities involved in being a merchant have an effect upon the culture of those migrants who undertook them?

This study of a trade, based on migration and credit, reliant on a structure capable of exploiting all institutionalized forms of freedom and of operating on the fringes of the law, allows us to shed a certain light upon questions posed by the development of merchant capitalism and the role played by both credit and the State in commercial networks. It also allows us to break down the oversimplified dichotomies often used in the study of emigration and immigration, and to refine certain concepts such as mobility, identity and interdependence.

Finally, peddling provides a way into remote rural communities with poor soil, who established a unique social structure based on the extended family and bonds of custom and dependence, the model of which is still in existence in numerous sites today, primarily – but not exclusively – outside Europe.

This book is the result of friendships forged in Florence which linked me with researchers, Jean Monnet Fellows, and lecturers in the Department of History and Civilization at the European University Institute in Florence between 1987 and 1990. I started the book whilst at the Institute as Jean Monnet Fellow in 1987–88, and its principal chapters were presented in a seminar which I gave in the autumn of 1990. I am delighted to thank the Department and, in particular, Franco Angiolini, Francisco Bettencourt, Jean Boutier, Philippe Boutry, Joachim Carvalho, Heinz-Gerhard Haupt, Dominique Julia, Wolfgang Kaiser, Dominique Poulot, Daniel Roche, Robert Rowland, Gabriela Solari, Stuart Woolf and my friend Peter Hertner, for his help on all things German.

Serge Noiret, the person in charge of the history section in the Institute's library, provided invaluable help and was always anxious to let me know of his finds in my area.

I should also like to thank those historians who took an interest in this book and shared their knowledge with me: Maurice Aymard, Roger Chartier, Geoff Crossick, Robert Descimon, Willem Frijhoff, Maurice Garden, Paul Guichonnet, Pierre Jeannin, Giovanni Levi, Renato Pasta, Ulrich Pfister, Jacques Revel and Bernard Vincent.

1

Peddling and Major Trade between the Fifteenth and Seventeenth Centuries

From the time it first appeared right through to the mid-nineteenth century, peddling was primarily dominated by the mountain dwellers. Indeed, for Western Europe, a map showing the origins of the first migrant merchants reveals three main places of origin: the whole of the Alpine curve (and, in particular, all high-altitude villages from the Savoy region to the Tyrol), the Pyrenees and Scotland. The primacy of these mountain regions as a breeding ground for pedlars has its roots in the Middle Ages when the complementary nature of high and low land was established, enabling the mountain regions to gain access to the European trading circuits and thereby make the most of a geographical position which placed them directly on the major trade routes. In fact, until the seventeenth century, the Alpine valleys were marginalized lands: the prosperous and most densely populated areas were the lowland valleys where the best land for growing corn was to be found. From the seventeenth century onwards, and particularly in the eighteenth century, the economic development of Europe, manifested in the expansion of the towns, the taming of the sea and increasing prosperity, and which could be seen in new fashions in clothes and food, rescued the mountain regions from their marginalized status. From then on, the building and ship industries needed a supply of wood; the clothing industry demanded an ever increasing quantity of leather and wool; and social distinction was flaunted by a diet which consisted of foods other than bread (such as meat). These new needs were the products of uncultivated regions – of the *saltus* – in other words, all that the mountain areas were *par excellence*.[1]

Mountain society was now constructed in response to the changing society of the lowlands: the breeding of livestock developed, small-scale transhumance farming (the seasonal movement of herds onto the slopes) was established and, with it, a system of irrigating the meadows was set up in the drier mountains. Surrounding these activities, on the edges of the mountains, fairs were created to cope with the new demands of trading.[2] At the same time a system of large-scale transhumance farming ('an admirable human construct' in George Duby's words) was set up, so that the sheep came down to the meadows, the higher valleys not being able to sustain them in the winter. The Savoy region joined Germany and Italy as suppliers to the leather trade[3] and Scotland challenged the Baltic, first with the wool of her sheep, then with her leather and pelts and finally, at the end of the sixteenth century, with coal and salt.[4]

As well as the increasing value placed on the products of the mountain regions, many mountain ranges discovered a new role as trade routes, right up until the opening decades of the eighteenth century. A division of trade was established: heavy foodstuffs, such as cereals, were transported by sea; luxury goods by land, along routes such as the Alpine ones. Mule trains, weighed down by silks, precious dyes, indigo, and gold and silver thread, took the mountain paths and every mountain pass had its share of traffic:[5] trade irrigated the mountains in a multitude of thin trickles, winter and summer alike, since the guides guaranteed a passage all year round.[6] These 'lofty trade routes' meant that one could avoid tolls and Customs: in the Pyrenees, just as in the Alps, there was 'a steady stream of those who cheat Customs on a daily basis'.[7] For the Baltic business markets, the ports on the eastern coast of Scotland served the same purpose as the Alpine passes.

The mobility of the mountain dwellers was not therefore a consequence of overpopulation, but an integral part of man's conquest of the mountain regions.[8] This complete change of perspective is essential to an understanding of the innovative nature of the migratory movement and of the densely populated societies which developed at this time close to the mountain passes, along the trade routes which, since the Middle Ages, people had used to travel between the uncultivated mountain regions and the main trade axes (north–south, joining the Netherlands and Italy via the Rhine Valley; and east–west, linking Italy to Spain through the South of France.)[9]

Later on, from the sixteenth century onwards, other focal points emerged: the valleys linking the great Italian lakes below the mountain passes[10] and, in France, the uplands of the Massif Central. Merchant migration in the Limousin and the Auvergne, however, had failed right from the start to get onto the dual commercial circuit. Remaining at a distance from the major routes, it developed along different lines, and the structure of its peddling activities was not in the same mould as that of the mountain valleys or of Scotland. It will be examined in the following chapter.

Since the Middle Ages, therefore, the pedlars from the high Alpine valleys had established a presence on the trade routes. Savoyards from the North and men from the Valle d'Aosta moved to the centres of commerce on the Swiss plateau and the mid-Rhine region. As early as 1336 the *Krämer* – pedlars selling haberdashery goods – were present in Zurich; at the beginning of the fifteenth century they had taken over the Zurzach region and, by the end of the century, they had reached Fribourg.[11] The other Savoyard valleys – the Tarentaise and Maurienne valleys – had been swept by the east–west trade movements, as had the mountain valleys of the Southern Alps in the Dauphiné, Briançonnais and Queyras, where families settled along the routes between Italy and Spain; even though the later adoption of Protestantism by a number of families in these Southern Alpine valleys upset the scheme of things by forcing them towards the Rhine regions and the Reformation. In the sixteenth century, the migrant merchants from the great Italian lakes moved on – some towards the North where they rejoined the original pedlars[12] and others towards Southern Italy, and towards Sicily.[13] Finally, from the seventeenth century onwards, the migrants from the South – the 'welches'* – met up with an influx of northern European merchants from Brabant in Holland.[14] The number of pedlars in Germany from the high Alpine districts reached its peak in the second half of the seventeenth century, to be succeeded in the next century by the itinerant merchants from the Italian lakes. Using figures showing definitive settlement, Karl Martin demonstrates the uninterrupted development of Savoyard immigration, its explosion after the Thirty Years War, its ineluctable decline at the end of the seventeenth century[15] and then its shift from German-speaking Switzerland towards Brisgau and the Black Forest.[16] The migratory movement from Brabant came to a halt during the Revolt of the Netherlands, only to start up again at the beginning of the eighteenth century.[17]

Scotland scattered her merchants, pedlars, leather craftsmen and weavers across all of northern Europe to Poland, Denmark, Sweden and Norway. The first settlements date back to the second half of the fifteenth century when Scots were to be found on both sides of the Channel, in western France, Norway and the Baltic. These migrations reached a peak between 1500 and 1650.[18] The Scots who settled in Poland were originally from over 140 locations, mainly in the north and north-east of Scotland. The majority arrived by sea, particularly via Gdańsk and the other Baltic ports. Some, however, following the main highways and rivers of Germany and Bohemia, spread out over Poland from the sixteenth century onwards and, in the first half of the seventeenth century, can be identified in more than 420 locations.[19] In 1621 the Scottish emigrant population in Poland was estimated at 30,000 people.[20] The last three decades of the sixteenth century and the first half of the seventeenth century were the peak periods (1580–1620). At the turn of

---

* *welches*: German word for 'foreigner', meaning especially those from the South or the Mediterranean regions. [translator's note]

the sixteenth and seventeenth centuries an influx of Armenians, a similar combination of merchants, pedlars and itinerant craftsmen, arrived
in the south-east of Poland.[21] In Malmö in Sweden, the Scots represented 2.6 per cent of the taxable population in 1518; their numbers
rose until the middle of the sixteenth century, when they constituted 3
per cent, and then declined to the point where, in 1596, they represented
only 1 per cent of the total.[22]

Whether one takes as a starting point the place from which the migrant originally set out or his destination, quantifying these pedlars is
an impossible task given the inexact and debatable nature of the statistical
evidence. Joannes Augel and Karl Martin, who set themselves the task
of identifying the Italians and Savoyards in the German archives,[23] provide
figures which are necessarily underestimated, since they represent only
permanent settlers and give no indication of the number of temporary
migrants. Alongside these impossible reckonings, however, there are
other traces which allow us better to imagine the importance of these
men in the lives and imaginations of the indigenous population. The
fact that, in Hünsruck, Mainz and Frankfurt, *der Italiener* meant 'a
merchant', a commercial trader; that the confusion between geographical origins and professional activity ran so deep that a German merchant
would find himself called *der Deutscher Italiener*; and that in Denmark
the word *scot* meant a pedlar provides us with another means of meas-
urement. Similarly, the presence of Scots in Poland manifests itself in
place names such as Nowa Szkocja, Skotna Gora, and so forth.[24]

The merchant structure

Because the peddling networks, with their sophisticated internal organization, are not easy to grasp or understand unless the historian addresses
their geographical source, they have remained largely misunderstood up
to now. In fact, these sources, in common with the more traditional
perspectives, can provide only partial insights. Seen from the lowlands,
the mountain was 'a factory producing men for others to exploit': local
government recorded their descent from the mountain and observers
noted their strange costumes.[25] Admittedly the city archives bear witness to the fact that this migration of the poverty-stricken concealed a
certain number of substantial fortunes, but the account books and the
inventories carried out after the deaths of these men do not yield their
secrets: they reveal merchants doing business with other merchants and
with other towns – all very traditional – and they highlight individual
successes. But, seen from the perspective of the mountain, these 'other
merchants' turn out to be relatives or pedlars who came from the same
villages; 'other people' were actually relatives or compatriots.

Analysis of the activities of these émigré city merchants brings to light a commercial organization which operated on two levels. The first level was made up of relatives and relations by marriage. It supported a family banking system and, through opening warehouses and shops in the city, was part of a vast geographical web. The second level was a distribution network linked to migratory movements. It had a rigid hierarchical structure, and was based upon temporary migration and the labour of men from the home village. We can penetrate these networks thanks to certain families favoured by the archives: the Bittot family from Montagny in Tarentaise, the Girauds and André Masson from La Grave in the Dauphiné, the Brentanos from the Alpine valleys of Lake Como, and other Alpine and Scottish family groups.

(1) On the first level then, we have a family network which traded over a wide geographical area. The network formed by the three Bittot brothers, originally from Montagny in Tarentaise, as reconstructed from the 'Record of Debts' owed to them in Strasbourg in 1611, shows that their business extended over dozens of towns located within the rectangle Venice–Lyon, Lyon–Haarlem, Haarlem–Gdańsk, Gdańsk–Venice.[26] An analysis of the family shows that the organization was set up over several generations and that it came about through a careful balance between marriages between mountain dwellers, and marriages linking them with the merchant families of their principal places of business. The father, the pedlar *Krämer* Gilles Bittot from Montagny in Tarentaise, married the daughter of a Strasbourg merchant, Georg Hellbeck, also known as Boheim l'Ancien, through whose intervention he was granted the *droit de bourgeoisie** in 1576. In such circumstances the *droit de bourgeoisie* was essential since it conferred the right to do business in the town. The couple had nine children. Two daughters married foreign merchants: the elder, Marie, married a Frankfurt merchant who settled in Strasbourg, where he became a burgher in 1595. The second daughter, Anne, was married twice, both times to Savoyard merchants who had businesses in Basel: first to Samuel Battier and then, the second time around, to Jean Sarrazin who, on becoming a widower, left to settle in Geneva. The uncle of the three brothers joined forces with Gilles in Strasbourg where he too acquired the *droit de bourgeoisie* in 1585. Within this structure, the Savoyard axis remained of great importance since two of the three brothers, Daniel and Guillaume, were married and resided in Montagny. The third brother, Jean, settled in Basel.

An analysis of the Savoyards living and working in Strasbourg at the beginning of the eighteenth century enables one to place a general value

---

* Being granted the *droit de bourgeoisie* was the equivalent of being made a burgher or burgess, and bestowed certain privileges, notably the right to trade or do business. [translator's note]

on a marriage strategy such as the one outlined above, and on the practice of mobilizing men between individual centres. The Savoyard Guillame Droz 'had been in Grenoble to learn the trade, then came here and married Jeanne Cannuelle from Lyon'; Etienne Romanet 'still has his shop in Besançon, where he has been established for seven years'; Claude-François du Puis 'lived in Lyon for seven years, where he did business as a full municipal resident'. Out of 24 wives of Savoyards in Strasbourg, nearly a third were originally from the home province and an appreciable number still lived there; the second largest group was made up of Alsatian wives.[27]

The Giraud family, originally from La Grave in Oisans in the Dauphiné, were part of a Protestant merchant network which can be partially reconstructed from Jean Giraud's record book, kept at the end of the seventeenth century. It extended over Switzerland, northern Italy and southern France: between Lyon, Geneva, Mantua and Perpignan.[28] Like his father before him, Jean had a shop in Lyon, his father-in-law a shop in Geneva. The Giraud family was only one part of a much larger network which linked other interrelated families from the same mountain range, such as the Bérard family,[29] the Delor family, the Horard family and the Vieux family from Mizoen. Thobie Delor was a burgher of Lyon and an influential member of the Consistory.[30] The family had been established for over a century in Geneva, where Antoine, Gabriel, Luc and Etienne Delor, all four haberdashers from Mizoen, were accepted as municipal citizens in 1572 and where Georges was accepted as a burgher in 1597.[31] The archives of the village notaries reveal that others settled in Grenoble, in Burgundy, in Italy and on the routes to Spain and Germany. All of these families were Protestant.

The Brentano family originally came from the valleys surrounding Lake Como. It relied on four family branches – the Brentano–Gnosso, the Brentano–Toccia, the Brentano–Cimaroli and the Brentano–Tremezzo – to form a network. The first Brentanos arrived in the sixteenth century as simple *Höcker*; itinerant merchants selling citrus fruit and spices. They turned up each year with their oranges and lemons, travelling between towns, fairs and weekly markets until, at the turn of the seventeenth and eighteenth centuries, they succeeded in opening a shop in the city. The first recorded Brentano appeared in 1640 in Basel, whence he was expelled; his son Carl turned up in Frankfurt in 1673. In the Tremezzo branch of the family, the first Brentano to come to Frankfurt was Martino. In 1662 he obtained permission to sell his citrus fruits from a table, as a *Hockerer* or 'squatting merchant', sharing this privilege with the old and infirm.[32] His son Domenico, born in 1651 in Tremezzo, developed the business in partnership with his brothers-in-law and, in 1698, opened a shop in Frankfurt. None the less he continued to travel between Frankfurt and his property at Lake Como where his family lived and where he died in 1723. The marriages which took place between Italian families over the next two generations enabled the Brentano family, by means of the businesses that they built up between themselves, to develop branches of the family business along the Rhine. Domenico Martino, the eldest son of Domenico (who died in Frankfurt) continued to live in Italy where his sons were born. We have to wait until the second half of the eighteenth century – in other words at least four generations after first identifying members of the family – before Domenico Martino's son Peter Anton (Pietro Antonio), who was born in 1735 in Tremezzo and died in Frankfurt in 1797, decided to become part of Frankfurt society. At the beginning of the eighteenth century, members of the Brentano family established themselves in Amsterdam, Bingen, Brussels, Koblenz, Cologne, Constance, Cracow, Diez, Frankfurt, Fribourg, Heidelberg, Mannheim, Mainz, Nuremberg, Rothenburg, Rotterdam and Vienna. If we also add to the above the towns where their relatives had opened shops, then their establishments covered all of northern Europe.[33] The most famous branch of the family, originally from the village of Tremezzo, produced the writers Clemens and Bettina. As the index drawn up by Augel and Martin shows, the history of these families was very similar to that of many other families from the Italian Alpine valleys. And, indeed, from the eighteenth century onwards from one end of the Alpine curve to the other, one could name similar families from numerous villages.[34]

Scottish merchant migration proceeded along similar lines. The merchants of Elsinore in Denmark married their daughters between themselves,[35] as did those merchants who had settled in Sweden, in Gdańsk, in Königsberg and in the North of Germany. Similarly, they chose godparents from among their close family, from their 'ain folk'.[36] Hans Macklier, who was born in Scotland and died in Gothenburg in 1666, had an uncle who was a merchant in Stockholm, who maintained close relationships with those Scots who had set up in business in Poland; Hans Spalding, who was born in Scotland and died in Gothenburg in 1667, had a brother Andrew who was established in Mecklenburg, and Hans brought his nephew Jakob to Gothenburg before setting him up in the town of Norrköping.[37] The road to success began with peddling on a small scale in Scotland. The profits thus earned then allowed the pedlar to extend his campaign into England, to become a 'traveller' or a 'merchant-traveller' there, then finally to gain access to the envied circle of those who adventured on the sea. Mathew Cuming, for example, travelled in England between 1683 and 1686. Profiting both from his income and from the credit to which he then had access, Cuming loaded up his ass with bundles of material, which he then took to London to sell in order to finance the importation of dyes from Holland, and to get a share in a boat bringing sugar and tobacco from Virginia.[38] He thus broke into the world of 'big business' and prepared to venture onto the Continent. When Brabant in Holland branched out into merchant migration, it was done according to the same basic plan: common origins and family links with the other itinerant merchants who had established themselves in the neighbouring towns.[39]

A family banking system bound the family network together and enabled it to maximize resources, since each member invested the best part of the family fortune into the firm. Jean Giraud's uncle and sister placed large sums of money with the Chicot, Monnet and Giraud business: the uncle deposited 6,000 *livres** and the sister deposited her dowry, the pension her late husband had left her and the entire fortune of her children, whose guardian Jean was. Jean Giraud regularly paid out the interest due and kept precise accounts of the money he was managing for different members of the family.[40] Vincent Pic from La Grave managed his three sisters' fortunes, despite the fact that they had all married merchants.

Commercial inter-marriage was one of the cogs in a mechanism which aimed to protect the banking system and the loyalty that each member felt towards the merchant network. The exceptions to this rule were the result of compromises that the migrants had to make in order to gain access to the markets of the countries in which they settled.

(2) These merchant networks, created from what was initially a small-scale migration from the mountains, expanded by relying on one town which became, in some ways, an epicentre for the immigrant pedlars: Fribourg served this purpose for the Savoyards, Lyon for those from the Dauphiné and Gdańsk for the Scots.[41] In such towns certain families from the original village managed to establish an initial centre for supplies. When they had made enough money, family members would then open a warehouse in another town and so the merchant network was gradually built up. The geography of the network changed as focal points were created and then shifted, according to where the money was, or where the law was weak enough to allow a shop to be opened without problems, or where low taxes meant a higher profit. Using these focal points as a base, a peddling trade developed which explains the central role played by the original villages and forces us to consider the mountain axis as closely as the city. High and low lands were mutually dependent and the Giraud, Bittot and Brentano families, even when they had been granted the *droit de bourgeoisie* in a town, continued to live in their home villages, or visit them regularly. It is often difficult to demonstrate this conclusively because the city sources conceal the double lives of these *bourgeois* and record only their status as city-dwellers.

* *livre*: historical currency, originally the equivalent of a pound of silver; but subsequently less than 5 grams with the introduction of the metric system in 1801. [translator's note]

(3)   These family networks organized themselves into very flexible firms, which could be set up and disbanded in response to commercial necessity, death, and the relative wealth or poverty of its members. Generally the association lasted between one and four years: each member invested a certain amount of capital and the profits were shared out in proportion to the initial investment. In this way, Jean Giraud's company was dissolved and re-formed every four years around associates including both family members and in-laws. The Giraud–Chicot–Grengent association was succeeded in 1670 by Giraud–Chicot–Monnet which lasted until 1674, and was then replaced by an association between Giraud and Chicot. The association between Simon and Claude Diaque and Vincent Albert was set up for a period of six years, with the right to dissolve the partnership at the end of three years; in the end each member took back his share of the capital and both profits and debts were divided equally, even if the initial capital invested had not been equal; the association looked after their members for a month, provided them with silk stockings, with shoes and with chausses* and allowed them to spend two months a year in the village.[42] Domenico Brentano's organization in Frankfurt, which was run by his four sons until 1703, renewed and expanded itself constantly from that date onwards as the firm conquered the trade markets to the North.[43] This type of contract 'of association' (sometimes called 'assousiette' in the Dauphiné) was to be found across all of Europe, sending families to the North as well as to Sicily[44] and to southern Spain. An analysis of the make-up of these family networks would doubtless provide a better understanding of this movable and varied geography, of how links were forged between merchants from the same home village whose trade took them in opposite directions; like the merchants of Stazzona in the Como, whose activities varied depending on the year.[45]

So, despite settlement in the towns, it was still a question of temporary migration, progressing imperceptibly from one activity to another more important one, and from one level of wealth to another; the length of absence being in proportion to these variables. It was quite possible for some of the more important merchants who themselves travelled between the different markets on their circuit to return to the village only once every two years. Others turned up briefly on a regular basis, like Jean Giraud from La Grave who chose to take 'the back roads' – those that went through his village – when he travelled from his shop in Lyon to that of his father-in-law in Geneva.[46] More often in Lyon than in La Grave, Giraud none the less thought of himself as a man of the mountains and talked of his 'French trips' even when he went to Lyon. At the beginning of the seventeenth century, André Masson went into partnership with Claude Carraud and Esprit Rome, all three

* Tight-fitting garment covering the feet and legs. [translator's note]

being merchants from La Grave. While the latter ran a shop in Lyon, Masson stayed for long periods in Paris, where he had rented a room and where he traded on behalf of the company. In 1610 he was in Paris from the beginning of February to the middle of March; in the second half of May and the first half of June; then from the end of September to the middle of November. The statements of debts owed for the years 1607 and 1609 show that in 1609 he was still in Paris at the end of July, and in 1607 didn't leave Paris until 4 August.[47] The Savoyard Pierre Chevalier was either travelling through Alsace, or in the Savoy, or in Geispolsheimau, the market town where he ran his business, but his home, wife and six children remained in the Savoy. The archbishop of Grenoble, Monseigneur Le Camus, remarked upon the long absence of the merchants when, in July 1678, he undertook a pastoral visit to Oisans. He found himself in the villages in the middle of summer, during the rush to get the harvests in, and yet found that in all of the higher-up villages a proportion of the merchants had not returned: 'because they live almost all year round in the place where they have their shop and merchandise, leaving their wives and children behind in the village.'[48] Again, in the eighteenth century, the grand Elector of Mainz, under pressure from the local bourgeoisie, ruled in vain that the Italian merchants who were 'citizens' or *bourgeois* in his towns should send for their wives and children. Few heeded his decree. In Bingen in 1712 only one obeyed the ruling.[49]

The refusal to allow pedlars to marry whilst in the lowlands also played an important commercial role, in that it allowed men to be moved around easily in response to the needs of the organization. It also enabled the rest of the family who still lived in the village to keep an eye on the pedlar and his would-be suitors. The Perolas were a Savoyard family who, in 1784, ran a business whose headquarters were in Piedmont, with warehouses and subsidiaries in the towns in the Black Forest. Like all other mountain businesses, they had built up their commercial supremacy through a combination of mobility and a limit on the number of marriages entered into outside the sphere of the Alpine valleys. The Perolas supplied the region and the annual fairs, using as a base the seven towns of South Baden, where they had been granted *droits de bourgeoisie*. The German merchants who were hostile to them laid stress upon the fact that these *bourgeois* were migrants and did not live there. The older members of the family lived in Italy while the younger ones were sent to German towns for lengthy periods. The company decided on the position and the function in the organization of each 'Kamerad' and decided who was to be recalled to Italy and, similarly, who was to be kept in Germany.[50]

(4) In order to develop their businesses, these merchants relied on village migration. At the top of the hierarchical structure was the *commis*

[clerk], who was in fact a salaried pedlar who travelled the town, fairs and surrounding villages selling the goods which the company had imported; as is suggested in the ruling of the Frankfurt magistrates in 1628, which forbade the *commis* from selling retail and which allowed instead all foreigners to sell their goods twice weekly in the market-place.[51] The *commis* were generally relatives of members of the organ-ization who, having completed their apprenticeship, remained in the service of the business until they had the capital necessary to set up their own business or take a share in the company employing them. There were other possible candidates for the post of *commis*, such as Jean Monnet, brother-in-law and business associate of Jean Giraud, who had to pull out of the business because his affairs were going badly but remained with the firm as a *commis* with his previous business partners, Giraud and Chicot, paying him a salary.

Alongside the *commis*, the merchants had numerous apprentices or 'Jungen'. These young men, sons of members of the organization or of their relatives, came to undertake their apprenticeship as packmen. There were sometimes a fair number of them in the town and this practice was denounced by the native merchants, who complained that all these young men not only were not registered with the town authorities but also peddled their wares with impunity.[52]

On a level below that of *commis* and apprentices were a great many pedlars. It is not always easy to highlight the link between the merchant businesses and peddling since the Italian merchants who had succeeded in getting themselves accepted as citizens of the town where they had their shop made every effort to conceal it. Such was the case of Antonio Rivolta who peddled fancy goods in the area surrounding Fribourg and who, once he had been granted citizenship, demanded – as he was obliged to do – that peddling be banned; whereas the inventory drawn up after his death bears witness to the fact that, despite what he said, his practices had not changed and he had continued to supply the pedlars who covered the surrounding countryside with his fancy goods.[53] The inventory drawn up in Paris after André Masson's death shows how he paid the fine levied against two pedlars from his village for selling his goods at La Ferté Allais.[54] Similarly, without the Bittot brothers' 'statement of debts' which showed the debts owed to them by other minor Savoyard merchants, it would have been impossible to highlight the ways in which the home village was used.

A hierarchy also became apparent within the peddling group. At the top were a group of travelling merchants who did not have shops, who were always referred to in texts as 'merchants' and who were numbered amongst the richest inhabitants of their home villages. Their absences corresponded to the seasons. From the end of the seventeenth century, notaries' deeds concerning travelling merchants demonstrate the essential role of these men as a pivot between the two halves of the organization.

In the lowlands they were part of the network developed by those merchants who had opened shops, from whom they got their supplies. One only needs to examine the stocks held by the merchant shopkeepers, and all is revealed: in his two shops and his stockroom, Jacques Bérard had a total of 195 pairs of stockings of all sizes and materials, 20 dozen bonnets, 360 woollen bootlaces, lots of braid, ribbons, laces of all possible colours and fabrics: cordillat, cadiz, serge, drugget, calico, canvas, ratine, muslin, wool, woollen cloth and homespun, of varied quality and origin. Documents confirm the pedlars as clients since most of Bérard's debtors were the same rich pedlars from the Alpine valleys.

In the mountain villages, the travelling merchants acted as intermediaries through whom one could trade in winter. Pierre Gourand, from Clavans in the Dauphiné, owed more than three hundred *livres* 'to Jean and Daniel Horard, brothers, merchants of Mizoen' in the form of four obligations dating from 1665, 1668, 1670 and 1672:[55] they bear witness to the winter activities of the pedlars whom Gourand deployed in Burgundy through the Horard brothers. The Horard family, linked by marriage to the Delors, and to the Vieux and Bérard families, were responsible for the Burgundy link in the network of upper Dauphiné merchants. In his turn, Gourand acted as a link between the families in the village and the merchant network of which he himself was part. He did so by finding work for other migrants, providing them with certain merchandise and acting as banker and intermediary between them and more important merchants, who were less often in the villages, and with whom, as with the Horard brothers, he enjoyed a special relationship. These pedlars, who were very much a part of the economic life of the village, were the pivots of the village migratory system.

In their turn, the packmen, who stocked up from the factories and warehouses established in the town by their compatriots, employed servants and apprentices. However, unlike the *commis* in the large firms, the pedlar's employees were not allowed any opportunity to line their own pockets: they were forbidden to act as wholesalers or retailers on their own behalf or to lend money (the other method of building up one's own business); moreover, any social activities likely to divert them from their work - such as dancing, playing billiards, or going to the theatre - were forbidden. The Perroman company made use of this structure from the end of the fourteenth century to distribute textiles, scythes, metals, saffron and saltpetre, which they imported in bulk; the packmen collected fresh supplies from a storehouse set up by their employer in the shop or hostel of a compatriot.[56] In 1591, a small band of nine pedlars from the Upper Dauphiné were robbed of their goods at Aubusson. The notary's report records that they were on the road between Lyon, where they had obtained their goods, and Limoges, where they intended to sell them on behalf of other merchants, and it was for the latter that the pedlars demanded a formal statement of theft. In this way the merchant hierarchies were united in a single act since the two pedlars, who each led a horse loaded with bales of material, were accompanied by seven other pedlars travelling with a pack apiece.[57]

Even allowing for exaggeration, the complaints that the German towns and guilds made regularly to the Diets indicate how far the peddling hierarchies had extended. At the Diet of Zurich in 1516, Schwyz, from German Switzerland, denounced 'those persons who travel around the region, hawking their cheap goods, from village to village, from farm to farm and from house to house, up hill and down dale. So much so that no home is safe: they worm their way in with their servants and children – even the lowliest of them has three or four. They also beg and live off the backs of the poor, without paying a pfennig to a single innkeeper.'[58] In the seventeenth century, the local spice merchants took every opportunity of denouncing Italian and Jewish organizations who used five or six boys to distribute their products, on public holidays as well as working days. The boys stopped off in inns, wriggled their way into the houses of the middle classes on wedding days, and knocked on every door.[59] The rulings in Mainz, just as in Cologne and elsewhere, railed against the practice of only employing one's compatriots because it brought about the ruin of the native traders by not allowing them the opportunity to benefit from the merchant network.[60] They also revealed the links which bound the wealthiest to those who could offer only a limited amount of craftsman's knowledge, or who had nothing more than a bear or marmot to exhibit.[61] In their own way, these complaints express the bonds which linked the various migrants from the same village, from the richest down to the most impoverished.

Similar conclusions can be drawn for northern Europe. In Sweden, the relationship between the important merchants, pedlars and craftsmen in the migrant community was a strong one. The pinnacle of social success was establishing a business, but, if things didn't work out, the backpack was abandoned in exchange for a sword and the army.[62] In Denmark both the business and industrial aspects of the clothing industry comprised merchants, pedlars, tailors, weavers, and leather workers from Scotland.[63] And, just as in the towns on the Rhine, Scandinavian complaints and rulings laid stress on the multiplicity of these commercial links: Gothenburg was envious of the business done by the rich Scottish merchants who dealt in the export of wood and iron and the import of fabrics, wine, salt and herrings. They were said to use 'the many young, foreign merchants' who hovered around the town 'on the pretext of collecting debts relating to their illegal trade' and who stocked up from the vast warehouses owned by the Scots.[64] The Danish rulings in the fifteenth and sixteenth centuries forbidding the Scottish merchants to send their *commis* and servants to hawk their wares in the surrounding countryside also bear witness to the existence of links between the now sedentary business community and the trade done by itinerant pedlars who came from the same original village.[65] From North to South, the existence of peddling reveals the extent of the recruitment which bound the migrant community together and included even its poorest members.

The peddling hierarchies were also visible in the contracts of apprenticeship: there were several 'business schools', depending on the extent of the family fortune and network. At the highest level, the youngsters were sent to the city as *commis* to learn the trade in a city shop. Those whose family means were more modest would become packmen for a merchant who was part sedentary and part traveller. Some of the contracts relating to the higher-up villages of the Dauphiné provide information on what such an education comprised: *sieur** Pierre Baille from the Villard d'Arène put his son in the care of *sieur* Laurent Eytre of Hières 'residing in the town of Nart in Piedmont', 'to learn the trade of being a merchant' and 'to serve said *sieur* Eytre in his business, either in the Savoy region or in Piedmont';[66] *sieur* Noé Aymond from La Grave 'put his son Claude into apprenticeship with *sieur* Christophe Juiller, native of Villard d'Arène and living in the town of Pau'.[67] Four years later, in 1684, the same Christophe Juiller, 'a burgher of Pau' took on a new apprentice for four years, the son of *sieur* Christophe Carraud, son of Felix, a merchant from La Grave, to instruct him 'into the art of being a merchant'.[68] Both contracts were made through the intermediary of the merchant's brother, *sieur* Pierre Juiller, parish priest in Chazelet. *Sieur* Etienne Girard 'gave his son Jacques as apprentice to *sieur* Jean Hugues, merchant in Turin'.[69] These deeds of apprenticeship, all somewhat different in their details, had the same basic structure: the child who went into apprenticeship was the son of a merchant who had the right to use the title '*sieur*'. The merchant who took him on came from the same village and was established in the city. The length of the apprenticeship was between four and six years. In two of the above cases, at the end of the apprenticeship the youth was given a sum of money (50 *livres* in one case and an unknown amount in the case of the Turin merchant); and in the other the apprenticeship was followed by a period of two years in which the boy stayed with his master and was paid a salary (90 *livres*). Moreover, certain merchants, at the end of the apprenticeship, promised a gift of clothing. The master undertook to 'initiate him into the practices of his profession as merchant, be it in buying or selling'; the boy to 'be at all times loyal and faithful' or to do 'all which is lawful and honest in pursuit of the profit of his aforementioned master'; and the father to 'return the boy to the service of his aforementioned master' if he were to run away. The period during which the master would look after the apprentice in case of illness,

---

* *sieur*: a historical title, equivalent of *seigneur*.

paying all costs 'be they to the doctor, the apothecary or the surgeon' was always stated: it varied between one and two months. In the contracts that Eberard Gothein came across, the merchant-pedlar paid for shoes and, in the case of illness, upkeep for the apprentice for a period of time varying between a fortnight and two months, but the apprentice was responsible for paying for the doctor and for medicine.[70]

Others served their apprenticeships as servants: 'honest Jean Arnaud, merchant of Villard d'Arène, entrusts Pierre Berthieu, son of Pierre, merchant of the aforementioned place, with his son so that he may be instructed in merchant practices.' This was for a period of eight months, with the boy receiving 11 *livres* in wages and 'a hat and a pair of shoes' while the merchant undertook to feed and care for him for a fortnight if necessary.[71] Other contracts allowed the son to visit his family for several months and fixed wages and duties.[72] The men from Savoy who were established in Strasbourg whilst their wives remained in the village, like the Italians had their children sent to them when still very young: Mathieu Gorel's wife lived in Savoy with five children 'of whom two are in Savoy and the other three travel from place to place to earn their living'; Jacques Chevalier's wife 'is in Savoy with three children whilst another roams Alsace'.[73]

Establishing oneself in the city

The peddling networks were organized around two mainstays: first, the formation of far-reaching family networks, with a common place of origin, who married amongst themselves and were supported by a family banking system; and second, complete coverage of the market through setting up warehouses and city shops and using village manpower. Establishing the latter – in other words, setting oneself up in the city and opening a shop – meant finding a way into two closed systems: one had to clear the political barrier of the *droit de bourgeoisie* and, later on, the economic barrier posed by the guilds.

Both these difficulties, which were linked to the political, economic and demographic climate of the cities into which the pedlars were striving to gain admission, partly explain the changes in the migrant population and their eventual assimilation into the cultural patterns of the lowlands. They had, in fact, to juggle three separate economic and cultural realities, with often mutually antagonistic interests – the sovereign power, the sedentary merchants and the consumer population. Despite differences in emphasis and geographical and chronological discrepancies, these evolutionary changes were globally similar.

Generally speaking, the ruling powers oscillated between two approaches towards itinerant merchants who sought to establish themselves in the cities: there were the princes, who needed men to populate or repopulate their towns and boost trade, as was the case in Sweden and Spain and in Germany after the Thirty Years War; and the governments, who had to reckon with a powerful city bourgeoisie, as in numerous towns on the Rhine, on the Swiss plateau and in areas already repopulated. In the latter case the contradictory wishes of the population complicated the rulers' decision since, as consumers, their attitude towards the travelling merchants, who supplied them with the cheapest goods, was positive. The towns themselves were divided: on the one hand they made money from the pedlars through the collection of customs taxes and city tolls; on the other hand the shopkeepers demanded their expulsion from the towns and markets. Lastly, the nation states were tormented by commercial worries as the money which the foreigners earned disappeared, and made nervous by organizations which were outside their legal framework and their authority. Between the sixteenth and nineteenth centuries, the legislation in European states alternated between these contradictory demands and the measures adopted affected in their turn the structure of the merchant networks.

The bourgeois communities of the Rhine were the first to try to break up the peddling networks, by refusing to accept their top ranks into their community. They prevented them from becoming members of the bourgeoisie, which would have allowed them to trade freely: refusal of this right was the surest means of weakening the whole network. Starting in the most important cities, the battle against the foreign merchants gradually reached the smaller towns, who learned of legislation adopted elsewhere and copied it.[74] In this way, after the sixteenth century it became almost impossible to be accepted into the bourgeoisie in the cities: in Zurich, the Savoyards were completely forbidden from exercising their profession within a radius of two leagues from the city walls. Only one immigrant was accepted into the bourgeoisie at the end of the sixteenth century, and in 1576 Horgen, a small town near Zurich, refused the request of the Savoyard Jacob Billeter to set up in business there and sell his produce, even though he had married a local woman. The pattern was the same in Berne between 1584 and 1594.

Whilst the doors were still open to them, the pedlars settled in the small market towns and medium-sized towns and, very occasionally, in the more important urban areas such as Fribourg. But, in their turn, these less important towns began to make them pay dearly for the *droit de bourgeoisie*, attaching various conditions to it – such as buying a new coat for the town policeman or pails for the municipal fire brigade – and the sworn promise to give up peddling. Moreover, very often the towns put up obstacles to their having political rights and only granted them reduced citizenship in the form of *Hintersässen* (or cotter) status.[75]

As the cities closed against them, some merchants took the only option open to them in order to be accepted fully in the towns of the

Rhine, and married the widows of local merchants so as to take over the latter's business and rights.[76] At the same time, the custom of choosing fellow countrymen as godfathers for their children became less common, and they chose instead the influential men of the town: burgomasters, state employees or sworn members of the guilds.[77] The strategy of marrying into the native community also encompassed business associations: the migrant merchants formed partnerships with their Swiss and German brothers-in-law so as to get round the ban which, as a way of reducing their business, forced them to sell only those products which were from their home country.[78]

In Spain in the sixteenth century, in an attempt to repopulate the kingdom, the monarchy sought to make the migrants settle there through marriage and granted those Frenchmen who were termed 'domiciliados' or 'avecindados' – in other words, those who were married to Spanish women – the right to trade in the towns and also the equally valuable right of trading with the Indies. Thus the latter became privileged subjects of the King, unlike the 'transeuntes' who were foreigners passing through and, as such, subject to the law but unable to engage in either retail trade or the liberal or mechanical arts. In order to penetrate the market, conceal their French origins, avoid the taxes to which they were especially subject and, in times of racial tension, to escape public condemnation, the migrants here too adopted the same strategies of marriage[79] and business associations with the Spaniards.[80]

This strategy would appear to be tactical rather than motivated by a real desire on the part of the migrants to become integrated into urban society since, as soon as the merchant had married a local merchant's widow or daughter, he re-established his links with his original network by marrying his children into it; as demonstrated by those Savoyard families who were established in Strasbourg: Noël Borel, who married a 'local bourgeois woman', 'had three married daughters in Savoy'; and Pierre Gorbai, who did the same thing, also had two married daughters in Savoy.[81]

However, in certain places, the whole business was complicated by the existence of an elite which included those who had been pedlars, but had been granted bourgeois status at a time when the country was in need of men. In these cases, it was not always possible to exclude them or close the doors of the town to them: in 1676 in Fribourg, certain Savoyards refused both to buy the *droit de bourgeoisie* in the period of time allotted to them, and to use the new weights and measures which the town had just adopted. Their refusal was supported by the Savoyard population which was both long-established and powerful: the most important innkeepers there were Savoyard, and the 1695 poll tax register in Fribourg records in the top band of 'grosse Kaufleute' two Savoyards who were members of the drapers' guild; in the second band, out of five businessmen taxed, once again two were Savoyards who belonged to the haberdashers' guild; and in the third band three-quarters of those earning a salary were Faucignerans.[82]

On the other hand, to satisfy the populace who wanted to buy on the most favourable terms – in other words, outside the corporative and shop system – and to compensate for the rise in the price of foodstuffs brought about by the monopoly demanded by the guilds, the rulers imposed compromises: at the fairs, days and places were reserved for the pedlars; these became more numerous and finally the pedlars were granted the freedom to do business at the fairs on a completely equal footing. Hence the poorer people, who were very much in favour of these steps, managed to procure specially reserved sites for the *Welches* everywhere. In Zurich in 1558 they were allocated the Wasserkirche, even though the porch of this church was used as a court to judge those who broke the rules. The same conditions applied in Fribourg, though here they had the added imposition of having to lodge in particular inns.[83] In Spain there were uprisings in numerous towns at the beginning of the seventeenth century against the proposed expulsion of the French; it was claimed in Toledo, Granada and Cordoba, for example, that life without them would be extremely difficult since they made up the majority of bakers in one place, of water-carriers in another. Differential measures were taken to protect them.[84]

However, the migrants were able to play on the rivalry between towns as well as on the conflict between the princes and the ruling bourgeoisie. As an example of rivalry between towns, in 1654 Thurgau banned all Savoyards from setting up goods warehouses within its territories. The Savoyards got round the difficulty by getting themselves accepted as *bourgeois* in the neighbouring domain of the abbey of Saint-Gall, despite the complaints of the Confederates who brought to the abbot's attention the irregularity of such a concession, given that the *Welches* left their families behind in Savoy.[85] In the same way, Mannheim, which had become a free zone after the Thirty Years War, attracted both Savoyards and Italians who settled there and established huge warehouses.[86] When Frankfurt closed its doors to the migrants they set up in the rival city of Mainz.[87] The pedlars turned to their advantage the conflicts between the two urban powers – between the princes and the town bourgeoisie – and hence most German towns with a prince's or bishop's court had its colony of migrant Italian merchants.[88]

The stage prior to requesting bourgeois status was acceptance into one of the guilds, which had shut their doors to foreigners at the same time. The peddling networks were made up of craftsmen as well as merchants, which increased the number of guilds who were hostile to them. In Zurich, as early as 1539 the guilds of the cutlers, locksmiths, clockmakers, makers of spurs, armourers and papermakers, as well as the burgomaster and the town council, enjoined the law-enforcing agents to rid the countryside of all Savoyard haberdashers.[89] Fribourg decreed in 1598 that no *Welche* would henceforth be accepted into the guilds.[90] During the whole of the sixteenth century and the first half of the seventeenth, the trade guilds in Poland multiplied the number of rules protecting themselves against Scottish craftsmen and merchants.[91] A century later, the guilds in the Spanish towns closed their doors to Frenchmen. In 1629 Barcelona banned them from holding representative office or honourable rank, then withdrew all voting rights from them and eventually expelled them completely.[92]

To find a way round exclusions such as these, the merchants adopted a variety of strategies. They united in religious brotherhoods and, using the patron saint as a pretext, they established meeting places in the town, and this gradually became familiar and accepted.[93] They banded together in interest groups: in Cadiz, they formed a French 'national corps'; in Palermo all foreigners met up in a similar type of corps, and the more modest villages of the Alto Lario, to the north-west of Lake Como, had their own organizations to rival those of Milan or Genoa. The national 'corps' did not exclude religious brotherhoods devoted to a patron saint being created, whose places of worship became regular and necessary meeting places, distant replicas of the village assemblies.[94] Lastly, they attempted – and often succeeded – in investing in, infiltrating and then hijacking the marginal guilds. The guilds gained power and money from the arrangement and the migrants the legal immunity they needed to develop their business activities: in Turin at the end of the seventeenth century, the guild of tailors thus accepted certain merchants from Savoy and the Dauphiné who used the guild to store smuggled goods and import forbidden fabrics.[95] Having specific meeting places simultaneously reinforced the identity and solidarity of the group from the home region as they confronted the city in which they were trying to establish themselves: it demonstrates that their desire to gain access to the city was a means to an end and not a search for a new identity.

The attempts made by the local bourgeois communities to prevent the peddling elite establishing themselves in the towns went hand in hand with attacks on the linking elements in the networks – the *commis* and the packmen – and the number of bans and the amount of harassment levelled at them increased. Just as had been the case with the *droit de bourgeoisie*, methods of dealing with the pedlars were passed on: in 1590 Rothenburg and Hörb asked Fribourg to tell them of measures being taken against the Italian pedlars and adopted these obstructionist tactics themselves.[96] A third legislative tactic which was deployed against the merchant network sought to prevent their development by forbidding the established merchants to employ people from their own country: from the mid-sixteenth century, the Swiss towns demanded that 'jobs be taken by natives of the town or its surrounding area, excluding those from Souabe or Gressoney'.[97]

The same legislation had developed in the towns and states of northern Europe. In Denmark the first decrees forbidding the Scottish merchants to allow their servants to sell goods in the villages dates from 1496; in 1551, the ban was extended to those pedlars who had been sent into the rural areas.[98] Poland from the end of the fifteenth century, and Sweden from the sixteenth century both tried to break up these organizations by issuing rulings which sought to restrain the trade of the travelling Scotsmen; they refused to allow them to buy goods, limited the length of time they could stay in town after the fairs, prevented them from forming illegal societies and made it an offence for anyone to offer them hospitality.[99] At around the same time, decrees were published which aimed to exclude them from municipal rights, unless they could prove that they were residents: the struggle began in 1457 in Gdańsk, the first base of Scottish commercial operations. Finally, the decrees concentrated on destroying the links of preferential employment which bound the Scots together: in 1534 the town of Ystad requested that these foreigners be refused access to the towns and that all Scots already established there be forced to employ only Danes or Germans as helpers and apprentices.

Opposition to the migrant network was just as strong in Sweden, as the example of Malmö demonstrates, where the inhabitants accused those Scots who had acquired citizenship of being bad citizens since they offered work only to those of their own nationality. The petition which they sent to the King refused the Scots the right of citizenship because they did not respect the responsibilities which went with it. Moreover, they were accused of falsely claiming poverty so as not to have to take in the soldiers who came to be billeted in the town; or even of moving town so as to avoid having to accommodate them; and, in particular, of buying up the stalls in the market in foreign currency – in joachims, thalers or Danish money, thus disadvantaging the poor bourgeois class who had only honest money to offer and who, unlike the Scottish merchants, could not bid up to two or even three times higher than the price asked. For all these reasons, the bourgeoisie of Malmö demanded that henceforth the Scots be refused the right of citizenship.[100]

An analysis of the geography and chronology of different rulings against the migrant merchants in northern Europe, Spain[101] and in the Rhine area[102] demonstrates the wide variety of local circumstances and the numerous changes in political direction, and also reveals the opposite side of the coin – the times and places which were favourable to the migrants, areas where institutions were more relaxed and where the migrant organizations could gain a foothold. This was the case in Sweden in 1612, after the destruction of Gothenburg by the Norwegians, when Gustavus Adolphus granted foreigners certain privileges and advantages in order to repopulate the town: straight away, a small colony of Scottish merchants established itself and secured a place on the town council, and a group of pedlars and craftsmen formed around them.[103] As soon as they had attained a sufficiently strong position, the *commis* and the pedlars began to avoid paying the expenses involved in obtaining the *droit de bourgeoisie*, to the point that, in 1638, certain Swedish towns had on their registers more than 70 who were engaged in business activities – some of them for more than ten years – but who had yet to buy the *droit de bourgeoisie*.[104]

In this way, the contradictory interests of the princes, the populace and the sedentary merchants, in conjunction with a lack of means to enforce the numerous rulings (which were successively contradictory) and, in certain areas, the strength of the peddling networks themselves, effectively disabled the strictest legislation. Merchants and pedlars always succeeded in gaining access to the city and disregarded geographical restrictions, institutional limitations and any form of specialization which was forced upon them.

Goods, banking and smuggling

These small business networks had a certain number of common characteristics. They relied on commercial diversity: merchants and pedlars traded in all types of merchandise, depending on the demand and the opportunities – even though each family had a relative speciality, which had its roots in the broad specialization of their home region – the southern Tyrol for carpets,[105] Lake Como for citrus fruits, or the Upper Dauphiné for gloves. Three factors forced them to offer a wider selection of goods: the desire to reach a larger clientele by offering the widest possible range of products; methods of payment in which exchange and barter played a large part; and the search for new or forbidden goods which would mean larger profits. Thus, in 1692, the stocklist for Antonio Brentano's shop in Nuremberg revealed that he had on sale salted herrings, salmon, beef, cheese (Parmesan in particular), tobacco and prunes: at his death 11 years later this also included 1537 pounds of coffee, 67 pounds of tea, 65 pounds of truffles – the first potatoes – oil, candy sugar, cotton, paper, Spanish and Rhenish wine, and Dutch and Spanish tobacco. During the same period, Carl Brentano's shop contained casks of capers, figs, salted lemons, Parmesan, bay leaves, rice, nuts, almonds, olives, oil, lemonade, 180 pounds of chocolate, a cask of dried truffles, four barrels of truffles in oil, Spanish wine, Brazilian tobacco, 34 pounds of Spanish snuff, two boxes of rubber, a barrel of indigo, a small cask of cochineal, 140 caskets of blue and pink wood, three bales of cotton and 16 bales of silk.[106]

Moreover, the peddling organizations turned all trade circuits to their advantage. The pedlars sold their goods on credit, and demanded repayment in the form of buying or renting fields; or as a share of the harvests, which they stored there in the village in rented cellars and barns. In this way they multiplied their access to other markets and short-circuited a certain amount of trade between town and countryside. From 1505, the tanners of Lucerne denounced the merchants and the *Gritscheneyer* for buying the hides of wild animals, thus doing great harm to their industry.[107] The Society of Souabe complained to the Diet of the Empire shortly afterwards about certain Savoyards whose business practices hindered traditional commerce: 'not content with offering the ordinary man commodities such as fabrics, spices and other indispensable goods right on his doorstep, they allow him to delay payment – while at the same time charging him more – and in the autumn they accept fruit and wine as payment. In this way they draw the poor people to them, all the more so because they are now in debt to the pedlar and, because of the difficulties in which they find themselves, can no longer visit the fairs and markets in the towns but must wait instead for these foreign pedlars to return. The latter come back when the wine and fruit have been harvested, demand their share and snatch from the poor wretch's hands all that he has to live on. Worse, in numerous places, they have even begun to rent or acquire cellars and coffers in which to store their fruit and keep their wine.'[108] In 1626, the community of Küssnacht in central Switzerland became worried by the number of coppersmiths and pedlars from the Valle d'Aosta who were renting fields.[109] During the same period, the spice merchants of Basel demanded the expulsion of Italian merchants who had set up shop in private houses.[110]

Similar complaints were registered in Poland against the Scots, who did business on credit terms or in exchange for farm produce or raw materials.[111] Malmö justified its refusal to allow citizenship to the Scots by arguing that they were only following the example set by Ystad, Angelholm, Roskilde and other towns impoverished by peddling; for as soon as the autumn fairs were over, the itinerant merchants and their servants then travelled from village to village with their clothes and pottery and, in the countryside, bartered and sold so effectively that the peasants no longer found it necessary to take their own wares to the town. In this way the pedlars rounded up all potential merchandise – commodities such as butter, animal pelts, tallow and leather – and bought them up. Furthermore, so as to carry out their business without fear of reprisals, they bribed the King's officers who were supposed to prevent dealings such as these.[112] Indeed, pedlars everywhere were paid in peasant produce which they then added to their stock. At the beginning of the seventeenth century, when the sedentary merchant structure was weak, the towns authorized the peasants to sell their goods to the pedlars[113] if their turnover in the marketplace wasn't high enough; and in response the town merchants never gave up trying to recapture the markets they had lost and attempted to limit the foreign pedlars to selling only those products imported from their own country. But the increase in complaints and rulings throughout the seventeenth century demonstrates the ineffectiveness of these measures.[114]

The activities of the craftsmen at the lower end of the migratory scale was repeated at the level of the elite, where, alongside their shops, they also established factories producing foodstuffs or other objects of value in peddling terms – hence there were factories producing tobacco, fancy goods and peddling record books. The Bolongaro family, for instance, who were originally from Stresa on the banks of Lake Maggiore, specialized in the tobacco business and opened a snuff factory.[115] In Strasbourg, Claude Droz, a merchant living in Chambéry, extended his activities in three directions. Firstly, with a tobacco factory, which he owned in partnership with his ex-*commis* Wandervieille, who was still a merchant at Pont-de-Beauvoisin, and with Peret who lived near Geneva. The running of the factory was entrusted to another Savoyard, Claude-François du Puis, who acted as 'clerk to the company, with a power of attorney in its affairs'; he had previously been a merchant in Lyon, which he left in 1702 to come to Strasbourg and look after the factory. The choice of tobacco is a good indicator of the practices of such merchant networks – it was a new and sought-after commodity, and an item of merchandise that was subject to strict controls in various countries. Similarly, the choice of Strasbourg as a place to set up a business was not a chance decision: the area benefited from a particularly favourable situation with regard to customs duties since it lay outside of the zone where the 'Ferme' tax applied. Moreover, the equipment required for tobacco production did not entail heavy investments: two bolting machines for the tobacco, one large wheel 'which moved eight pestles to crush the tobacco', nine sieves of brass wire, two millstones to grind the tobacco and one large empty vat. As well as the tobacco factory, the Droz family also had a wholesale haberdashery shop which the son Guillaume Droz managed. The stock inventory of the shop lists significant quantities of light articles of clothing, haberdashery, hosiery and fancy goods, precisely the goods which were attractive to the packmen. Finally, in yet another house, Droz had set up a ribbon factory containing eight looms of which four 'were in working order and on which there were about six ounces of silk' and a few other instruments for working the silk. The business papers for the shop demonstrate the connection between big business and small-scale peddling: there are lists of letters and bills from Geneva, Amsterdam, Basel and Lyon – an essential stopping place, whose fair was a particularly important centre for redistribution. The record of debts, which confirms the close links with the Savoy and its migrants, points to the fact that the knife-grinders, in collaboration with the packmen, played a part in the expansion of the business.[116] Only through a study of the Drozs' home village – and Chambéry was probably only a place to which they emigrated – would one be able to pick out the family names and links and to reconstruct in full what the inventory drawn up after Droz's death only hints at. This would also bring into sharper focus our knowledge of the links between the various migrations and the strategies of diversification adopted by the pedlar-merchants established in the city.

In addition, the itinerant merchants continued to act as money-lenders. Jean Giraud and André Masson both kept a special account book in which they made a note of the money they had lent in the different places in which they did business; Jean Giraud even accepted deposits of money and paid interest to those who entrusted him with such sums.[117] That the business network relied on attendance at the fairs is demonstrated by a map showing where the Bittots' debtors lived. The places where payment was made were the Easter and September fairs in Frankfurt; the Saint-Michel (29 September) fair in Leipzig and, from the beginning of the seventeenth century, the Saint-Martin (11 November) fair in Besançon.[118] Naturally, the sedentary merchants denounced the credit arrangement which bound the peasant clientele to the itinerant merchants and allowed the latter to arrange repayments at a rate which was very favourable to them: either taking a share of the harvests, or waiting until autumn when the peasants had just sold their crops.[119] The authorities had no idea what to do in response to these practices apart from blaming the peasants for their 'thoughtlessness' as the Austrian government did; because, it explained, to tax the travelling merchants more heavily would only make the goods more expensive, since the merchants would immediately put the cost of the new taxes onto the prices: however, to deprive the pedlars of their concessions would ruin the peasants who were in debt to them. After having tried in vain to restrict their access to these numerous markets, finally the government could only come up with the internal workings of the market itself as a weapon, and the competition it fostered: but the competition was between similar parties, Savoyards or Italians, since the Germans 'were not very good at business';[120] in other words, they did not have at their disposition an organization which was as much in tune with the economic climate.

Through their financial dealings, the migrant merchants rose above the framework of family and peasants and gradually became merchant-bankers who boasted a clientele where craftsmen rubbed shoulders with lords and members of the lower middle classes. In 1574 there were 18 *welsche Firmen* in Nuremberg who traded in silk, velvet and spices and ran a bank. They sent representatives to the Frankfurt and Leipzig fairs. In 1625 a merchant from Nuremberg complained that the *Welschen* dominated the business of bills of exchange.[121] The success of certain merchants, such as that of the Brentano family, was striking but should not conceal the fact that many important German companies and banks started out in this way, using both the income from itinerant sales made to the poor on credit terms, and that from lending money to the wealthiest members of society. Among the most famous companies, mention must be made of Perrolaz de Magland who, in association with Belmont, Lichier Ribola and de Casal from the Valle d'Aosta, and with the Brentanos of Lake Como, monopolized the retail trade across the mid-Rhine region in the 1700s, and simultaneously joined the ranks of the bankers; or, equally, the Favre company, established by a family from Tignes in the Upper Tarentaise, which, in the eighteenth century, was nicknamed 'Fugger of Lake Constance'.[122] As their range of debtors now included increasing numbers from the upper classes, the merchandise sold echoed this, given that the pedlars could supply on demand any item desired.

One last feature, there beneath the surface in all aspects of the merchant organizations: men and merchandise circulated and worked on the fringes of the law. This constant is, of course, the most difficult to establish, even if one can hazard a guess at the profits gained from the skill with which these men manipulated the rules – at all levels. Goods were transported along routes where it was possible to avoid customs and tolls, especially when some of the goods were of smuggled origin, as was the case with raw wool and, in particular, tobacco, which was grown on a large scale (despite the ban on this) in the Alpine valleys of Lombardy[123] and processed in the towns of the Rhine where the laws were more flexible. As soon as a new market opened up or circumstances allowed and, in particular, as soon as war began, smuggling and illicit warehouses multiplied.[124] Armies and war always created places where there were excellent profits to be had: it is difficult to imagine an encampment during the Thirty Years War which didn't have its pedlars, its own community of suppliers, *vivandières* and merchants.[125] Before they settled in Strasbourg, the Savoyards were often to be found in garrison towns, depending on the military events of the time, until the royal powers established a large garrison in Strasbourg, thus increasing the opportunities for trafficking in the town itself.[126] When the war moved south the merchants and carters from the Dauphiné and Briançon went with it.[127] A fondness for military routes was one of the constants of the profession.

The pedlars also circulated in this legal twilight: the richest tried as hard as possible to avoid paying costly registration fees in the city, thus confusing both urban and peddling hierarchies. We have already observed this in Sweden and Switzerland; we can also see it in Strasbourg at the beginning of the eighteenth century. The Savoyard Guillaume Droz (whose business activities were many), like Claude-François du Puis who ran the tobacco factory, went no further than paying fees for residency – just like Estienne Romanet who had opened a shop in Strasbourg even though he was a burgher in Besançon; or like the Roche brothers, married to two sisters, where one had been accepted to the rank of *bourgeois* and the other simply registered himself as being a resident – in other words, on the first rung of the ladder towards recognition as a citizen, the same rung as the legions of knife-grinders (something the native merchants never passed up an opportunity of denouncing).[128] A society based on order and status here came up against the organizational logic of the peddling network: thus, as soon as one or two members of the family firm were legally established in the city, the others saw no advantages in paying duties and taxes which they would have to add to the sale price of their goods. It was also a sign that they didn't yet share urban values. These same merchants were careful not to register with the local administration the vast number of young men who came to work for them several months of the year, nor to purchase status for them; however they didn't miss an opportunity to send them out on business.[129] A substantial amount of the profits no doubt came from the accumulation of all such fraudulent practices and irregularities.

These networks operated at the margins of the law, on the level of community states within constitutional States, complete with their own internal bodies of justice and policing. In effect, the interdependency of the migrants was indispensable for the prosperity of the whole. Information and surveillance mechanisms, which we will examine later on (chapter 6), were there to monitor this. In actual fact there were very few instances where the migrant merchants openly quarrelled between themselves and called in the legal authorities to sort it out: they preferred to resolve any difficulties before an informal tribunal made up of their merchant compatriots.[130] In the same way, merchants stated categorically in their wills that the inventories and declarations that they had made between themselves were to be respected. The closing lines of Paul Delor's will, made in Lyon on Monday 15 May 1656, were 'expressly forbidding that any inventory be made of his goods by the forces of justice, requesting the forces of justice only to take notice of the last inventory which they will find to have been drawn up between himself and his associates and by which his heirs, testamentary guardians and trustees agree to be bound.'[131]

As the Genoese withdrew to Genoa, the migratory movements of the smaller merchants represented a new strategy – through the use of the whole village migratory system – for building up an extensive business. At a higher level the temporary migration of the merchants from the Savoy and the Dauphiné in the sixteenth and seventeenth centuries was perhaps not so different from that of the Genoese merchants between the twelfth and fifteenth centuries:[132] just like the latter, they thought of themselves as 'merchant-travellers'; like them, they relied on their families, friends, servants, agents and book keepers; like them, they endeavoured to conquer the market by covering and infiltrating it,[133] and, like them, they kept themselves to themselves.

It is more important to take note of the extraordinary capacity of the migrant merchants for exploiting all opportunities for profit, the ease with which they adapted between the diverse locations within their network and the balance between its various axes, than it is to note the diverse receptions which greeted them. This balance between locations was the basis of the migratory structure, at the centre of which were several powerful families from the Alpine villages. Because of this structure, despite the constant friction with the sedentary merchants, and in defiance of the political moves to contain them and change their trading practices, the links established at the end of the Middle Ages between town wholesalers and itinerant pedlars from the same region lingered until the end of the eighteenth century.

2

The Eighteenth Century: a Return to the Regional Areas

Between the seventeenth and eighteenth centuries, the vast peddling networks became fragmented and withdrew to regional areas. The chronology of this withdrawal, a result of the encounter between internal changes in the adopted country and those in the home villages, had its own logic and periods of inertia: the break-up was sometimes abrupt and sometimes the result of a gradual change, depending on the region. But by the end of the eighteenth century, this transformation had been accomplished everywhere.

In the French and Savoyard Alps, the first crack in the migratory system was a political one. In France the affirmation of royal sovereignty, centred on religious unity and the war, upset the balance of the mountain economy between 1685 and 1715. The decision to go into exile taken by the majority of the peddling 'elite' as well as by a significant proportion of the Protestant population of the villages threw the networks into disarray. In the Oisans region, almost the entire population of Mizoen, half that of Besse and Clavans and around a third of La Grave set off into exile; in Queyras and in certain villages in the Briançonnais similar losses were experienced. The mountain valleys became correspondingly poorer, and the fairs which had been set up a century before under the stimulus of the Protestant merchants did not survive the Revocation of the Edict of Nantes.[1]

The war brought its own difficulties and, in 1713, the loss of the Briançonnais valleys of Outremont, accomplished by the Treaty of Utrecht, established for the first time a border between the two sides of the same mountain. In Savoy, the conflict between the Sardinian states and the French monarchy forced the merchants to choose sides. A small proportion chose to stay in France, partly in order to avoid paying the taxes that the Sardinian king intended to impose on the repatriation of capital. In fact, once he became ruler of the Outremont valleys following the peace agreed in Utrecht in 1713, the king of Sardinia blocked the Alpine passes and raised customs duties[2] so as to encourage the development of his own manufacturing industries. The obstacles to free circulation and the increased price of transport now redirected the movement of trade, accustomed to the southern valleys, towards Mont-Cenis.[3] The French Revolution and the Napoleonic Wars completed the process of fragmentation which had begun a century earlier by discontinuing relations between France, Savoy and Germany, thereby forcing the Italians to settle in Germany;[4] but the flow was already greatly reduced through the combined effects of national politics, municipal obstacles and the merchants' growing lack of interest in the highlands.

The politics of affirmation of the nation states was set against a background of profound economic change: the real business was no longer being done on this side of Europe. Since the beginning of the seventeenth century, European business had gravitated towards England, north-west France and Holland. Only the comparative inertia of the migratory movements – mostly due to the fact that the credit networks encouraged the profession to develop within the same regions[5] – maintained the old movements of trade alongside the new movements to other more promising and active markets.

In addition to the business world's economic swing towards the north-west, a new imbalance was introduced between lowland and mountain: the new coastal and urban centres favoured the development of nearby (and easily accessible) regions[6] and the mountain economies found themselves further marginalized and confined. For those who had emigrated to the city, the profits to be gained from mountain manpower were now in competition with what could be gained from investment in the lowlands. In the areas of protoindustrialization, the strategies of credit and payment-in-kind meant that the pedlars were natural intermediaries in these developments. Moreover, the social make-up of these migratory movements strengthened the traditional practice of the peddling 'elite' investing in – and, in some cases, creating – such forms of industrialization. The putting down of economic roots in the lowlands and the subsequent impoverishment of the mountain regions spelled the end of their double lives for the important Alpine merchants – the Bettots, Brentanos, Girauds and Delors. Little by little the mountains became obstacles, isolated communities.

The networks which had been built up between Scotland and the Baltic States, despite a new lease of life between 1716 and 1745 which corresponded to the rise of the Stuarts, underwent the same transformations.[7] The dominant position occupied by the Dutch in Baltic commerce for over a century,[8] and the opening up of the English market following the Act of Union with Scotland, had already signalled the decline of Scottish merchant and pedlar migration: since emigration was no longer as widespread, men gradually integrated into new communities and, towards the end of the eighteenth century, the transformation was accomplished in Poland and Denmark.[9] The renewed activities of the sea adventurers can be traced in the customs records, where names changed after a number of decades.[10] The same phenomenon had occurred a century earlier in Sweden where political expediency had led to gradual integration, via settlement and marriage into native families: once a family had made its money, relations with the home village became strained and the family turned to more profitable activities, and to new family networks and loyalties. The search for new loyalties and a new identity can be read into the choice of godparents and witnesses at family ceremonies, who were no longer exclusively Scottish; and subsequently, from the end of the seventeenth century, into the choice of first names – young David, Robert or Alexander became young Eric, Gustave or Olaf.[11] In the eighteenth century, large companies such as the Swedish Company of the East Indies replaced the Scottish merchant families as a means of support for the poorest migrants, recruiting Scotsmen at all levels who, after ten or twenty years' service, set up their own business in Sweden or returned, rich men, to Scotland.[12]

However, those peddling networks that were organized around the east–west commercial axis, that looked towards Mediterranean Europe, benefited from the shift of the main trade movements towards the Atlantic coast and continued to profit from commercial structures which remained weak in the Iberian peninsula.[13] The families from Briançonnais and Queyras, forced to abandon the Italian market in the eighteenth century, now directed their attention in the opposite direction, towards Spain, Portugal and their American colonies.

Other migratory movements took advantage of the change of direction in the peddling networks to set up their own commercial organizations, as did men from the Auvergne and the Bas Limousin in Spain. Similarly, ethnic minorities – particularly Jews – took a further step towards integration by moving into the place left vacant by the Italians and Savoyards and by extending their activities towards western Europe.[14]

The geography of the merchant networks changed and redefined itself as the profession altered. The number of Savoyards to be found in the German-speaking areas of Switzerland fell dramatically after 1750, and even the Valle d'Aosta began to turn its attention towards France (first towards the Dauphiné, then the South and finally Paris); only those communes which had retained the German dialect – both Gressoneys and the Upper Sesia region – remained loyal to Bavaria and Breisgau. This shift took place after a transitory period in the intermediate zone comprising Franche-Comté, Burgundy and Lorraine. These regions which, from ancient times, had had a certain German-speaking population, now took the ascendancy: in short, now that the great period of migrant settlement which followed the Thirty Years War was over, establishing oneself in even the smaller towns became increasingly difficult.

Such changes took place slowly and overlapped each other: the assimilation of certain migrants did not prevent other families coming to take the place they had vacated, but the influx was greatly reduced. It was not a clean break in the Alps either, and the pedlars from the Varaita valley continued to migrate to the South of France, maintaining a route which became extremely popular again in the nineteenth century.[15] In the eighteenth century, men from Savoy established or re-established merchant networks in France and Germany; men such as André Cleaz from Montcharvin in the Upper Tarentaise, who set up in business in Augsburg in the second half of the eighteenth century, and sent for his cousins and brothers-in-law; at the same time he also had relatives living in Vienna and yet more were established in Ratisbon. But such networks were on a smaller scale and more strictly family-based. These family ventures are recorded in the parish registers of the home villages: once the entire family was integrated into the new commercial market, the family surname disappeared from the village records. A counter-example and a borderline case is that of the Walser enclaves around Gressoney in the Italian Alps, which maintained sufficiently powerful networks to be able to retain both their German dialect and their enduring commercial success.[16]

A withdrawal to the regional areas and the beginnings of protoindustrialization

In order to analyse how this process of dismantling came about, we shall take a closer look at the experiences of two families: the Ratton family from Monêtier (today Le Monêtier-les-Bains) in Briançonnais, who founded a family line in Portugal; and the Brentano family who attempted to settle in the Zurich region. Each represents one of the two main evolutionary models adopted by the peddling elite within the host country: the Ratton family continued to sell merchandise; the Brentanos took part in the process of protoindustrialization.

The Ratton family, originally from Monêtier, reveal much about those families who opened shops in one of the merchant network's earlier locations, where the family had been working for several generations. They achieved this by relying solely on family loyalties and by abandoning their traditional role in the mountain migratory system. At the same time, by ceasing to use village manpower, the family had no further interest in investing in the home village and severed their links with it in favour, in this instance, of gaining a much sought-after entry into the elite class of the country in which they settled.

In the seventeenth century, the Ratton family[17] was part of one of the major Alpine merchant networks which traded between Lyon, Franche-Comté, Italy and Spain. The grandfather, old Jacques Ratton, divided his time between Monêtier and Franche-Comté, where he was a pedlar.

His wife, Jeanne Orsel, was the sister of one of the most important merchants in Lyon, and originally from Briançonnais, and their sister was married to a Briançonnais merchant who had settled in Portugal. Jacques Ratton, the father, peddled between the Alps and Portugal until 1736 when, enticed by his brother-in-law Jacques Bellon, he opened a small retail business in Porto. Less than seven years later, the two brothers-in-law signed a deed of partnership: Bellon stayed behind in Porto and in 1747 Ratton set up a second business in Lisbon where his son Jacques, born in Monêtier in 1736, came to join his parents.

The next generation abandoned the policy of marriage and kinship used to extend and consolidate the network, in favour of assimilation into the chosen region: Jacques Ratton's son married Isabelle de Clamouse, the daughter of an honourary consul of France in Porto and one of the town's most important businessmen. Henceforth, the family fortune was amassed primarily in Portugal, even though they sought to maintain their double identity. The family's entry into the world of the business elite was also reflected in the sons' apprenticeship. The latter no longer learned 'the art of being a merchant' behind the shop counters of relatives who had migrated to different spots in the merchant network; instead their education was entrusted to educational establishments. They were sent first to France to follow the *collège* classes, then abroad – to Saxony or England – to institutions responsible for finishing their education.[18] The family first got rid of property in Monêtier so as to invest in the traditional migrant destinations (Franche-Comté and Portugal) and then, in the wake of the upheaval of the Revolution, opted for Portugal alone.

In those areas where the processes of protoindustrialization were already at work, the migrant elite divided into those who concentrated solely on commercial and financial transactions and those who invested in the dawning industry. These two developments – which remain largely unexplored – cannot be comprehensively differentiated, since more often than not the activities of the former supported those of the latter: the banking arms often enabled other family members to set up manufacturing ventures. Thus the Litschgi family from Gressoney, who had settled in Baden, invested in the exploitation of the mining resources of Schau-im-Land, and established the textile industry in the valleys of the Black Forest and the smelting of iron in Kollnau, near Waldkirch. The Castell family developed handloom weaving in the Elz valley and then, aided by their own banking organization, based in Offenburg, set up a powerful group of wool merchants.[19] In the second half of the eighteenth century a clock-making industry developed in Savoy, driven by the families of the migrant merchants.[20] Investment in local industry and the setting up of firms which specialized in manufacturing those commodities which were particularly attractive to pedlars was not a new idea; indeed it was a strategy characteristic of the merchant networks and the role of peddling in the development of protoindustrialization has undoubtedly been underestimated, as Ulrich Pfister demonstrates using as his starting point the activities of the Curti and Brentano families in the Zurich area at the beginning of the eighteenth century. These initial investments were characterized by the same features as the peddling business: business ventures relied on family associations, with limited capital at the outset, but with the best part of the profits being made through exploiting the limits and loopholes of the system – without being afraid, if the need arose, of embracing lawlessness and smuggling. Where rural production was concerned, one essential element was invariable: the workers were paid in kind.[21]

Indeed, the combination of the migration of pedlars who were tied to a wealthy city business and payment made in kind for the pedlar's goods – a combination which had been at work from the very beginning – carried within it the essence of protoindustrialization. In August 1604 in Paris, César Eustache, 'a merchant residing at Besse in the Dauphiné', went into partnership with Jacques Blattier, 'a haberdashery merchant attached to the Court and presently in this town', to trade in and supply mulberry plants and seeds. The partnership was established for this sole purpose, on the basis of all gains and losses being shared equally. It specifically forbade César Eustache from entering into partnership with anybody else. The company took up residence at the house of an eminent merchant, one *sieur* Olivier Picque, 'a merchant resident in this city of Paris',[22] and, like Eustache, originally from Oisans. On 2 July 1705, César Eustache undertook to supply an association of Parisian merchants (who had signed a contract with the clergy of France to plant a nursery of 50,000 white mulberry bushes in every province of France) with 800 *livres* worth of seeds of white mulberry bushes from the Dauphiné and Languedoc regions and transport them to Lyon at the end of the summer. Five days later he signed a bond for 600 *livres* with the merchant who ran the association's offices because the latter had supplied him with stocks of lingerie, braid and lace: the deed stipulated that the merchant would be repaid with the initial payment from the sale of the mulberry seed.[23] Such deeds allow us to piece together a circuit which began with a rich merchant from the Dauphiné established in Paris, who used pedlars from the mountain regions to collect and transport commodities acquired from the peasants from the Dauphiné and Languedoc regions, which the latter had exchanged against the fancy goods that the pedlars had bought on credit from the original Paris merchant.

The demand from sedentary business

The break-up of the large networks, the shifting destinations and the return to the regional areas all brought about change within the profession of travelling merchant. Admittedly, the new methods of peddling did not develop at the same pace everywhere: things began to change in England at the beginning of the seventeenth century following union with Scotland and the border peace treaty, and in the eighteenth century in France and in the Rhine regions. The new peddling model was fully established at the beginning of the nineteenth century in England and during the second half of the nineteenth century in France.

The geography of the places of origin was always the same: border mountain regions or outlying areas. In France, pedlars came from the Alps, the Pyrenees and the Massif Central area as well as from the Jura mountains and from Brittany.[24] In Britain, although migration was less dominated by the highlands because of the existence of a peddling structure organized around the industrial zones, none the less Scotland invariably accounted for the largest number of pedlars.[25] In Belgium it was the Hainaut region which upheld the old tradition[26] and in Italy, pedlars always came from the Alps or the central region of the Apennine mountains. On the other hand, Spain, at that time, did not appear to have developed an indigenous peddling network.[27]

In comparison with the peddling which occurred in previous centuries, this new structure was distinguished by an increase in the number of pedlars; by the use made of pedlars by all urban commerce and no longer just by the village 'elite' who had settled in the towns; by the wider range of goods offered by the pedlars; and by the disappearance of the multiple transactions involving the pedlar (in which payments in foodstuffs and goods bypassed other markets) in favour of credit alone.

The increase in the number of pedlars was vouched for everywhere, although it is still just as difficult to assess precisely how many men this nomadic population comprised. That England had an early start is obvious, as much from the upsurge in numbers as by the subsequent decline, which had begun even before peddling in France really took off.[28] England thus had a century's head start over the Continent: from the end of the seventeenth century the distribution network covered by the travelling merchants had reached the furthest corners of the land,[29] whilst on the Continent the rural areas had only been partially conquered. In France, the growth in numbers was significant from the 1760s onwards: this is evident from the notaries' records in the home villages, along with the appearance of the term 'pedlar' itself. In the seventeenth century, the records still referred only to 'merchants'; from the eighteenth century, the 'pedlars' appeared in their droves in administrative and legal documents and the migrant hierarchies thereby became more clearly defined, since henceforth 'merchants' were distinguished from 'merchant-pedlars' and from 'pedlars'.[30] In the passport records of the Dauphiné, the balance between the categories is interesting – six merchants (there were doubtless more, but since the writer gives no indication of where they came from, one should treat this with caution),

57 merchant-pedlars and three pedlars – since it reveals the gradual drop in status of the former in favour of the latter which took place during the eighteenth century.[31]

This upsurge was the consequence of the general development of urban business. Henceforth, the pedlars no longer worked solely for merchants who came from the same valleys as themselves but also bought their stocks from other city merchants who used the pedlars to further their own business concerns. This new development brought with it other changes: the better-off pedlars neglected the products of family industry to devote themselves solely to the resale of goods; the less well-off, who were selling their craftsman's knowledge, gradually abandoned this in favour of city goods. Thus the knife-grinders and scissor-sharpeners tended to give up these humbler professions and concentrate solely on trading.[32] This broadening of the range of goods peddled went hand in hand with similar changes taking place in sedentary business.

At the same time, the widespread migration of craftsmen such as the masons became a phenomenon which was independent of merchant migration, as the craftsmen organized themselves into stable communities. In the Giffre valley in the nineteenth century, a guild called *Des Trois Couronnés* brought together all those in the building trade: builder's mates, mortar-mixers, stone-cutters, masons, chief masons, works foremen, overseers and building contractors as well as those in related trades: carpenters, joiners and roofers. In the nineteenth century, they had a virtual monopoly over the building trade in Geneva.[33] The identification of certain villages with the migration of craftsmen demands a comprehensive study which would enable us to understand the various choices facing the mountain communities, and examine the bonds which initially linked the merchants and craftsmen of these villages.

Eventually large quantities of a new product – printed material – became part of the pedlar's range of wares. Initially this was distributed from centres of production in eastern France and the German regions of the Rhine, from Paris and Lyon: by the mid-eighteenth century it had reached most of the rural areas.[34] Before specific peddling networks were built up around it, printed matter was an extra commodity much valued by pedlars of haberdashery: so much so that trade in this alone supported most of the haberdashery businesses in eighteenth-century Troyes, for example, as the aldermen of the town illustrated in a statement in 1760 supporting Jean Oudot IV's widow against the Paris *Parlement* (regional supreme court). 'The majority of the haberdashery business in the city of Troyes is done with the packmen who come to stock up with volumes from the *bibliothèque bleue**. Should Widow Oudot's printing

---

* The *bibliothèque bleue* was a popular collection of titles in the eighteenth century.

press be closed down, then this source of business in Troyes would soon dry up and become exhausted, since M. Garnier's printing press which competes with that of Mme Oudot in producing this type of book could never provide for the considerable demand which occurs every year. The packmen, no longer being able to stock up with titles from the *bibliothèque bleue* as before, would not make a deliberate detour to Troyes (as they do now) solely to buy haberdashery goods which they could find as easily anywhere else.'[35]

Trading in prohibited books became a very attractive business for the pedlars, since there were large profits to be had. Paul Malherbe, who ordered books from Neuchâtel, stored them in a secret warehouse and resold them to pedlars because they were 'the goods with the biggest turnover at the moment... The pedlars are extremely eager for this type of book; they earn far more than on other works, because the price is perfect, a snip given the demand for the book.'[36] The pedlar Personne bought four copies of the *Traité de la Tolérance* for 4 *livres*, 10 *sols** each, and resold them for 7 and 9 *livres*.[37] This, naturally, was only one way in which prohibited books were distributed. This was also carried out through channels which mixed business and friendship: letters were exchanged and books ordered from the friend who was on the spot, who waited until the package was sufficiently full before sending it on to its recipient.[38]

In the mid-eighteenth century, most large towns in northern and central France boasted a bookseller-cum-printer who catered for pedlars.[39] At the same time as printed material was finding its way into the haberdasher's backpack, certain regions were beginning to specialize in this type of peddling – Cotentin and Briançonnais in the eighteenth century, then the valleys of the Pyrenees[40] in the nineteenth century. We shall return to them again in the following chapters.

Finally, in certain areas the disintegration of the previous migratory movements allowed men from other regions to occupy the positions thus left vacant, and, in their turn, to build up an organization of shops and pedlars and to assume a virtual monopoly in a variety of businesses within the chosen region. However, these later networks, like the one found in the Massif Central, only operated within a single country, or indeed, within certain areas.

From pilgrim to pedlar

The Massif Central had not experienced a steady flow of goods through it since the Middle Ages, and so its migratory system developed along different lines. In the case of the Auvergne and Bas-Limousin regions,[41]

* *sol*: old French currency.

the earliest documents indicate that the migrants initially followed the same routes as the pilgrims to St Jacques de Compostelle and Notre-Dame de Montserrat in Catalonia, then a second wave followed the paths taken by the *Reconquista*. In which case the migrants would initially have followed in the footsteps of the clergy, then later followed the nobility who were engaged in battle against the Infidel.

Several facts support this theory. The Limousin population to be found in Christian Spain in the Middle Ages had settled along the routes taken by the pilgrims and the armies.[42] Abbeys such as the Saint-Géraud in Aurillac or the abbey in Tulle owned property in Spain along these holy roads and religious orders were founded in the wake of the *Reconquista*. The noblemen of the lower Limousin region took part in the *Reconquista* and many of the bishops, themselves of Limousin origin, who were elected to Spanish dioceses in the sixteenth century, came from the same region which was subsequently to provide the largest number of migrants to Spain.[43] This first migratory movement was primarily concerned with populating Spain: it was to 'build, sow and prepare the ground for' Frenchmen 'of mainly Auvergnat and Limousin' origin 'who go one after another to Spain' and were 'almost always the vinegrowers, farm labourers, masons, joiners, stone-cutters, turners, wheelwrights, carters, rope-makers, quarriers, saddlers, and harness-makers' in Navarre and Aragon.[44]

From the fourteenth century men from the highlands of the Massif Central as well as those from the high valleys of the Pyrenees repopulated Catalonia and Aragon, finding in these areas towns to rebuild, land to cultivate and business to revive.[45] Yet in the seventeenth century, an analysis of Barcelona's French colony revealed that the French merchants in Catalonia did not have their origins in that migratory movement, but came from Marseilles and Languedoc with the Pyrenees and the Auvergne providing an unskilled workforce.[46] As far as the richer provinces of Andalusia were concerned, despite the differences in their figures the testimonies of the Golden Age tally with those of Antoine de Montchrétien over the importance of itinerant commerce – which was almost exclusively the province of the French – and on the role played by the men from the Auvergne: 'Most of them come and go still and the others return home when they have earned a certain amount of money in the richer Spanish provinces such as Seville, Toledo, Granada, Valencia or at the Court itself, where they carry out several offices; water-selling, peddling ironmongery and cloth, and selling hardware and cutlery.'[47] In 1705 Père Labat described how the Auvergnats infiltrated the lower ranks of itinerant trading, and how some of them made a success of it:

Not counting the craftsmen with open air stalls, nor the merchants, of whom there are always 20 foreigners for every Spaniard, whilst I was in

Cadiz, I was assured that, in Andalusia alone, there were more than 20,000 Frenchmen from the Auvergne, Marche and Limousin regions and the area around the Garonne, whose job was to take water to the houses, sell coal, oil and vinegar in the streets, serve in the inns, plough the land and bring in the harvest, and work in the vineyards. These men almost always return home every three years, taking with them three or four hundred piastres, and often more. . . . There are a great number of coal merchants who, after a few years, were in a position to return to Spain with a backpack containing fabrics and other petty goods and who are now the most important merchants in the Kingdom.[48]

During the same period, one can identify the beginnings of specialization in the emigrant's declared line of business when he left France: the men who later developed businesses came from the same regions which already sent men into Spain to trade mules, horses and silver[49]: using the capital represented by their animals, the Auvergne merchants thus gradually succeeded in breaking into the lucrative gold and silver market, which brought the largest profits. In Spain, they were accused of disguising their dealings in gold and silver jewellery behind the cry of 'fil de Flandres' [thread from Flanders] which is what they were supposed to be selling – to the point where the expression became a password to alert those who wished to get rid of old jewellery or valuable old crockery.[50] As well as trafficking in metal and piastres, they also exploited activities which were prohibited, such as the exchange of silver coins, which always brought a 20 per cent profit; or the circulation of merchandise, which they managed to do despite the laws against foreign merchants, or by getting round these laws.[51]

Those involved in this particular migratory movement none the less remained for a long time at the bottom end of merchant society, as though other groups who had long monopolized the retail trade were holding them back in their bid to acquire that indispensable shop: when, in 1625 and 1674, the Spanish authorities seized the goods of French merchants, the number of men from the Massif Central region who were affected by this was absurdly low;[52] the same hierarchies were revealed a century later in an analysis of the French colony in Cadiz. At the head of this colony, which consisted of some 150 important businesses in the town, were the Protestant merchant-bankers. After them came two distinct groups of merchants from the mountain regions: firstly the Basco–Béarnais valleys of the Pyrenees, and secondly a group from the Upper Dauphiné region. However, there were virtually no men from the Auvergne and Limousin regions to be found at the head of any of the 145 main French firms in Cadiz. All 366 Limousin men, bar one, belonged to the service sectors or artisan class: out of 160 servants, 104 were of Limousin origin, as were 73 out of 74 bakers, and 17 out of 33 cafe owners and waiters; and all of the 50 chairmakers, 35 water-carriers, 19 colliers and 16 cooks were from the Limousin region.[53] At the end of the eighteenth century, the French consul in Cadiz, Mongelas, analysed the migratory situation: those from the Auvergne had achieved a kind of monopoly in a number of professions, which they defended from within a professional organization with communal funds at its disposal. When somebody left he passed on his share of the market to a member of his family or, failing that, sold it to a third party.[54]

In the eighteenth century the migratory movement underwent a gradual reorganization, shifting towards the higher echelons of the migrant hierarchy: at the lowest levels, knife-grinders and water-carriers from the Auvergne and Gascony abandoned the journey to Spain in favour of closer French destinations and they were replaced by Spaniards from Galicia and the Asturias.[55] At the same time, the migratory peddling 'elite', who had secured themselves a monopoly in those areas of the Spanish economy which required little or no capital investment, gradually built up firms which were based around the extended family on the model of those which were so successful for the pedlars from the high Alpine valleys.

Admittedly the terrain was no longer as favourable and these firms were being established at the same time as the country was closing its doors to foreigners. In Madrid in 1730, the 'Cinco Gremios Mayores' [five major trade unions], having fought for this throughout the Golden Age, were granted the monopoly on the sale of fabrics and haberdashery goods, thus pushing back foreign competitors to beyond a five-league exclusion zone and forcing them to reorganize themselves using the medium-sized towns as a base.[56] Moreover, from 1627 onwards, laws against peddling abounded,[57] even though they didn't manage to prevent the merchant network's continued growth.[58]

In the last 30 or so years of the eighteenth century, the network was established, and a report of 1770 gives an account of the 'considerable' numbers of men from Gascony, Limousin and Auvergne who were spreading throughout Spain 'and peddling their wares from village to village, trading as coppersmiths'; they created 'reasonably large businesses in a few places in each province, whence they spread into the villages' and they 'all return to France from time to time, whither they take the fruits of their labours, and another comes in the place of the one who has left'.[59]

These merchant companies came out into the open in the nineteenth century. In 1812, the prefect of Cantal estimated the number of people involved in them to be at least 400. They were constructed upon a family network and banking system, and the labour supplied by village manpower. The principles behind their organization all aimed to keep the migratory chain as self-sufficient as possible, by preventing its shareholders from breaking away from the family banking system and by keeping the tightest possible hold over the migrant manpower, in order to guarantee the loyalty of the members to the venture. They adopted the principles of the Cadiz businesses which, from the eighteenth century, imposed celibacy upon their shareholders whilst they were in Spain (thus, in 1754, a report on commerce in Andalusia stated that 'the French merchants very seldom marry Spanish women').[60]

The organization was based upon close family links: upon the sons and sons-in-law of shareholders. Out of the 102 members of the Chinchón company, 40 individuals from around 20 parishes in the northern canton of Aurillac had six surnames between them.[61] Recruitment from within the family went hand in hand with extremely strict rules regarding time spent in France and investment of capital: each new partner or young apprentice had to contribute an initial capital sum, and only a quarter of those shareholders travelling between France and Spain could return to France each year. After two years, those who had the right to return home were not allowed, however, to take all their profits with them: a certain amount had to be reinvested to boost the capital investment in the Spanish business.[62]

With the built-up capital, other shops were opened, enabling the pedlars to circle ever further afield into the rural areas:

the main shops were established about 15–20 leagues apart, under the management of two or three shareholders. Each shop served a surrounding area made up of a good number of towns or large villages where other shareholders went to sell on a retail basis merchandise which they obtained from the region's shop – some operated from the fixed base of an open-air stall in the larger towns; others peddled their wares using mules in the villages assigned to them, travelling there each week on set days. Opening a new shop at a suitable distance from the others was enough to provide work for 12–15 new shareholders. Many of these businesses consisted of 100 partners or more, who traded over an area of 30–40 leagues. They had a very considerable amount of capital, with established credit arrangements with factories in France, Switzerland and Spain – and they realized profits in proportion to this. It would be no exaggeration to value them at 2,000 francs for each full shareholder, although they didn't reach this point until after a period of around 16 years of partnership, during which time the business had increased in value over a series of 4-year periods.[63]

Their system therefore, which functioned on several levels, was based on a twofold selection process: both in the village and in Spain. In the village only close family had access to the foreign business and to the criterion of family membership was added discrimination in favour of the wealthiest. Sons-in-law had to be rich enough to contribute their share to the business and fathers who introduced their children into it had to provide an initial outlay of 3–4,000 francs for each child. Apprenticeships, which lasted seven years, were another form of selection, this time determined in Spain since, 'depending on their diligence and intelligence, their interest in the profits developed accordingly during

the last four years'.[64] At the end of the first seven-year period, the young
migrant went back to his family for two years; this was usually the time
when his family married him off. The selection process for assessing
business acumen was reinforced by a strict monitoring of the migrant's
conduct, similar to that carried out by numerous Italian firms: it was
forbidden, under threat of expulsion from the organization, to marry in
Spain, to bring one's family there or make it one's home,[65] to gamble
for money or to behave disreputably. A social life with those from the
same background, organized around hostels run by one's compatriots,
card games and hunting expeditions took up the young migrant's free
time.[66] Any lapse was judged by the shareholders and the penalties
ranged from a cut in one's share of the profits to being expelled from
the business.[67]

The family functioned as a supply and information network between
the different sites, and between the home villages and the places of
settlement: letters carried back and forth meant that supply and demand
could be adjusted and that all markets could be exploited.[68]

In Spain, the peasants almost always paid the travelling merchants
and coppersmiths in wheat, flour, wine and wool for the essential goods
which local industry could not offer them. The consequences of these
methods of payment were twofold: on the one hand, the travelling
merchants profited from the share of the agricultural market which
came their way and thus, along with the land-owners, they prevented
the peasants from getting a foothold in the market;[69] on the other, the
vast quantities of cereals they received in payment engendered a parallel
industry, that of breadmaking, in which the men from Cantal gradually
acquired the monopoly, right up to the end of the nineteenth century.

These family firms continued none the less to provide work for the
men from the village by employing them as domestic servants.[70] This
explains the continued need for trips back to the homeland and also the
fragmentation of families between the two sites. In Auvergne, apprenticeship contracts varied between 400 and 10 *livres*; the parents of a
child who was to be apprenticed for two and a half years to a copper-
smith based in Spain, and whose uncle took him there, were charged
400 *livres*; in the middle price range many were the boys who, between
the ages of 12 and 19, were taken with their father or a relative on their
rounds. At the bottom of the pile, a parallel industry was created in
which a few men who were little more than smugglers sold dreams of
Spain and offered, in return for an all-inclusive sum of 10–45 *livres*, to
act as a guide, and to feed and find a place for the would-be migrant
on arrival in Spain.[71] It is none the less difficult to understand what lay
behind this system of recruitment which, given the customs of the time,
would seem to augur merciless exploitation of the migrant, unless it was
simply to conceal a 'migration of exclusion', as was practised at that
time in the Haut Dauphiné and in the Apennines.[72]

The large merchant firms disintegrated in the agonies of revolution. Already, during the final decades of the eighteenth century, the merchant-migrants were hindered by the measures taken to protect the Spanish market and Spanish industry; in particular by the customs tariff of 1782, which got rid of most of the peddling merchandise from the market by making it impossible to import needles, hats, shoes, playing cards, soap or fancy fabrics from Lille or Armentières. Opposition to revolutionary France, and then the Napoleonic Wars, finally destroyed the links between the two countries: on 20 July 1791, a royal edict ordered 80,000 Frenchmen domiciled in Spain to swear allegiance to King Charles IV or leave the country. In 1793, and once again in 1808, in the midst of pillaging and demonstrations against the French, they were expelled from Spain and their goods confiscated.[73]

3

The Eighteenth Century:
the Networks of Booksellers
and Book Pedlars in
Southern Europe

In the eighteenth century, peddling on a large scale – where the entire population of the home village benefited from the network of shops established by the wealthiest families – was only made possible by the market for printed material. This durability is explained by the choice of product: printed material was a new commodity, very much sought-after, likely to bring in substantial profits and one where there was a market for both legal and smuggled goods. In 1754, François Grasset, formerly chief clerk with the Cramer booksellers in Geneva, wrote in a letter to Malesherbes that

> the bookselling trade in Spain and Portugal, as well as that of many Italian towns, is totally controlled by the French; all of them from a village in a Briançonnais valley in the Dauphiné. Active, hard-working and moderate, they make successive trips to Spain and almost always marry amongst themselves . . . not only is the bookselling trade in their hands, but also the market for geographical maps, prints, clock-making, cloth, printed calico, stockings, hats and so forth.[1]

In his letter, Grasset suggests that a significant share of the book market was seized and controlled by a single village community. We shall see how far this statement was true, and then attempt to understand how this network of booksellers established itself and what its links with peddling were.

Let us quickly review the nature of publishing in Europe, where first

France and then Switzerland played a leading role in the publishing industry of Southern Europe. In the seventeenth century, European publishing was characterized by the dominance of Holland and England and by the weakness of Spanish[2] and Italian[3] output – this being especially so from 1620–30 onwards. Spanish publishing in the seventeenth century was, in fact, completely stagnant:[4] the risky formalities of preventive censorship, harassment by the Inquisition, the excessive privileges granted to certain religious orders, the inadequate supply of paper and steadily increasing taxes forced Spanish authors to have their works published abroad, especially in Lyon. Censorship, however – which was as much the result of secular demands as a result of the Inquisition – could not hold back the trade in 'free' books despite the rigorous border controls and the heavy fines imposed.[5] Thus, from the end of the sixteenth century, booksellers in Paris, Lyon and Rouen sent their publications to the Iberian peninsula, where there were significant colonies of foreigners.[6] This state of affairs meant that first France and then Switzerland played the part of intermediary between northern and southern Europe.[7] In the eighteenth century, Geneva became a key centre of the European market for printed matter, both for redistribution and for production.[8]

Some figures as proof of the importance of the Briançonnais community in the book trade: the list of those individuals who had an account with the Cramer bookshop between 1755–60, as published by Giles Barber, reveals a minimum of 38 names of booksellers originally from Monêtier or the surrounding villages who were then established booksellers in France, Italy, Spain and Portugal. The confiscation of goods from the Briançonnais population of Spain during the Terror of 1793 revealed that 45 families originally came from Monêtier alone.[9] Similarly, Aristide Albert has published a list of 51 booksellers, originally from the very same villages, who were in business in the same places (as well as extending their activities into the Brazilian market) at the end of the eighteenth century and beginning of the nineteenth.[10] Naturally, these lists are open to cross-checking. Other names from other sources can be added to this provisional list, revealing nearly 50 Briançonnais family names (referred to 140 times) amongst those who ran bookshops in Europe in the eighteenth century (see appendix).

Is it then possible to assess the part played by the Briançonnais population in the book trade? Admittedly they were not the only ones who traded in books in Mediterranean Europe: if one examines this market using the Cramers' business as a starting point, it becomes clear that a network of Protestant merchant-bankers,[11] who were active in the granting of loans to bookshops and the distribution of books, also played a key part; as did national business correspondents in Italy and Spain. However, in Portugal all booksellers were foreign and almost exclusively from the Briançon region: in the second half of the eighteenth century at least 14 of the 17 booksellers in Lisbon were originally from Briançonnais; in Coimbra there were five of them, and in Porto, six.[12]

Amongst the Cramers' correspondents, there were two main types of customer: individuals who bought for personal consumption, or for a small family circle, and whose turnover of business was modest and irregular; and then there were the bookshops. The list of their Italian customers ran to 79 names, of which only 22 appeared for more than three consecutive years. All the Briançonnais booksellers were on it: the Faures in Parma; Joseph Bouchard in Florence; the Graviers – Jean, Yves and Joseph-Antoine – in Genoa and Naples; Reycends and Collomb in Milan, and Reycends, Guibert and Sylvestre in Turin (who subsequently became Reycends and the Guibert brothers). If one looks at it in terms of turnover, 23 customers, of whom most were private clients, did 100 *livres* worth of business; 35, a mixture of booksellers and private customers (including the Reycends and Collomb booksellers in Milan and the Bonnets in Parma), did 1,000 *livres* worth of business; above 2,000 and 3,000 *livres* and this was really the domain of booksellers. Nine booksellers fell into this category (all of them Italian apart from the Faure family); seven of whom did between 5,000 and 12,000 *livres* worth of business and stood apart from the others. Certain of the latter – Reycends and Guibert in Turin (11,000 *livres*), Bouchard in Florence (10,000 *livres*), Gravier in Genoa (11,000 *livres*) – were Briançonnais; the rest (one of whom did 5,000 *livres* worth of business, two did 8,000 *livres* and one 12,000 *livres*) were Protestant merchant-bankers – in other words they belonged to the other powerful network which supported the Cramer bookshop. This latter network was significantly different from the one under consideration since it did not function in terms of temporary migration. If one adds up the amount of business done (somewhat complex, since beyond 2,000 *livres* one has to take numerous bad debts into account) one arrives at a total of 121,300 *livres*, of which a good half, 65,000 *livres*, can be traced back, in almost equal proportions, to the network of Protestant merchant-bankers and the Briançonnais network.

In the Iberian peninsula, 63 correspondents are recorded. In comparison with Italy, there were far fewer small accounts. Seven correspondents did business up to 100 *livres*; 26 generated 1,000 *livres* worth of trade, of which four were Briançonnais booksellers (these were Dubeux, Reycends and Collomb in Lisbon, Dubeux in Coimbra and Bérard in Seville); then one reaches the 3–5,000 *livre* mark which comprised 14 booksellers – seven native booksellers, three Protestant merchant-bankers and four Briançonnais booksellers. Lastly, the most important clients were of a slightly different ilk to those in Italy since two Protestant bankers, Pascaly and Larralde in Madrid who traded to the sum of 59,000 along with Caylan, Cabenas and Jugla in Cadiz (34,000) and a

Spanish bookseller, Mutis of Cadiz (27,000), easily topped the list. Behind them were two Briançonnais booksellers, who did between 10,000 and 16,000 *livres* worth of trade – Bonnardel of Lisbon (16,000) and Mallen in Seville and Valencia (11,000). Finally there was another important group consisting of seven booksellers, who did between 6 and 9,000 *livres* worth of trade, of whom five were native (Alvera and Mena in Madrid, Pi in Barcelona, Mendoza in Saragossa, Espinosa in Cadiz) and two were Briançonnais (Ginioux in Coimbra and Bertrand in Lisbon). The business done by the Briançonnais booksellers was 56,000 *livres* out of a total figure of 265,200 *livres*; in other words they accounted for between a third and a fifth of the Cramers' market.

This is only a partial overview of the book trade since the Cramers were not the only ones supplying these markets; but, equally, it is only a partial evaluation of the activities of the Briançonnais booksellers, who also worked for other publishers, in particular for the Gosse family and for La Société typographique de Neuchâtel.[13] Other names make an appearance: Gendron and Reycends in Lisbon, who were the Gosses' most important correspondents around 1740; still in Lisbon, Borel, Ginioux, Martin and Bertrand, and Jean-Baptiste Reycends had accounts with the Gosses, as did Reycends and Guibert in Cadiz. Mention must also be made of Joseph Collomb, in Marseilles, who was the Cramers' general agent, responsible for debt collection and supplying booksellers: he was good for 12,000 *livres* worth of trade. And not mentioned on the Gosses' and Cramers' business records were even bigger fish, such as Jacques Barthélémy, known as Don Diego of Madrid, one of the most important booksellers in the capital.

Some of these booksellers published Spanish and Portuguese authors in France; booksellers such as Delorme in Avignon or Pierre Gendron who, after leaving Lisbon, set himself up in Paris and became Camoens' publisher. We can assume that they used their family network to distribute their publications. In concluding this overview, mention must be made of another Briançonnais publisher: Marc-Michel Rey of Amsterdam, Rousseau's publisher, whose relationship with the Reycends in Turin, for example, is well documented.[14] And finally, let us add that Jean-Jacques admitted in Book VI that, when he was at Charmettes, he was a customer of Bouchard, a bookseller in Chambéry.

This begs an initial question: how did this network, which we discover fully formed in the eighteenth century, come about? Its beginnings can be reconstructed from certain scholarly works[15] and family archives: it developed from the Protestant merchant-pedlar network of the Upper Dauphiné, which was first visible in the sixteenth century, and which we have already encountered in the seventeenth century in chapter 1. Destroyed by the Revocation of the Edict of Nantes, the network shifted its focus several times before re-forming in the eighteenth century in the neighbouring villages of the Guisane valley.

To understand how such changes were possible, we need to go back to the old merchant network to see how the links forged between families in the mountains in the sixteenth century still held firm in the eighteenth century, despite the dispersal of the families. Let us take another look at this network of people involved in the book trade – this time from the perspective of the Nicolas family from La Grave, who had a bookshop in Grenoble in the seventeenth century.

First, however, one must understand the fundamental reason why the existence of such mountain networks has eluded researchers until now. Booksellers, like haberdashery merchants, have always been studied as part of – and from the point of view of – the town in which they set up shop. Their account books played their part in perpetuating this idea, since when they recorded who they had done business with they made no mention of the shared village origins of certain merchants (which was obvious to them), but noted instead the place where they had their business, which was the only information which mattered in the transaction. For example, Nicolas the bookseller records in his account book his business dealings with Pic and Rome of Paris and with Giraud, Chicot and Grengent of Lyon; he does not record that they were all Alpine merchants. Jean Giraud makes reference in his account book to Salomon, Arthaud and Pic in Turin and the Nicolas family in Grenoble, Arles and Le Puy but not to the fact that all of the above were originally from La Grave. Such practices are understandable: one does not set down that which is obvious and worthless but that which is likely to change, or cause confusion: the merchants moved around and, moreover, each family could have shops in several places – like the Pic family who were to be found in Paris and in Turin; or like the Nicolas family itself. And, of course, the information to be gleaned from the city does not make reconstruction any easier since, most of the time, it says nothing about the origins of the merchants and generally makes no mention of the temporary nature of their settlement in the city. Thus the merchant networks are invisible unless viewed from the starting point of the mountain village. Let us bear in mind that, as research currently stands, the network in which the Nicolas family played a part was active between Switzerland, northern Italy and southern France: between Lyon, Paris, Geneva, Mantua and Perpignan[16] – but that does not mean one should give up hope of uncovering a possible Iberian dimension.[17]

To prove the durability of networks which relied upon the continuing relationships between families, our initial task is to demonstrate a continuity of business. What did the Nicolas family do? Before running a shop in Grenoble, in the sixteenth century they were pedlars who added a few books to their wares, which Benoit Rigaud,[18] the bookseller from Lyon, sold to them on credit terms. The Rigaud family made their fortune in bargain books and were perhaps the first to specialize in publishing and distributing books specifically aimed at pedlars.[19] The success of the Nicolas family in peddling meant that Jean Nicolas I was able to rent a bookshop in Grenoble in 1608. Nicolas' account books, like those of Jean Giraud, bear witness to the fact that the business links forged by previous generations were maintained by those that followed: having supplied the Nicolas family as pedlars in the sixteenth century, the Rigaud family continued to work with them as booksellers in the seventeenth century; moreover Nicolas' account books and those belonging to Giraud were consistent and corresponded to one another, proving that the families never stopped working together. Jean Giraud did business with the Grenoble branch of the Nicolas family, as well as with those established in Arles and in the Puy de Dôme area.

A closer analysis of these account books reveals, furthermore, that these families did the majority of their business with one another; that they were related, naturally;[20] and that they kept close links with their home village: they all married women from La Grave, had at least one family member living there and all returned from time to time. Thus Jean Nicolas I married the daughter of a merchant from the Oisans, Marthe Jullien. His brother Moyse, also a merchant, lived in their home village in Les Terrasses and managed the family fortune. Jean Giraud, his father and grandfather all married daughters of merchants from La Grave – from the Chicot, Monnet, Mallein (the same family who later re-appeared in Spain) and Galot families: all names which go on to pepper each other's account books. Although Jean was considered to be a Lyon merchant, his family and a certain amount of property remained in La Grave. It was in La Grave that he renounced his faith in 1685 and from La Grave that he left France for Vevey in 1687.

Moreover, Nicolas' account book reveals that, though each family specialized in a particular area (in their case, stationery and books; in the case of the Giraud family, silk and fabrics), this specialization came within a wider framework which made use of the manpower and money from the mountains. Hence, in addition to books the Nicolas family also stocked many other types of product in their shop, which filled the pedlars' packs of the time. As well as a wide range of paper, they also dealt in medical supplies, spices, haberdashery and, above all, in furs and gloves on a large scale: between 1646 and 1650 they received 14,000 gloves and 3,744 chamois leathers, and they sent out from Grenoble 23,532 gloves and 4,698 chamois leathers. These figures, which also demonstrate that not all of Nicolas' transactions were recorded in his account books, place him amongst the most prominent glove and fur merchants in the Dauphiné region and put into perspective the part played in his business by the bookshop.[21]

Most business was therefore done between merchants from the Dauphiné region and it was with those particular firms – Chicot, Grengent and Giraud from Lyon, and Rome and Pic from Paris – that the Nicolas family did most business. Jean Giraud's account book, whilst not going into too much detail, reveals that most of the people who owed him money came from the Upper Oisans. Business revolved around the sale of peddling goods and money-lending. An example of this: in 1646, Nicolas sent to '*sieurs* Chicot, Giraud and Grengent 4 dozen scriptures, 1,000 quill pens, several sorts of paper, 62 dozen gloves and an Amsterdam bible'. Moreover, they all lent money, either directly or by using one of the others as an intermediary; thus Nicolas sent clients who were in need of capital in Paris to Rome and Pic.[22] A third aspect of their shared activities was to join forces with other families from the Upper Dauphiné region to set up various business ventures outside of their specialized field of merchandising – such as the partnership which brought together Nicolas and Elisée Julien in building bridges over the Isère river.[23] Without spending too long on the complex family strategies used by these merchants, who were both city and mountain dwellers, it should none the less be noted that, either directly or through the intermediary of a brother or brother-in-law, they put money into government expenditure and into the legal and financial systems of both the mountains and the lowlands.

Following the Revocation of the Edict of Nantes, most of these Protestant families left their mountain villages and Catholic France. However, the links forged over a number of generations were not broken and, after several upheavals, the merchant networks rebuilt themselves. The first development was in human terms: certain families who were partly Catholic, or newly converted to Catholicism, who had up until then been on the fringes of the network, such as the Gravier or Hermil families, now took the place of Protestant families who had been forced to emigrate. The second development was geographic and involved a shift towards other mountain villages. This was the case of the Gravier family, most of whom were Catholic, who were originally from Bez de Monêtier. A Jehan Gravier appeared in La Grave in the sixteenth century, where he married and founded a family line. In 1578, along with other pedlars from La Grave, he was to be found amongst the debtors of the printer Benoît Rigaud of Lyon.[24] A century later in 1671, this branch of the family was still in evidence.[25] They were among the relations and clients of Jean Giraud – Jean Gravier married Suzanne Chicot, Jean Giraud married Marie Chicot and Gravier was one of his debtors.[26] They were Protestants and, in 1686, were scattered between Vevey, London and 'La Carroline'.[27] What is important is that the family links between the Protestant Graviers from La Grave and the Catholic Graviers from Monêtier were never severed and the latter were in a position to replace the Protestant Graviers who emigrated. However, to do this, they relied upon the villages in which they lived, in this case on Monêtier and the surrounding hamlets. The Hermil family illustrates a different type of geographical shift: they never moved from

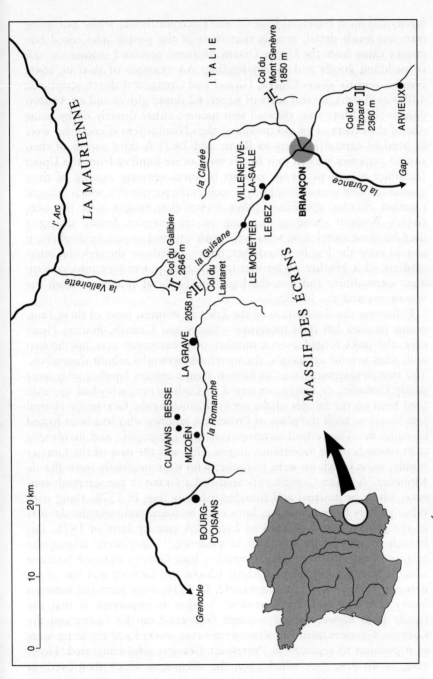

Map 1 The massif des Écrins

the Briançonnais, were related to the Graviers by marriage and, from the seventeenth century, were part of the Giraud merchant network. Once Giraud had left for Vevey, the Hermils were in a position to act as intermediaries. This first geographical shift was not a large step, since it only took in those villages closest to La Grave in the direction of Briançon, and also because in the seventeenth century the bonds of family and work between the Monêtier Catholics and the Protestant network of Haut Dauphiné merchants were already numerous. One final example: in 1690, amongst those in debt to Jacques Bérard – a newly converted Catholic from Mizoen, established in Lyon and 'compère' (family friend) to Jean Giraud (Giraud's own words) – were several of the families who were to form the wide circle of Briançonnais booksellers in the following century. Thus there was Antoine Gravier, in partnership with Blaise Arnoux and Jean Gautier, who signed a credit agreement for 1,040 *livres* in 1688; also Bompart who undertook to repay 62 *livres* and 10 *sols* in 1690; and Bouchard, in partnership with Manissier, who signed another agreement for 3,705 *livres*:[28] all these families were already related by marriage in the seventeenth century.

A third development: Geneva took over from Lyon. The family links between the two towns were long-standing.[29] From the end of the sixteenth century, all the merchants from Oisans had relatives who had been accepted in Geneva as *bourgeois* (citizens with full municipal rights) or *habitants* (citizens with residential rights);[30] in the seventeenth century, Jean Giraud's father-in-law ran a shop there and Giraud himself travelled there on a regular basis. In the previous generation, the Geneva booksellers Chouet and de Tournes were already Nicolas' principal correspondents in Switzerland: in exchange for paper, they supplied him with Protestant devotional books and acted as intermediary for him in his dealings with the Dutch and the Germans.[31] In 1676, following the bequest from his uncle Paul, Jean Giraud paid Perrachon and Philibert 300 *livres*, to be passed on to Noël Clot's heirs.[32] It was thus that, through their mother (whose maiden name was Jeanne-Louise de Tournes), in the eighteenth century the Cramer family inherited networks of relations established in previous centuries by the de Tournes, Chouet and Perrachon families.[33] They also inherited long-standing business links with Italy and the Iberian peninsula, via Lyon.[34] Around them, and around Geneva, the old business activities, destroyed by the Revocation, now took on new life.[35] The families who first came to our notice in the seventeenth century were naturally clients of the Cramer family in the eighteenth century – the Bouchards of Metz and Florence, the Graviers of Genoa and Naples, the Bérards of Seville, the Hermils of Cadiz and Naples and the Mallens of Valencia and Seville. There is no doubt that those such as the Graviers from Genoa and the Bouchards of Florence, who regularly received packages worth almost 10,000 *livres*, also supplied their relatives – Thomas Gravier, the Bouchards of Bologna

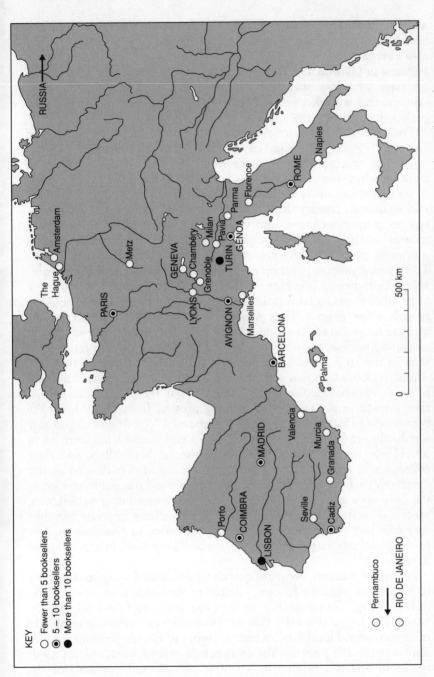

Map 2 Distribution of booksellers originating from the Briançonnais in Europe in the eighteenth century

and the Bouchards of Rome[36] (and this is exactly where the Cramers' list of business contacts is almost completely lacking in names).[37] They also almost certainly supplied Thomas' first cousins, who had set up in business in Livorno and Florence, as well as the Bomparts' relations by marriage who had opened a bookshop in Genoa in the seventeenth century, then a further one in Naples in the eighteenth and, in the same period, had crossed the Atlantic to open another in Rio de Janeiro.[38]

The fourth shift was to Avignon as a central focus, in addition to Geneva. Avignon, a 'foreign' city not subject to the constraints of royal legislation or corporative organization, was one of those havens of freedom which pedlars had always been able to recognize as somewhere to set themselves up as merchants or businessmen. In Avignon, until the mid-eighteenth century there was effectively no structure to the profession of printer-bookseller and little outlay was required to become a 'master' of the trade. The equipment required by the guild's statutes – a printing press and three sets of characters – meant that with 1,000– 1,500 livres, one could set up one's own business and wait for a profitable return before investing in more costly equipment. Moreover, a large amount of capital was not required to print pamphlets or booklets of only a few pages.[39] Thus Avignon was the perfect place to become a centre for pedlars to stock up with merchandise. In fact, the recruitment of printer-booksellers was socially and geographically far more open than in the large cities in France, and the colony of pedlars from the Alpine region which had settled there was a substantial one.[40] Because of its exceptional circumstances, Avignon was the only city to experience growth in the number of printing presses, from 12 or 15 at the beginning of the century to 40 or 50 around 1760; whereas Lyon saw a reduction in her facilities from 90 to 53 and Rouen's fell from 52 to 39. Hence the complicity between provincial booksellers and their colleagues in Avignon: since the former did not always dare to reprint those titles which were in public demand – the Paris publishers being the only ones allowed to do this – the booksellers left it to Avignon, protected by its status as foreign city, to publish the forgeries and then they sold them throughout the country, preferring to give their support to the papal city rather than to Paris which kept them in a position of dependence.[41]

In foreign markets, Avignon quickly appropriated a significant share of business in southern Europe,[42] thanks to the freedom she enjoyed and to her strategic location, close to both Marseilles and the land route to Spain. The favourable rates that her bookseller-publishers were able to offer encouraged local activity (the inventory of Claude Delormes' goods drawn up in 1753 reveals the existence of several thousand copies of works in Spanish, printed by Delorme himself and destined for the Iberian market)[43] and spurred foreign printers to do their printing in Avignon.[44]

The specific nature of the third and fourth developments outlined above leads to the fifth and final development: the network's growing specialization in the market for printed material, whereas in previous centuries the book had been merely a pack-filler. It also explains why, whilst all over Europe the peddling networks were breaking up and withdrawing to regional-based operations, the older type of peddling which operated over a wider area held firm around the market for printed matter – a much sought-after commodity which Geneva and Avignon produced at the most competitive prices.[45]

We shall use the Delorme[46] and Gravier families as a way into this network of shops and pedlars, which carved out an important place for itself in the market for printed material in Mediterranean Europe. Both the Gravier and Delorme families established themselves in the various locations vital to the book trade in southern Europe.

The basic characteristic of their networks remained the practice of endogamy within the narrow group of merchants who originally came from the same village: this was still the key to the arrangement and the effectiveness of marriages. Both the Graviers and the Delormes married within this group. Jean Delorme, originally from Monêtier, established himself in Avignon around 1692 as a bookseller, then as a printer. He married his two oldest sons, Claude and Jean-Baptiste, to two daughters of Joseph Josserand, a merchant – but not a bookseller – from Monêtier. Josserand traded in Lyon, Avignon and La Rochelle, amongst other places. Of Claude's three daughters and two sons who survived, two (Anne and Joseph) married into the Collomb family, who also came from Monêtier but had been established in Marseilles for a generation. Through these marriages the Delormes penetrated to the inner circle of the bookselling network, since the father, Joseph Collomb, was one of the Gosse family's correspondents and the general agent for the Cramers in Marseilles, responsible for recovering debts and bills of exchange on behalf of the Geneva bookshop; and also because Marseilles was one of the central locations in the Mediterranean business world.[47] Claude's other son, Charles-Joseph, married Jeanne Jourdan, the daughter of a Lyon merchant whose family was still in Monêtier. Through the Jourdans, the Delorme family gained links with other merchants from Monêtier, notably with Jean Reycends, a cloth merchant, related to another important bookselling family.[48] After the death of Jean-Baptiste, Claude's brother, in 1732 his widow got married again to Jean-Joseph Guibert, a bookseller born in Turin, but whose parents were originally from Monêtier. At that time Guibert was a bookseller in Lisbon where he had set up a company in association with another Reycends, also born in Turin. The Delormes' family network thus included a number of the established booksellers in Southern Europe; the Gravier family's marriages achieved the same ends.

However, what is important is not so much those marriages which brought booksellers together, but those that brought merchants together irrespective of their business specialization, and any list drawn up which was confined solely to booksellers could easily conceal this. First let us take into account the extent of the coverage – both in geographical and human terms – created by these alliances. In fact, all these merchants were initially a combination of haberdasher, cloth-merchant, ironmonger and bookseller, and a number of printers started out in this way, beginning with Jean Delorme, the founder of the dynasty; or the brothers-in-law Chaillot and Jouve, originally from the Dauphiné Alps, who were first recorded, around 1735, as itinerant 'ironmongers' who added books to their array of wares. Specialization was something which was somehow imposed on them by outside forces, with the merchants trying every possible trick to avoid it: Chaillot's son continued with the threefold occupation of bookseller, haberdasher and ironmonger until 1783, when the threat of the suppression of a certain number of positions for master-printers forced him to make a fictitious sale of the haberdashery and ironmongery businesses to his brother.[49] Those who were able, such as French booksellers in the kingdom of Naples,[50] in Spain and in Portugal, continued to run various types of business.[51]

This system of family alliances showed itself to be extremely flexible and effective when faced with the weakness of the economic, legal and police machinery of the time, which was unable to control the itinerant merchant population; or when up against the illness and death which left families in despair.

The five essential elements and traditional foundations of the migrant merchant organizations can be more closely examined in the case of the network of booksellers; and they demonstrate how important family and business strategies were:

(1) By creating a genuine family banking system, such alliances meant that an initial capital sun could be raised, in which the dowries and personal fortunes of family members were invested.

When Claude Delorme married his son to Jeanne Jourdan, she brought with her a dowry of 8,000 livres, which was invested in Delorme's business. The young couple undertook to live with the father and work at developing the business, and Claude Delorme promised his son and his wife that they would live with him and he would support them, as well as paying them 1,000 livres a year as remuneration for their work. He left his son half his property at his death and promised to give him 20,000 livres worth of merchandise out of that half, if his son so wished, should working together prove impossible.[52] François Guibert's inheritance was also invested in Delorme's business, in particular the 10,527 livres which made up his share of the Lusitanian firm. In 1754, when he married the daughter of a jeweller from Avignon – one of the first marriages entered into outside of the home valley – he settled up with

Claude Delorme, his guardian, and set up in business on his own account. The collapse of the Delormes' business confirmed the necessity, for a successful business, of having family agreement concerning the joint management of inheritances. In fact, François Guibert did not go into business completely on his own, since he set up a company with his cousin Jean-Baptiste Delorme.[53] However, Jean-Baptiste's incompetence, his risky property speculations and, most importantly, the fact that François Guibert withdrew his money from the business, forced Jean-Baptiste to borrow money from outside the family – close on 10,000 *livres* over four years from Daniel de Beaucaire, a Jew from L'Isle. Consequently, from 1765, although the printing works in Avignon was still holding up well, the Delormes' firm was in a state of collapse. In 1772 – at which point the Avignon bookshop was approaching the end of its life – another challenge to the accounts between guardian and ward arose, this time between François Guibert and his ward, Jean-Baptiste Delorme's daughter and wife of Jean-Denis Gravier, which brought about Guibert's final ruin.

(2) A system such as this meant that one could always have someone at the vital points in the network – which can be represented as a tree in which those who were installed on the far end of the branches were likely to be moved if a place fell vacant on a more central branch. An individual did not, therefore, have any geographical stability and, according to the necessities of business and of biological chance which left family firms without anyone at the top, each individual moved between businesses throughout the Mediterranean basin.

The concept of mobility was instilled as early as childhood through apprenticeship. Simon Gravier, who himself always lived in the valley, thus sent his four sons to different countries to learn the merchant profession, both from booksellers and haberdashery merchants: Thomas Gravier was a clerk with the Bouchard bookshop in Rome; as was his brother Jean-Baptiste in Turin in 1762,[54] and then with the merchants Bérard and Tardieu[55] in Moutier; another brother, Antoine, was sent to Marseille;[56] and the youngest brother to Bardonnèche.[57] Clerks and apprentices were despatched at an early age, as young as 13, to these firms which acted as schools for the use of the network. The clerks who were in service with the Delormes, or those who were recorded with the Graviers of Turin, were part of this family strategy of the apprenticeship of mobility.[58]

Moreover the clerks might move from business to business, depending on the departures of the main shareholders. Whichever family one studies, one comes across such movements within the merchant network. Jean-Joseph Guibert was born in Turin, married a Delorme in Avignon and, in partnership with one of the Reycends family, set up as a bookseller in Lisbon. When he died in 1736, his widow, with their son

François (who was born in Lisbon) and Jean-Joseph Delorme, the child of her first marriage, returned to Avignon to live with Claude Delorme, who was her first father-in-law and uncle and guardian to young François, and would later employ him in his business. Turning to the Gravier family, Thomas summoned his nephew Jean-Simon to Rome as a clerk as soon as he himself had been able to establish himself as a bookseller. Ten years later, in 1796, Jean-Simon left for Genoa,[59] where he worked for another bookseller, Yves Gravier, taking the place of Fantin who had left to set up a bookshop in Paris; another Briançonnais, Billaud, came to take up the post of clerk in Rome left vacant by Jean-Simon. Finally, on 12 July 1801, Jean-Simon joined forces with Fantin in Paris, initially as his clerk, later taking over from him as bookseller at the shop at 55 quai des Augustins;[60] in 1809, Pierre Joseph Rey, a native of Villeneuve-la-Salle, a hamlet of Monêtier, and formerly a bookseller in Lisbon, withdrew to Paris to continue his business. There he met up with Jean-Simon Gravier, who had then been in charge of the Fantin bookshop for 12 years, and in 1815 they set up in partnership together and applied for a bookseller's licence. In the Iberian peninsula, the two Orcel brothers – relations of the great Madrid bookseller Diego Barthélémy, and related by marriage to the Bonnardel family – set up their first bookshop in Madrid. Jean-Baptiste then opened a subsidiary shop in Lisbon; then, when his brother Joseph died in 1758, he went back to Madrid to run the parent shop.[61] One final example: in 1747, Pierre Gendron and Joseph Reycends were booksellers in Lisbon; ten years later Pierre Gendron set up in business in Paris – again on the quai des Augustins – and Joseph Reycends went back to Turin where he went into partnership with a Guibert; they were replaced in the Lisbon bookshop by two relations, Bonnardel and Dubeux.[62]

(3) Mobility assured the continuing activity of the important markets and ensured that families were scattered between the main Mediterranean towns and ports on the one hand, and the Alpine villages on the other. It also meant that if the need arose the mountain routes, neglected by official surveillance, could be used. In this way the networks became effective and flexible, allowing goods and books to be circulated between all markets, without using the traditional channels and away from foreseeable inspection by the authorities. Traditional routes or unofficial channels were used depending on the political circumstances. When Gosse the bookseller had to send his catalogue to Jean Baptiste Reycends in Lisbon, he sent it first to Yves Gravier in Genoa, asking him to make sure it got to Reycends.[63]

Joseph Collomb, who had set up in business in Marseilles, was thus an essential cog in the network, not only dividing the books he ordered from the Cramers between his relations in Italy, Spain and Portugal – between 1755 and 1764 he was sent over 12,000 *livres* worth of books[64]

– but also playing a part in all smuggling activities: on 11 August 1761 the Venetian bookseller Albrizzi suggested to Gosse that he sent him his books using 'a trustworthy neutral vessel' and that he ought to go to M. Joseph Collomb of Marseilles for this service.[65] When Reycends left Lisbon for Turin, he broke his journey at Diego Barthélémy's shop in Madrid, to deliver some Portuguese publications to him. Gendron made use of his successors in Lisbon to introduce Portuguese books into the market, particularly the works of Camoens which he published in Paris; similarly Jean-Baptiste Orcel retained close links with his old Portuguese customers after he left Lisbon.[66] When it became difficult to introduce French books into Italy, Lisbon became the transit town between France and Italy.[67]

The example provided by this network of booksellers and pedlars from the Upper Dauphiné demonstrates, not without a certain irony, that the pedlar was first and foremost a merchant who understood the expectations of his customers and who gave them what they wanted. In fact, one could summarize the history of peddling between the seventeenth century and the end of the eighteenth century as being a network of mainly Protestant pedlars who transported books on theology and religion throughout Catholic Europe; which a century later became a network of Catholic pedlars who, hidden under the covers of the same works, circulated the writings of the Enlightenment at the end of the Ancien Régime. Thus, Benoit Rigaud who supplied the Protestant pedlars of La Grave at the end of the sixteenth century specialized in spiritual works; the first publisher of the *L'introduction à la vie dévote*, he was also renowned for having introduced spiritual texts from Spain and Italy into France.[68] In the final decades of the eighteenth century, treatises on canon law served to conceal other, less edifying works: in 1772, Georges Rey & Co. of Lisbon made the following request to the Société typographique de Neuchâtel: 'Amongst the books we are ordering from you, there are some which are prohibited in this country. Would you be so kind as to insert those marked with an asterisk inside some other work, in such a way that they will not be discovered upon inspection'; Bertrand requested that *Crival ou les aventures d'une guine broche bien battue* be delivered to him as 'individual sheets, mixed in with the interleaves, so that they will not be seen'. In 1780, the Société typographique de Neuchâtel sent Reycends of Lisbon the complete works of Voltaire, whilst Gosse sent Borel those of Montesquieu.[69] In Parma in 1776, Faure had in stock 60 prohibited books from Geneva, mostly French, including works by Rousseau and Montesquieu.[70] In Spanish official circles, complaints were made about the brazen advertising done by the French businesses in Seville and Cadiz who were illicitly importing revolutionary and subversive French literature into the peninsula.[71] In the 1780s, the Reycends' catalogue, unlike those of the other booksellers in Turin, was cosmopolitan and dominated by Enlightenment culture;[72]

and Yves Gravier of Genoa was one of the main suppliers for devotees of Louis-Sébastien Mercier's writings.[73]

The Graviers' business dealings demonstrate how well integrated members of the network were. Thomas Gravier of Rome printed books which he then sent to Agazzi to be bound. He also coloured prints and maps, a proportion of which he then sent to Genoa where Yves Gravier worked.[74]

> We're at work on the colouring of the 15-leaf map of Italy, and when you wish, I'll send you a dozen copies. We're also at work on the tinting of the four copies of the *Hortus romanus* which you asked me for.[75]

Up until his death, letters referred to deliveries of prints and books to his nephew in Genoa; Genoa being one of the large commercial ports for the Iberian peninsula. Moreover, since these booksellers had an extremely good knowledge of the different clients whom they supplied, they were able to take advantage of new markets as they arose. This is demonstrated by Reycends of Turin who printed different catalogues, according to the subsidiary to whom they were to be sent;[76] or Thomas Gravier who took advantage of the revolutionary wars to buy up the convent libraries and thus to supply the Iberian market, where large quantities of devotional books were consumed: 'We can make a good deal out of the theology books, since I think we've got enough to be able to throw them away.'[77] As François Grasset emphasized in his letter, as in the previous century, business specialization remained relative and the same trade in gloves continued: between 1782 and 1785, Joseph-Antoine Gravier of Naples put in seven orders for gloves, to a total value of 8,160 *livres*, to Claude Bovier, a glove merchant in Grenoble.[78] Thanks to their extensive links, these booksellers sold as many books – with which they mutually supplied each other – as coffee and chocolate if a customer requested them.[79] And, naturally, money and letters of credit circulated between all locations where a member of the network was established.

(4) The strength of this mutual dependence between members, further bound together by family ties, ensured the greatest degree of security against the extensive web of debt upon which the network was based: in every town there was a relative, haberdasher or bookseller on whom could be bestowed a power of attorney to look after one's interests where the estate of some merchant or pedlar with whom one had done business was concerned.

In 1747, Pierre Gendron and Joseph Reycends, then booksellers in Lisbon, bestowed a power of attorney upon Diego Barthélémy so that he could recover as best he could money owed to them by Pedro Simond who had recently died in Madrid.[80] Claude Delorme granted Jean Reycends, a cloth merchant, a power of attorney so that he could collect his dead son's personal effects from Lyon.[81]

(5) Peddling and the mountain village, which were at the root of the shopkeeping network, remained essential ingredients for its smooth working, providing the potential for geographical expansion, as well as the network's flexibility: for the family, in times of economic difficulty, taking to the road with one's pack was still the obvious last resort. With establishments in all four corners of Europe, the merchants none the less remained Briançonnais first and foremost, and it was this that enabled them to wield their power over village life and also to organize redeployment, should circumstances demand it.

Until his death Thomas Gravier, who ended up spending his life in Rome, retained property in Monêtier. Through their management of his private income, rent from tenant farmers and loans, his relatives nurtured for him a fortune that he would never have the opportunity to enjoy, and at his death on 12 October 1797 he passed it on to his nephew, making a settlement on him of 'all profits, income and revenue from all his property in France, as much in recognition of the past, since the death of his father, as for the future, for as long as he judges it fit'. The joint heirs estimated his fortune at 50,000 francs.[82]

If, on the one hand, pedlars who had made their fortune extended the network of shops, on the other, the mountain village was a reserve of men who could be used as clerks or pedlars when necessary. Such was the case with the youngest of the Gravier brothers, Jean-Pierre, who, having served his apprenticeship in Bardonnèche, arrived on the job market just as the bookselling trade was in crisis. Unlike his brothers, he did not go into service in a shop and can be discovered in the nineteenth century as a pedlar selling haberdashery goods. His account books are a history of sorts of the development of the family. One book begins with an account of a stocktake in a bookshop, and continues with the usual business of loans; deals with the management of the family fortune for those family members who had emigrated – in particular that of the Raby branch of the family,[83] who had established themselves as merchants in Turin; then continues with deals concerning livestock and their by-products; and indicates the supplying of a wide variety of goods, thus pointing to his role as village merchant, working in conjunction with relatives abroad. The next account book bears witness to the return to winter peddling of haberdashery goods and to the combination of itinerant selling with the trafficking of mules between Saintonge and Briançonnais.

This network, bound up with peddling through its origins and through its potential developments, simultaneously supported different temporary migrations as well as a web of shops. Firstly there were cases where young pedlars were employed by a specific firm for several years: Pierre Borel and Chaffié Nel both hired themselves out for three years to their compatriot Jean Jouve, a bookseller in Avignon, one in 1769 and one in 1771

> to work as pedlars and travel to all the towns and villages of the surrounding provinces, and particularly to the fairs which are held there to sell all the goods which will be supplied [to them] by the aforementioned Jouve.[84]

Then there was the seasonal long-distance migration: in the words of Malesherbes '[they] come down from their mountains every year to assemble a selection of books from Lyon and elsewhere, and convey them themselves as far as Cadiz or Sicily.'[85] Traces of such peddling in foreign lands are difficult to find – the report by the Spanish library authorities in 1757–8 proves the existence of stallholders ('*copleros con puesto*') and travelling salesmen alongside the bookshops, and in conjunction with the complaints from booksellers against the haberdashers and street pedlars vouches for the fact that peddling and various other businesses had introduced the book into the rural areas and towns of Spain where there were no bookshops.[86] However, only from brushes with the police or with the Inquisition can we identify these pedlars as coming from France. Thanks to such encounters Ramon Gravier, '*un extranjero que va de pueblo en pueblo con una librería*', first emerges from the shadows in Carmona, where he was required to draw up a list of the books in his possession which were imported from abroad; and subsequently in Malaga in 1766, when once again he got into trouble with the authorities because of the prohibited publications he had in his cart.[87] A happy sighting, which thus allows us to locate a book-peddling Gravier[88] in southern Spain and which confirms Malesherbes' accusations that the travelling merchants of the Briançonnais region themselves took charge of the transporting of books, often illicitly, into Italy, Portugal and Spain.[89]

Finally, in addition to those pedlars who travelled abroad, there were the men who came down from the Alpine valleys every year to sell books and printed matter, together with haberdashery and ironmongery goods, in the rural areas of Provence and Languedoc.[90] According to a contemporary report, there were more than 500 of them who came regularly to Avignon to stock up,[91] and, following his visit to the fair at Beaucaire, the Parisian bookseller David wrote in 1745 that there were

> more than 200 men from the mountains of the Dauphiné who, having tilled the land for six months of the year, at the onset of winter come down to the Comtat region, collect considerable amounts of books and introduce them into Provence, Languedoc and other neighbouring provinces.[92]

As far as the Parisian bookseller was concerned, the pedlars were primarily responsible for the circulation of the unauthorized editions produced in Avignon, 'the consumption of which is mainly achieved through the pedlars or packmen who travel from town to town and from fair to fair.'[93] The Intendant of la Porte reinforced this:

> Two book pedlars usually appear in Gap twice a year. The first comes in May, the second during September. They are not in any way authorized to trade in this way.

They came from Avignon and their trips took them to Apt, Forcalquier, Sisteron, Gap, Embrun, Briançon, Nyons and Buis. They sold devotional tracts and books of ethics, law, history and poetry.

> For the most part, these various books are rubbish. They buy them in Lyon and they also buy many unauthorized editions of books in Avignon. It is claimed that they make their largest purchases in Avignon, which, however, cannot be sizeable if one reflects that in all of Gapençais they only sell two hundred francs worth of books in a year.

He mentions the part played by men from Monêtier:

> Certain pedlars from Champsaur and Monestier les Briançon are in the habit of attending the fairs at Embrun and Guillestre every year. They sell devotional books. They display their wares to the public and, as soon as the fair is over, are off to seek their fortune elsewhere.

These pedlars, along with four other merchants in the ironmongery trade (one of whom was from Monêtier and travelled constantly between the principal towns of the Dauphiné) who also dealt in school books, history books and devotional books, do not seem, however, to have dabbled in the traffic of prohibited books.[94]

If this network of booksellers and book pedlars emanating from the Briançonnais appears to be the most important network, it was not by any means the only one. The Remondini publishers of Venice, originally from Bassano, made their mark in the second half of the eighteenth century by means of a similar network, at a time when the Venetian publishing scene as a whole was in crisis.[95] De Lalande, in his book Le Voyage en Italie, points to the printing operation run by the Remondini family as the largest establishment of its kind in Europe; the only one to have a completely integrated production process, from the paper manufacture to the sales network.[96] The firm employed a thousand workers, 1,500 business correspondents in Italy and a further 50 in Europe; and, in particular, more than 2,000 travelling salesmen, all originally from the Ticino valley, who covered Italy and Europe.[97] From

1708, there is evidence in legal records of the practice of selling books on credit terms to people in the Ticino region; in 1781, 170 company bosses (*Capi-Compagnia*) were working for the Remondini and distributing their products in Italy, Germany, Hungary, Poland, Russia, Flanders, Holland and Spain; and in 1881, there were 552 pedlars holding a trading licence.[98] Remondini's pedlars began to cover Spain from the 1730s. Made wealthy by the sale of prints of a religious nature produced by the Remondini family, some of them opened shops, providing in their turn a point of entry into the rural areas for the Remondini's books. They were extremely active in Spain from where, using their base at Cadiz as a point of departure, they crossed the Atlantic to Latin America.[99] They began to set up bookshops at the end of eighteenth century; the Tessari family opened a shop in Augusta in 1786, followed by one in Paris and one in Warsaw, and to the bookshop they added a publishing house. In 1790, the Buffa family set up in business in Amsterdam and also launched out into publishing. In the first half of the nineteenth century the number of shops opened grew, with the Pellizaro family in Besançon; the Tessaro family in Gand; the Fiettas in Strasbourg and Metz; and the Daziaros in Moscow, St Petersburg, Paris and Warsaw.[100] Endogamy and mobility between different locations were once again distinguishing features of the business organization.[101] Good relations were maintained between the two networks, the Italian and the French,[102] and in September 1776, for example, several French books were brought into Italy via the Lisbon–Venice route: that particular month Giuseppe Remondini received packages from Lisbon containing 34 different titles, ranging from Montaigne's *Essais* to a copy of *Pouvoir des Evêques, Plaisirs du chevalier d'Eon*, and works by Beaumarchais and so forth. Borel and the Dubeux brothers happened to be among Remondini's correspondents.[103]

Similarly, a peddling network for books and other printed material developed in Northern France around Cotentin.[104] We shall return to it again in chapter 4, but let us mention here its international dimension and the relations it maintained with the Briançonnais network. The inventory carried out in regard to the firm of Le Père and Avaulez, dissolved in 1777, demonstrates how this commercial network also covered Europe, although it was strongest in northern Europe, with which Normandy had the strongest links. Hence we find, running shops, Mondhare in Seville and Cadiz;[105] Lemière in Bilbao; Augustin Leroux in Mainz; Leprès in Antwerp; and others in Ferrol, Madrid, Lisbon, Brussels, Amsterdam, Basel, Geneva, St Petersburg and Moscow.[106] Particularly close ties naturally linked the pedlars from Cotentin, who stocked up in Paris, to those who were established, or getting themselves established, abroad. Finally, the Briançon network and the Cotentin network were also linked by the usual trade practices: Noël Gille, for example, on 5 June 1780, sold Delorme in Avignon 248 volumes from the Societé typographique de Neuchâtel for the sum of 833 *livres* and 14 *sols*.[107]

One should also examine the smaller networks more closely, such as that comprised of pedlars who stocked up at Toulouse, Bordeaux and Bayonne and who, since the seventeenth century, had travelled to Aragon to furnish regular customers with packages of books they had ordered.[108] Initial evidence reveals that they were originally from the same villages in the Pyrenees that also spawned the bookselling pedlars of the nineteenth century who were studied by Darmon.[109] Equally, there was a network in the Apennines in Tuscany, based around the village of Pontremoli where, at the turn of the sixteenth and seventeenth centuries, there was already a family printing in Parma, one of the important centres of Italian publishing; also in Pontremoli itself and in Oppenheim in Germany – and here research remains still to be done.[110]

Affected by the crisis in publishing following the collapse of the Ancien Régime, the network of Alpine booksellers did not survive the Revolution. In France the exceptional and unique role played by the bookshops of Avignon came to an end with the decrees of 1777 and the Concordat of 1785. In fact, from 1777 the royal government, which had decided to tackle the problem of forgeries head on and to review the concept of author's copyright, announced a series of decrees limiting the duration of protected copyright, finally authorizing provincial booksellers to publish a great number of widely distributed works themselves, and, at the same time, determinedly outlawed unauthorized editions from abroad. Driven to the verge of bankruptcy, the Avignon printers demanded that concessions be made to spare them the universal fate of French booksellers, which the Concordat granted them. Subsequently, Avignon returned to her modest status as a regional centre of book production and trade which she had previously been in the seventeenth century. Before Avignon was effectively reintegrated into France (in 1791), the political decision to battle against unauthorized foreign editions had crippled a vital link in the Briançon network, as well the bookshops of Avignon.[111]

The Genevan publishing environment, which had been afflicted by the tax on imported books or books in transit introduced in France in 1771, also suffered, as a centre of distribution, from the disappearance of Latin as the language of science in favour of national languages.[112] Finally, the expulsion of the Jesuits from the Bourbon States and the suppression of religious institutes had a profound effect on the number of publishers, rendering obsolete at a stroke the literature which constituted the mainstay of their business.[113] In Portugal, even the prosperous Bonnardel had to abandon virtually all activity.[114] In Spain the governmental assaults began in 1752, with the publication by Juan Curiel of the new regulations controlling the bookshops' trade, which, in order to put a stop to Spanish books being printed abroad, ordered that all bookshops in the kingdom should be inspected so that a list of all

Spanish books printed outside Spain could be drawn up, and also ordered that the customs were to be watched vigilantly. This inspection was carried out quickly and effectively between 1757 and 1758.[115] The Revolution and the Napoleonic Wars ultimately threw the circuits into disarray. When the Bouchard brothers wrote in 1798 'our business has completely collapsed; however, we could go on if we had in stock all the works which people ask from us',[116] their words prove that the business circuits were no longer functional and that all French firms in Italy were affected.[117] In Spain in 1808, the confiscation and looting of French merchants' goods triggered the return to France of a fair number of them. The great pedlar-merchant networks were definitively a thing of the past.

4

A Flexible Typology

Following the break-up of the great merchant-pedlar networks, when those who had been the 'elite' of the mountain villages had left and integrated themselves into the lowland towns, the migratory patterns which adapted to this new situation – and which are the most familiar to historians – are the most consistently similar throughout Europe. The only meaningful criterion for distinguishing between types of travelling merchant is not in terms of distance covered, or even goods peddled, but concerns the way in which the trip was financed. This allows us to identify three groups of pedlars in terms of the estate which they could offer as security to the city merchants in return for the goods they supplied. The importance of the amount of credit allowed thus serves to distinguish the half-starved pedlars with nothing to offer from the regular pedlars who had enough of an estate to guarantee their loans and the merchant-pedlars who, with a solid financial base, could travel by cart and who opened shops. A typology such as this has two distinguishing features. On the one hand it is flexible: the pedlar who carried a pack could hope to attain the higher ranks of the profession; for many, it was seen as a career with scope for progression, depending on how successful one was, as far as opening a shop in the city. On the other hand, these different types of pedlar were bound together as much by family ties as by the business links which existed within the profession.

A potential career

We can reach a better understanding of the links between the various levels of the profession, and the movement which took place between these levels, if we take the book pedlars of Cotentin as an example. Cotentin, to the north-west of Coutances, was the land of migrant

merchants: 'Every year in March a significant proportion of the inhabitants of ten or twelve parishes by the sea, around the *élection** of
Carentan, set out from their homes, some to sell books, prints and maps
in the kingdom's provinces, the others taking their packs and peddling
haberdashery and ironmongery goods', reported *l'Etat statistique de
l'élection de Coutances* in 1727.[1] Anne Sauvy and Robert Darnton's
work on Noël Gille and the more general analyses by Pierre Casselle,
Jean Quéniart and Jean-Dominique Mellot lend prominence to the pedlars' peasant ties, the way in which the profession was handed down
within the same families, and the main stages in a pedlar's training.

First of all, pictures and almanacs were sold by the children, who
served their apprenticeship from the age of 12 or 15 in the company of
an old pedlar, subsequently remaining with him as a servant until their
inheritance allowed them to become pedlars in their own right. At this
point, they progressed to selling books: Noël Gille, like his brothers,
took this particular route.[2] There were, admittedly, older pedlars who
never sold books and continued to sell cheap pamphlets which brought
in very little money: these were pedlars whom poverty or ill-fortune had
prevented from obtaining credit in the city and who supplemented an
array of haberdashery and ironmongery goods, prints and playing cards
with a few *brochures de lettres* and booklets from the *Bibliothèque
bleue* series. Moreover, in some municipalities the right to sell almanacs
was reserved solely for this destitute group.[3]

Progression to a grander lifestyle was dependent upon the family
assets, which the merchants accepted as security for the credit they
allowed the pedlar. The sounder the pedlar's inheritance and network
of family connections, the greater the access he would have to good
quality merchandise, to bulk stock and to credit. Generally speaking,
these newcomers were not unknown quantities to the city merchants:
they would previously have frequented the merchant's booth as servants
of pedlars who were long-standing clients, and their old masters would
unfailingly recommend them to their regular suppliers. Noël Gille, for
example, wrote the following to the widow Machuel, a Rouen bookseller: 'Since my boy has just left my service . . . and he will doubtless
be needing your goods, you can safely let him have them . . . I hope you
will be satisfied with him'.[4]

At this stage, the pedlar was able to afford a horse and cart and
become a stallholder at the fairs, specializing in books. Although they
were neither prosperous nor highly respected, and moved from fair to
fair, they were closer to the established booksellers, carrying a great
number of books, offering classics as bound editions, new books and
the full range of forged editions in paper covers.[5] They would settle in
a single town for anything between a fortnight and a month and send

* An *élection*: a fiscal region of France.

their apprentices and servants out to cover the countryside and sur-rounding villages.

Entry to the higher ranks of the profession became a reality when the pedlar rented a shop, initially for a couple of months, followed by the establishment of one or two booths in the towns in the areas he cov-ered. The Chauvigneau brothers thus criss-crossed the Loire Valley, Beauce and Perche, until 1771 when Charles Chauvigneau set up in business in Vendôme. In July 1772, he didn't regret this decision:

> It was reason alone which made us settle, given that we had such difficulty in supporting ourselves. . . . Setting ourselves up cost a good deal of money . . . but we have never been in a position to earn our living as we do today . . .

However, setting up in business did not mean that the pedlar was withdrawing from the migrant network, nor did it mean that he was abandoning his former practices. In the case of the Chauvigneau broth-ers, one concentrated on developing the shop, even attempting to add a bookbinding workshop onto it, while the other brother continued to cover the fairs.

Setting up a shop did not mean that the pedlar carried out his business differently, nor did it mean that he had moved into a world of different cultural practices and relationships: if the business was not successful – and this might have been what happened to the Chauvigneau brothers – these newly settled pedlars did not hesitate to take to the road again with their cart in an attempt to rebuild their capital: 'since they had neither hearth nor home, no rent nor expenses to pay out, they often gave the books away at very low prices'.[6] Once they had built up their profits again, they made another attempt at setting up in business. This was also the route taken by Noël Gille (also known as *La Pistole*) and his brother Pierre, who opened a shop in Montargis and one in Aire-sur-la-Lys, went bankrupt, had a taste of prison life, took to the road again, and finished life as established bookseller in Montargis.[7] The important thing was that, even if their creditors had shown their impa-tience by having Pierre thrown into prison, the long chain of credit which kept them within the community of Cotentin migrants was never broken. On the other hand, by refusing to grant credit to the Euvremer family, the widow Machuel cut them off from the network, despite their bitter letters – 'I cannot set up shop without your support. If I ask you for credit, you refuse it. . . . you grant it to people who are in no po-sition to repay you. Respectable people are always ignored'; and their bragging, 'It seems to me that you only recognize those who pay you money. And yet I have been doing business with you for three years. But no matter, I still have goods to tide me over, even without yours'.[8] In barring them from credit and from access to her money, the widow

Machuel condemned them to remain on the fringes of the network, and thus blocked their future success.

Like all peddling networks, the success of the whole relied on a few members setting up in business in the vital supply centres. This meant Paris, which was at the time an important supply centre and a very profitable place to sell goods; and also abroad where one could take advantage of several supply centres and become part of a wider market.

The first pedlars from Cotentin to settle wholly in Paris were Louis-Joseph Mondhare and Gilles Rosselin who, before 1770, had established themselves in the traditional commercial centre for prints in the rue Saint-Jacques. For them and others like them, this step had been made possible by government intervention. Effectively, the monopoly granted to the Parisian booksellers by Colbert, in conjunction with the Malthusian policies of these booksellers, who only took on apprentices in exceptional circumstances, brought about too great a reduction in the number of shops at precisely the moment in mid-century when business was picking up. The government then decided to inject new life into the profession by bringing help in from outside. Thus, for example, in 1767 Malesherbes had 17 new Master Booksellers appointed, exempted from apprenticeship; and once again ordered that the pedlars, who shortly before had been considered a risk, be accepted.[9] After 1770, a second influx of pedlars-turned-booksellers settled in the rue Saint-Jacques, then in the newly fashionable parts of town – the quays, the boulevards and, in particular, the Palais-Royal. Pierre Casselle has compiled a register of a dozen firms and sets out the family links which bound together many of these merchants.[10]

The chain of trade was well established at that time, linking to the homeland all the migrant merchants who had set up business abroad, all those with shops in Paris, those who travelled back and forth between Normandy and their stall on the banks of the Seine, those of wealth and standing in a provincial town, those who travelled to the fairs, and finally all those who sold pictures and booklets, either as their only merchandise or included in their packs along with haberdashery goods. A network structured in this way meant that a printer could sell to a bookseller, who would then supply merchandise to pedlars of sufficient standing. In their turn, the latter would distribute this merchandise to other, more lowly packmen.

The migrant merchants' fortune was primarily a paper fortune: all the inventories drawn up after death point up the inadequacy of furniture and real estate in relation to debts owed and loans outstanding. From top to bottom, the peddling hierarchy was awash with goods supplied on credit, cash loans and guarantees, not just in Cotentin but elsewhere in France,[11] in England,[12] in Belgium[13] and in Germany.[14]

Letters received by the widow Machuel, a bookseller in Rouen, in

1768 and 1773 testify to her close links with the Normandy pedlars – out of the 56 travelling salesmen who did business with her, 52 were originally from Cotentin.[15] The debts owed to the Gille brothers reveal the overlap between income from their farm and income from merchandise. In March 1771, whilst held in prison at Châteaudun, Pierre Gille drew up a statement of all the debts owed to him to prove his solvency. The bulk of it involved other migrants: pedlars to whom he had sold on one occasion a horse, on another pictures or a few books, or to whom he had lent money. Established, or supposedly established, booksellers also featured in the list.[16] The book in which his brother Noël Gille recorded debts, which was kept between 1770 and 1776, attest to the profits which he could accrue in his role as intermediary between booksellers and pedlars: on the one hand, the book reveals ten or so important sales to booksellers and 22 sales to fairground booksellers, all for a large number of books and worth several hundred *livres*;[17] on the other hand it vouches for the fact that Noël Gille did not neglect more petty peddling, since the most sizeable part of his assets consisted of the debts owed to him by other pedlars to whom he had sold a few books and prints.[18]

Finally, the settled merchants retained property and family links with their home region, which meant they were guaranteed a supply of peddling manpower and also enabled them to keep an eye on this. Gilles Rosselin, a merchant selling prints who had a shop in the rue Saint-Jacques in Paris between approximately 1760 and 1772, had kept a house back in his home parish of Anneville. Those notary's deeds which we have been able to locate reveal on the one hand his role as lender and supplier to temporary merchants; and on the other the chains of credit which criss-crossed village life, since some people repaid their debts by passing on debts which they were owed. In October 1776, the widow of Jacques Rivière, who had been a farm labourer in Geffosses, made over to Rosselin '50 *livres* as a fief payable for life . . . in return for the sum of 1,000 *livres*'; in May 1767, the Regnault brothers, Louis and Pierre, 'merchants normally residing in the village of Créances', and staying for this occasion in the Hôtel Saumur in the rue Saint-Jacques in Paris, agreed to pay Rosselin the sum of 20 *livres* a year, in return for 500 *livres*. In May 1768, another Louis Regnault, 'a fairground merchant . . . from the parish of Anneville', exchanged 40 *livres* income a year for 1,000 *livres* upfront; and on 1 June another pedlar, Pierre Maçon, 'a merchant originally from the parish of Créances', made over to Rosselin 5 *livres* a year, in return for 100 *livres*. In October 1769, Jacques Lelong, 'a merchant selling prints, from the parish of Montsurvent', also staying in the Hôtel Saumur for the occasion, agreed to pay Rosselin instalments of 26 *livres* to repay the 650 *livres* he owed, of which 500 'had been borrowed by him from the aforementioned Sr.

Rosselin to discharge the various sums which were owed to Srs. Crépy, Chéreau, Mondhard and others by the late Pierre Lelong, brother of the man now entering into this agreement'; in other words, sums owed to other merchants selling prints in the rue Saint-Jacques.[19]

These merchants, like the Alpine merchants, gradually extended their banking activities to other strata of society. Once he had made his fortune, Rosselin did not confine himself to lending money to the peasants from his village and the pedlars who worked for him, but also lent money to the lord of the region, to 'Messire Nicolas Néel, knight, lord and patron and High Justice of La Haye Picquenot and other places, previously squire to the late Dauphine'. In 1771, the latter agreed to pay 60 *livres* in income from his land in return for 200 *livres*; as well as 'the quantity of thirteen bushels of wheat as income from the land . . . to be taken as a fief from Champagne en l'Interville, of which he (Nicolas Néel) is the lord and owner, in return for 1,000 *livres*, in gold louis, the coin of the realm'.[20]

Merchant structures of this type, networks on the basis of family connections and a common homeland, which both supported and were dependent upon one another, were perfectly suited to operating on the fringes of the law. To preserve their adaptability and flexibility, diverse trades were practised within the family unit. Such ambiguity ensured that a change of direction was possible if the specialization adopted ceased to be profitable. It also facilitated illegal trafficking by providing hiding-places which were not immediately obvious: Louis Ibert, a 'pedlar of prints, with a stall on the boulevard, first on the right through St Martin's Gate', was thus supposed to have used his brother's shop – 'a haberdasher in the place Maubert' – to hide the 22 *Dictionnaires philosophiques* which he had just bought.[21]

Moreover, by taking advantage of the various corporate affiliations within the network and by exploiting the opportunities offered by particular towns, the pedlars managed to circulate prohibited books without any problems, as the Intendant of Caen remarked in 1730: 'In spite of the rules, books coming from abroad have no difficulty getting into the city, since there is no inspection either on the way in or the way out – because Caen is not an official port', he wrote. He also pointed out that this illegal traffic did not pass through the hands of either the printers or the booksellers, but through those of 'the uncouth pedlars' who 'bring in prohibited books and editions with their other goods' and 'who store them in warehouses two or three leagues from the city, which are ideal for illegal distribution'. Other pedlars then came to collect these books from their hiding-place and spread them throughout the French market. Thus, in 1765, an anonymous denunciation brought about the arrest of Alex Marais in Le Bourget with 40 copies of the six volumes of *L'Espion chinois* in his possession. He was a pedlar from Coutances, who had just arrived from Liège, where he had gone to obtain the goods. Laisné, who was from the same place, was also arrested. In the same year another pedlar was arrested in a hostel in Mortagne: his baggage contained works considered pernicious or licentious, such as the *Cousin de Mahomet*, the *Anecdotes jésuitiques*, *Angola* and *La Nouvelle Héloïse*.[22]

Such structures were all the more effective because there was little competition between the different networks – each had their own geographical territory – and they maintained good relations, working together when the need arose. Hence papers belonging to Noël Gille of Normandy and those of the Briançonnais merchant Jean Delorme reveal that Gille occasionally acted as a middleman between Delorme and the Société typographique de Neuchâtel; and that Jean Delorme introduced the forgeries he manufactured into northern France using the Rouen booksellers, who supplied the Norman pedlars on a preferential basis.[23]

For the upper echelons of migrant merchants, an organization based on the wider family unit and extended by a workforce who were dependent and supervised was the most reliable structure for running a business in which a large part of the profits came from trafficking unauthorized editions and distributing prohibited books. The versatile nature of each family and the information network in place meant that corporative constraints could be manipulated, and that there was an awareness of the needs of the market and the weak links in the mechanisms of the establishment and of the police. Haberdashers, booksellers and pedlars thus formed a double-sided network: they were working for the development of trade in general, which gained both profit and security from the network's solidarity, and they were also working for the continuing wealth of the family network and its regional client base.

The peddling physiognomy

There were three distinct stages in the career of a travelling merchant. Depending on the ability to obtain credit and city goods, three prototypes stand out: the destitute pedlar, the regular pedlar and the merchant-pedlar. However, alongside these three a new model emerged in England: the 'Manchester Man', who heralded a radical innovation in that his ties with his home community were relaxed in favour of his firm, for whom he worked on a virtually exclusive basis. Four groups then, each with their own methods of selling, obtaining their supplies and attracting customers. It is the specificities of the way in which culture was incorporated into the very act of selling, and how the meeting between the potential customer and the pedlar was engineered, which I now want to bring to the fore.

The destitute pedlar

The sociological diversity was greatest amongst the destitute pedlars, since they had nothing to offer as security against goods and credit. Their trade thus slipped easily through the net of interdependency and restraints which bound other pedlars together. Destitute pedlars might be from anywhere, could have uprooted themselves and changed class. Chance acquaintances, opportunities, and municipal policies[24] produced these destitute wanderers and occasional pedlars in all places. These men were on the fringes of peddling, they were the most visible and the most disturbing, overshadowing the profession as a whole: they were the multifaceted figures who caught the imagination of their contemporaries, the essential characters in novels of the city and the open road. This was Victor Hugo's Paris in 1793:

> In the rue Saint-Jacques, the street-pavers, barefoot, stopped the wheelbarrow of a pedlar who was selling shoes. . . . Few of the big shops were open; women dragged carts containing haberdashery goods and knickknacks, lit by candles, with the tallow melting onto the merchandise; . . . Newspaper sellers raced around, selling newssheets. [. . .] Strolling singers were everywhere.[25]

Other figures, involved in the trafficking of illicit books, emerged. An analysis of those imprisoned for distributing prohibited books reveals that, alongside the merchants with whom we are already familiar, those reduced in status were to be found in a variety of circumstances, prepared to risk much in an effort to make ends meet again: there were workers from the printing presses who both manufactured and distributed, increasing the precariousness of their situation; many women from the poorer classes; and some men – teachers, doctors, clergymen, soldiers – who were looking for work or money.[26] Even though they worked on the black market and society liked to think of them as belonging to structured frameworks and organized groups, the vast majority of them were solitary, perhaps joining forces briefly if they encountered one another on the road. But this latter group was sociologically on the fringes of the infrastructure which now occupies our attention.

Amongst the destitute migrants, special mention ought to be made of three groups who did belong to a structured whole. Firstly there were those who, in villages where there were craftsmen and pedlars, had been expelled from credit circles; secondly, those who came from villages which specialized in the sale of devotional images, where the profession came within the framework of family interdependency, like the 'santari' from Campli in Italy, or the 'Chamagnons' from the Jura;[27] and finally, the blind, who in Spain succeeded in obtaining a virtual monopoly for themselves in the sale of printed sheets. The first group took any work which came along, and in between jobs went hawking their wares and begging. Their ties with the home village had not been broken and their temporary itinerancy was primarily an economy of absence – a saving of the bread that they would not be there to eat in the village in winter. In the Alps, in the Auvergne or in the Apennines the police archives tell their pitiful tales of misery and itinerancy, humble occupations, petty thieving, sometimes stints in prison or hospital, and often death on the road.[28] On the other hand, the blind in Spain organized themselves into a guild, dominated by a group of about 20, some of whom were far from destitute and a few of whom actually published stories in the form of small booklets, 'pliegos sueltos' or 'pliegos de cordel', which other pedlars would distribute throughout Spain, and even as far afield as Latin America. Gradually they assumed the monopoly for distributing this type of printed material.[29] A blindman seldom worked alone, and for the most part was accompanied by his wife, another blindman or a child.[30] However, there were vast differences in status, and at the bottom end of the ranks of blind pedlars were those who had nothing to sell but their life story, their wailing voices intended to arouse pity, or those who turned themselves, like living calendars, into heralds of the forthcoming saints' days.[31] In Portugal, as in Spain, they were partially united by a Brotherhood. In the eighteenth century, the struggle between the different types of pedlars and between pedlars and booksellers was fierce, and the boundaries remained blurred. The legal archives kept a record of the repeated clashes between the booksellers' guild, the blindmen's brotherhood – to which had been granted the exclusive right to sell printed sheets – and those pedlars who were termed 'volanteiros', who did not belong to any of these organizations.[32]

For these pedlars, who were half-beggar, half-tramp, more important than the goods was the act of selling itself. They put on a show and sold entertainment and dreams. As intermediaries between their public and other worlds, they took their audiences into the realm of the imaginary, into other ways of knowing oneself, to other places, and to new understandings. Ultimately, the pedlar was selling himself and all that his words – spoken or sung – could stir in the imagination of his listeners. They were not seeking one-to-one contact with the purchaser, nor the intimacy of the home, but the public square, the fairs, places where people passed through, times of festivity when a crowd might form around them, might share values other than those that they lived by, vying with each other to attain this difference.

The richest of these itinerants had a few goods to offer – a small amount of haberdashery, toys, some printed material – and to sell them they would play out the peasants' dreams and expectations. In *A Winter's Tale*, the ballads and news stories that Autolycus had in his knapsack opened up the minds of the isolated villagers to what was happening in the world, to how strangely people behaved and to the movements in current affairs. It little mattered that what they related was both fanciful and magical; what was important was that the narrator swore to its novelty and accuracy: all the stories that he brought with him were 'true' stories, and 'less than a month old'. Next he crooned his goods, the fabrics and the ribbons, which contrasted starkly with the drab clothes of the peasants, the pleasure to be got from giving and wearing them, the fashionable status they would thereby acquire:

> . . . if you did but hear the pedlar at the door, you would never dance again after tabor and a pipe; no, the bagpipe could not move you. . . . – He could never come better: he shall come in. . . . He hath songs for man or woman, of all sizes; . . . Has he any unbraided wares? – He hath ribands of all the colours i' the rainbow; points more than all the lawyers in Bohemia can learnedly handle, though they come to him by the gross; inkles, caddisses, cambrics, lawns: why, he sings 'em over, as they were gods or goddesses. You would think a smock were the angel, he so chants to the sleeve-hand and the work about the square on't.[33]

Like Autolycus, the pedlar whom Jacques the Fatalist met a century and a half later also crooned about his wares and the new fashions – fashions with which he opened windows onto other ways of knowing oneself, other ways of life.[34]

Others turned themselves into storytellers, recounting the adventures which had brought them to their current audience and, like Ulysses, described the worlds through which they had passed, transporting the villagers to other places.

> I now intend a voyage here to write/ From London unto York, help to indite,/Great Neptune lend thy aid to me who past/Through thy tempestuous waves with many a blast,/ And then I'll true describe the towns, and men,/ And manners, as I went and came agen.[35]

Le Mercier Inventif (The Resourceful Haberdasher) declared:

> As a haberdashery merchant who traffics on the seas/ From on high have I seen many foreign countries/ I have travelled through Canada, Vaugirard, Etruria/ Montmartre, Papagosse and all of Sierie/ Thence have I come to these unfamiliar woods/ And so many people! I am so lucky/ to have come to this place to sell all my haberdashery from my wicker basket straight away/ I shall approach them to cry my wares.[36]

Lace and laces became props for adventures which could be lived by proxy through the travellers – and the latter were laden down by such wares.

As well as revealing a way into other worlds, certain pedlars offered the prospect of new knowledge to be shared, or the soon-to-be-realized dream of restored health, or the future revealed. The charlatans who brought with them potions, pills, powders and ointments claimed to be putting medical knowledge and power over illness and death within the reach of all. Certain Englishmen have remained famous, such as Martin von Butchell who created a colourful personality for himself, with eccentric behaviour and an extravagant style of dress, in order to sell his remedies;[37] or Samuel Solomon, who made his fortune selling a miracle cure – the balm of Gilead – at the end of the eighteenth century; or Isaac Long who held a mini-lottery to win worthless items at the same time as selling his powders.[38]

By playing on these expectations, those who had nothing to offer but themselves, and nothing to sell but words and a few printed sheets, moved into the slot vacated by the theatre which, between the fifteenth and seventeenth centuries, became institutionalized and moved into the cities, leaving the market squares and the fairgrounds to the pedlars. Indeed, from the sixteenth century, city gates were closed against itinerants who were suspected of 'acting out' false social personae, bogus beggars and charlatans.[39] Similarly, between 1570 and 1585 certain cities – first Florence, then Venice, Madrid, Paris and Naples – set aside closed rooms within the city walls for companies of actors to give performances. At the same time, definitions of what constituted an actor were developed,[40] even though the authorities – such as those in Milan in 1578 – often still confused travelling salesmen and actors.[41]

The theatre's move into the city relegated those excluded from institutions to the margins, to the fairs, the small towns and villages.[42] Here, a combination of hawking, entertainment and begging was still practised. John Earle, in his *Microcosmography* of 1628, paints a picture of one of these men who, too destitute to afford other goods or have them vouchsafed to him, has only printed sheets bearing his words to offer – stories, tales, ballads or homages to the glory of God. Earle describes him, travelling from market to market, singing his pitiful verses, which were patched together like his clothes and accompanied by a 'vile tune and a worse throat', offering them for sale for a few halfpennies.[43] If the occasion was not propitious for selling, some would take advantage of it to steal, as an article in *Fog's Weekly Journal* remarks in July 1732: 'an Irish ballad seller, who used to entertain the good people of England with a song, while his companions were picking their pockets, was taken up and committed to Bridewell.'[44] Autolycus was guilty of the same thing.

The *cantastore* and the itinerants, the charlatans, teeth-pullers, hernia-shrinkers and Bergamasque maskers spread prophecies as they travelled from one town square to another in Italy.[45] Those from the Ticino region who sold pictures and small booklets threaded them onto a piece of string and told their story using a hazelnut twig to illustrate the tale.[46] In Germany the pedlar resorted to large illustrated boards

(*Bild*) whose tale he told as he sold his booklets;[47] as did his French counterpart[48] – as painted by Moreau the Younger – who, violin at his shoulder, the song to be sold in his right hand with other copies arranged in a bag attached to his belt, had behind him a picture illustrating the story which he sang and sold. One of Pellerin's woodcuts captures him on a town square with his wife, violin in hand, indicating with his bow a scene in the painted canvas, whose pole his wife holds in her right hand, whilst in her left hand she holds up a satirical sketch entitled 'crime'; middle-class onlookers in Louis-Philippe period dress and ordinary people listen to his patter.[49] These wandering singers preferred the busiest streets and squares, and church gates; and if they left the city it was for the crowds at the fairs. In Paris, they set up their pictures at strategic points: on the Pont Neuf, the boulevards and the squares.[50] The following is taken from Louis-Sébastien Mercier:

> Some chanted lamentations and hymns, others came out with bawdy ditties, and often there would not be more than 40 paces between the two of them . . . The scapular seller's audience deserted him for the happy song; he remained alone on his stool, pointing in vain to the horns of the devil of temptation, the enemy of humankind. All forgot the salvation he promised to run after the song of damnation. The reprobates' singer sang of wine, good food and love and extolled Margot's attractions; and the 2 *sol* coin which was poised between the hymn and the vaudeville was to fall, alas, into the pocket of the worldly minstrel.[51]

On these fringes of entertainment were to be found the destitute vagrants who exhibited curiosities, such as the marmot which accompanied the mountain dwellers of the Savoy region; the bear which certain dwellers of the Pyrenees brought with them; or the Mohawk Indian put on display by a Jewish pedlar from England in 1765.[52] Acrobats, organ-grinders and bear-tamers from the mountain villages of Tuscany all became familiar figures in the city.[53] And the mendicant forger, dressed as a monk, 'carrying a box of tricks . . . which contained an *Ecce Homo* and four figures from the Passion which he displayed to passers-by'[54] was similarly part of the entertainment.

The blindmen of Madrid gathered around the Puerta del Sol, which was in the centre of the city and was the meeting point for the three sources of news: official information circulated through the newspapers and 'relaciones'; news from the outside which arrived by post and unofficial news which was spread by word of mouth.[55] They battled against a city anxious to rid itself of its beggars by periodically reminding the authorities that they should not be included in that category on the grounds that since the end of the eleventh century they had been exempt from taxes as blindmen who exercised a profession.[56]

Thus the *pliegos de cordel*[57] were in part circulated by a network of blind pedlars who sang the text in verse.[58] Once in possession of the printed text, the blindman turned to the services of a reader, who read him the text as many times as necessary for him to learn it by heart so that he could then recite or sing it, either in snatches or in its entirety.[59] Work initially had to be done on the title, which was always extremely long and descriptive; it emphasized the originality of the tale, gave a flavour of the *romance* or story, described the main characters, indicated where the action took place, heralded the most important episodes and hinted at how it would end, whether happily or tragically.[60] The title acted as bait and the written text was converted into an oral history with all the resulting superfluous additions, discontinuity of structure and tenses, and an increasing number of digressions. The blindman proclaimed his tale over and over again, embellishing it, adding more exciting touches when necessary, constantly updating the dialogue to make it more appropriate to the gathering and to attract those passing and whet their appetites, all the while giving the impression that he had other, better tales to reveal. Obscenities and coarse expressions were the most common additions. To avoid this, the authorities demanded that only the title be proclaimed and eventually they banned the proclamation of printed texts.[61]

The manner of rendition depended upon whether the text was a newspaper text or 'relaciones' [narrative] in prose, which was merely proclaimed; or a 'romance' which would be sung. When he sang, the blindman accompanied himself on a guitar or violin or, increasingly in the twentieth century, on an accordion.[62] Sometimes he introduced visual images into his recitation and used illustrations from the 'pliegos sueltos', or posters stuck on canvas sheets, or 'cartelones' [placards].[63] On occasions, he acted out what he recited, especially when his subject was a religious one such as Christ's Passion.[64] Whenever possible, the storyteller embellished the tales he recounted with extracts from his own daily life or experience, and with the supposed expectations of his audience, as well as with their sorrows and desires.[65] And perhaps, like the Italian 'cantastorie' of the sixteenth century, he would pause from time to time to gauge his audience's reactions.[66]

The path common to both actor and pedlar is magnificently described by Corneille in *L'Illusion comique*, performed for the first time in 1635 or 1636. In Clindor's social itinerary, Corneille represented that of the French theatre – the 'Théâtre françois' – in its transition from fairground attraction to an art form valued by society's elite. In the wandering years of Clindor's youth, as recounted to Pridamant by Alcandre in Act One (lines 163–87), the different functions of role, place and audience are clear:

Your son's was scarcely an immediate rise;/ . . . /To get to Paris, whilst on the road he sold/Quacksalves to cure fever and migraine/And to get there, he also told fortunes. Once there, he lived by his wits, as many do/ . . ./ Tiring of being a scribe, he left his post suddenly,/ And had a dancing monkey in Saint-Germain./ He took to writing rhymes, and his scribblings/ Made a fortune for the vagabonds to sing/ . . ./ After that he traded in rosaries and balms, and, as a master of his trade sold mithridate/ He returned to the law courts and became an advocate/ In short, Buscon, Lazarille de Tormes, Sayavèdre and Gusman never took on so many different guises;*

Thus Clindor, who had explored all the picaresque paths of itinerancy – played the charlatan, paraded animals both on the road and in the fairs, acted as lyric-writer for wandering minstrels – left peripheral places and base activities behind and entered into the heart of the city and the favour of the highest society. The places he left behind henceforth belonged to the destitute vagrants.

The regular pedlar

The regular pedlar, who had established suppliers, faithful customers and enough of an inheritance to guarantee his credit, was the pedlar *par excellence*. Generally speaking, he set out between the end of August and the end of November, depending on the demands of farm labour, the dates of the livestock markets and the number of people in the household. Those pedlars who did not rear livestock left the village as soon as the harvest was in, the rest waited until the end of the autumn fairs, for in several regions the sale of livestock was men's business alone.[67] The make-up of the household was therefore of vital importance. In the mid-nineteenth century, in the Gourand household in Clavans in the Dauphiné, the father, Didier, previously a pedlar, lived with his sons Didier and Jean, his daughter-in-law and their three children. Didier had taken over his father's rounds in the Yonne, whilst Jean covered neighbouring Nièvre. Both of them went down to the lowlands as soon as the farm work was finished. In the Eymard household, on the other hand, there was only Jean, his wife and their children. Since there was no one to whom he could entrust the responsibility for selling livestock, Jean never set out on his rounds before November.[68] Joseph Nogeret, a 'vendor of cast iron cooking-pots' from the Auvergne, and his brothers divided the time spent away between them, so that Joseph set off on his rounds in the springtime, when his brothers, older than him and married, were returning home to farm their land.[69] The dates they returned, however, demonstrated that the demands of business were more important than those of farm work, since no pedlar

* Translation taken in part from Ranjit Bolt's translation and adaptation of *L'illusion comique*, Absolute Classics, 1988, Bath. [translator's note]

returned in time for the earliest farm tasks. In the Gourand household, the father helped his daughter-in-law to manure and sow the land; and Jean Eymard was always insistent in his letters that his wife took on hired help to assist her with these tasks. For the pedlars, the end of springtime was the time when the two halves of their lives coincided and clashed: they were required at home on the land, but if they went back too early they would forfeit two of the best months of business.

On the other hand, those pedlars who specialized in books and printed matter were not troubled by the constraints imposed by the land in exercising their trade. Those from Cotentin, like those from Campli who sold religious images, left in the spring and returned home at the beginning of the winter; those from Lorraine, the Pyrenees[70] and the Ticino region[71] divided the seasons up between themselves: some were away in the autumn and others in the springtime.

The pedlars stocked up primarily at the shops opened by émigrés, then made up the rest of their stock from other merchants. They made the bulk of their purchases from the former, and borrowed from them all or some of the money they would need for their campaign. As the years passed, a family tradition was forged with the latter suppliers and between the seventeenth and nineteenth centuries one can trace from generation to generation particular relationships maintained by peddling families with the same families of suppliers. The politics of purchasing remained the same, organized around a principal supplier who also acted as banker, and supplemented by stocks from specialist shops or regions encountered in the course of their travels.[72]

In contrast to the scattered nature of suppliers of goods in France, London was the place where the more minor English merchants filled their packs. At the end of the seventeenth century, over three-quarters of the supplies of fabrics were still bought there.[73] The city was also the major centre for the redistribution of porcelain imported from China.[74] To the supplies purchased in London were added more specialized products from the provinces. At his death Thomas Teisdale of Lincoln owed 192 pounds to five London merchants; he made up the rest of his stock in Glasgow (for Scottish cloth), Manchester (for needles and small articles of ironmongery) and Newport (for braid). Long-standing personal relationships developed between pedlars and London suppliers to the point where certain among the latter remembered their 'faithful' pedlars when they died and left them some money so that they might buy a ring of mourning or remembrance in memory of them.[75]

These packmen generally undertook one or two small-scale predetermined trips. They kept account books. In the course of his campaign Jean Eymar, a pedlar from the Oisans, covered a circuit of 15 kilometres in the Nièvre, between Corbigny and Epiry-Montreuillon. The Yonne canal lay at the heart of it with tiny villages of 100–400 inhabitants clustered around the locks. Pierre-Joseph Barret of Monêtier in the

Briançonnais extended his business over eight *communes** to the extreme west of the Beaujolais mountains, covering between 9 and 13 kilometres a day depending on the month.[76] The campaign of a pedlar from the Auvergne in south and south-west France followed a similar pattern: they covered small areas, but this did not preclude longer journeys, which were regularly undertaken to visit the important fairs. The 'Scotch Draper''s campaign was no different from that undertaken by the pedlar from the Auvergne or from the Dauphiné.[77] The cramped nature of the Belgian territory influenced the way in which the campaigns were organized: usually the merchant would travel in the area surrounding his house for several days or weeks. The goods being peddled subsequently dictated how extensive a campaign it would be. Certain pedlars, who travelled for three months, rented an attic in a city as a base from which to travel around the surrounding countryside for several weeks, then moved on to another area, where the family had taken care to send a replenished stock.[78]

In the same way that they divided up the seasons between themselves, the Pyrenean pedlars also divided up the area covered:

> The summer pedlars covered the South of France, the Alps, the upper Loire valley, Brittany and Normandy. The winter pedlars split up into groups and went directly to Toulon, Limoges, Bourges, Guéret and Auxerre, where they collected their first purchases, which they had ordered from Paris. From these starting points, they took short cuts to spread themselves over all regions, getting to within 60 leagues of Paris and meeting up to travel there together, with some arriving at the beginning of January, some only in the springtime.[79]

Noël Gille also undertook two campaigns: one in the North and the Pas de Calais, the other near Paris in a quadrilateral between Pontoise, Nogent, Bourges and Amboise. His marriage settled him in Montargis and the latter campaign subsequently won the day. He often stayed in a town for a week or fortnight, sometimes even for a month – which did not however prevent him from making brief forays into the surrounding countryside. He travelled 'everywhere'.[80]

One must, however, look separately at book pedlars, who reached all markets:

> If one were to suppress these Mountain Pedlars, one would be doing a considerable wrong to provincial bookshops, who would be deprived of a consumer demand for which these people are absolutely essential, be it for the conveyance of ABC books, books of hours or devotional books etc., which one cannot do without in small towns and villages, where there are

* A *commune* is the basic administrative unit of France for local government purposes. [translator's note]

no established bookshops. Those members of the nobility who spend part of the summer months in the country, a number of gentlemen and women whose income does not allow them to live in the big cities where the price of goods is high – all these people, members of the State, useful to society and whose time is often spent in studying literature or mastering the arts and sciences; all these people, I contend, would be deprived of a number of works which are of great importance to them, were the pedlars to be completely suppressed . . .[81]

Noël Gille's biggest customers were civilian officers, those in the legal profession, the bourgeoisie, doctors and the clergy. There were few members of the nobility amongst them.[82] Nor should one overlook the inroads made into the poorer classes by pictures, songs and playing cards; or that the strength of the itinerant merchants and their biggest sources of profit were dependent upon their belonging to a network which allowed them to work on the basis of orders and to supply one and all with their chosen reading matter, even if it meant going to Paris to get it. 'I intended going to Rouen', wrote a Norman pedlar, '. . . When I saw from your catalogue that you do not have the book I needed, this meant my travelling to Paris.'[83] The police denounced this role played by the 'Normans', whether they went to Paris 'from time to time', stayed with relatives or 'compatriots' and 'circulated immoral books';[84] or 'returned home in the winter and came back to Paris in the summer' to run a stall on the quays,[85] since 'most of them never fail to bring the most dubious books back with them, which they pass on to private customers or pedlars, risking almost nothing, except at the tollgate, because they are not known'.[86]

As for the haberdashers, up until the nineteenth century, evidence shows that their clients were not solely from the lower classes, and that the aristocracy did not turn up their noses at what the haberdasher had to offer.[87] However, reflecting the development of the profession, their clientele became increasingly proletarian: in the nineteenth century, when the pedlar visited a middle-class home, it was to sell to the maid or manservant, and when an account book referred to a 'gentleman', it was solely because the sale had taken place on his premises, or because he had stood as guarantor to his servants. Jean Eymar's customers were all village people of modest means, as were those of Pierre-Joseph Barret and Jean-Pierre Gravier-Cheville.[88]

Jean Eymar's account book, which he kept between 1858 and 1870, helps us to understand how the regular pedlar became part of the geographical and social fabric of the few villages to which his campaign was confined. The area was too small to be able to talk in terms of an itinerary: Eymar travelled constantly between one village and the next, from lock to lock. He mapped out the landscape in his head, and it was this mental topography that provided him with his initial landmark: each new client was first identified in relation to the position of his house: 'in Mouche-Pazy, the house above the farmyards', 'the house nearest to the tilery', 'the lady in the house nearest the wood' . . . The pedlar would then concentrate on situating his customers in social terms, within networks of relationships, family connections and occupations. He noted down all these links in his notebook, along with any nick-names, how the customer was addressed in the village, and how they presented themselves during his conversations with them. It was a strange business relationship, where transactions were carried out with people whose names he never asked, and who were defined through their position in village society. The life and culture of these villages in the Nevers region is reconstructed through the pages of this notebook: a landscape of large farms; tiny hamlets scattered amongst the hills and woods; a small number of 'gentlemen', the only ones to employ any servants; the factory with three workers; and the world of lock-keepers who worked on the Yonne canal. Subjugation can be read in its pages – that of nameless women and servants who only existed through their husband or employer, or that of the workers who were dependent upon their employers, although some male servants had dealings with the pedlar themselves.

It was to the women that the pedlar sold his goods, but it was the man's name that he recorded: 'Roubi's mother'; 'Mourau's wife'. Widowhood bestowed a first name: thus Pierre-André Gavillon's wife was not Widow Gavillon for long, but quickly became Joséphine, from Chaise-Pazy; just as the widow Davaud became Jeanne from Sardy. The pedlar pinpointed the personalities, the key players in the community (Jacob the treasurer à la boite aux loups, André the musician) and their geographical, professional and family itineraries. The family connection was the first thing Eymar noted down, as both a landmark and a moral connection, drawing another map for him, which he gradually mas-tered, leaning on some people to gain access to others. All the brothers, brothers-in-law, sons-in-law and children often had no label other than their family link with one of his better-known customers: 'Brûlé's brother from Collancelle' or 'Charles, son-in-law to Philippe from Marcilly-Cervon'.

In this way, the pedlars almost surreptitiously became part of village culture. Their presence on the roads or at the inn, initially disturbing, then visible and familiar, lost its strangeness as, thanks to their knowl-edge of the local population, they became part of the social fabric of the lowlands. Finding the keys to gaining access to these hamlets was a very slow process, which demanded total flexibility from the pedlar and where time was not important. Hence, on average, Eymar only profit-ably visited between one and four houses a day.

Knowledge of the places and the people went hand in hand with another relationship, one as much economic as cultural – that of credit. This was the basis of the relationship between the pedlar and the villagers: the account book, which has no record of a single cash sale, bears witness to this. Without exception, all Jean Eymar's customers paid him on credit. They paid him back over the year, in dribs and drabs, payment being made when the pedlar turned up again, and always coupled with a further purchase and thus further credit. The more months that passed, the fewer people settled their debts before the pedlar's departure, to the point where, from May onwards, those customers who paid him the following year outnumbered those who paid him during his campaign. Sometimes the pedlar and the customer decided to go over their accounts with each other, and Eymar recorded that the account was 'settled', whilst none the less indicating a total amount still outstanding, which could be paltry – 0.75 francs for Nolot, a servant; 1 franc for Claudine Saulin – or more substantial: 22 francs for Sautran, la Mignauve's manservant. What was important was that the debts were, in fact, never completely paid off; the remaining symbolic debts prove that the reason behind them was not economic but was concerned with forging links. The business relationship was friendly and based on trust, and accounts were always kept open. To close it would have meant the end of any relationship, business or social. The outstanding debts were also the migrant's guarantee that he would reclaim his customers during his next campaign.

Just as he bought on credit, the pedlar also sold on credit. Lack of money was not the only reason, even though the money came in irregularly from the peasants. Deferred payment was at the heart of the relationship between the migrant and his customers: it was a guarantee that a relationship had been formed, and it gradually opened the village doors to him. Since the packman covered a limited area, travelling constantly from one location to another, each time he passed through a place it was an opportunity for him to recover a small amount of the money he was owed, and to offer a few more goods on credit. The account books from the first half of the nineteenth century, like the letters which families kept, show that when his campaign was over the pedlar hadn't recovered the credit granted.[89] This meant that he was sure of reclaiming his customers in the autumn but, if the campaign had not been too fruitful, could also mean that he was unable to repay the city merchants, forcing him to borrow money in his own village.

Prices were not fixed. They were negotiable within the context of a personal relationship, and through the manoeuvrings of trading and bargaining. The only precautionary measure taken by the pedlar to remind himself of the purchase price and to enable him to recognize his goods should they be stolen, was to mark them with symbols known only to him or to his close relations. Those from Cantal, for example, wrote the cost price on each article of their merchandise using a ten-letter code which corresponded to the ten figures: Azuqueca's was ABSOLUMENT; Usano's was SAINT FLOUR.[90] In his memoirs, another such pedlar remembers the mark which allowed him to prove that he was correct when he recognized his stolen goods.[91]

This continuation of credit from one year to the next confirmed the pedlars and their families in the profession. In the mid-nineteenth century, Jean-Pierre Charpenel, a pedlar from Barcelonette born in 1804, wrote his father's life story. The campaign he described was similar to that carried out by Jean Eymar, and, as in his case, credit was at the heart of his custom:

> As regards private customers, . . . it is imperative to grant them credit on at least a part of the amount: as these are regions where assets are almost entirely tied up in wine, figs, almonds and olives, and since these are all harvested in late autumn, this means that they are often short of the money at the time of year when they need to buy clothes. Of course, they have the silk-worm harvest which comes very early, but that money is already far behind them when the question of winter clothes arises. Thus, if one wishes to make a sale, one is obliged to allow credit, but the risk is not great with these people. If for some reason they are unable to pay one year, they pay the next. Taken as a whole, there is no doubt that you will lose some money from them but, taken together, although they are only small accounts, they make up a considerable sum at the end of the day.[92]

However, the winter that his father fell ill, the son was obliged to leave Lyon to take on his father's rounds and attempt to recover the money owed. He had made the choice not to be a pedlar; the death of his father forced him into it.

The merchant-pedlar

The merchant-pedlar, who rented a shop but was prepared to go back on the road if business went badly, employed the newest sales techniques: from the moment he appeared on the scene, he used the press as an advertising medium; if he was a bookseller he would have catalogues printed.[93]

The Manchester Man

The new figure to emerge in the seventeenth century in England was the Manchester Man, who was to a certain extent the first sales representative. He could be distinguished from the traditional pedlar by the way in which he obtained his supplies, through his customers and his sales techniques. The Manchester Man was a pedlar working for a factory, who did not travel from door to door but from shop to shop.[94] He remained an itinerant merchant, but the vital difference was that he operated as a middleman between the manufacturers in the north of England and the retailers, shopkeepers and pedlars across the country. As early as 1685, the existence of the 'Manchester Men' was well established. They criss-crossed England with their mules or horses loaded with cheap fabrics and clothes, ironmongery and cutlery, to which assortment they also added watches and almanacs. A bell worn by the lead horse signalled the arrival of the convoy. They travelled along lonely roads in bad repair, primarily in summer to avoid the rigours of the winter weather.

As an intermediate stage in the distribution network, they sold in bulk to the shopkeepers and to the pedlars whom they met when visiting the fairs, thus competing with the London merchants for the custom of the itinerant merchants. They all attended the fairs, which became places where deals were struck between, on the one hand, the London merchants or their agents and the Manchester Men and, on the other, the pedlars, who took this opportunity to settle their previous debts and to obtain the necessary goods for their next campaign. The London merchants, like the Manchester Men, offered extensive credit to the packmen.[95] In addition to offering credit the Manchester Man, who in the eighteenth century was one of the preferred agents of the manufacturers as they set out to create a mass market, played on his respectability, creating the illusion that he had the same social status as an established merchant. To lend substance to this impression, he had ostentatious decorated visiting cards and headed notepaper printed, which he left with businesses to indicate that he had called, or published in the local newspapers to advertise his imminent arrival.[96]

The ways in which a peddling campaign was financed, together with an assessment of recruitment procedures, thus allow us to distinguish the various categories of itinerant merchants. And, because these criteria take into account the pedlar's roots in a village community, they bring to light one of the major divisions in the profession. Indeed, for some, whatever position they occupied on the scale of activity, belonging to a community promised the possibility of success, which became more real as the pedlar gained access to the ranks of those who 'were creditworthy'; it also meant that, should business fail, then the latter could count on his home community to provide him with what little merchandise or work he needed to see him through the period he was out of business. For the others, for those who did not belong, or no longer belonged, to a network of compatriots, taking up the profession meant a drop in status and social marginalization, and left little hope of future success. Finally, these dual criteria also brought about the emergence of the developing figure of the sales representative, marking the beginning of a movement towards the world of employees attached to a firm.

5

In the Village: Reasons for Itinerancy and the Structures Supporting It

Since the home village was as important to the network of merchants – both itinerant and settled – as the changing cities in which they established their businesses, we should now turn our attention to the communities which were their point of departure so as to understand the nature of the social organization which was the driving force behind migrations so economically diverse and yet so closely bound together. What was it that bound the burghers of Strasbourg, Lyon or Frankfurt so closely to their Alpine villages? And how did changes in their business affect the home communities?

From the Middle Ages in the Alps, mountain society developed around the concept of migration. Moreover, the population was unevenly spread, with the higher-up villages having a clear advantage in population terms since they were close to the passes and mountain pasture-lands. This distribution of the population – which is surprising if one adheres to the school of thought that believes that the peasant societies had to share limited agricultural resources – points to something which is essential to an understanding of 'overpopulation' in the higher villages and helps us to unravel a society which seems, from the outset, to have developed with scant regard to the poor and easily damaged soil.

This change of perspective necessitates some close questioning about the way in which the traditional image of the mountain villages was constructed. The usual analyses of Alpine valley society rest on a certain number of assumptions and archival sources. The archives are riddled with complaints against the 'poor land', cries of despair which are echoed from one valley to another, from one mountain to the next. Snow, torrents of rain, avalanches, rockfalls – all forced the peasants to develop their land with their bare hands, which required too much manpower during the short farming season for a harvest which was never sufficient. Taking the shortage of cereals as a starting point, historians have explained the mountain migrations as a function of the mountain ecosystem, of the way in which the mountains' resources were exploited. Sensitive to the grievances of the population, they also blame the tax system which meant that money had to be found to pay the rates.[1] Such analyses rest on the conviction that nature gives man no option as to the way in which he exploits her; they explain everything in terms of the agro-pastoral system in use in the French Alps in the nineteenth century, the 'loi de transhumance',* as described by Raoul Blanchard.[2] The other constant theme in their analyses relates to the social structure of the mountain communities, which are always described as 'republics' of small landowners, all equal in their mediocrity:[3] the land records bear witness to this, urban observers remarked it, and the memories of the mountain folk both then and now confirm it.

Yet this emphasis on nature over culture remains to be proven. If migration was a factor of dense population, then the discourse which sees it as the 'oxygen bottle' of overpopulation conceals the interdependence and essential links between the migrants and the settled population: it sees migration as a necessary breaking away whereas it can also be a way of occupying territory. In fact, those analyses which classify the inhabitants of a community according to their stability or mobility – using space as the only analytical criterion – are describing migration from a completely different perspective which, at least up until the eighteenth century, was completely foreign to the logic behind village migration.

In order to grasp a different reality, we have to open up our approaches to migration, change where the lines are drawn and not think solely in terms of competing spaces, groups of individuals (with a distinction between the mobile and immobile) and levels of wealth in terms of land (by constructing hierarchies based solely on the ownership of land). In other words, considering society as made up of hierarchical and autonomous groups which can legitimately be studied without taking into account the bonds which link them to each other, or confining oneself to an analysis which takes as its starting point the narrow family unit or the individual, means one loses sight of the context in which all these realities are rooted and, in particular, does not allow for the emergence of other, more pertinent social configurations.

The next step then was to try to establish how groups evolved (refusing to take emigration as an a priori sign of entrenchment of the village community) and how links were established between individuals, within families and between families; to ascertain what lay behind such alliances and how the actors in this social drama went about preserving or destroying them. This approach, which takes as its starting point the interactions of the actors themselves, means going back to the village, piecing together the families and their collective wealth, and tracing the

* System of transhumance farming. [translator's note]

formation and evolution of the networks of relationships of which the families were a part, both in the highlands and elsewhere. This complicates issues of mobility and identity by demonstrating, on the one hand, that the nexus between those who stayed and those who left did not create two distinct family units but was the basis of all family and customer networks, and marriages; and, on the other, that identity was constructed as much through social relationships – and sometimes more so – as spatial.

An analysis of this type, of course, can only be conducted on a small scale. We shall proceed using as a starting point the geographical origins of the merchants and packmen of the Upper Dauphiné peddling network – the villages of Besse, Clavans and La Grave (all at a height of 1,400 metres or more in the Upper Oisans), and Monêtier in Briançonnais on the other side of the Lautaret pass in the Guisane valley. Using these 'laboratory' models, we will then try to ascertain whether the other important peddling regions differed significantly from the Upper Dauphiné model.

Land and credit

Was it then love of his native soil that kept the *bourgeois*, newly accepted in the city where he conducted his business, in his village? Was it because of his attachment to his plot of land – no matter how tiny – that the peasant travelled constantly between highlands and lowlands? Since the economic and emotional role of the land is at the heart of all problems relating to rural societies, and because the representation of the mountain dweller as poor, free and solitary has developed alongside the concept of land being meanly but equally distributed between the landowners, it is important that one assesses carefully how important land was in the economy of the mountain valleys.

What follows is an analysis of two valleys at the end of the seventeenth century: La Grave in 1671 and Besse in 1685. The tallage register of La Grave had 449 landowners on its records and the source specifies that it was calculated on the basis of the actual surface area of the land recorded on the cadaster and 'at the rate of 40 *sols* for each *sétérée** on the cadaster'.[4] The tallage register of Besse includes 227 landowners. If one confines oneself to defining wealth in terms of land, then the classic analyses demonstrate their validity: social hierarchies based on property reveal that inherited wealth was not widespread and that fortunes were generally paltry, since nearly 70 per cent of the inhabitants of La Grave

---

* 1 *sétérée = c.* 38 *ares.* 1 *are* = 100 m².

Table 1 **Percentage division of land, measured against average land value**

Average = 1	<0.5	>0.5 <1	>1 <2	>2 <3	>3 <4	>4 <5	>5
La Grave 1671	39	29	22	6	2	0	2
Besse 1685	32	25	33	6	4	0	0

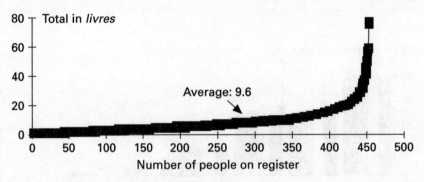

Figure 1 **Tallage register: La Grave 1671**

owned land whose surface area was less than the average surface area in the village (obtained by dividing the total area by the number of landowners), which was 4 *sétérées* and 3 *quartélées* – about 1.7 hectares.[5] In Besse, less than half the population attained this average, which was slightly higher here – 5 s, 2 q or about 2 hectares. In both cases, certain families stand out. In La Grave there were two merchants who owned more than five times the average land surface area and in Besse the four richest inhabitants each owned between three and four times the average (table 1). The graph (figure 1) showing the total amount of contributions paid by the population of La Grave in 1671 clearly illustrates the situation in such communities, where the majority owned tiny areas of land, more or less equal in size, with a few individuals standing out from the rest.

The development of land-ownership in Monêtier during the eighteenth century does not reveal any significant changes or original features in relation to the other villages of the Upper Dauphiné.[6] In Monêtier for the first three quarters of the century, between 60 and 70 per cent of the inhabitants owned less than the average surface area and only one or two families stood out from the others, owning more than five times the average. At the end of the century, one can see a definite concentration of land wealth within the most powerful families.

Table 2 **Percentage division of land, measured against average land value**

Average = 1	<0.5	>0.5 <1	>1 <2	>2 <3	>3 <4	>4 <5	>5
Monêtier 1713	38	28	20	10	2.6	0	1
Monêtier 1741	29	36	21.1	9.4	2.7	2.7	0
Monêtier 1761	37.1	22.9	25	10.8	2.7	1.3	0
Monêtier 1770	42.2	19	23.2	11.3	2.8	1.4	0

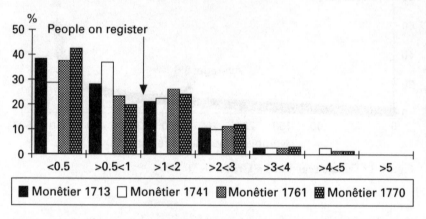

Figure 2 **Changing division of land-ownership in the eighteenth century**

However, several facts make it necessary to reconsider the relevance of hierarchies constructed on the basis of land and tax.

(1) An analysis of the way in which the tallage registers were compiled reveals that those who owned the land weren't necessarily those who farmed it: such registers mask the importance of tenant-farming. Moreover, a knowledge of the families involved enables one to see that members of the same household could be scattered over different property ratings, thus piling false divisions onto real divisions. For an understanding of the real divisions between ownership and exploitation, between owning land and working it – without taking into account, of course, that one has to weigh up the discrepancy between the amount of property declared and what this actually represented in the context of the family's total income – it is essential to cross-reference the tax registers with other source documents and to compare them with case studies.

What can we learn from wills in comparison to these tax registers? Jean Giraud from La Grave kept a record of his property in the hope that on the day when Protestantism was once again accepted in France, he could reclaim the assets which he left behind when he fled the kingdom. Jean summarized the amounts recorded in the wills of his father and mother: he recorded 3,913 *livres* for his father and 2,000 for his mother. Then he summarized all that he had inherited. According to the terms of the will, Jean should have inherited 1,957 from his father – in other words, half the total amount declared by his father, his two sisters sharing the other half between them; the mother's inheritance was shared equally between all three children. However, his account book, which summarizes and values the various elements of his father's fortune (fields, meadows, woods, numerous houses which had been in the family a long time, goods acquired by his father in repayment for debts) indicates that his portion adds up to 6,512 *livres*, or three times what was actually declared. In order to arrive at the total estate of the father, one would also have to add his sisters' portion which should double this figure. Thus estimated, this inheritance – already more sizeable – still doesn't take into account the business affairs. If one remembers that in 1670 – in other words, two years before his father's death – Jean invested 6,000 *livres* in capital in the company which he had set up with Monnet and Chicot, one can imagine how much the tax records of the past – just like those today – were misleading when it came to the actual wealth of the elite classes: even if one assumes that property always constituted the major part of an inheritance, the tax records made the community seem more equal than was the case, by not including the few large fortunes which were at the head of the field in the village.[7]

(2) By dividing society in terms of the head of the family, the tax sources established the household as the basic unit of mountain society. Yet business practices demonstrate that a more relevant division was a larger unit: that of the extended family, both present and elsewhere, in which larger structure the head of the family played a part. Rereading the tallage registers from the perspective of this wider network of relations alters the hierarchies and makes them more visible. In La Grave in 1771, three of the eight richest inhabitants were members of the same family: Blaise, Pierre and Vincent Pic. Everything would seem to point to the fact that these Pics were related to, amongst others, the Picques of Paris who, from the beginning of the seventeenth century, had been part of the Parisian merchant aristocracy. The clue which leads us to believe that this was so is the fact that Olivier Picques, who was a *bourgeois* of Paris, acted as a correspondent and business address for César Eustache, a merchant from the Upper Oisans, in his business dealings with other important Paris merchants.[8] This same Olivier Picques, who had inherited more than 50,247 *livres*, left 607,796 *livres* to his seven children when he died in 1635.[9] He was consul of Paris in

1608 and a consular judge in 1623. His son, Olivier the younger, was himself consul in 1648. A Nicholas Picques was then a town councillor in 1664 and an alderman of Paris in 1668.[10]

In considering these men separately, one overlooks two important dimensions of their power: the family banking network which supported their business activities and the migrants who had opened shops with whom they were closely linked. However, if we consider the extended family network as an indissociable whole, regardless of whether its members were sedentary or mobile, we can locate these elite classes in terms of other activities which were not based on land-ownership but which commanded just as much power in the village. Seen from this angle, the influence of the Guerre, Masson and Arthaud families bore no relationship to the modest place which they occupied in the hierarchy of land-ownership: no member of the Guerre family was in the top band; the richest, Claude, owned land only three times more than the average holding. Yet in 1670 he was a *bourgeois* of Lyon; and in 1680 he had sold all that he owned in the village.[11] Felix Guerre barely owned three times the average property, but his son who lived in Lyon was a *bourgeois* of La Grave.[12] In the Masson family, the richest, André, came only seventh on the tallage register; yet the inventory carried out on the death of his ancestor, André Masson, detailing only his merchandise and letters of credit, which were kept in two trunks that he had rented in a lodging-house in Paris called the Pomme d'Orange, revealed that for 1610 alone, the business deals he had conducted with around 30 Parisian merchants had left him with more than 26,350 *livres* in debts owed to him. In Paris, he was sometimes referred to as a merchant from La Grave, sometimes as a merchant from Lyon, which demonstrates the extent of his business.[13] No member of the Arthaud family owned more than three times the property average, yet Jean Arthaud was successful enough to become Rector of the Lyon Hospital in 1656[14] and subsequently an alderman of the city.[15] His widow, who resided in La Grave, lived very comfortably on the pension he had left her. In the case of the Guerre family, as with the Arthaud and Masson families, a strategy of detachment from the mountain was at work; these families no longer invested in the village but, whilst they had not completely severed their links, they none the less remained no less powerful – and perhaps even more so – than those who occupied the top rank of the land hierarchy: their potential for providing employment and for intervention, allied to their social success, no doubt compensated substantially for their partial retreat from the land-owning world. The tax records, in leading one to think that the village history was confined to its geographical territory, whereas it actually encompassed the places where the family network was at work, hide the real hierarchies. These hierarchies, shaped by the dynamic of migration, were consequently subtle and fluid.

Table 3 **Distribution of sales agreed in the notary's practice in Besse (1684–90)**

Value *in* livres	Number	Sum total	Percentage of total amount
Less than 25	9	104	1.5
25–49	13	503	7.4
50–99	12	869	12.9
100–199	11	1385	20.5
200–399	4	950	14.1
400 and above	4	2945	43.6
Total	53	6756	100

(3) To understand how the elite built up their capital, one must look beyond wealth solely in terms of property. A systematic analysis of notaries' deeds allows us a first glimpse of the respective roles of land and credit. From the list of all deeds drawn up by the notary in Besse between 1684 and 1690,[16] several conclusions can be drawn concerning the constitution of family fortunes:

(a) The notary drew up almost as many deeds of sale as bills of debt and more than half the deeds concerning land were leasing agreements.
(b) An analysis of the deeds of sale confirms that the market for land was almost totally immersed in the market for credit. In fact, during the six years covered by the register, there were only seven sales paid for in cash and these sales, with the exception of the most modest (3 *livres*), all took place in the presence of the merchants.
(c) Although the total movement of sales differed very little from that found in the lowlands[17] (less than 7 per cent of land was put on the market), the movement was three times more significant for meadows than for grassland since barely 20 *sétérées* of farmland (about 7 hectares) changed hands in comparison with 60 *journaux* of grassland (about 20 hectares). To this must be added items which were not set down as part of an inheritance (six cases of this); or were attached to a house (four cases); as well as a wood and three 'montaignes' (alpine houses with mountain pasture-land).

At first glance (tables 3 and 4), the obligations concern the greater sums, but the imbalance is introduced by a substantial letter of credit for 3,400 *livres*. This amount apart, the sums in question are very similar: 6,510 *livres* for 54 obligations against 6,756 *livres* for 53 sales. The average obligation would be 180 *livres* including the substantial letter

Table 4 Distribution of obligations agreed in the notary's practice in Besse (1684–90)

Value in livres	Number	Sum total	Percentage of total amount
Less than 25	4	80	0.8
25–49	10	415	4.2
50–99	25	1929	19.4
100–199	10	1500	15.1
200–399	2	523	5.3
400 and above	4	5463	55.2
Total	55	9910	100

of credit, or 119 *livres* without it, against an average of 127 *livres* for the sales.

The distribution of sales and obligations according to their frequency and the amount they were for highlights different patterns: minor sales were numerous whereas minor obligations were less so: the higher brackets (100–400 *livres*) were more frequent as sales than as obligations. Sales therefore took place at the two extremes of the scale, tiny plots of land or vast areas. This divergence brings us back to the characteristic features of the credit market: merchants sold animals and cereals on credit and lent money on numerous occasions. The transactions would pile up one on top of the other and were recorded as promises – spoken or written – in which the debtor undertook to repay the debt in the shortest time possible (between six months and a year). But such deadlines were never respected and from time to time, at times which depended largely on family factors (illness, fear of death, the need to set up one of his children) or economic factors (unfavourable circumstances, doubt about the solvency of the debtor) the creditor would go to the notary to insure the sums lent and make the debtor sign an obligation. In this way, the money lent was officially recognized. Then, once again, delays in repayment of the capital would build up, the interest would be paid more or less regularly and new transactions would be added to old debts. Lender and borrower would go back to the notary to record a new obligation, with the capital being increased by any arrears in interest repayments. Selling land would therefore seem to bring to an end a long chain of debt which stretched back over long periods of time (some for more than 40 years). Ten years was a completely standard period of time, at the end of which the debtor's heir would sell the whole of the estate, crippled with debt, which he had inherited on the death of his father: this would be worth between 100 and 500 *livres*.

Table 5 Table of obligations signed in favour of the tax collector of Besse (1684–90)

Value in livres	Number	Sum total	Percentage of total amount
Less than 25	0	0	0
25–49	3	128.13	8.5
50–99	8	648.19	42.9
100–199	5	736.2	48.6
200 and above	0	0	0
Total	16	1512.52	100

Money circulated seldom: the economic life of the village was run along lines of credit and exchange. Land was exchanged for animals, in return for debts, for work, for personal relationships and for power. Village life appeared to be dominated by a handful of merchants who were as much in control of the local markets as they were the links with the city markets. They were important pasture owners (the most important deals were, moreover, the ones involving pasture-land) and dominated the only lucrative market, the livestock market. They were also the major providers of farming salaries and incomes, in particular through leasing out animals which they were unable to feed in winter.

Among these merchants, the tax collector played a predominant role, which the notary records allow us to discern clearly: he was ubiquitous, as much as a purchaser of plots of land as in the role of guarantor. He played a part in almost a third of sales and obligations, and he held more than 15 per cent of the total sum owed in obligations. An analysis of the sale contracts in which he was involved shows that he accumulated small plots of land and petty bills of debt: he was only involved in purchases of more than 100 *livres* four times and never in those over 150 *livres* (table 5). The total amount of his acquisitions represented nearly 14 per cent of the total value of all acquisitions. Like his purchases, his letters of credit were to be found in a narrower band than the full range of obligations represented.[18]

This approach to the respective importance of land and credit demonstrates that there was no strategy for the accumulation of land,[19] but rather strategies for accumulating letters of credit. This being so, the image of the smallholders, all equal in their mediocrity, is destroyed. In fact, a fair number of these smallholders were only viewed as such in the eyes of the legal system, since many of them owed more than the value of their property – and this wasn't only true of the poorest. As for the elite, they rarely owned more than 5 hectares. It was neither the land nor the business conducted over it, therefore, which allowed the accumulation of capital but rather the profits to be had from other markets controlled by means of letters of credit, in particular the labour market. Many of those who emigrated did not do so to pay their taxes, but to pay the man who paid them for them – which is not at all the same thing. One can therefore understand how merchant migration supported other types of migration: it was a case of offering one's labour elsewhere as repayment for debts contracted in the village.[20] Social bonds were thus greatly transformed.

Tracing the politics of land acquisition by certain families over several generations demonstrates that it had a threefold function: to form the basis of future matrimonial alliances; to gain access to communal grazing land, since the number of animals that one could graze on this land depended on the importance of one's landed inheritance (to this end, the merchants extended their networks of debtors to neighbouring villages so as to multiply the accessible pasture-land); and finally to use the land as a guarantee for credit granted by city suppliers.

Open hierarchies and family networks

The mountain communities were not, then, so many 'little republics' as urban observers so liked to remark,[21] as did the historians, labouring under the combined effect of analytical methods perfected for the study of peasantry on the lowlands and the recent picture of mountain society which gives no hint of previous riches under the cloak of past poverty. On the contrary, these villages sprang up between the fifteenth and seventeenth centuries, composed of extremely unequal social groups and ruled over by certain families, who were scattered over several geographical locations. We shall be looking at the histories of Jacques Bérard, Jean Giraud, Vincent Pic's widow, Jean Bernard, Pierre Gourand, Jean Pellisier and a few pedlars who died on the road to gain an insight into the variety of roles and the wealth of these different groups.

At the top of the village hierarchy were men like Jacques Bérard, who died in Lyon in 1690. An inventory of his belongings was drawn up 'at the request of Jeanne Vieux, wife of *sieur* Jacques Bérard, merchant of the town'.[22] Bérard was described as 'a merchant of Lyon', although he was born at Mizoen, married there, was a pedlar until 1676 and continued right up until his death to go to the village regularly, where he still had property and did business.[23] The Revocation of the Edict of Nantes took place whilst he was at Mizoen and it was in the mountain village in 1686 that Jacques, his wife Jeanne Vieux and their children Jean, Suzanne, Simon, Marie, Jeanne and Jacques all renounced Protestantism.[24] At his death in Lyon, four children were still alive: Jean, Suzanne and Marie were present when the inventory was drawn up and Simon was away, having enlisted with the royalist army.

When Jacques Bérard settled in Lyon, he was far from being a poor man: his family was rich and his wife, Jeanne Vieux, daughter of a merchant from Mizoen whom he married on 15 April 1658, had brought with her a dowry of 15,000 *livres*. In 1676, a year before discharging the dowry, he opened a shop in Lyon. During the first three years that he was in business in the city, he was in partnership with his brother Jean and with a relation by marriage, Jean Delor. Subsequently, Jean and Jacques remained the only partners. The reports of the village meetings in Mizoen show that although Jacques more commonly stayed in Lyon, his two associates lived in Mizoen where Jean was Consul in 1674–5 with Jean Delor succeeding him in the post in 1676–7.[25] Both remained active in village affairs until the Revocation.[26] In the years that followed, Jean Bérard and his family, like the Delor and Giraud families, emigrated to Switzerland: only Jacques remained behind to carry on the business in Lyon.[27] This strategy, similar to that employed by numerous lawyers, merchants and noblemen who made arrangements to protect the family inheritance (by reviving debts long paid, or inventing contracts and obligations so as to render themselves insolvent and leave their property with a relative, who had volunteered to stay so as to continue looking after the family inheritance), should also be put in the wider context of the family network.[28]

Effectively, studying individuals in their nuclear family means that one overlooks the importance of the wider context in which choices were made. For example, a decision as fundamental as where to settle the immediate family was discussed first within the close family circle, taking into account the opportunities offered by more distant relatives. In this second, less well-defined set of relations, more distant family links were strengthened by religious family bonds: hence Jacques was *compère*** to Jean Giraud; and Simon Delor, a relative of Jacques through his wife, was chosen as guardian of their younger children. The two main registers – creators of identity and solidarity – of real and invented family relationships were superimposed upon one another and supported each other to implant in each member of the family the sense of belonging to an extended family group. The history of nuclear families only makes sense, therefore, in the context of these larger family networks which encompassed them.[29]

The inventory carried out after Jacques' death explains both why his associates continued to be active in the village and his own comings and goings: the 19,002 *livres* and 17 *sols* worth of letters of credit which he possessed, divided into eight obligations and 45 promises, highlights the essential role played by the exploitation of mountain manpower in building up the fortune of the elite. At least 34 of the letters of credit were signed by men from the Upper Dauphiné. Moreover, the notary's

---

* Godfather from the mother's side of the family.

archives in Oisans indicate further letters of credit from other mountain villages which the inventory does not mention, such as that signed by Michel Durif from Villard d'Arène who had owed Jacques Bérard of Mizoen 300 *livres* since 1672, the interest on which had been due for two years. Furthermore, this letter of credit represented only half of Durif's debts because in 1684 he owed a total of 590 *livres*, in other words, as the deed states, more than the value of his father's and grandfather's property.[30]

Agreements made privately, which bear witness to the increasing prosperity resulting from mountain peddling, also, with the beginnings of loans to private individuals (and even to the state itself: barely had they arrived in Lyon before the three business associates signed a contract for 20 *livres* income a year, guaranteed by the Hôtel de Ville in Lyon), point to a still tentative but original strategy of involvement in public money-lending. Unfortunately, such agreements do not enable us to understand the business dealings themselves since the inventory confines itself to recording only the number of account books. Bérard had five of them: a ledger, an invoice notebook, a daybook, a purchase ledger kept jointly with his brother, and a small notebook containing the rent receipts for his shop in Lyon. However, to place the peddling elite within the merchant hierarchy in Lyon, we have put together a list of the costs incurred in each of the 41 inventories drawn up the same month as that of Jacques Bérard. The fees which had to be paid according to the amount of time spent on each inventory can also be of use in establishing the relative importance of each estate. In these terms, Bérard ranked among the richest Lyon merchants since he came in third place with 179 *livres*. Above him were two merchants: one was worth 205 *livres* in fees and the other, Octavio Mey, a *bourgeois* of Lyon and one of the most important merchants of his time, incurred 355 *livres* in costs: the average was 70 *livres*. His wife's dowry had already given some indication of how wealthy the family was before he settled in the city.

Jacques Bérard had rented a house overlooking the rue de Grenette and the rue Tupin. It comprised three bedrooms, a cellar, an attic, two shops and a storage space behind the shops. The total value of his property in Lyon came to 42,840 *livres* and 7 *sols*. Included in this were furniture and foodstuffs worth 1,153 *livres*. Ready money, which he kept in different bags according to its value and country of origin, amounted to 3,735 *livres*. Thus, the bulk of his wealth came from the merchandise found in his shop (fabrics, articles of clothing, all kinds of braid and ribbons) which had a value of 18,948 *livres*, and from his letters of credit, kept in a chest in his bedroom, which totalled 19,003 *livres*.

His furniture in Lyon was of walnut and adorned with tapestries. The bedroom in which he kept his papers and his money was carefully furnished: the chairs, bed, pedestal table and cabinet were all of walnut; green velvet and silk tapestries surrounded the bed, framed the windows and lined the chairs. Another bedroom, probably intended for the children, was more perfunctory – although still entirely of walnut – since it contained a table, a large bed, two smaller ones and yet another on wheels (but the inventory experts did not deem it necessary to note the colours of the fabrics). In the kitchen, a large walnut wardrobe contained his underwear: 15 pairs of underpants, a dozen pairs of socks, two dozen slipper-socks, two dozen handkerchiefs, a dozen items of black headgear, two dozen linen undershirts, another six undershirts, two jerkins and a pair of breeches. The absence of any kitchen utensils – apart from the instruments used to roast and grill in the fireplace – and the more general absence of objects which would reveal the day-to-day life of a family of six or seven leaves one with the impression that this rented house was primarily intended for the merchant lifestyle and for various people passing through. But perhaps this is a consequence of the inventory, which was only interested in valuing the deceased's property.

There is no document which would allow us to value the property that Bérard had kept in the village. His *compère* Jean Giraud – about whose business in Lyon we know nothing, apart from the fact that, following in the footsteps of his father, he too rented a shop there – nevertheless gives us an indication of what an important mountain merchant could retain in his mountain village. The total value of the Giraud inventory, including almost 3,000 *livres* from his two successive wives, amounted to 9,955 *livres*. However, the Giraud family were not highly placed on the tallage register since none of them owned land which was more than twice the village average. None the less, they married into the richest families: the Chicots and the Massons who were part of the most highly taxed group. Jean Giraud left assets to the value of 5,301 *livres*, divided more or less equally between grassland, farmland and houses. The house in which he lived in the hamlet of Hières had four storeys and a garden and was valued at 1,400 *livres*. Next to this he owned another garden in which he had had a small building erected. A house in the high mountain pasture-land which was worth 500 *livres* and a few woods, which counted for little in the valley, made up the rest of his property. The furniture in his main house was made of walnut and he had furnished his bedroom with curtains and wall hangings in red damask caddis.* The value of his furniture amounted to 1,186 *livres*, a little more than that in Bérard's house in Lyon. His wife also owned a house in the village in which she often stayed.

It is very difficult to follow Jean Giraud's business operations because he only gave summaries or partial accounts in his various account books, jumbling up information from them all. It nevertheless emerges that the capital invested in the company in 1670 was 6,000 *livres* and this rose

---

* Caddis was a worsted yarn, or crewel; also lint. [translator's note]

to 8,000 *livres* in 1674. Between 1671 and 1678 the company's accounts fluctuated between 12,000 and 18,000 *livres*. Once again, it is difficult to know what to think of these figures since, in the same year 1674, he recorded in his ledger that he was personally worth 18,046 *livres* and in his 'secret notebook' that it was 31,048 (although it is true that his secret notebook also usually included the value of his inheritance). In the same year, the inventory of his goods valued them at 10,480 *livres* – a little more than half the value of Bérard's shop goods, which represented none the less a well-stocked shop. As with Bérard, the relationship between credit and goods was the same and the same patterns emerged: 54 merchant shopkeepers, among whom were many names recognizable as being from Oisans and Briançonnais, owed him a total of 11,226 *livres*.

He recorded in a special account book the transactions he carried out in his home village. The account he gives shows that 42 people owed him a total of 9,145 *livres* when he left La Grave. In certain cases he gives details of their accounts with him or the place where the transaction took place – in Lyon for Claude Arthaud, in Grenoble for Félix Arthaud. He mixed business between the highlands and lowlands, selling Pierre Pic 'a small bale of silk', Michel Girard a horse, and Martin Berthieu a mule. For all these men he acted not simply as a backer and supplier but also as a banker (some of them had accounts in credit in his books) and an intermediary, since he took it upon himself to pay the debts that they owed to others. Apart from playing the markets for credit and goods, he occasionally also dabbled in small short-term speculations involving land: in Oisans on 4 July 1684, he acquired, in the course of an exchange, a plot of land valued at 6 *livres* which he then sold two days later for 10 *livres*, allowing six months' credit on the transaction:[31] naturally the profits from the credit he had just granted would count for more than the profit he made on the resale of the land.

Bérard and Giraud were not unusual. *Sieur* Vincent Pic's widow left a total of 5,000 *livres* in personal effects, without taking land into account. The tallage register allows one to place the family on the landowners' scale: her father-in-law paid five times the average rate of those on the register and her own father paid four times this rate. The personal effects that she left included 877 *livres* in cash, a little more than 1,800 *livres* in terms of furniture in the house (and so more than Giraud owned) and animals: a young mule, two cows, a calf, and 20 ewes, as well as two cows and six ewes which she 'had leased out for the winter' in Saint Jean d'Arves in the Savoy. Finally, there were 2,230 *livres* worth of letters of credit, divided into three categories: a loan of 1,680 *livres* to her brother-in-law (which brings us to one of the ways in which the family banking system functioned: once the husband was dead the banking system did not break down and the widow continued to invest his money in the family business affairs); debts owed to her by the ordinary

people in the village, and more than 25 small debts from insolvent villagers and Savoyards. This inventory also demonstrated that, in everyday
terms, the borders between Savoy and the Dauphiné meant very little.

These rich Dauphiné merchants now in business in the city had much
in common with the Motte family – who were originally from Savoy
but then settled in Beauvais – with whom, moreover, they had business
relations. In 1650 the Motte family, who were the first to open up the
trade route between Beauvais and Lyon, were owed 14,730 *livres* in
Lyon, 9,868 *livres* of which was owed by Jean Arthaud, Guillaume
Arthaud, Henri Raymon and Guerre, all merchants from La Grave then
established in Lyon.[32] Pierre Goubert summed up the originality of the
merchants of the Motte family thus:

> Nobody knows where the Motte family came from, perhaps from Savoy
> towards the end of the sixteenth century, but in Beauvais they have always
> displayed an admirable originality. With very few exceptions their fortune
> has been almost entirely in personal property and business. A Motte would
> almost certainly have a house 'in the Square' and would furnish it luxur-
> iously, with furniture and *objets* which were expensive, loud and gaudy. . . .
> You would never catch a Motte patiently building up a country estate, or
> going to spend the summer in a farmhouse to supervise the farmers and
> weigh the ears of corn. . . . They were always born merchants. Their passion
> was for handling and transporting thousands of pieces of unbleached linen,
> bleached cloth, sheets even, travelling further and further afield in pursuit
> of new markets and larger profits. They liked to circulate bills of exchange
> and cash rapidly and frequently, in the same way as they circulated cloth
> and sheets. Did they love money for its own sake? One may suspect as
> much. They loved it for the splendour and social status it bestowed upon
> them, for the feelings of inebriation that they must have experienced in
> earning it, in moving it around, and sometimes in losing it. However, as
> players in the game, they neglected to secure themselves something to fall
> back on, which might have provided them with a solid property base. If
> one compares them to so many others, wiser and more enduring, the wealth
> and power of the Motte family passed over Beauvais like a comet.[33]

A refusal to put down roots by buying land; a distinct reluctance to take
on local responsibility; marriage strategies which were oriented towards
the major centres of trade; the mobility of men, money and goods;
splendour in clothes and personal property: all went to make up a
merchant prototype which was new in northern France, but archetypal
of the 'merchant elites' from the upper villages of the Alpine ranges,
who reinforced their position using family ties and adopted the lowlands, not because they thought to find land there less barren than their
own, but because there was profit to be gained there, goods to be
circulated and money to be earned. Were circumstances to change, the
sources of profit to dry up, or other more promising markets to open
up then these men, whose stability lay in people rather than places,

would leave the towns in which they might have lived for over a century without putting down roots, and set out for other cities which promised a brighter future.

On a rung below these few families on the social scale, the pedlars acted as a link between merchants who had emigrated and packmen from the village, and made their living either from the continual to-ing and fro-ing of men and merchandise (for instance, the mule-drivers and the guides who ensured the safety of travellers and goods in negotiating mountain passes or dangerous routes) or from the migratory craftsmen. Both the merchants and the pedlars sought to use the mountain for rearing animals rather than for growing crops. Jean Bernard, a merchant from Besse, is an example of the second group. The inventory drawn up in 1685 after his death shows that his wealth in terms of land (just under 5 hectares) placed him on the tallage register amongst those who paid tax at a rate which was two to three times the average rate, and that he was therefore among the 24 richest inhabitants of the village. He left his heirs more than 14,000 *livres* in letters of credit, goods and cash. In other words, his land represented less than a tenth of his estate. The debts owed to him accounted for the lion's share, totalling nearly 11,000 *livres*. This was divided between three groups of related importance: loans to individuals, loans to the community, and loans to other merchants; in addition to which there was the 800 *livres* of dowry returned to him on the death of his daughter. The 43 obligations signed by villagers represented the repeated accumulation of petty loans: some rye for food or seeds, a little money to pay the taxes, the master-builder, the price of a cow or of some goods – 3,665 *livres* in all. The money that he had lent to the poorest people, to the 'less well-off' as he wrote, was recorded in a special book and represented 82 *livres*. These loans were not secured by any land and would never be repaid. In most cases, they were not even readily convertible into labour and these people were added to the network of debtors. Since she could neither recover nor make use of these debts, Bernard's widow later sold them on *en masse*. Next came four obligations owed to him by the community, totalling 3,776 *livres*. These marked repeated advances for taxes, municipal works, legal costs and loans in times of food shortages. These debts gave him a certain amount of power within the community and meant that it was easier for him to gain access to the mountain village pasture-land. Then came six obligations all relating to other village merchants and totalling 2,063 *livres*. In addition to the above, he also had livestock, goods and cash: more than 3,000 *livres* in 'gold louis, Spanish pistoles and other legal tender'.[34]

On a smaller scale, other pedlars built up their capital in the same way. In 1676 Pierre Gourand, Thomas' son, from Clavans was numbered among the 15 richest families and his land was two and a half times the size of the average holding. However, the man who paid the highest taxes in the village was André Gourand – who was almost certainly Pierre's uncle – who paid nearly five times the average. In 1702 he was amongst the group of the ten richest families, and in 1717, he was amongst the five most powerful families. From 1733, his only son Noé, who succeeded him in 1721, was the richest man living in the village. Using this family as an illustration we can see how, by gradually taking control of the internal and external village markets, the pedlars amassed sufficient capital for one of their descendants to have at his disposal a large enough fortune for him to open a shop in the lowlands. In the lowlands, their peddling activities – because they only left the village during the slack season – slotted into the network established by the Bérard, Delor and Giraud families. Back in the village, they became peasants once again, but also small businessmen, merchants and middlemen, which made it possible for them to engage in business in the winter as well.[35]

At the bottom end of the migrant merchant scale, the inventories drawn up after death reveal the overall paucity of inheritances. Jean Albert from the Villard d'Arène died on his rounds, leaving behind him in the lowlands 270 *livres* worth of goods and 267 *livres* of debts owed to him; back in the village his furniture was valued at 50 *livres*.[36] Pierre Gonnet's goods came to 139 *livres*, the debts he owed to 240 *livres* and his property to 33 *livres*: *sieur* Jean Rimbaud wasted no time in setting about seizing his assets as repayment.[37]

The remainder of the village population – the majority – lived for and through this elite class, which provided them with credit and supplies and hired village manpower. In these communities two methods of exploiting the soil were in conflict and concealed two contradictory ways of using the mountain. On the one hand, there were those who were settled permanently in the village, and the temporary petty migrants (craftsmen or beggars), who sought to establish farming concerns in which grassland and farmland complemented one another, which considered the breeding of livestock as secondary to the growing of crops, and which required interdependence and community constraints to survive. On the other were the merchants who had a shop in the lowlands where they spent most of the year, and who, on their return, were still involved in running the business, and invested the money they had made in far-off places in the more profitable activities of rearing livestock and money-lending. The interests of the latter were thus in conflict with the idea of community constraints. In particular, the use to which the communal mountain grassland was put was at the bottom of bitter disputes between the migrant merchants and the others: the merchants who sought to appropriate this grassland for themselves and graze their large herds on it were in opposition to the rest of the community, who were anxious to preserve the grass, vital to them all as manure for the fields.[38]

Conflicts such as these went hand in hand with a great degree of interdependence between one group and another, since the merchants used village manpower to farm their land, look after their herds in summer and feed the animals which they looked after in winter. Moreover, the merchants made money from the non-agricultural activities of the villagers by selling the articles that they produced at home. Through granting credit, they also reaped the benefit of the artisan skill which some in the village used as the basis of temporary migration.

Amongst the group of sedentary villagers was Jean Pellissier, whose family was originally from Savoy, who had come to La Grave to lease farmland from merchants who were too involved in their business to have time to devote to farming. At the end of the seventeenth century, the Pellissiers were settled in the village, and some of the family had taken the first step towards gaining access to merchandise by acting as packmen for a pedlar in the village. Jean was one of the large majority of very small land-owners; in 1671 he paid six *livres* in tallage, three-quarters of the average rate paid by those on the register. He had a son and two daughters. At his death in 1680, his three children divided between them an inheritance of 758 *livres*. This included their father's property, that of their mother and bequests which had been left them by other relatives. They had a house in the mountain pastures, valued at 24 *livres*, and a house in the village valued at 150 *livres*, an old mule, farmland to the value of 519 *livres* and grassland totalling 135 *livres*. This inheritance clearly illustrates the difference which existed between the two cultures living in the village, between the merchants and the rest. Besides the significant difference in value between the houses, the major contrast can be seen in the relationship between farmland and grassland. Whilst the pedlars owned both in roughly equal proportions, the Pellissier family had nearly four times more farmland than grassland; the most important thing for them was to be able to support the family. In terms of value, the division between the three children was more or less equal: 267 *livres* for Françoise, 274 for Marguerite and 310 for Louis. However, closer examination reveals that it was not at all equal, since all the livestock was left to the son, who also kept the house in the mountain pastures and the mule, as well as being left twice as much grassland as his sisters put together. The son was left property which could gain him entry to merchant circles. The sisters kept the house in the village and each had a deal chest, valued at 2 *livres*. We should not forget that, at this time, the Pellissiers did not have any livestock of their own; in fact, the only animals that they looked after were those entrusted to them by those richer than themselves. Lastly, Jean was one of Pierre Pic's clients – Pic was one of the richest men in the village, numbered amongst those who paid nearly eight times the average rate of tallage. Jean owed him 100 *livres* and Pic used the Pellissier family as labour in the village.[39]

Such families, through their land and their houses, confirm the information contained in the notaries' records: as a result of the credit mechanisms which permeated village life, everyone had a part to play in the merchant migration, even if they were neither migrant nor merchant. Firstly, there are examples of temporary migration at all levels, from the servant working for a pedlar to the man who had opened a shop, who might be away for longer and who had started to climb the social ladder, via the packman who came in the winter to fill up his pack and returned home in the spring. Moreover, each level of activity in the migrant merchant hierarchy had its extension in the work allotted to those who stayed at home, which related to cultivating the land, rearing livestock or other tasks in the village. At the top of the hierarchy, those merchants who had a business in the city leased out all or part of their property to other villagers and employed men to ensure that all ran smoothly on their farms when business detained them in the lowlands.[40] They used their debtors' grassland and entitlements to feed and winter more animals than would normally be possible. The length of these agreements for 'overseeing' or 'wintering' varied between a single winter and several years. Lessor and lessee came to some sort of agreement, either that they would share the livestock products, or the eventual sale price of the animal, or, less frequently, they agreed upon a pension.[41] In September 1684, Jean Aymard from the Villard d'Arène, who had opened a shop in Turin, leased out all his own property and that of his sister for three years. His asking price released him from his responsibilities in the village: the price of the pension he and his sister had undertaken to pay their mother (3 setiers* of rye wheat and 4 livres, 10 sols) and the tallage and charges relating to property. The lessee would also have to pay both himself and his sister 6 livres in silver,[42] this arrangement being more to create bonds of dependence than to constitute a real source of income. In addition, Jean Aymard also supported the small-scale migrations of pedlars: Pierre and Jean Finet from the Villard d'Arène owed 39 livres to sieurs Salomon, Aymard and Co., merchants in Turin, which they borrowed 'for business they did both within the province and outside'.[43]

Agreements relating to the wintering of livestock were one of the features necessary for these communities to function properly, and the extent of their existence was a good indication of how open the village hierarchy was. These agreements meant that the poorest people had access to livestock produce and to a certain amount of income. In the seventeenth century, the local people of Clavans justified their refusal to

---

* A setier (also called sétérée) was an old land measure, meaning literally the surface which could be sown with a setier of seeds. A setier was also an old measure for seed or grain, representing about 150–300 litres or, for liquids, 8 pints.

change their tallage tax collector by explaining that such a change could bring about the ruin of the poorer members of the community, who survived because the present tax collector entrusted them with animals to look after during the winter and the income from this meant that they could more easily pay tallage and rates.[44]

These client societies spawned three categories of migration:

(a) The definitive migration of an individual, which affected both the richest and the poorest. The migration of the richest members of the community was the cornerstone of village society, since they constructed networks in which the mountain axis was only one constituent, but a constituent which determined the other migratory movements. Migration of the poorest members of the community concerned those who no longer had land or manpower to offer in exchange for their requirements – the old, widows with no means of support, orphans from poor families.[45]

(b) A temporary migration, linked to the migration of the rich merchants. The 'petty Savoyards', the 'gavots'* from the southern Alps, the 'Dauphinés' from Oisans, all the knife-grinders, pedlars, packmen and haberdashers who were scattered across the countryside and the markets in small towns – all were linked to these rich merchants by a double relationship of dependence: they were indebted to them in the village, and reliant upon them in business. In Savoy, at the end of the seventeenth century, a new type of migration developed which used children as chimney-sweeps. This involved master sweeps and merchants on the one hand, and sweeps and small-time pedlars on the other. This occupation should doubtless be set within the context of the network of credit and clients which was the basis of village life. The master sweeps came from the higher *communes* of the Maurienne and Tarentaise, specializing in business and recruiting mostly in the poor areas of the lowlands in the valley below the Arc, aside from a few children from their own villages.[46]

(c) A mass migration of the poorest people who, in times of economic crisis when their village creditors (who themselves were under pressure from their own creditors in the city) all demanded repayment at the same time, would leave their worthless land and abandon the village. One comes across such departures in Oisans, as in Queyras and doubtless elsewhere, from the Middle Ages onwards. They meant that a significant amount of land was left neglected since no one, not even the creditors, would agree to take responsibility for it.[47]

Mass migration was none the less linked to the emigration of the elite classes by the information which the latter brought back with them: in

* *gavot*: a term for someone originally from Gap in the Upper Dauphiné.

other words, it took place within the geographical horizons of the merchants. When, in 1687, the inhabitants of the mountain villages of the Oisans who had been arrested in Savoy as they fled Catholic rule were questioned, they replied that they had left their homes 'to seek the word of God' and because they had been promised attractive properties in Brandenburg. Merchants had come back expressly to show them the way:[48] and the departure of the poorest had been made possible by the merchants, as much by keeping the far-off country alive in their imaginations as by providing them with useful information. Similarly, in the eighteenth century, there were men from the Massif active in Maurienne, whose job was to recruit men to go to Spain.[49] Similar mass exoduses were recorded in the Auvergne and Limousin regions in the sixteenth century, when the local people abandoned the area 'to leave for Spain in search of bread', to the point where the spectre of the 'desertion' of entire populations haunted the administrative imagination in these regions; a fear which the local people, moreover, did not hesitate to use in order to obtain benefits and alleviation of taxes.[50] In 1708, and again in 1777, the authorities noted that, because of extreme poverty, 'many people have left the country and gone to Spain'.[51] On the other hand, in those valleys where migration of the elite classes was unknown, as in the lowland valleys of the alpine baronies, or in the Chartreuse, men died of starvation, without ever dreaming of other places, of lush foreign lands.[52] When the social structure of the mountain valleys changed, in other words when the merchants abandoned the village without there being other families able to take their place, winter migration dried up and the community very quickly became impoverished, since the land alone could not feed the same number of people that the credit structures and the sale of merchandise could support. This was the situation in 1678 in Saint-Christophe-en-Oisans, for example. The bishop of Grenoble, on a pastoral visit, remarked that previously there had been rich merchants there but that today

> this parish is one of the poorest in the diocese; there are many families who do not have any bread for three months of the year and only survive for the rest of the year on herbs cooked in skimmed milk with no salt. They put rape leaves to dry and live off these in the winter . . .[53]

All of which underlines the interdependence of the rich merchants who emigrated and the poor farmers who remained in the village.

Was the Alpine model unique?

Analyses which take into account land and personal fortunes and wide-ranging alliances which bind individuals together – whether they be family networks or groups which have formed around credit networks – have not yet been undertaken for other peddling regions. We will therefore confine ourselves to highlighting those elements which indicate that the social structures and structures of relationships existing in these other regions where merchant migration took place were broadly similar to those in the Alpine mountain regions: in other words, characterized by an extremely open social hierarchy, by the prevalence of credit (with land-ownership occupying a minor role in comparison) and by relationships organized within the context of large extended families (even if these networks were not used to their fullest extent), which were extended to a client base bound by debt.

To the south of the Italian Alps, the Val Varaita was similar to those French valleys onto which it opened. The vast majority of the village population owned less than five hectares and a quarter of them possessed property only in a nominal sense.[54] Contracts for the wintering of animals – called contracts of 'meyrie' in these parts – which were widespread in the seventeenth and eighteenth centuries,[55] indicated the existence of a rich merchant elite. These merchants did business along the route leading into Spain: some had businesses in Bayonne or Pau, others in Catalonia. The Vassal brothers from Chianale doubtless took advantage of the two-way relationship between the villagers and the migrants, since at the beginning of the eighteenth century one was doing business in the Dutch Indies, the other was head of the Irish postal service in Bristol and a cousin was a fairground stallholder – 'banchiere' – in Barcelona. The departure of the 'merciajuoli ambulanti' recorded at round about the same time continued until the middle of the nineteenth century.[56]

The success of the merchants from the valleys surrounding Lake Como, which was among the most spectacular in Alpine peddling, had a trickledown effect in their home villages until the middle of the eighteenth century. The Brentano family were important members of the community in Tremezzo for four generations and relied on the village to extend their credit and business networks. In 1662 Martin Brentano, for a yearly fee of a florin, was satisfied with a stall in the market at Frankfurt to display his fruit. At his death in 1723, Domenico Brentano, who had inherited 1,816 florins from his father, Stefano, left 116,000 florins in his turn. As they amassed their fortune in this early period, the Brentanos invested in the village: around 1710, Domenico and his brother Paul bought two houses in Tremezzo, as well as two large estates and a vineyard in the surrounding villages. It was not until the end of the eighteenth century that the family integrated into German society: the million florins which Peter Anton Brentano left when he died in 1797 were the fruit of his Frankfurt business affairs and firm.[57] With a few minor differences the histories of the Guaita, Allesina and Bolongaro families follow the same pattern.

In the Auvergne and Limousin, the land was of little value.[58] From the end of the seventeenth century, there were numerous examples of land neglected due to the lack of people willing to farm it, a neglect to which Turgot draws attention.[59] Lease contracts reveal the meagre income from the land, which the migrants abandoned for the price of *'la façon d'une barrique'* ('the making of a barrel'); and there were frequent legal actions which brought owners and tenants into conflict with each other because the latter refused to pay for land which yielded nothing.[60] In these medium-sized mountains, as in the others, wealth could be amassed through migration and from the chains of credit which ran through and between families: one borrowed money to travel, to 'support oneself during the aforementioned journey', 'to make the aforementioned journey'.[61] Debts circulated within the village, between the village and Spain, between the migrants: all were secured on the family inheritance. In 1780 in Cadiz, Jean Puydebois borrowed 350 *livres tournois** from one of his countrymen, a baker, securing it with 'in particular, the property that he owns in France in the village of La Brande which comprises woods, grassland and arable land which he inherited from his parents'. The poorest, without land to guarantee their borrowing, were unable to leave.[62]

Inequality was sustained by the successes of certain migrants and, as a result, the village hierarchies widened. An analysis of family inheritances and dowries hints at the extent of social division. The widening gap in the range of inheritances in the eighteenth century is demonstrated by taking a sample of 70 men who emigrated to Spain and looking at the patrimony they passed down: this varied between 36 and 5,904 *livres*, in other words a difference of 1 to 165 *livres*; the greatest concentration was around the 200 *livre* mark and the average was for 677 *livres*. At the top of the pile were the rich merchants who migrated to Spain, men like Jean Vigier, an associate of the large Chinchon merchant company, who gave both his sons 6,000 *livres* when they got married, his youngest daughter a dowry of 10,000 *livres*, and anticipated boosting the dowries of his three already married daughters by 2,000 *livres*. Moreover, according to the terms of the youngest daughter's marriage contract which appointed her as sole heiress (and which he used to settle his estate), he kept back 24,000 *livres* for himself for his old age. Thus his assets amounted to 75,000 *livres*.[63] For the less well-off, the migration of merchants and craftsmen was primarily a means of paying the family's debts.[64]

The migrant merchant society reproduced the social hierarchy of the sedentary population, even if most of the merchants were to be found towards the top of the scale: out of 60 dowries bestowed on their sons

* *livres tournois*: money minted at Tours, which eventually became the royal coinage.

by 'Spanish' merchants in the eighteenth century, 12 were equivalent to those given to the younger sons of labourers; nearly half of the sample, with sums ranging between 300 and 900 *livres*, came into the same category as those given by working farmers; and more than a dozen young men benefited from a share of an inheritance worth more than 1,200 *livres*, in line with the youngest sons of *bourgeois* or of rich peasants.[65] Between 1761 and 1791, out of 152 marriage contracts of young men who had emigrated to Spain, 16 received more than 5,000 *livres* of dowry, 51 between 2,000 and 5,000, 53 between 1,000 and 2,000 and 30 less than 1,000. Of this number, 42 were designated their parents' sole heirs and 108 married a woman thus designated. The majority of the sons who were designated heirs were at the top of the scale of dowries, whilst those who received a dowry alone were amongst the middle ranks.[66] Similarly, dowries for girls were higher: those bestowed on Jean Vigier's five daughters were around the 10,000 *livres* mark; Marie Dandurand, who married a son and heir, received 8,200 *livres*. At the other end of the merchant scale, 20 per cent of sons received less than 1,000 *livres* in dowry and some, even when designated heirs, married women who brought with them less than 400 *livres*. But one should beware of these figures which very often underestimated the amount that the child could rely on. Moreover, since the merchant firms were rigidly organized around the family, one should examine the ways in which the family networks functioned from a village perspective in order to understand the matrimonial strategies.

The links between migration and life in the Pyrenean communities are yet to be elucidated. Always presented as 'little republics', the social structure of these villages nevertheless appears to have been just as riddled with inequality as that of the valleys high in the Alps. At the end of the seventeenth century in the Upper Vallespir, one-tenth of the families owned more than two-thirds of the farmland, and the system of 'métayage' (where the farmer pays rent in kind) was widespread. On the eve of the Revolution, while the consuls deplored the existence of large numbers of 'poor wretches steeped in destitution' and thus reduced to smuggling, two families received an annual income of 12,600 *livres*.[67] These few facts help us to understand the importance of the credit networks. If one also takes into account the enormous range of the migrants' activities, and the development of a cottage weaving industry in the valleys, then the argument that, like the Alpine communities, these were client-based communities, reliant upon credit and manpower, merits serious consideration. The work currently being done by Jean-Paul Zuniga on migration from the Béarn and Basque regions to Latin America confirms this analysis.[68]

The question of pedlars' ties to land and to the home village still remains to be answered for Scotland and England. The bonds seem to have been very loose in England where inventories drawn up after death show that, apart from very small land-owners in the rural areas of Nottinghamshire, Lincolnshire and Herefordshire, there were few pedlars who were linked to a rural community.[69] In Scotland, the development of peddling was concurrent with the growth of the towns,[70] and a certain number of travelling merchants were burghers of a Scottish town. This type of membership brings us to the rules of business: to trade in goods as mundane as butter, oil and eggs, one had to have paid to become a burgher. This meant that one could engage in two spheres of activity which brought in more substantial profits: the cloth trade with England and the sale of certain other goods to Ireland. However, to enjoy full business rights – in other words, the right to sell goods imported from Europe and to take part in cross-channel and Baltic trade – one had to belong to the guild, membership of which was three and a half times more expensive (500 Scottish merks) than the status of burgher.[71] As in France, the rules of business and the urban source documents perhaps mask a still active involvement in a village community. Only by reconstructing the families and the business networks can the question be answered.

Initially, as in all mountain regions, livestock trading was the way into other markets. Following the union of the Scottish and English crowns in 1603 and the pacification of the Borders, the growing demand from the English markets for lamb's wool and for mutton between 1650 and 1760 bolstered the rearing of livestock. This then spread from the south of Scotland and dominated all of the Lowlands; in the middle of the eighteenth century, the farms of the Southern Uplands specialized increasingly in the production of wool, hides, sheep and lambs. A new model of society emerged from these changes, one closer to the Alpine model in which, taking advantage of communal grassland and weak seignorial control, an elite class of merchants asserted itself and introduced new-style domestic industries into the villages. The list of *Pollable Persons* confirms the expansion of rural industry: in the Aberdeen region the parish of Clatt boasted 51 full-time merchants, who were weavers, pedlars, tailors, cobblers, carpenters and smiths; another parish of Monymusk registered 52 full-time merchants as well as a number of cotters and tenants, the majority of whom were weavers, as in Clatt. Moreover, such lists conceal the part played by women and children, who carded and spun the wool – payments made in pieces of material and account books bear witness to this.[72] But we need to be able to study the links which existed between the craftsmen, the local pedlars and the merchants, who were further afield. How was the market divided between the pedlars, who siphoned off a large part of the domestic production, and the merchants of Aberdeen, Glasgow, Edinburgh and other places? It appears that the village pedlars and shopkeepers were the link between peasants and merchants,[73] as was the case in the Zurich region.[74]

The union with England, which expanded Scottish markets and boosted the demand for livestock produce, also brought about the Scottish agricultural revolution of the eighteenth century, thanks to the accumulation of capital from business dealings. The Glasgow merchants turned their attention to land investment. In turn, these changes had an effect upon social structures, with the disappearance of the *fermtoun*, the shrinking number of peasants and the concomitant rise in the surface area of land owned: many of those who had been unable to buy property became day labourers or abandoned the land to swell the ranks of the urban proletariat. The traditional links between landlords and farmers were broken when this new social group – merchants, industrialists and lawmen – moved into the land market.[75] The irreversible decline in peddling took place at the same time. Studying the network of relationships would doubtless provide us with an understanding of the position occupied by the migrant merchants in these developments.

On the other hand, in the Highlands there were no elite classes to act as intermediaries between the peasant weavers and the high-ranking merchants for whom they worked. The pedlar in the far-flung *touns* who bought up the local craftsmen's work was not a part of the community with which he did business, but an agent for the big city merchants,[76] and thus brought no flexibility to the migratory system of villages which were gradually losing their poverty-stricken population, in trickles or floods depending on the agricultural circumstances.[77]

The complex nature of Scottish society and the absence of any studies looking at family networks and migrations within the context of a social analysis prevent us from seeing whether the occupation of pedlar was constructed along different lines here than in the villages of migrant merchants on the Continent; or whether the same developments are discernable here a century earlier, relating in particular to the transition from an organization based around the extended family, to a withdrawal into the immediate family, with peddling finally existing only as a residual activity on the fringes of the family (see chapter 7).

6

Credit and Social Relationships

Contradicting the myth of the pedlar as vagrant, socio-analytical studies of the condition of migrant merchants stress their geographical and family roots; running counter to the myth of pedlars as free spirits, they demonstrate instead how they were prisoners of various financial dependencies, caught in a system of social relationships which both supported and controlled them. The business of credit was at the heart of the peddling culture, forging links which created the enforced interdependencies to which we must now turn our attention.

The profession of pedlar depended upon three separate places: the home village, the town in which the pedlar acquired his supplies and the region in which he undertook his campaign. In each of these different locations, the business of the itinerant merchant was dependent upon deferred payment. However, the relative importance of the part played by each of the three locations varied according to the era and how peddling fitted into the contemporary social framework. In the first example of peddling that we studied, that of the sixteenth and seventeenth centuries, the town played a limited part in terms of the circulation of money, since most financial transactions took place between men from the same region. However, when peddling withdrew to the regions in the eighteenth century, the use of a growing number of suppliers from outside the mountain valleys complicated the credit structures. The migrant was completely absorbed into three separate credit networks: credit in the village, the credit granted during his rounds, and the credit which the city merchants granted him. The interrelated nature of these networks, their flexibility when faced with economic setbacks, in addition to the guarantees provided by backers and the pedlar's possible standbys were the vital ingredients for the continuation of the profession.

An analysis such as this, which, as yet, has only been carried out in relation to the Oisans mountains in the Dauphiné region and not in other sites, means that one has to deconstruct the credit mechanisms largely using this one framework. However, work done elsewhere allows us to glimpse that, from one end of Europe to the other, the profession was based on similar webs of debt; and that the pedlar's fortune was always a paper fortune made up of debts resting upon other debts.

The chain of credit

Time was central to the credit mechanism. Effectively, in order for the system to work, the time allowed for payment had to be congruent between the different locations. In the home village, the debt could run over a long period of time: the time allowed for the repayment of obligations or promises agreed in the village was anything between six months and ten years, with a year being the most common period; but, in fact, the sum had accrued over much longer periods of time, since the obligations which were recorded in the notaries' offices were the accumulation of numerous petty promises, both verbal and written, made by the debtor and partly honoured during the preceding years. An obligation was therefore seen as a guarantee for the lender and a way of including the unpaid interest in the capital sum. It is difficult to know how much interest was actually charged. Legally, the recorded rates could not go above 5 per cent and the notaries' deeds refer to rates of between 4 per cent and 5 per cent. Certain lawsuits in the nineteenth century refer to much higher rates (20 per cent and above), but these were the exception. Far from being usury, the way in which debts were settled demonstrates that the lender often made a loss on the interest, if not on the capital itself. None the less, it remains the case that there was a tendency to absorb unpaid interest into the capital owed. When the debt was settled, the deeds often recorded that the sum 'has been decreased', or that a 'reduction has been granted', a reflection of what actually happened rather than merely a contractually cautious form of words. Sometimes the deeds specify that, since the interest exceeded the capital owed, it was reduced to the same level as the capital.

In contrast to the lengthy credit periods granted in the village was the short time span allowed for city credit. In theory, the pedlars bought on credit terms in the autumn and paid off the debt in the spring when they returned from their campaign. Some merchants even demanded a first instalment halfway through the campaign. The credit granted was thus short term – between six and nine months. But in the same way that the more important pedlars acted as a support for the smaller pedlars by transforming their city debts into village debts, similarly émigrés from the village who had opened a shop in the city acted as intermediaries between the pedlars and the city merchants by allowing longer repayment times: from their remaining family in the village they knew about individual business affairs and fortunes, and the money that circulated between the city and the village brought them interest and gave them a certain amount of control over manpower.

In between the long-term and short-term credit arrangements were the medium-term credit arrangements (two years on average) which were agreed by the migrant pedlar during his campaign.[1]

Peddling was thus based upon three geographic, economic and social realities: the home village, where the pedlar had land and money owed to him which opened the doors to city credit for him; the lowlands, where he earned enough money to preserve and enlarge his fortune; and the town which provided him with the wherewithal to do business, and where emigrants played the part of intermediaries, an interface between the various temporalities and economic forces. The length of credit in the village and that allowed by the pedlar on his rounds was evidently not at odds, and the money he made from his campaign was used in the highlands either to repay his debts or to increase the number of people indebted to him, or the amount of land he owned – in other words, his basis for being granted credit. Even though it had its setbacks, the double time of city credit, in the global context of economic development, meant that the whole fitted together perfectly, since the pedlar was traditionally paid for goods he had sold during his previous campaign at the beginning of the next, or at the end of his trip by those who settled up with him before he left. He could thus pay the city firms for his goods at the beginning and end of his campaign, even though this might mean delaying settlement of goods and money supplied to him by the émigré merchants, who thus absorbed the discrepancy between lowland deadlines and those imposed by the city merchants.

For other peddling regions, little is known about how these networks functioned or the varying time periods allowed for repayment of different types of debt. On the one hand, we have the example of the English importer of Dutch fabrics, who, in 1732, in justifying his delayed payment to his suppliers, complained that they customarily only allowed him eight months' credit, when the London cloth merchants took 16 months to pay him.[2] On the other, at the beginning of the seventeenth century, the important English merchants tried to insist upon credit periods of not more than six months, and discounts of not more than 7 per cent for those who paid in cash.[3] However, we lack precise knowledge of the credit periods granted to the pedlars by the merchants, and also of those granted by the pedlars to their customers, which is necessary for an understanding of how the whole network fitted together, and where the most fragile points in the structure were.

The city was the site of the principal tensions: the main problem for a pedlar who had just experienced a bad campaign was honouring his debts in the city. Right up until the middle of the nineteenth century in

France – and probably earlier in England – those pedlars who had emigrated and set up in business in the city provided vital assistance to the itinerant pedlars, allowing them to cope with temporary financial difficulty. These émigré merchants gained from both economic systems. In their business dealings with city merchants they granted only short credit periods: in the inventory drawn up in Paris after André Masson's death in December 1610, which referred to his business dealings with the merchants of the capital, there were only two letters of credit not bearing that year's date; on the other hand, both Jacques Bérard and Jean Giraud had much longer-standing debts owed to them by men from their village. As they were the principal employers of peddling manpower, and knew both the men and their families, they were prepared to allow the debt to run from one year to the next and to act as intermediary between the different temporalities and economic systems. In their dealings with the mountain folk, they operated on two levels. At first they accepted a longer credit period before repayment, thus allowing the pedlars to settle up first with other city merchants. Later they turned unpaid debts in the city into village debts.

In practice, once the newly agreed credit period had elapsed, if the pedlar still had not been able to honour his debt, the city merchants passed it back to the home village. Depending on the merchant's connections in the highlands, the debt could then take one of several routes. When he had relatives in the village who could take care of his business affairs, the émigré merchant would entrust them with the responsibility of those debts owing to him. A second option was to call on the services of the village notaries, who were to stand in for the absent family. This was the solution chosen in 1764 by the Avignon bookseller Jean-Joseph Niel, Abraham's successor. He granted a power of attorney to a notary from Valbonnais in the Dauphiné, so that the latter could recover for him the 394 livres he was owed by two pedlars for goods he had sold them.[4] Certain notaries in the Auvergne were well known for acting as intermediary between emigrants now settled in Spain and those living in the home village: they settled pending inheritances and defended their clients' interests. Thus, in 1788, Lady Elisabeth Mathé, widow of the late Jean-Baptiste Legay, 'a merchant in Denia in the kingdom of Valencia', authorized M. Parieu fils, a lawyer from Aurillac, to recover the 376 livres and 15 sols from Pierre Buc of Saint-Santin, which he and his brother Jean had had in goods on credit from her husband's shop.[5] Similarly, Widow Machuel of Rouen left it to Maître Roux, chief bailiff of the bailiwick of Coutances, to keep her informed of the solvency of her debtors.[6]

A third option involved other merchants from the mountain village, reproducing on a larger scale the transfer of debts commonly practised between the most powerful families in order to build up clearly defined and manageable client bases. Merchants thus authorized one another to recover money lent to pedlars. This is doubtless the meaning of the receipt given to Jean Delorme, a merchant bookseller of Avignon, on 11 January 1700 by one Bonnardel for 210 *livres* and 13 *sols* which he had collected from different people in Monêtier in his capacity as Bonnardel's attorney.[7] This system worked both ways, and the migrant pedlars used their family back in the village to settle their debts and realize the few assets that the migrants who died whilst on their rounds far from the village left behind them. There are innumerable examples of the assistance provided by the city dwellers in settling the estates of those from the mountains, where part of the assets remained in the lowlands. The system functioned in the same way for those merchants abroad.

Alongside the emergence of debts contracted in the city, outside of the village network, there developed a system of sponsorship of the younger pedlars by the older, who introduced their protegés to their own suppliers. An older pedlar recommending another who was at the beginning of his career also implied a certain responsibility and moral engagement from the former for the conduct of the latter. The merchant naturally turned first to the 'patron' to get his money back. Thus, in May 1754, Jean Gourand paid out the 253 *livres* owed by Jean Aubert for goods that he had had 'from *sieurs* Gallant and Parrain, merchants in Lyon'. Without being asked for a formal guarantee, Gourand, who had introduced Aubert to this firm, knew that he had staked his own relationship with the Lyon merchants on it. Gourand, then, paid for the goods which Aubert had been unable to do when he left the lowlands. Before the new autumn campaign, since Aubert had not been able to repay Gourand during the summer, they both went to register the debt, now transformed into an obligation by the notary in the mountain village. The obligations which bound merchants together from unpaid debts in the city were very seldom found in notaries' deeds before 1760, but multiplied rapidly between 1760 and 1780. If this betrays the difficulties experienced by the profession in the unfavourable economic circumstances of the time, it also demonstrates the increasing need that the rapidly expanding sedentary businesses had for the mountain pedlar.

There are two important consequences of the way in which the chain of credit functioned to be emphasised. Through its shortcomings, it points to the gradual transformation of the role of émigré merchants: from being the real entrepreneurs of peddling with almost total control of the migratory process they became a flexible link in the credit chain, advancing money and repaying debts contracted with other merchants when the credit deadline could not be met. In times of successive economic crises, the fact that debts generally found their way back to the home village meant that families found themselves deeply in debt. Fortunes built on credit and merchandise were fragile, and good luck rapidly turned to bad. The city merchants knew this and set up regulatory systems which were intended to foresee failure and limit their losses. These systems were reinforced by information networks which could update the merchants on the financial affairs of the migrants to whom they entrusted their goods. Mechanisms such as these had a profound effect on the migrants' conduct and had a trickle-down effect in the villages where all social relationships were controlled by them: such mechanisms might well force the migrants into interdependency, but this same interdependency could also be costly for those who accepted it.

Enforced interdependency and recourse available to the pedlar

Business association, financial guarantees and sponsorship were the main instances of enforced interdependency. From the beginning, the first two had been vital to the success of peddling: at no time would the smaller merchants have had enough capital personally to be able to open a town warehouse, or obtain the necessary credibility to acquire the *droit de bourgeoisie*, which was indispensable to those doing business in the lowlands.[8]

For some, a business association was a necessary prerequisite for going into the profession; for others, a joint capital outlay allowed them to undertake a larger-scale campaign. Thus, as far back as the texts can take us in tracing the ways in which the profession was practised, business associations are to be found in all shapes and sizes: joint financial outlay, where the profits were shared out pro rata, depending on the amount invested; but also, as demonstrated by a contract of partnership of 1631, where the contributions were unequally divided – one partner provided a horse and a certain amount of money, the other his labour and goods.[9] Whether they were booksellers from Cotentin or haberdashers from the Alps, there were few merchants who travelled alone. In most cases, they set out in partnership with one, or perhaps two or three, members of the family; brothers, cousins and brothers-in-law for the most part.[10]

The importance of the business association was such that its various rules were taught in the village school, where children learnt to solve the problems that it raised in terms of the capital invested and the duration of the association. The Gravier family from Monêtier kept a child's exercise book from 1788, used by the children to learn how to calculate individual profits in a variety of situations which might be encountered in business partnerships. Here is one of the exercises as an example:

> Three merchants formed a company. In which the first invested 598 *livres*, taking back his money after 4 months; the second invested 748 *livres*, taking

back his money after 8 months; and the third invested 846 *livres*, taking back his money after a year and three months. They made 643 *livres* in profit. How much will each one have received in proportion to his contribution and the amount of time they kept company?[11]

But this interdependency, which was a prerequisite for setting out on the road, was also an ambiguous and extremely uneasy bond, since it implied that individuals were jointly and severally responsible for losses as well as profits. Evidence shows that the imbalances inherent in interdependency made it more and more difficult to bear in times when economic crises were eroding profits. On 9 August 1830, Laurent and Jacques Collomb left La Grave in the Dauphiné and set out on business. Laurent died during the winter whilst on his rounds and was pronounced 'insolvent'. Their backer, Victor Nicolet, asked his brother to settle the promissory note for 157 francs, which they had signed together, but Jacques refused to accept this betrayal by fate and would not agree to pay more than half the debt. 'I will not be deflected from the justice of my cause, which is that one of them must pay', wrote Nicolet to the bailiff who worked for him. He thus asked the bailiff to visit Jacques and have the 157 francs repaid, with interest naturally, which had been owing to him for three years. Foreseeing the inevitable haggling, the glove merchant suggested that the bailiff calculated interest on the basis of 7 or 6 per cent a year, when the legal maximum was 5 per cent; and finished his letter by saying that he still had 50 or 60 francs worth of gloves, which Jacques had left in his keeping until he next passed through, and it was through them that the interest would be repaid if necessary. Of the brother's goods, there remained nothing bar two trunks that were to be opened so that an inventory could be drawn up, and Nicolet told his bailiff to 'have the widow brought to Grenoble, and if there is anything left after I have been paid back what he owes me, then she may have it'.[12]

All the pedlars whose letters and memoirs we have condemned the tyranny of business partnerships. Jean-Pierre Magne tells of his partnership with 'a perfectly honest man with a good heart, but no merchant' only 'to illustrate to my children, and warn them, that in business one should count on oneself and never on others.'[13] In fact, it was widely recognized that a business association was a direct product of financial necessity; to be able to say that one was travelling alone was proof of great success, and in autobiographies betrayed the writer's desire for social distinction: a harmonious relationship was not easy, and when business went badly one's partner quickly seemed a scapegoat for all disappointments. Behind the self-justification, the difficulties of enforced cooperation are plain to see.

The second enforced interdependency developed under pressure from the financial backers: this was the system of financial guarantees. For the smaller pedlars, for whom paying for their own purchases was already difficult even before a slightly poor year came along, interdependency threatened their very existence. The development of financial guarantees which linked individual fortunes together meant that the failure of one pedlar weighed upon the others and introduced a further imbalance into the network of relationships. In times of growth, the most fortunate could help those who were less well-off, but in times of recession it was the whole economic and social structure of the villages that shook.

The system of sponsorship, which was no more than a disguised financial guarantee, could, like this latter option, land the mistaken or over-optimistic sponsor in difficult financial circumstances. If, as in the case of Noël Gille, who owed 3,430 *livres* because he had acted as guarantor for his brother (who was in the same profession), it was the merchants who had trusted him who were the victims, in the majority of cases it was the sponsoring pedlar who incurred the costs of the dishonesty or failure of those whom he had introduced to them. Jean Gourand had agreed to act as sponsor for Michel Arnol in his dealings with the Druart Brothers firm in Chalon and to stand guarantor for his purchases for the 1857–8 campaign, which was close on 1,600 francs. A year later, the bill still not being paid, the Druart firm turned to the guarantee and Jean Gourand spent the following years paying this outstanding amount in instalments, even though it meant asking for expensive credit periods from other firms, getting into debt in his home region and spending longer each year in the lowlands in the hope of making more money.[14] By hitching the shakiest fortunes to those of the wealthiest individuals, in times of economic recession guarantees and sponsorship weakened the whole merchant body, or, in other words, the entire fabric of village society. However, this interdependency also had two sides to it: for those who acted as guarantors, it provided a hold over the pedlar's labour and assets. In times when land was in short supply in the home region, when power was bitterly disputed between a few powerful families, more than one man used the offer of financial backing to gain access to the coveted farmland. This interdependency must always be set within the context of power in the village, where financial ties were many and where the pedlars' debts easily outstripped the value of their assets.

For the financial backer, the extremely hierarchical structure of village migration, in which the peddling 'elite' classes functioned as anchor, acting both as contractors of labour and privileged intermediaries between city business and itinerant selling, provided him with as many guarantees as he needed. The financial guarantee, whilst enforcing interdependency, also spawned a climate of denunciation: should a pedlar attempt to escape his creditors, the guarantors, their own existence threatened, would join forces with the merchants to find him and make him pay. Therein lies the first ambiguity of merchant interdependency which encouraged the elimination of the black sheep and forced the peddling body to shoulder the failure of certain individuals. This moral code imposed on the group was reinforced by the strategies employed by the village elite, who carefully monitored all changes in an inheritance and were on the alert for any change in fortune.

As the city increasingly assumed the role of main financial backer to the pedlars, and, at the same time, the merchant elite gradually distanced themselves from the home village in favour of integration into the city, in response the system of migrant surveillance underwent a transformation. Up until then, it had been the responsibility of family members who had remained at home: in the absence of family, the responsibility was gradually entrusted to certain people of standing in the village.

Letters written between 1828 and 1842 by the Grenoble glove merchant Victor Nicolet,[15] who, as he himself writes, did most of his business with 'his' merchant pedlars, reveal in detail the links which bound city merchants to the important people in the village. Nicolet was originally from Oisans, and had been manufacturing and selling gloves since 1792. In the 1830s he ceased manufacturing gloves so as to devote himself solely to marketing them. Through the 234 pedlars whom he mentions in his letters, he could sell his gloves virtually anywhere in the world.[16] The role of glove merchant was twofold: he supplied pedlars with gloves and, more importantly, he advanced them the necessary money for the trip and for acquiring other goods.

Although Nicolet was originally from Oisans he no longer had goods or family in the mountain region. By means of a regular correspondence, he charged a handful of notaries, two bailiffs and the tax collector of the principal town of the region with the responsibility of looking into the conduct and fortunes of the pedlars whom he entrusted with money and merchandise. The glove merchant paid them 'for their trouble and labour', and took every opportunity of providing them with a financial incentive when the matter in question was a delicate one; he also never failed to reward them with gifts at the beginning of each new year. Nicolet expected all sorts of information from his agents: firstly concerning the pedlars, because he had to be able to distinguish between men with the same names and place the pedlars in the context of their family connections. Secondly he needed information on their fortunes, since the extent of this would dictate the credit and merchandise he allowed them. In July 1836, for example, he wrote the following letter to one of the bailiffs he employed:

Before the coming campaign, let me have details of the solvency of those people with whom I do business, or am likely to do business with this year. Attached are all the names currently on my books: put the letter B against those who are sound, D for those who are in doubt and M for those who are a bad risk . . . I beg you to count upon my total discretion and to be kind enough to return the completed list to me within the fortnight.

During the peddling campaign, especially if the pedlar had not settled his bills on time, he made enquiries as to their movements. Finally, his 'spies' always kept him informed of events in the migrants' family lives, since a death, family settlement or marriage could change an inheritance and were opportune moments for Nicolet to call in his debts.

Faced with credit systems which were based on information and enforced interdependency, what possible recourse did the pedlar have? Secrecy was the most important safeguard or precaution; secrecy concerning his creditors so that he could borrow money from several sources, secrecy concerning the state of his inheritance, especially if it was crippled with debts, so that he could find guarantors and sources of funding. One can imagine the type of poisoned atmosphere which was created in these communities, where any confidence could backfire on the person imparting it. Against the power wielded by those of standing in the valleys, playing one's cards close to one's chest and drawing on a range of creditors were the only weapons available to the peasants in their struggle to preserve freedom of movement by lessening their dependency.

Letters exchanged between Nicolet and Jean Ramel, who acted as guarantor for Laurent Balme, allow us to gauge the level of secrecy surrounding the multiple financial links, and at the same time bear witness to the ambiguities inherent within these links. In 1833, Laurent Balme had three bills outstanding in Nicolet's favour – one for 948 francs, which he had reduced to 403 francs; another for 1,000 francs, reduced to 870 francs but with interest of 7 per cent owed over two years, which actually brought the total to 1,010 francs; and a third for 650 francs, with a further 192 francs owed in lapsed interest on an obligation. The two latter debts were guaranteed by Jean Ramel, one of the most reliable pedlars in the valley. In the spring of 1834, Laurent Balme put part of his property up for sale and it was only at this point that Ramel learnt the names of the remaining creditors on the mortgage deeds: three were important people in the mountain region (a notary who was owed 138 francs, 305 francs to a clerk of the court and 257 francs to the tax collector), the fourth was the widow Cambon, a stockist of fabrics and hosiery in Lyon, who was owed 540 francs, and the remaining creditors were other pedlars. After this sale, Nicolet wrote as follows to Ramel:

> It must not now be concealed from you that, despite the interest that you take in Laurent Balme, it is none the less true that quite apart from all these recorded debts, the man owes more besides . . . which compels me not to hide from you the fears that you should have concerning his situation. . . . I am recommending that you take the initiative and have his remaining

property sold to you, or at the very least a part of it worth a minimum of 1,200 to 1,500 francs, which you will have registered straight away before others have the chance to claim, so as to cover your guarantee. Should you allow him to repurchase his property within a fixed time, at least in this way you will be covered. . . . Time is against you, make haste to do this now, it is vital for your peace of mind.[17]

It was well-informed advice; as early as August Jean Ramel found out about two other debts, making a total of 1,200 francs – money borrowed in the Oisans, where the two lenders were preparing to buy what remained of Laurent Balme's property. It is rare to have such a wealth of detail on the multiplicity of loan agreements and for the relationships which they created and the conflicting strategies which they concealed to be so crudely displayed: if some were tricked by those whom they agreed to help, others agreed to act as guarantor in full knowledge of the situation for the power which it gave them over that person's labour and property. All village relationships were marked by ambiguity, and the notion of interdependency went to pieces the moment that the means of existence were threatened.

The break-up of the credit network

These analyses demonstrate that peddling brought different economic cultures and social organizations of relationships face to face. This encounter was characterized by two major imbalances: the guarantees on which credit was based and the period over which the debt could run varied from place to place. On the one hand, the city and its merchants were committed to a capitalist rationale in which land served as a security for credit and which sought to avoid all non-profitable immobilization of capital; on the other, the villages survived through the labour of men rather than through the produce of the land and so, to retain control over their manpower, they deliberately used the granting of credit as a weapon. For the elite classes from the migrant villages, the lengthy time periods allowed for the repayment of debts responded to a different economic rationale: the creditors would have a hold over the labour force constituted by their debtors and their families all the longer. This same rationale helps us to understand why, endemically, the villagers were in debt well beyond the value of their land: it was because their debts were based on both their land and their labour. We have already seen the links forged between these two worlds by the more important pedlars and the émigré merchants: by agreeing to take on the debts incurred by smaller pedlars, they allowed these two different economic cultures to function side by side.

It was this vital link in the credit chain which, in the first half of the nineteenth century – from the 1840s onward – gradually lost its flexibility as the rules of the game changed. The new order thus established destroyed the balance between the links in the chain and brought into question the existence of the whole, forcing the merchant pedlar to make changes in the credit he granted and, in particular, to reduce the amount of time over which a debt could run: he had to get his money back from the lowlands and from the village in a shorter space of time.

The repeated economic crises of the nineteenth century effectively increased the number of unsuccessful campaigns. In the lowlands, the pedlar sold less and debts were not being repaid; in the village he was constantly having to find someone to borrow money from. It became increasingly difficult for the established émigré merchants to get their money back and they hardened in their attitude towards the pedlars. Nicolet's correspondence shows how his demands increased as crisis followed crisis. Initially he worked on the family units in an effort to make family members responsible for one another's fates; then he turned his attention to the whole village network and, by demanding guarantees, tried to hitch the debts owed by the poorest members of society to the fortunes of the most important. At the beginning of the century, it was only very rarely that Nicolet asked for a loan to be guaranteed. From 1828 onwards he informed the bailiffs who looked after his affairs in the mountain villages that henceforth they were only to allow credit after having obtained 'an appropriate guarantee'. In 1831, he initiated the practice of demanding a double guarantee in the case of a lapsed debt that was being renewed. In 1833, he directly intervened in the choice of guarantor and was against one single family guaranteeing several pedlars. The crisis came to a head in 1837–8, when he changed his practices and decided to reduce the credit periods: he would no longer allow any credit extensions. At the same time he continued to demand more and more guarantees: he required two guarantors before he would even entertain a new arrangement. When this strategy failed, he resorted to legal intervention and thus leant on all his debtors at the same time: he was anxious to settle business which had dragged on for several years, and not to allow any more late payments of account. In order to compensate for the amount he had been forced to lose in agreed reductions, he put his interest rates up to 6 or 7 per cent, sometimes even 8 per cent for certain migrants, the decision on which rate to charge being made on an individual basis. For example, to guarantee a loan, Nicolet insisted that the pedlar registered an obligation in the presence of a notary:

> I prefer to pay something towards the legal costs, which, however, you will have them pay to the notary straight away afterwards, as well as the costs you have already incurred. Even though it costs me 5 or 6 francs, I shall recoup that on the interest which you will put at 8 per cent.

On the other hand, he proposed a reduction in interest rates, from 7 to 6 per cent, in order to encourage the brother of another pedlar, with whom the latter was in partnership and who had died on the road, to accept joint liability for the debt.

Urban economic practices and ways of thinking forced their way into the village. Against a background of repeated crises, in which directions did the two economies adapt, and what possible negotiations were there between them? Initially the city merchants resorted to traditional measures and put matters in the hands of the law. For the pedlar, the possibility of being seized, stripped of everything, even driven out of his home was the threat which lay beneath all negotiations. For him, his only defence and the only means of bringing pressure to bear lay in destitution itself, whether feigned or all too real. This was what was at stake in the struggle that was waged between a capitalist rationale and the rationale of the peasant economies which were founded on the basis of migration.

Negotiations always began with the defaulting merchant suggesting a reduction in the sum owed. Faced with such a demand, the creditors were in a difficult situation. On the one hand, they calculated the potential loss and the legal costs, and tried to guess at the value of the pedlar's present and future assets. On the other, they were worried that this would become a widespread occurrence, and that the precedent created would serve as an example for others. Fundamentally, the city merchants were fighting a losing battle, because village wealth amounted to far less than the total debts of the villagers, and the system could only function if the creditors refrained from all demanding their money at the same time.

So as to salvage part of their property, the bankrupt migrants usually resorted to a fictitious sale of their goods, preferably to their wives. Nicolet complained of this. A similar system operated in the Auvergne where, to escape their creditors, the itinerant merchants would put all their property in their wife's name, even though it was mortgaged to the hilt; at the beginning of the nineteenth century, it was claimed that 'from La Rhue as far as Puy-Chavaroux, the women own all the property'.[18] Nicolet the glove merchant dealt with these matters as they arose, using his knowledge of the families to anticipate future inheritances. He in his turn was secretive and was extremely concerned that his negotiations and their outcome should not spread to other families who were in debt. None the less, more often than not he had to agree to a 50 per cent reduction of the debt.[19]

The second strategy adopted by the pedlars was to declare themselves bankrupt so as to be free from all debts and thus put themselves in a position to continue trading after a certain amount of time had elapsed. That the practice was both common and profitable is demonstrated by the story of Augustin Barelle from the Briançonnais, and Nicolet's letters concerning him. In 1835, Augustin Barelle had had an outstanding promissory note for 756 francs with the glove merchant for five years. Barelle had not paid the bill, but had paid the forthcoming interest, which satisfied the glove merchant, until the pedlar 'was arrested and stripped of his goods by some Lyon merchants, after which he ended up enlisting'. However, despite this, not all the promissory notes had been redeemed and, four years later, his brother Joseph came to visit Nicolet, on his way back from business, to propose to him that he, Joseph, redeem Augustin's debt 'if a 2/3 reduction could be agreed, saying that he had come to a similar arrangement with several other creditors'. Nicolet entrusted one of his bailiffs with settling the matter:

> I turn to you, dear sir, to ask you to be good enough to see these gentlemen and deal with them, encouraging them to agree to split the difference, in other words to pay 50 per cent, and furthermore, I beg you to do this in such a way that nobody hears of it, because it would be a disastrous example to those who owe me a lot of money and who are always ready for some dirty trick.

Then Nicolet went on to explain the strategy that he guessed lay behind these requests:

> Doubtless this family has a certain amount of income. They'll get Augustin out of the army, then provide him with the means to start up in business again, but first they want to rid him of all his debts.

Bargaining began the following summer. Nicolet did not want to go below 300 francs: 'If he should refuse this latest arrangement, then tell him that I prefer to wait until he comes into his inheritance, when he can pay me all his brother owes me intact; both capital and interest, as well as the costs I shall have to incur to cover myself'. But, as a post-script, Nicolet added: 'Wrap the matter up, unless you learn that what he is likely to receive from his father would be enough for us to hope to lose nothing. Deal with him, and make sure you get your fees paid; it will be a job well done.' A month later, the bailiff had concluded the business for the sum of 230 francs – Nicolet had lost more than three-quarters of the original capital sum, and the pedlar was now ready for a new start.

In fact, tracing those pedlars who had declared themselves bankrupt reveals that this did not signal an end to their activities, and that this was a strategy adopted from time to time to re-establish a more man-ageable situation when pressure on the credit networks became too fierce. Hence Noël Gille's announcement of bankruptcy on 7 August 1776 did not prevent him from starting up again in the same business. When he appeared before the King's notaries in Versailles, he did his utmost to prove that, on the one hand, ill-fortune was the sole cause of his bankruptcy, and, on the other, that he would agree to pay the sums he owed – 'the capital sums alone' – if his creditors would agree to let him have 'enough time and appropriate terms'. We do not know how the situation was resolved, but two years later he was once again a merchant bookseller. In 1779, he renewed contact with the Société typographique de Neuchâtel, even offering to pay in cash if they would agree to a 12–15 per cent reduction, as if he were one of the long-established clients in whom the publishers had complete confidence; however, the Société typographique de Neuchâtel had learnt to be on their guard and did not follow up his request. When he died, in 1824, he was referred to as a merchant bookseller.[20]

An analysis of the fraudulent bankruptcy registered by André Reymond, a haberdashery pedlar from the Dauphiné, shows that he was a pedlar all his life whilst declaring himself bankrupt every ten years or so. Each time, he came to an arrangement with his creditors, and each time he changed his suppliers and the location of his operations. If his third declaration of bankruptcy did not go as smoothly as the previous ones, this was because one of his creditors – to the amazement of the solicitor responsible for the matter, and despite the latter spelling out to him how much money would be lost by all the creditors if he put the matter in the hands of the law – refused to agree terms with Reymond. But the Lyon merchant wanted to 'make him truly bankrupt, and have him imprisoned, if only to make an example of him'. At the end of this first court case, Reymond was acquitted and his creditors, instead of receiving 40 per cent of the total amount, as previously agreed, had to settle for 17 per cent. The pedlar was able to tell the innkeeper, with whom he had stored some goods, 'that he had settled all his affairs, and that he would soon return with his son-in-law and sell his goods as in the past'. Due to a slip on his part, his caches were discovered, the court case was re-opened and this time Reymond was sentenced for fraudulent bankruptcy.[21]

Over and beyond the basic changes in the relationship between merchants and pedlars, these transactions all demonstrate the new development which had taken place in the town–mountain relationship: the latter had drifted a little further towards the margins of the European economy. The network of village informers, whether it was composed of family members or relied on the pillars of village society, was costly in terms of both time and money, and only those men who earned the major part of their income from lending to pedlars were able to devote enough time to the painstaking task of getting to know both the families and those with similar names. Increasingly, the elite classes were severing their links with the mountain, and the merchants were moving out of itinerant commerce. Their evidence in cases of bankruptcy clearly indicated how this type of business had become marginalized and, over and above the case in question, also indicated the new merchant practices.

On the face of it, little had changed. As in the first half of the century, the pedlar bought his goods on credit and paid for them when he returned from his campaign. However, two developments should be noted. Firstly, the sums involved in the transactions became smaller and smaller. As early as October 1776, Paul Malherbe, agent for the Société typographique de Neuchâtel, wrote in a letter 'I sell them very little, and yet still cannot avoid being tricked by them. Now Noël Gille has declared himself bankrupt. Very few of them can be trusted.'[22] As the receiver in charge of Reymond's bankruptcy revealed, the pedlars paid dearly for the few goods they bought: 'Reymond was doing business at a bad time: in common with most pedlars, he was paying vastly inflated prices for his goods.' Another receiver gave figures: almost all pedlars had to settle for maximum discounts of 2–5 per cent. Only the very important pedlars, and those who paid in cash, could expect discounts of 10 per cent.

Secondly, it became rarer for suppliers to ask for a guarantee: only one creditor would agree to supply Reymond with extra goods if his son-in-law, who was judged to be 'extremely solvent', guaranteed the debt. In this way, the merchants were attempting to limit the effects of disinformation: they sold little and at extremely high prices. If the pedlar did not repay what he had borrowed, the merchants took no steps to recover their debts since they lent the money without any illusions.

In eighteenth-century England, the following announcement printed by a merchant on the back of a chap-book demonstrates, if not actual success, at least a desire to open up the market for peddling articles to all those prepared to pay in cash, or in scrap iron and rags, which was the other currency between the pedlar and his customers:

ADVERTISEMENT. S. Rudder, Printer at Cirencester, Sells the Following Articles to Shopkeepers and Dealers, at the Wholesale Prices, viz., ALL Sorts of Threads, Bindings, Tapes, Inkles, Gartering, Laces, and other Haberdashery Goods – Stone and Smalt Blues of different qualities, which he will warrant upon his words, and sell as cheap as the Makers. Starch of different Sorts. Birmingham and Sheffield Goods in no less Quantities than Half a Dozen of each Sort together. Pins, Needles and many other Articles, which he will sell for ready money, on the same Terms as they are sold by the Manufacturers themselves. N. B. He gives the most Money for Rags, Horse-Hair, Old Metal, &c. &c.[23]

At the same time as peddling was becoming a more marginalized activity, firms were establishing a network of 'travellers' who visited the shops in the countryside for them. The point of contact between pedlars and suppliers involved an ever decreasing number of mountain dwellers and more and more men from the lowlands: travelling salesmen became the new middlemen.

Finally, the building of roads and railways made getting to the city shops far easier: in this sense, peddling lost its *raison d'être* as the network of shops developed. According to Daniel Defoe, the success of sedentary business had initiated the decline of peddling in England as early as 1745: 'several observers have remarked', he wrote, 'that there are fewer pedlars than in the last century, and many of them have set up "shops, or chambers, or warehouses, in the adjacent market towns, and sell their goods in the village round".'[24] The doors of city business were thus closed to the pedlars, and the packmen had only one choice left: either they managed to get themselves taken on by some of the firms and thus benefited from discounts of 8–10 per cent, which was the only way of making a profit, or, and this was the fate of the majority, buying few goods at exorbitant prices meant that the only way they could survive was through a combination of begging and stealing.

At the same time, new economic attitudes were forming. Enforced solidarity had collapsed in the face of business difficulties and it was increasingly difficult to make business associations work. Subsequently the idea of the guarantee was no longer accepted, thus spelling the death of the migrant communities, since in refusing it the elite classes demonstrated that having control over men, and hence over their land, no longer mattered to them. Consequently, not only did Nicolet several times come up against pedlars who refused to honour the guarantee they had made, but he also realized that the solidarity which this represented was losing its importance in the village: 'I have refused to allow Pierre into my house since he informs me that he will only pay what he owes, and will not pay the debts of those for whom he is guarantor.'[25] Finally, from the moment that city business had no further need for itinerant trade, rivalry between pedlars deepened and a climate of betrayal often replaced that of solidarity. The blackmail carried out by the agents of the Lieutenant General destroyed the harmony between the Cotentin pedlars, important distributors of prohibited books: Gandelin denounced two of his compatriots – 'Jean Leclerc, a merchant selling prints which he displays on the quai des Théatins; and Lange, also a merchant selling prints, who travels the countryside' – on condition that he was allowed to sell almanacs.[26]

Those families who were less involved in this centuries-old form of migration found their sons a place on the building sites of the new industrial infrastructure, thus creating new role models of success in the village. Jean-Joseph Ranque's letters[27] echo this shift in thinking which placed value on time and labour. Henceforth he praised the 'many young people' who had found other professions which 'ensure that they do not consume more than they can own'. This spirit of self-interest was based on hourly rates of pay for workers, and undermined the economic ethics of the village. The renunciation of this ethic emerged in attitudes to credit. All the letters written to Joseph Ranque by his

father reminded him that times had changed and 'that the number of
people who can be relied upon to pay up are very few'. Ranque told his
son in his letters that his insistence upon continuing his peddling activities would ultimately mean that 'he could not dare show his face in
society' because the village was no longer prepared to forgive stub-
bornness which was so unprofitable, any more than they would forgive
an unsuccessful campaign carried out on the basis of credit: 'People
would no longer refer to it as credit, but as reprehensible behaviour.'
Jean-Joseph Ranque's realization of this state of affairs is obvious from
his first letters dating from 1864. In the face of it, Jean-Joseph saw only
two ways out: one could either henceforth sell solely on cash terms, or
one could leave the profession – and the latter seemed the only truly
practical option to him.

> If you wanted to please me, you would recover however many debts are
> owed to you while you can, abandon this way of life and take care that
> nothing happens to you.

And yet he himself had 'travelled' in the past and carried the pack, as
had his fathers before him.

In the Auvergne, the pedlars who worked in Spain had the same tale
to tell:

> Whilst there, they too traded in livestock and sold on credit. They were
> accused of charging usurious rates, which were not actually excessive if one
> took into account the labour involved and the difficulties they had in
> recovering their debts – how many visits they had to pay to the peasants
> before dawn or late at night, how many burdensome legal proceedings it
> involved – especially when one considers that their customers were only
> farmers and that they had to rely on their goodwill rather than on non-
> existent securities. A law of 1908 forbade loans at more than 6 per cent
> interest. Since cash sales were rare, it became risky to place all one's hopes
> on there being a good harvest (oranges, rice and cereals). The only thing
> to be done was change profession, first attempting, if at all possible, to
> recover those debts which were in abeyance. Many of them returned to
> France.[28]

In the Auvergne too the chains of credit had dissolved and those in
business together, who had lost their assets in Spain and been unable to
recover their debts, now found themselves hounded by their French
merchant suppliers who, like Nicolet, were putting increasing pressure
on them. Faced with the combined demands of their creditors, the
relationship between business partners broke down and each sought, by
means of interminable legal proceedings, to extract themselves as best
they could from their collective ruin.[29]

The urban capitalist rationale had forced its way into the village. All creditors had simultaneously demanded that their debts be cleared, unmasking the weakness of economies based on credit and migrant labour. The harsh demands of the city creditors revealed just how extraordinarily fragile village credit was. Normally the extreme levels of debt between different people in the same village meant that those who were wealthiest had time on their side and they only went to work on their debtors one by one, depending on their own needs; depending also on an economic ethic which was based on the community, in which matters were only usually settled when the debtor died and which demanded that, if it proved impossible for the creditor to wait, then the debtor should not be stripped of all his property – land and houses were exchanged instead and the sums owed were reduced. The economic crises of the nineteenth century, in conjunction with the changing practices of city business, turned this economic balance on its head by forcing most of the richest members of society to put pressure on all their debtors at the same time. On the one hand, the majority of the villagers were unable to pay, and, on the other, the amount of money which the debt represented – in theory based on the value of land – turned out to be illusory in that the money owed was secured by property which already supported a level of debt far beyond its value. Thus the chain of credit dissolved. For three centuries, however, the system had worked because of the men who acted as a link between the different groups in the chain and, because they belonged to two separate cultures, allowed continual adjustments to be made to the overall mechanism.

The domination of urban logic also changed the way in which the peddling families considered the pedlar and the profession. They learnt to value time and labour differently. Itinerant commerce, which up until then had been respected by the community, was now disparaged and accepted with difficulty, and the entire social organization of peddling found itself discredited as did the culture of credit which was at its foundation. In the sixteenth century, this social structure which put most of the village's wealth in the hands of a few was praised, because the way in which the client culture operated allowed the poorest members of society to subsist and to pay their taxes. In the nineteenth century, this same system of credit had led to a drop in social status for the village elite class. This change in how the old practices were perceived brought with it radical disruption. The old hierarchies were neither transformed nor modernized by capitalism, but shattered. Reflecting the lasting depreciation of the relationship between capital and labour on which the mountain economy depended, the villages emptied inexorably.[30]

The break-up of these credit networks marks the demise of peddling and of those societies which, thanks to merchant migration, managed to support a far greater number of men than their natural resources would have allowed.

7

The Demise of the Profession

Marginalized in the business world and discredited in the home villages, peddling began to decline as early as the eighteenth century in England[1] and from the middle of the nineteenth in France.

On the other hand, in Spain, where there was still a dearth of diversified and easily accessible shops, there was a peddling revival in the nineteenth century.[2] After the Napoleonic period, the communities from Cantal once again established themselves in New Castile. The same families returned there: the Vermenouze family to Chinchón, the Rebeyrols to Vallecas and Ciempozuelos, the Sourniacs to Villatobas, the Lafons to Santorcaz, and so forth. However, the wide family groups which had constituted the framework of migrant trade in the previous century did not re-form after the financial ruin and liquidation of their Spanish assets brought about by the revolutionary wars. Those families who returned were of limited means and were not linked by common business interests; they covered by mule a diminished territory centred on the shop – the 'lonja' – which they had re-opened or newly established. Sometimes a strategically placed warehouse allowed superior distribution and slightly increased the area covered.

In comparison with the communities of the previous century, in addition to the withdrawal into a narrow family structure, investment in the region where business was conducted disappeared, the merchant network was no longer expanding and the firms grew smaller in size. Between 1879 and 1931 in Parla, the average number of people working for the firm fell from eight to six, then to four – of whom one was a Spaniard who would eventually take over. In Humanes, of the six shareholding members present in 1900, there remained only one in 1929; and the wife had been in charge of this trading-post before the family settled in Humanes. The business unit was reduced to a minimum: three migrants to maintain the trading-post, the related peddling and then the return home. The family banking system had disappeared, and so if each pedlar remained in Spain for two years he came away again with his profits. The map drawn up by Rose Duroux showing the places where the Cantal migrants lived in Castile demonstrates that this reduced form of peddling, which was limited to the family unit, none the less had considerable impact overall, since there were few villages without a settler from Cantal.[3] Like the regular pedlar of the rural areas of France in the eighteenth century, he covered a modest area, calling in at the inn to offer linen, household sheets and all sorts of ironmongery, and sleeping where night overtook him, more often than not in the stables of one of the farms he visited. In these poor regions of Spain in the Meseta, credit and payment in harvested crops remained the key to business: in order to understand the vast quantities of cereal revealed in the balance sheets, one would have to look more closely at how these merchants fitted into the workings of the market, and link their activities to those of their compatriots who, around the same period, started up numerous bakery ventures.[4] The slump in Spain in 1898, the war in 1914 and the excellent exchange rate of the peseta in 1920–2 led to the migrants abandoning Spain for good.[5] There was indisputably indigenous peddling which subsequently took over; as early as 1815 the Cantal migrants reported that there were now Spaniards working as coppersmiths, bakers, horse-dealers, itinerant stallholders and gelders;[6] one glimpses this occasionally in literary texts or comes across evidence of it when researching, but as yet there has been no Spanish study devoted to the phenomenon.[7]

The break with family tradition and eschewal of peddling as a source of income

To study the final changes in the profession, we must once again take France as an example. Following the rejection of organizations based on extended family groups and the withdrawal into a narrow family structure, the end of the profession was distinguished by a double breakdown which put an end to all future development: both family tradition and credit structures were demolished. This final stage reveals that behind the continued use of the term 'pedlar', there lay a radically different way of thinking and of operating as a migrant merchant.

Regular salaries had transported these families into another economic universe. On the one hand, the temporary migrant's age-old fear of never being certain of being able to return home honourably, boosted by the money to pay off one's debts, had disappeared; on the other the attractions of the possibility of getting rich quick after a successful campaign were, in the context of this new economic ethos, dismissed and discredited. A psychological malaise had set in; the reversal of values was complete – farmwork and credit had lost their prestige to the city and salaried status, which were henceforth the only measurements of value. The migratory movements thus changed direction and nature: merchant migration dried up and was replaced by the quest for jobs as minor public servants, in domestic service or as unqualified labourers. In France, all those pedlars whose descendants we have been able to trace are proof of the new values which permeated the village. In 1858, Jean Gourand, the last in a line of pedlars which can be traced back to the seventeenth century, asked his wife whether their son, then 18 years old, intended 'to become a merchant'; her answer was that 'his main enthusiasm was for a career in the Sciences, but he understands that our financial means are not such to allow him to do this'. The son travelled as a pedlar for a while, then settled in the valley as a schoolteacher. At the beginning of the twentieth century, Cyprien Balme, another son of a pedlar, was a monitor in a religious school in Sassenage. He wanted to get his certificate and work for the railways, or find a job as a tax collector. His ambitions came to naught and, in 1906, he was a pedlar.

During the 20 years which followed the great agricultural crises of the mid-nineteenth century, definitive emigration supplanted seasonal emigration. However, traditional peddling emigration, even though it was affected by this development, nevertheless managed to hold its own and even expanded round about 1875. The French institute for alpine geography, which studied this phenomenon in the 1920s, basing its conclusions on oral surveys, even claimed that there had been a maximum escalation in peddling during the last quarter of the nineteenth century.[8] Who were these end-of-the-century pedlars, who were still present in such significant numbers, and who were probably more numerous than we can deduce from the documents consulted?

An analysis of the censuses of 1896 and 1901 for the peddling villages in the valleys of the Oisans[9] reveals an initial development – the profession, which up until then had been passed down from father to son, now only survived on the margins of families. In 1896, only single men who belonged to atypical families still practised the profession – these were brothers living together or men who were the only wage-earners in the family. Married pedlars were no longer heads of household but young men living with their in-laws, and there was one case of a servant supplementing his income as a packman. In those villages where the pedlars had specialized particularly in the grocery and seed business in the nineteenth century (such as Villard-Notre-Dame), this specialization had, for a time, helped them to preserve the profession – in 1896, there were still 17 pedlars who were also heads of household in this village. However, five years later, only four remained and those who persevered demonstrated that the family structure was no longer self-perpetuating. Only a handful of men in their fifties with families to support still peddled. Their children would become pedlars too, but only for a couple of years before they emigrated for good. At the end of the nineteenth century the great tradition of peddling families had been destroyed.

An analysis of the records for military conscription[10] for this same group of villages bears witness to another aspect of this marginalization. If one takes into account all those conscripts who had been pedlars – 405 of them – then it would appear that a third of the pedlars who emigrated, if not for good then at least for most of their active lives, had only been occasional pedlars. The majority of them only peddled for a year or two before or after military service; others 'travelled' between jobs; lastly, some returned home and became packmen after having failed in other careers. Finally, slightly less than 60 per cent of pedlars returned to their home region and slightly more than 40 per cent left. For all of them the search for work was a long process and they rarely settled straight away, or after one move, but generally after having moved at least three times.[11]

The fundamental transformations in the profession are thus concealed by the overall figures, and only an analysis of the families allows us to perceive them, and recognize that the basis of peddling had shifted. And from this, even if in absolute terms the number of pedlars leads us to believe that the profession had stood firm against the movement towards definitive migration, a study of the families involved shows the opposite to be true: the old profession which was practised by both father and son had been swept away, and other men had appropriated it and adapted it. If one relies solely upon quantified sources then one is led to describe a reality which no longer existed. The need to move on from all-encompassing statistics to look more closely at the families involved is compounded by the need for caution when faced with the weight of words and official categories. The way in which people accept and make use of the categories offered to them should also be questioned.

A breakdown of the applications for peddling permits reveals the changing peddling population. The law of 27 July 1849 and the circulars from the Ministry of Police of 28 July and 12 September 1852 placed peddling under the jurisdiction of the Prefect and made it compulsory for migrants to have permits. The analyses done by Rudolf Schenda of the applications for peddling permits made by itinerants selling books and printed material in the 1850s have pinpointed a turning point in the evolution of the profession. On the one hand he discovers whole clans of book pedlars with the same name, from the same villages in the Vosges and the Haute-Garonne; on the other he finds lone individuals of all ages, emanating from communities in crisis, without jobs and, finding no other way of earning a livelihood, seizing upon the profession in droves when they can no longer continue in their stated occupation: 'bookbinder', 'labourer', 'stallholder', 'haberdasher', 'war veteran', 'mason', 'rag and bone man', 'deaf and dumb' [sic], 'day labourer'.

Furthermore, illiteracy was the norm and applications for peddling permits were usually written by a public scribe or in uncertain handwriting with shaky spelling.[12]

The applications for peddling permits analysed by Dominique Lerch for the years following (between 1849 and 1870) reveal the rapid decline of traditional peddling: out of 1,140 applications registered in the Bas-Rhin region, only 8 per cent came from career pedlars who had applied over at least five years; the others were only occasional pedlars. Twenty-four per cent had renewed their application fewer than five times and 68 per cent had only peddled on one occasion. These declarations also allow us to apprehend the emergence of the travelling salesman, employed by one firm for whom he worked exclusively: out of the 52 career pedlars, seven were from Wissembourg in Pirmasens in the Bavarian Palatinate, and exclusively employed to sell prints for the Wentzel firm.[13]

It should however be noted that the low prices for which the prints were bought and sold were extremely well suited to this type of peddling which was on the financial borderline between an income and an appeal for charity. In fact, at the end of the nineteenth century, the print was more often given away than sold by the more successful pedlars and became a small gift with which they presented children in order to attract their mothers' attention, or to pay them for their indirect collaboration, whilst at the same time assuring themselves of a warm welcome the next time they passed through.[14] Similarly, the rag and bone men paid the children who brought them bones, ash or animal skins in pictures.[15]

At the end of the century, the applications for peddling permits studied for the Isère region between 1897 and 1902 vouch for the disappearance of the old networks: there were only two applications made by members of the old peddling families in the Dauphiné. The remaining applications demonstrated that the profession had become an occupation in which economic profitability took second place to its function as a symbolic protection against a life of begging, and also that it had been appropriated by the elite classes who used it as a medium for the propagation of their ideas. Hence two groups rubbed shoulders in these permit applications which have been analysed for the turn of the century: the militant and the beggar. The first group sold books, pamphlets and newspapers; their applications were curt – 'Desiring henceforth to sell Le Socialiste in the Isère', one ran; and the mayor of Allevard added to the application from the church sexton, 'The applicant, who already sells the newspaper La Croix, doubtless means to conduct a fierce campaign on behalf of the Church in the canton, under orders from the archbishop of Allevard.' Others claimed to be part of the Salvation Army. Yet more went begging with their newssheet, moved people to pity and made excuses.

Amongst this last group of applicants, two populations overlapped:

the beggars and the vagrants who sought the right to peddle so as to escape from one fate or the other. Amongst the vagrants, many were only passing through the Isère: 'Being unemployed, and wishing to leave Grenoble for Paris...', 'To get back to Lyon, his home town...', 'Almost penniless and exhausted, since I have come from Geneva on foot... to be able to take the train'. But vagrancy and mendacity were two sides of the same coin and one or the other always lay behind these requests: 'I am sick... I wish to sell goods on the road, so that I can get home without being reduced to begging....' For many, it was sickness which had left them with no other choice: 'I have been declared unfit for military service because of the bronchitis which I have suffered from since 1893... being unable to do any work which is at all heavy, I would wish to sell thread, needles, laces, etc....'; 'Occupied as a pedlar, given that I suffer from exacerbated progressive myopia and am thus incapable of doing any work requiring the slightest keenness of sight...'; or age: 'An old soldier of sixty-two, I find myself without work'; or family circumstances: 'I am unemployed and alone with my mother, having lost both my brothers in the space of eight months.' But in all cases, peddling was not considered even by those applying for permits as a profession, or a job. It was precisely because they were 'without work', 'unable to work' that they were making such an application.

Allow me respectfully to beg of your kind indulgence a peddling certificate. Suffering from a medically certified disability, my right leg having varicose ulcers which makes it impossible for me to work and forcing me, in order to escape from the dreadful situation of having to beg, to become a pedlar for which I seek your kind permission...

Finding myself crippled and unable to work...

Finding myself presently without work, I should like to sell songsheets or newspapers, which would enable me to subsist whilst waiting to find work.

All these letters are permeated by the interiorization of the Christian doctrine of the poor man as being a good man: the reference was often quite plain and contrasted with the image of the dangerous populations of brigands and vagrants which had haunted Western imaginations from the Middle Ages:

Having had the thumb of my left hand amputated, finding myself unemployed at the present time and with extremely modest resources, I hope that, equipped with this document, I shall be able to obtain my daily bread...

My wife and myself find ourselves without work, and wishing to extract myself from this situation in an honest manner, I should like to sell a little stationery, haberdashery...

Finding myself in dire straits... my left leg was devoured by a bear...

But the line between itinerancy and delinquency was a fine one:

> I was placed under arrest . . . and released today for the crime of vagrancy
> and begging. Not being able to work in my professional capacity as a
> carpenter since my sight has weakened considerably, I beg you, Monsieur
> le Préfet, to have the kindness to grant me a peddling certificate so that I
> may earn my living, without asking for public charity, as far as Bordeaux
> where I have acquaintances and friends.[16]

Thus the profession was one no longer, but a stop-gap between two
jobs, a haven for those left-overs of the job market.[17]

In the migrant villages, peddling also concealed a forced migration of
the poorest, of the old who had no means of support and of children
between the ages of eight and twelve. There are numerous examples of
children taken off by a pedlar *affinchè lo conducesse seco nel torinese
onde istruirlo alla mercatura* ('to take them to the Turin area to teach
them the merchant profession') and, like Michele de Castagnetoli from
the Apennines, later found in Paris *assieme a un parmagiano che faceva
ballare una volpe* ('with a man from Parma who had a dancing fox on
display'); or left behind at an inn; or lost in a strange town.[18] Others,
such as Tarantola Alessio di Stephano de Castevoli, sent them to beg for
alms. An *espositore di panorama e venditore di canzonette e stampe*
(tour guide and vendor of song sheets and prints), he was arrested in
January 1874 for having made his eight-year-old son beg and sell
songsheets, as well as another 14-year-old child whom he had hired
specifically for this purpose.[19] In the final decades of the nineteenth
century, the ratio of children to adults within the groups of travelling
musicians, originally from the mountainous provinces of the kingdom
of Naples, underwent a complete reversal: the number of children, usually
limited to one or two, now increased to the point where there were
companies formed entirely of child musicians (aged between 6 and 14),
led by a single adult.[20]

The practice of excluding young children, mostly orphans, from the
mountain villages by putting them into apprenticeship was an ancient
one in the Alps. In France, contracts relating to this are to be found in
the reports of meetings held by 'relatives, neighbours and friends' responsible for deciding the fate of orphans: they record how a migrant
was to be paid to find the child a master – a 'padrone' or 'capo' in
Italy.[21] At the beginning of the twentieth century in the Apennines and
Southern Italy, the migration of children took on such alarming dimensions that the authorities and the charitable organizations became
concerned.[22] Excluding them in this way was the last resort for the
villagers, who were unable to feed children who could not contribute
their labour in return. But once they were beyond the critical ages of
eight to twelve years old – from the end of infancy to adolescence –

their relatives sometimes became worried and tried to discover the whereabouts of the child, who had then been gone for two or three years.[23] On the other hand, once the child was 15 there was no further possibility of their being abandoned, and the travelling pedlars who employed these adolescents allowed them to return to the village in time to help with the farm work.

With this new preponderance of destitute pedlars, those who earned their living through peddling had disappeared and had been replaced by those who asked for charity or enlisted in the army. The authorities had not been mistaken: in instituting a system of applications for peddling permits, they sought as much to control the destitute vagrants as the churches and political parties who used travelling salesmen as a way of spreading their beliefs. Indeed, in France the active Society for Religious Treatises in Paris paid missionary-pedlars to circulate their Protestant pamphlets.[24] Jean-François Botrel gives two contrasting examples of how peddling was used in Spain to militant ends: firstly, in 1869 the republican José Estrañi entrusted two blindmen, also republicans, with the circulation of a propaganda *romance*, in which miracles were re-counted, but miracles which favoured republican ideals; and secondly, in 1876, the very Catholic Carlo Maria Perier gave out free copies of the popular newssheet *La Hoja popular: Apéndice a La Defensa de la Sociedad* 'to the blind and the poor, so that they could sell them for not more than a *quarto* each, and thus be a means of aid for them'.[25] Income from peddling had become a secondary consideration, as it had been at the beginning of the sixteenth century when a multitude of wandering prophets travelled across Europe, bareheaded, with long beards and crosses in their hands, living echoes of John the Baptist and the prophet Elijah.[26]

Specialist pedlars

Certain traditional pedlars, however, managed to continue in their pro-fession for a few decades longer. They survived by specializing in new, luxury goods, or goods which were very much in demand, which sometimes reintroduced an element of craftsmanship, as in the early days of the profession. In each peddling region there were a few families who turned their attention to a new specialization. In the Dauphiné, haberdashers became opticians, seed merchants or florists; in the Pyr-enees they became booksellers; in the Auvergne, wine merchants; in the southern parts of the Black Forest they peddled glass jewellery; on the other side of the Rhine it was pictures.[27] Some villages in Savoy were split between two specialities,[28] and in the upper Rhine regions certain communes specialized in selling almanacs in winter.[29] In the Tuscan

Apennines, pedlars selling shaving stones now also sold books;[30] in the Blenio valley in the Ticino region the pedlars cultivated their old tradition of chocolate making,[31] and the picture-sellers gradually abandoned printed material in favour of spectacles.[32] In the Apennine valleys of Lucques, pedlars became known as *figurinai* because they sold plaster figures.[33] There was a wide range of specialities and the organization of itinerant trade was not confined to one single model since, depending on the markets canvassed, the goods offered and the village traditions, either the old way of doing things was resurrected, or original ways of selling were invented to fit in with the new economic constraints of the end of the nineteenth century.

The Pyrenean booksellers were within the mainstream of eighteenth-century migration. They came from the mountain communities of the Haut Comminges on the one hand, and from the Garonne on the other: they were called *Gascons*. Around the bookselling villages a triangle could be drawn, its points being Saint-Gaudens to the east, Bagnères-de-Bigorre to the west and Bagnères-de-Luchon to the south. Many pedlars also had another specialization, bookselling alone only representing a tiny minority of interrelated families.[34] This is a very good example of how the network changed, because we know that, from the end of the Middle Ages, the men from these mountain valleys were part of a complex structure of merchant migration, directed towards Spain and combining rich merchants with a business in the city, packmen and a migratory movement of poor knife-grinders and water-carriers. Doubtless the book had already made its appearance in the pedlar's pack in the eighteenth century, but it was not evident as a specialization until the 1820s.

Pedlars divided France and the seasons up between them: some set out in the winter, from October to June, and covered the eastern part of the mountain region of Armorique, Normandy and all those regions within a 270 kilometre radius of the Paris Basin; others went in the summer, between April and September and covered southern France, the Alps, the upper Loire region, Brittany and Normandy. In this way they covered almost all of France, with the exception of the Saône plain, the Jura mountains, Lorraine and Alsace,[35] regions which were doubtless supplied by German, Italian, Swiss and Savoyard pedlars who stocked up from firms in Lorraine or Alsace, and by the Chamagnon pedlars who were originally from the Jura mountains.[36]

If one is to believe Charles Noblet, printer, publisher and bookseller who specialized in producing popular booklets and was the spokesman for his profession in 1869 and 1874 in their dealings with the authorities:

Pedlars always follow the same itinerary: it's a real annual circuit that they accomplish; their campaigns . . . extend over a predetermined radius and they invariably end up back where they started. . . . Consequently, nothing is further from the truth than what has been said about the irregular nature of their appearances in the village, or about the impunity they would thus enjoy were they to be involved in some trickery. I repeat that the pedlars always visit the same spots in the same localities.[37]

The role of credit granted to the clientele developed along the same lines. These pedlars did not just sell books: in their cart or pack they also had writing-paper, pictures and etchings, purses, chains, glasses, wallets, notebooks and diaries. Only very occasionally were almanacs also present.[38]

The peddling organization was traditional – based around a few interrelated families who formed an interest group and who protected their sales territories by splitting the itineraries between them, keeping each other informed of changes in the market. Charles Nisard, assistant secretary to the Committee for Peddling, pointed out that 'if, for example, a Parisian bookseller were to lower his prices by a *livre*, a week or ten days later the entire guild of pedlars knows about it; and therein doubtless lies one of the reasons for their strength and the confidence they inspire.'[39] The pedlars were organized in hierarchical groups; 'the master' remained in a given site, distributed the goods and decided on the area to be covered by the 'servants' whom he had brought with him – these were generally young men who were serving their apprenticeship in this way. They then spent five to six days selling the goods, after which the servants rejoined their master at an agreed spot and the group set out towards another major town.[40] In comparison with the Briançonnais or Norman pedlars of the eighteenth century, or the Ticino pedlars of the nineteenth century, the Pyrenean network did not seem to be attached to any structure of migrant-owned shops: there was no pinnacle to the merchant hierarchy, which had lent the migrant networks of previous eras their originality.

In the middle of the century, this type of peddling found itself in crisis: it experienced considerable decline between 1850 and 1860, carried on for a few more years and then practically disappeared during the war of 1870. Before this crisis, the size of the group comprising the 'masters' was put at between 150 and 300 people who, according to the sources, each employed between 6 and 12 'clerks' or 'servants'; in other words, a group of around 3,000 people. In 1874, there were no more than 400–500 left.[41]

One can pinpoint the obstacles put in the way of itinerant commerce[42] as being behind this decline, as well as the development of other merchant outlets for the sale of books. The prefect of Cher, for example, announced that peddling 'has been destroyed by the commercial possibilities which bookshops have managed to create for themselves in the rural areas'; his colleague in the Orne department added that, if pedlars were becoming more scarce, it was because 'people prefer to get their books from bookshops'; and the chief of police in Falaise reported that peddling 'has lost much of its importance since the arrival of newspapers costing 5 centimes and novels in instalments at the same price, which are sold by the sedentary booksellers'. In Lorraine, Baudot, successor to the well-known Oudot from Troyes, one of the largest publishers for pedlars in France, went out of business in 1863, the same years as the *Petit Journal* appeared, priced at one *sou**.[43] Books were distributed in the rural areas though other channels: 'In this area,' protested a bookseller from Nancy to the Director of the Library, 'there is not a single village, however small, where the schoolteacher, the Holy Sister, and one or several of the grocers are not selling books. . . .' Books were cheaper, and 1 *sou* newsapers, such as, from 1863, the *Petit Journal*, made the peddling booklets unfashionable. In addition, of course, the railways burst onto the scene, bringing the rural areas closer to the town.[44] Cafes and reading-rooms were only of interest to the elite peasant classes. However, the end of book peddling finally came about when the pedlars themselves abandoned it. The book was no longer profitable; it was becoming a humdrum commodity and, with the abolition of bookselling licenses in 1870, could be found on grocer's shelves, a sure sign that, along with its status as a luxury object, it had lost the quality of rarity that gave it its value.

In England, the same phenomena eradicated book-peddling around 1830, with the distribution of cheap periodicals replacing it:

> The extinction of the chap-book was as sudden as its reign had been long and prosperous. About 1830, cheap and respectable periodicals like *Chamber Edinburgh Journal* appeared and like summer mists before rising sun the chap-books vanished, and with them their worthy and unworthy vendors.[45]

In the nineteenth century in Spain, when the fashion was for novels published in instalments, publishers set up distribution networks using salaried employees who were responsible for the promotion and sales of these publications. The 'repartidor', who was the key player in the system, sold the present and forthcoming instalments door to door, so as to build up a clientele whom he would visit at home to deliver the booklets and collect the amount owed. After the First War, the product changed: and the 'repartidor' then distributed de luxe editions of encyclopedias, books and periodicals to his subscribers.[46] As the sale outlets and channels for printed material multiplied, the pedlar found himself universally marginalized.[47]

Around the same period, there were a few Italian peasants who specialized in book-peddling. They came from the Valle del Magra in the area covered by the commune of Mulazzo, and in particular from the

---

* 1 *sou* is roughly equal to a shilling.

village of Montereggio in the Tuscan Apennines. They were known as the pedlars from Pontremoli. In this instance also, specialization was the business of the wealthy minority. Towards the middle of the century, the register of emigrants from Mulazzo, a village of some 400 peasants, recorded six book pedlars, against 65 whetstone pedlars, who peddled a few pamphlets in addition, and 142 pedlars who made their living solely from selling whetstones. Over half the migrants (69 out of 122 in 1843) claimed that they travelled to France, and sometimes to Belgium too; the others went to Venice, Tuscany or Piedmont; a few travelled to Corsica or Germany. The numbers varied from one year to the next, but the ratio of the various specializations and destinations remained broadly the same. Most of the whetstone pedlars set out for Piedmont, a small minority continuing into France. They usually emigrated for three or four months, setting out in April and returning in June – only the booksellers might return later.[48] A second and less common period of emigration fell in the autumn, from the end of August until October or December. The destinations were different: the pedlars travelled to Corsica and Sardinia to sell whetstones, books and pictures.[49] The books peddled were primarily short novels, stories and devotional books, but there might also be Italian vocabulary books.[50] These pedlars of printed material were often arrested by the authorities on suspicion of all sorts of trafficking – carrying forged currency, smuggling tobacco, or selling obscene books.[51]

The bookselling pedlars got their supplies on credit and settled up when they got back from their campaign.[52] In its organization, this campaign was similar to those carried out by the Pyrenean book-pedlars: the pedlar set himself up in a town with his cart, and sent his young sons and servants (children of between 14 and 18 years old), whom he rented from other families, with the books into the surrounding inns and villages *con una gerla o una cassetta a tracolla* (with a basket or box slung crosswise). A few days later they moved to another town and started all over again. The same peddling hierarchies were to be found, from the packman to the pedlar with his own harnessed cart.[53]

Le bancarelle, the little shops which sprang up everywhere, were first mentioned as early as 1855. At the beginning of the twentieth century, the booksellers limited the area they covered to a single Italian town, and sold only books and pictures, with a few knick-knacks and alabaster objects thrown in. In the first 15 years of the twentieth century, the booksellers settled in town with their families. In 1890 there were still 57 itinerant booksellers recorded in the registers; in 1916–17 there were fewer than ten, and in 1936 no more than four remained.[54]

Eberard Gothein has described the organizational structure of the glassware pedlars from the southern parts of the Black Forest which, in the nineteenth century, mirrored that of the Italian alpine companies of the previous centuries. It also had similarities with the structure which made possible the emergence of the extensive Auvergne companies in Spain. Established on the basis of the family and generally bringing together the brothers of a single family, the company decided on the basis of its profits where each 'Kamerad' was to be stationed and how he was to be used, just as it forbade him to trade on his own account, lend money, spend time in cafes or at parties, or take part in entertainments such as dancing or playing billiards.[55]

In Limousin, the end of the Spanish trade coincided with the emergence of a new type of peddling which specialized in wine from Bordeaux. The villages from which this originated – Meymac, Argentat and Egletons – were villages from which merchants had previously emigrated towards Spain. The first wine merchants set out around 1880 to test the markets in northern France. They gradually extended their sphere of activity into Normandy and eastern France, then Belgium, Holland and French-speaking Switzerland. After the Second World War, there were nearly 150 wine merchants who travelled to non-wine-making countries to sell bottles of wine from catalogues. Once an order had been placed, the bottles were delivered when the merchant returned to his country. These were individual ventures, swathed in secrecy by the families concerned, who kept particularly quiet about the merchant's intended destination. Here again, specialization had meant the creation of a new campaign and the breaking away from the shackles of credit. The merchants effectively became part of the banking circuit and, in return, from the beginning of the twentieth century the bank installed branches in their home villages.[56]

The most profitable forms of specialization combined luxury goods with the conquest of new markets. We shall take as an example the florist-pedlars from the Oisans in order to understand how this new type of peddling was organized. Originally from traditional families of cloth merchants and haberdashers, they gradually discovered new markets, new customers, new ways of selling and of financing their expeditions. The florists soon became the 'aristocrats' of peddling, as did all pedlars who adopted new specializations. Pinpointing the beginnings of the florist trade is difficult since it was the result of a slowly developing specialization, which was part commercial and part geographic. Some point to the first voyage to America in 1825,[57] but the family in question already travelled to Spain in previous generations.[58] Whatever the truth is, the tradition of ocean-going florists has its origins in these expeditions, which, as early as the sixteenth century, took men to Toulouse or Bordeaux, then from there to Spain, whence they crossed the Atlantic to the old Spanish and French colonies.[59] This particular type of specialization was also linked to the rise in cheap colour prints and natural history books which had familiarized the bourgeois classes with exotic plants, and thus made them desirable.[60]

The florists sold all sorts of fruit and ornamental trees, decorative plants, rosebushes and various sorts of bulbs and seeds. They packed them in sturdy wooden boxes, added a few baskets, and picked a destination, depending upon the time of year when they were setting out. Those who set out in autumn headed for Latin America, the Mediterranean basin or the Middle East; those who could only leave at the beginning of winter went to countries where spring came later: the Northern States and Russia. Jean-Pierre Magne, one of the first great florists, born in 1806 in Mont-de-Lans in the Dauphiné, travelled all over Europe from Ireland to the Baleares, North Africa, Egypt, Russia, Brazil; and over seven trips visited all of the eastern part of the United States, from the Great Lakes to New Orleans. Claude Chouvin, born in 1853 in the neighbouring village of La Garde, travelled to Mexico, North American and to Canada and then specialized in trading with Latin America. Others went as far as the borders of Russia and of Iran.

Their target customers were dignitaries and the rich middle classes: their sales pitch combined evocations of luxury, the imaginary and the exotic. Once they had reached their chosen destination, they set out to look for a shop to rent in a busy shopping street and then got their name known. In Latin America, where the rich middle class was relatively large, they placed advertisements in the newspapers. In Russia and Egypt, where those in power constituted a limited elite, before putting their wares on display they first presented them to the local dignitary, in the hope that by gaining favour with the prince they would attract the small number of people of standing into their shop. Whatever the circumstances, they had to make a sale quickly: customers were few, and the plants, which had already undergone a long journey, either withered or demanded too much attention. They hoped to sell most of their cargo within a fortnight, or a month at most, then sell the remaining plants by stopping off at one or two other towns on the way back.

As well as the plants, they were offering dreams to the rich bourgeois classes, and their sales pitch primarily targeted the imagination. They had calling cards and invoice slips printed – often in the language of the country – which created the impression that this shop on foreign soil was a branch of a large business which counted amongst its customers the most important people in France. They hung pictures of flowers in their shops, generally painted with stencils, reproducing the descriptions in the advance catalogues they published. The flowers, seeds, bulbs and the bare trees advertised as being on sale took on surprising and unexpected shapes and colours in their promotional material: green and blue roses in the shape of a turban, up to 14 cms wide, three-coloured hyacinths – white, blue and red – all from the same bulb, gentians with thousands of red flowers, strange orchids, flowering ferns. . . . The fruit trees matured incredibly early and produced vast quantities of fruit: strawberry plants bore berries as big as oranges, cherry trees produced clusters of fruit like grapes, peach trees produced peaches with no stones, apple and pear trees bore fruit weighing as much as two kilos, raspberries grew as big as hen's eggs, and the numerous dwarf varieties of pear, cherry and peach trees, intended as house plants, 'produce delicious fruit twice a year'. Finally, these catalogues also systematically exploited the idea of exoticism: strawberries destined for the American market naturally came from St Petersburg, whilst, for the inhabitants of Tashkent, the fruit and flowers came from America, apart from the cluster-producing cherry trees which came from . . . Siberia.

The financial structure of their business was similar to that of other pedlars, in that the florists approached the important people in the valleys for backing, including Nicolet the glove merchant, who, more-over, never failed to supply them from 'the coffers of the Grenoble glove shop'.[61] However, there were three important differences. Their suppliers were outside of this circuit, the merchants only borrowing money, never merchandise: the invoices which have been preserved show that the great majority of plants were paid for in cash. Since the initial capital outlay was the most important, business associations involved more people than for other types of peddling: the florists set out in groups of three or four, and sometimes more. Their partnership was usually agreed verbally and lasted for the duration of the journey; two months after the merchants returned home they settled their accounts and dissolved the partnership.[62] Finally, this type of business made use of the nascent banking services, whether for insuring their goods or transferring money.[63] In the early days of the banking industry, the city merchants acted as intermediaries to ensure that all necessary precautions were taken. At the end of the nineteenth century, using the bank in this way had become commonplace.

More than any other type of peddling, the flower trade was an extremely risky business with uncertain profits. The merchant could lose his merchandise at any point in his campaign. To begin with, once his plants had been taken out of the nursery soil they were at risk from frost if the weather was too cold (this was Claude Chouvin's misfortune in 1899 and 1901). If the sea was too rough they might rot during the crossing, as Claude Chouvin found when he travelled to Costa Rica in 1884–5. Once on dry land, the florist never knew what sort of political and economic climate he would encounter: thus Jean-Pierre Magnes arrived in Buenos Aires in 1829 during the troubles which were to take Rosas to power. And all the way along the line, whether they wanted to obtain the right to trade, or simply to travel, the pedlars came up against the authorities of the different countries. In addition to the dangers which threatened their cargoes were the dangers which the pedlars themselves faced as they travelled through countries which were unhygienic for the most part, and where tropical diseases had reached endemic proportions, with only a very limited supply of drugs for protection.

Profits were in proportion to the risks taken by the pedlar. Especially in the early years, some made enormous profits – such as Jean-Pierre Arnol and Jean Ronna in 1834: 'I have just been informed by M. Giroud the younger', wrote Nicolet, 'that his agent in Paris has received the sum of 14,015.65 francs, which you have paid from the 2,800 piastres which M. Gautereau from Lima sent you on behalf of Messieurs Arnol and Ronna.'[64] For the later periods, oral tradition puts the average profit from a campaign at 3,000 francs. Of the five campaigns which Claude Chouvin mentions in his letters, only two were successful (with profits of 3,000 and 5,000 francs); the others were at best mediocre (900 francs profit), or disastrous. Over his 18 campaigns Jean-Pierre Magne made an average profit of 2,934 francs, with the highest point being 8,000 francs and the lowest a 250 franc loss. One should calculate an average of 4,000 francs per campaign in capital outlay. When measured against the 600 francs that a cloth merchant might make for a capital outlay of around 3,000 francs, there is no comparison in the scale of earnings.

The customers they were targeting and the way in which the campaigns unfolded both permitted and presupposed that transactions were free of credit, and that this was a business in which purchases were paid for in cash. Credit then came into play in the sales pitch as a promotional ploy, and no longer as an economic or interactive necessity. To lend more credibility to their publicity and encourage customers, some pedlars arranged to be paid a supposed half of the purchase price in cash, the other half to be paid when the plant flowered – by which time they had obviously left the country.

These pedlars thus managed to get round the major problems which beset the pedlars who travelled in France: by choosing countries with loose business networks and a rich clientele who were able to pay cash, they were able to continue practising the profession profitably without being constrained by the traditional shackles of debt. Village credit was no longer the basis of their wealth – Chouvin was under no illusions as to his ability to recover the few debts he was owed in the village. Credit was no longer granted during the campaign and the pedlars' only ties were with the city merchant bankers who, as long as the market was profitable, were unstinting with their assistance. Similarly, the old solidarities which had provided the migratory movement with its financial basis were henceforth rejected: the pedlars formed business partnerships for the duration of the campaign because it was impossible to do otherwise, but they were suspicious of one another and deceived one another. It was each man for himself.

Despite the profits to be had, the village and the families wanted no more itinerancy: henceforward success meant a settled life and a fixed income, albeit a small one. Every letter expressed this sentiment: 'It seems to me that all those around us are happier than we are: they never have to part, and those who do are not apart for such a long time. . . . I pray to God with all my heart to take care of you. What should I become without you? Everything would be lost. And what would become of our son . . .', wrote Céleste Chouvin to her husband in January 1894. Jean-Pierre Magne gave up earlier, immediately after his second marriage in 1846. In partnership with one of his brothers-in-law he became a mule trader. In five years he earned 2,500 francs profit from this business – barely the equivalent of a single florist's campaign. These figures demonstrate the reversal in village values.

The economic slump that hit South America at the end of the century was the final factor in dissuading florists from a profession which had been depreciated despite the potential earnings. Claude Chauvin's last campaign was to be in 1901, as he wrote to his son in April, from Rio de Janeiro: 'I shall do my utmost to make as much as I can from my plants, but I think that if I manage to return home in good health, then this will be my last voyage. I am completely fed up with it. There is nothing left to be done here, apart from running the risk of having all one's money eaten up: the Americas are completely ruined and everywhere is the same.'[65]

Finally, along with the traditional ways of life, the high altitude mountains were rejected and became more than ever places where people no longer wanted to live. None of the florists went back there after making their fortunes; they opened a shop in the lowlands in one of the traditional peddling villages.

Such individual ventures were also to be found in the Auvergne, but only on the fringes of society. Augustin Jauriac tried his luck in Mexico because, as he wrote to his sister from Mexico on 23 August 1851, 'if fortune does not favour you in one way, then you must approach her in another . . . I would find it unbearable to return to Auvergne just as poor as when I left; besides I have my pride to prevent me from returning.' In all likelihood, he worked for a merchant from the Dauphiné selling fancy jewellery and watches. He was following in the steps of a relative who had been successful and had used the money he made to buy a bakery in Madrid.[66] However, certain places developed a type of peddling concerned with 'large-scale ventures': in Arconsat, pedlars sold ironmongery, cutlery from Thiers and the renowned Catalonian rugs to the Americas, the West Indies, Russia, and as far afield as China and the Indian Ocean. Other families specialized in a two-way trade with the Mediterranean Basin: they sold cutlery from Thiers, fabrics and a great number of weapons from the Saint-Etienne munitions factory to Greece and Sardinia; and on their way back, they imported untreated animal hides into France, which made them net profits of nearly 50 per cent.[67] Here, as in the Dauphiné, venturing abroad was a necessary evil and, once business affairs had been settled, business associates liked to dream of the eagerly awaited moment when they could return home for good:

We much be patient and endure it all. Perhaps the day will come when we will all be able to return to our homeland, to our village, and we will go and sit under an enormous fir tree and celebrate Midsummer's Day and drink to the good health of the Spanish *douros* and the Italian *scudos*. We should rest after having travelled the world over, like the wandering Jew.[68]

At the same time as these individual ventures were taking place, certain villages in the southern Alps had managed to recreate the circumstances of the great peddling era under the Ancien Régime. Admittedly, the trade routes had changed because of the merchant ventures which were being set up in the Americas, but they had merely followed the shifts in the profitable markets. The goods were no longer the same: after silk, citrus fruits, tobacco and printed material, at the end of the nineteenth century the Alpine merchants turned their attention to luxury goods. Yet the merchant structures remained remarkably faithful to the old way of doing things, which fixed the family and village migratory movements firmly within a network of shops run by their compatriots. This return to the great networks of shops and pedlars took place primarily in the southern Alps.[69]

According to tradition, capital was accumulated in the place to which the pedlar first emigrated. The Falque brothers from Aiguilles in Queyras had set up in business in Nice, Turin and Chambéry. Then Claude, who had left Turin for Nice where he rejoined his brother, went into partnership with Augustin Vasserot, who, like the Falque brothers, was originally from Aiguilles, and in 1835 the two of them went on their first trip to Rio de Janeiro. They set up a firm there and brought over the other Falque brothers, apart from one who settled in Lyon and took on the ordering and the shipping of goods to Latin America. Having opened up this new market, the partners called on migrant merchants from their home village to try out this new country, pack on back. Thus other firms were set up and gradually the area was covered. At the same time, purchasing firms were set up in France to ensure that the American shops were always supplied with goods: Paris had up to 13 of these. In the 1870s there was at least one firm in all the states of Latin America, apart from Paraguay: there were ten in Rio, six in Montevideo, five in Buenos Aires, five in Valparaiso and in Santiago, four in Guatemala, three in Mexico, three in Santa Fe de Bogota, two in Lima, one in Cochabamba, La Paz and Aréquipa, and doubtless another in Brazil; as well as two in Colombia, one in Equador and one in Venezuela which were established later and were somewhat shortlived. From there, the Alpine merchants tried to establish themselves elsewhere. Around 1865, a small colony settled in Petrograd, whilst others tried their luck in Istanbul and Turkey, and in North Africa. Others set up in business in Sydney selling fabrics, then went to Nouméa where they won the contract to provide supplies to the prisons and then went into the cafe business. Others went to Bombay and Hanoi. The latter, who had first set up in business in Mexico, then established a firm in Montevideo which they left to their nephew when they went to set up the business in Hanoi, thus continuing in the traditions of the great eighteenth-century networks.[70]

Barcelonnette in the Ubaye valley invested exclusively in Mexico. The first trip was undertaken in 1820. In 1846, there were 46 retail firms.[71] French intervention, which made settlement easier, also meant that, in addition to the Mexican market, the French army and Imperial Court were also potential customers.[72] By that time, a sales force covered all of Mexico and the pedlars from Barcelonnette, who up until then had bought goods from the English, the Germans and the Spanish, who controlled the market for wholesale goods, now opened up purchasing branches in France and England. From 1890, these families went a step further in their distribution business by building department stores in Mexico, similar to those which had been built in Paris, with names like Le Palais de Fer, Le Port de Liverpool, Le Centre Mercantil, Le Port de Veracruz. . . . Alongside these, they set up 110 shops across the entire country. In 1910, the year of maximum prosperity, they opened 214 shops which served as a base for the travelling salesmen, all originally from the home village, who criss-crossed Mexico.[73] The Mexican Revolution spelled the end of this prosperity:

> without this troublesome revolution, [wrote Pedro Fortoul to his family in 1913] I would perhaps have gone to France, but what can I do? – the few savings that I might have had, I invested in industry and in the agricultural and mining businesses, along with many of my friends, and that's worth practically nothing now; I've got to start all over again. Things are bad inland; Zacateus has been looted, the Jacques family have had their shop burned down and ransacked: in Durango all the French businesses – the Lombards and the Bovallons etc. – have been looted and burned down.[74]

These firms only recruited people from the home village. When there were no longer enough young people in the family to fill the gaps, youngsters from the village or the valley took their place, both in the Mexican firms and in the firms in Queyras.[75] Once again, employees were recruited through a guarantor: debt bound the migrant hierarchy together and guaranteed the power of the employer, since a migrant's departure cost a lot of money:

> You will have to give him a thousand francs for his outfit. The firm will take care of his purchases in Paris. He will also need six hundred francs to buy a third-class passage on the ship. On top of that, you must given him two or three hundred francs to tide him over for the rest of the journey.

In 1910 it cost 1,900 francs.[76] There were few families who could afford to pay the cost of the voyage and the outfit and they were forced to borrow money, either in the valley or directly from the business that was taking the youngster on. In return the boy was bound to the Mexican firm for a minimum period of three to five years, 'the symbolic length of time for the debt to have run its course'.[77]

Just like the apprentice of the old merchant traditions, the newly arrived immigrant was subject to his master and worked only for him: he was not allowed to change employers or get married. Once he had served his apprenticeship, he climbed more or less quickly through the ranks of the business and saved his salary until the amount he had put aside was enough to allow him return to the valley, leaving two-thirds or three-quarters of his capital in Mexico, and live off the income from this. He could then get married. He had to spend between five and fifteen years in Mexico before he could contemplate returning. The migrant's social origins played a large part in how long he stayed there and the likelihood of his returning.[78]

Control and selection were present at all points in the migratory chain. They were present where the migrant set out, in the role played by the guarantor who introduced the child into the business, and in the obligations which were created for the family by forcing them into debt to pay for the journey. When he arrived, all his material and recreational needs were taken care of by the community. He was fed and housed, but the money for his board and lodging and for the furniture with which he was provided was taken out of his salary. Thanks to the charitable organization which was formed in 1842, and the links which it had with other French associations (the gym club, the cycling club, the French Club, the philharmonic society, the choral society, the 14th of July society, the French guild) and the Saint-Louis-des-Français church, his free time was nothing of the sort. The company hostels organized gatherings of employees from different department stores and they were invited regularly by the French Club; lastly, all were obliged to go to the French parish church

so that they may meet in Christian surroundings, carry on their customs and traditions and perhaps, who knows, rediscover a certain flavour of France.[79]

Emigrating, which for most of them would be permanent, was initially presented as a temporary move. It was based on an illusion, that of democratized merchant apprenticeship, which was open to all and not, as in previous centuries, just to the sons of merchant families. The outfit which was put together before the migrant's departure was the symbol of this:

two pairs of shoes without studs (which I had never come across); two three-piece suits, like those which my uncle from America used to wear; a bowler hat and a trilby! Four shirts, not forgetting the starched sleeves, and three vests. I wondered what possible purpose all this could serve; three pairs of longjohns; a dozen handkerchiefs; six pairs of socks; four splendid ties and basic bed linen. It was all brought to me at the hotel. What an honour![80]

His return was present, symbolically, in his departure. At the end of a traditional apprenticeship, the apprentice was given a collar, a shirt, and some underwear to lend him a certain elegance when he returned home. Now, right from the moment he set out, the pedlar appeared to himself as he intended to look when he returned, unaware that his chances of returning were slim. The success of some pedlars kept the dream alive of making a possible success out of emigrating. Indeed, the first pedlars to return, between 1860 and 1865, had superb villas and grandiose monuments built for themselves; they held receptions, balls and banquets, which perpetuated the magnificent lifestyle to which the returned migrants had become accustomed on the other side of the Atlantic. This way of life illustrated the success of the migrants and stimulated the imaginations of those who were not part of it.[81]

In actual fact, very few came back; one in ten, on average. 'Out of 100 young people aged 20 who set out between 1870 and 1892, 77 were still alive at the age of 45 and only ten had returned home.' According to Arnaud, who provides these figures, the other 67 'were defeated by the struggle and dragged out their miserable existence, not daring to come back'.[82] This didn't mean that they set up in business in Mexico however, and for the most part they remained single.

At the end of the nineteenth century, political upheavals and economic crises in Latin America meant that profits became more uncertain and this type of migration or 'large-scale venture' – whether of individuals or by organized networks – disappeared.[83]

The emergence of the travelling salesman

The return to the old peddling structures should not conceal the modern innovations; in working solely for one firm, the last of the mountain pedlars had, in fact, become travelling salesmen. The restrictive nature of the structure in which the migration of itinerant merchants took place meant that the move from pedlar to travelling salesman was extremely specific. In fact, in the traditional areas where migration took place, it was not the natural development of the profession: we saw in chapter 4 that sales representatives were primarily recruited through other channels, heedless of the structure of relationships in the home village, which was henceforth unable to offer the degree of control over men and their property which previously constituted the strength of the migrant merchant networks. Only a few of the old-style pedlars became part of these new business circuits.

However, at the beginning of the twentieth century some pedlars – such as François Balme from the Dauphiné – managed to sustain a special relationship with certain firms without, however, becoming sales representatives in the strict sense of the term. In addition to the fabrics and items of clothing that the pedlar had always carried in his cart, he also began to take orders for goods using catalogues and samples, which replaced many of the goods previously bought at the start of his campaign. He bought and sold on credit terms only very peripherally, contenting himself with deducting his commission as intermediary between the business and the clients, and with ensuring that the goods ordered were delivered.[84] At the same time, commerce increasingly gained the upper hand over farming, and François Balme set out earlier and earlier, and returned later and later, only coming home for a few weeks in August. But this timorous entry into the new distribution circuits remained marginal, all the more so because, as of the end of the nineteenth century, businesses preferred to tap their markets by mail order. The Frette business, originally a Grenoble firm, thus managed to become established across the Italian market by publishing sumptuous catalogues and sending them to those shops which were likely to stock their products, with the business partners undertaking to travel and make the necessary contacts for the expansion of the business in person.[85]

Like the 'Manchester Man', these men who canvassed their market with catalogues and samples altered their sales techniques. They played on the idea of respectability and on the established nature of their business in contrast to the perception of the itinerant pedlar as a disturbing and despised figure. Like François Balme, they approached their customers by means of calling cards and sumptuous headed paper, which concealed their itinerancy and left the customer believing that they owned a solid business in the city.

Finally, there was one last type of peddling which developed out of the areas in which certain luxury products were manufactured, independently of the existence of a tradition of migration. The 'alabaster salesmen' from Volterra thus gradually developed as an organization throughout the nineteenth century and at the beginning of the twentieth. At the outset, a few manufacturers of alabaster went into business together to sell their goods in Europe and America. Then, from 1850, their sons and grandsons went on regular trips to sell the family products. Their passports reveal how far afield they travelled: Paris, London, Hamburg, Bremen, Rio de Janeiro, Constantinople, Rumania, Portugal, Spain, Havana, China, Japan and Australia. As well as the finished object, many took blocks of stone with them which they worked on wherever they were;[86] thus craftsmanship augmented merchant income.

The ways in which words developed are a clue to the tensions and difficulties experienced by the itinerant merchants in defining their identity. The permanency of the official term of 'pedlar' conceals the profession's history. In effect, the administrative labels did not record the changes in peddling activities and many pedlars no longer recognized themselves in the proposed classifications and refused to adopt them as their own. In government surveys, and especially in censuses, they kept silent about their occupation, preferring to put themselves down as farmers or land-owners.[87] They liked to style themselves merchants, sometimes specifying their particular field. This attitude was a systematic one, as true of the florists selling seeds and plants, whether in France or abroad, as of the spectacle-makers who had exchanged their pack for a small suitcase and their traditional selection of goods for spectacles.[88] Louis Giraud from Venosc who was in the plant business in France styled himself as either merchant florist, plant merchant or horticulturist, and from 1877 adopted the title of merchant horticulturist. The bookselling pedlars from Cotentin called themselves 'stallholding bookseller', 'book merchant' or simply 'merchant bookseller'.[89] Traditional peddling, which, swept along like everything else, had become something different in its attempt to adapt to changes and survive, had experienced a drop in its status, which was reflected in the pedlar's unease in stating his occupation.

This rejection of the term 'pedlar' by those who still saw the activity as a profession meant that the meaning of the word gradually became more precise, and its usage was confined to the packmen who had no fixed campaign. At the end of the nineteenth century, the word found itself sidelined and devalued, and new classifications were created. Effectively, sixteenth and seventeenth century texts recognized three categories of pedlar: 'merchants trafficking in . . .', 'petty chapmen' and 'haberdashers'. In the eighteenth century, *pedlar* became a more general term referring to all migrant merchants; in the nineteenth century the classification was initially a somewhat uncertain one and the term varied from one administrative document to another. In passports in the first half of the century, they were referred to as 'merchant-pedlars'. In the latter half of the century, since the sums payable were different, the register of trading licences made a distinction between pedlars who carried a pack and the stallholding merchants with their beasts of burden, with a final distinction for those who travelled around in a cart concerning the number of beasts pulling it. Between themselves, they referred to one another as 'travellers'. After 1870, the word *pedlar* gradually disappeared; and they found themselves called 'merchant' opticians, ironmongers, florists – or even flower senders or horticulturists – or 'merchant' something else. The pedlars had once again become merchants, just as the richest inhabitants in the village had been several centuries earlier. Lastly, the sales representatives also wanted to disassociate themselves from a profession which was no longer respected and wished to be called 'merchant-travellers' and nothing else 'for both moral and professional reasons'.[90] The word had thus run its course and once again conjured up the same images as it had given rise to at the end of the Middle Ages: the pedlar, excluded from the world of work, had once again become the 'fraudulent beggar', suspected of all crimes and debaucheries.

The death of peddling in Europe, marked by the great variety of pedlars, can be seen as symbolic of the migrant merchants' final attempts to adapt to the explosion of new sales methods which were forcing them to the fringes of the market. The increasing number of sales outlets, the new distribution networks, the opening up of the rural areas and, of course, the rapid development of mail order – all made them redundant as intermediaries.

8

The Culture of Itinerancy

These 'travellers' who came from the furthest-flung regions, who were at once strange and familiar to the inhabitants of the regions they covered, were the meeting point of several economic and social functions. They were eagerly awaited in the villages they travelled through for the dreams and the objects they brought with them, and, at the same time, repulsed because they were an unknown quantity and their apparent freedom was disturbing; and, moreover, opposed by the sedentary merchants who were fearful of the competition. Yet the vast majority of them had hearth and home, a family to feed and their own good name to protect or gain. Between these representations and tensions, the pedlar's own relationship with the settled way of life varied depending on the era and the place he occupied in the migrant hierarchy, although it was always ambiguous. Arising from the conflicting and hostile social values of itinerant merchants and sedentary merchants in the lowlands, these manifold tensions were intensified by the specific practices of a profession which was based on merchandise, novelty and itinerancy. However, they also created specific cultural phenomena.

In the lowlands: attraction and repulsion

The normative discourse of scholars which we have used to introduce the portrayal of the pedlar proposes a sociology of the profession which is both unstable and undifferentiated: according to this, the places and the specializations change, but all itinerant merchants were people who had little, united in their common marginality, and who had to be held in check. The pedlar was effectively reviled and obstructed everywhere and before the middle of the nineteenth century there were very few who spoke up to put forward a different reality; with the notable exception of England where, as early as the middle of the seventeenth century, there were men found to defend in Parliament the essential role played by the pedlar and his respectable connections, and to situate the debate within the context of the struggle between different distribution methods.[1]

From the point of view of the itinerant merchant, the double identity which the regular pedlar had gradually acquired through always visiting the same places was based on a tension arising from an imbalance between conflicting social positions, which were both, for a time, equally untenable. The regular pedlar knew the villages he covered as well as he knew his own and yet he was still perceived by the villagers as an outsider who was not to be trusted; a character on the fringes of society who could not be assimilated into the village hierarchies – unaware that, in his own village, he was one of the top land-owners, numbered amongst those who held municipal office, who was a consul in the seventeenth century, and a mayor in the nineteenth. He and his fellows were seen as nameless foreigners, all exactly the same and considered as one person, from one end of Europe to the other: in France there were the 'Dauphinés', the 'Gavots' and the 'Gascons'; in England, the 'Scotch Drapers' and the 'Manchester Men'; and the 'Saphoyer', the 'Augstaler', the 'Gryschneyer' and the 'Brysmäller' (from Prissmell, now called Alagna) from the German-speaking countries.[2] Such terms, in which differences in status had been ironed out so that only the place of origin stood out, registered both rejection and contempt. Spread by the sedentary middle classes who were opposed to the competition which the itinerants posed, this linguistic marginalization entered into the language and became part of the vocabulary of insults and of proverbial 'wisdom'. There was a Swabian saying that all Jews, itinerants, Savoyards and the like ought to be thrown into the same pot;[3] in German-speaking countries, to be a 'Saphoyer' was also to be a crook or a forger, half a Jew or 'halbe juden'.[4] The term 'pedlar' had derogatory connotations everywhere.

From the start, the complaints lodged by the guilds as well as the bans promulgated by the urban authorities used the non-differentiating collective term of place of origin. Their arguments veered almost surreptitiously from one linguistic register to another more abusive one, from the singular to the plural and from the plural to an uncontrollable mass; or from questions of merchant activity to accusations of stealing, from references to the man to references to the foreigner. In Berne in 1523, there was a call for measures to be taken against foreign pedlars – these *Kräzenträger* and carriers of lice[5] – and, in 1556, a sentence was passed outlawing *Schwaben, Waalen ... Brysmäler und Gryschneyer.*[6] In 1590, seven years after the decree issued by the archduke Ferdinand against the *Welsche Krämer*, a notice relating to those of doubtful reputation linked together Savoyards, pedlars and gipsies. From the seventeenth century, from Switzerland to Brandenburg, the Diets were bombarded with complaints against the migrants, who were described as 'a veritable deluge' [*Überschwemmung*], or 'a plague on the land' [*Landplage*].

We shall not go into any further detail concerning the endless ways in which the sedentary merchants and the guilds excluded and harried the pedlars in their efforts to drive them even further away from their own markets, or to make itinerant commerce a virtual impossibility. By increasing the number of constraints and bans, they aimed to demonstrate to everyone that, although they were tolerated, these men were none the less different and dangerous and had to be watched closely. As long as the townspeople were getting something out of them, repeated regulations and harassment had been more effective in formulating the negative image of the pedlar – which had been branded for so long in the collective imagination – than in creating any real obstacle to their trade.

The negative image of the pedlar which scholarly or official discourse created, and which literature imitated, remained in the popular imagination until the profession died out. He was the scapegoat, the immediate suspect whenever a theft had been committed or there was a suspicious fire: as early as 1565 in Glaris, Johannes Markandi from the Aosta valley was automatically thrown into the cells because he was suspected of belonging to a band of pillagers, bandits and arsonists. When it was discovered that he was innocent, he was released.[7] In Meaux in the seventeenth and eighteenth centuries, illegitimate pregnancies were always attributed to a passing merchant or carter.[8] They were the favourite suspects when there was rioting or violence and, once peace had been restored, they made convenient culprits. Moreover, the police reports to the police chief provided him with a ready-made classification of those dangerous social groups who needed to be watched carefully, with 'stallholding merchants, pedlars and second-hand dealers . . .' at the top of the list.[9] The itinerants' foreignness and bad reputation was thus reinforced at the same time as reassuring the sedentary population of its own worth. In Ireland during the troubles of the 1790s, all travellers were suspected of being conspirators and here too pedlars were the first to be arrested, even though they might be released a short time afterwards.[10] In France in the nineteenth century, if a pedlar was being pursued by his creditors, those in the lowlands would help to track him down, by indicating those from the same region who had been in the village for several generations: the old mistrust and xenophobia persisted, fuel for which was provided by the fact that many of these families continued to play the role of intermediaries in the peddling networks.[11] But this global rejection of the pedlar did not prevent a certain ambiguity in the way he was perceived: for a long time there were goods which only the pedlar sold, dreams and entertainment which only he brought with him and he was welcomed at weddings just as he was in the fairground.

More than all other pedlars, those who sold printed material were portrayed in a contradictory manner by the ruling classes, consumers and those who upheld the established order.

> The liking for literature is so widespread that it would be extremely difficult to put a total stop to this type of business. To do so would be to deprive of an important commodity the noblemen who live off their land, the country priests and the many private individuals who are cut off in small towns and villages where there are no bookshops.

Thus wrote Malesherbes, Director of the Library in France from 1751 to 1763, to the intendant at Besançon in 1752.[12] In Coutances, the inventories drawn up after death at the end of the eighteenth century confirm that so-called 'popular' literature was primarily of interest to the nobility and councillors, since they were the only group to own vast numbers of peddling chap-books.[13] Indeed, for those who liked printed sheets and the popular chap-books, the pedlar was eagerly awaited, an acquaintance known to you by name, because he was the person who brought you reading material that no one else could easily come by. In the battle between the police and the book pedlars, it was not uncommon to find the Parisians on the side of the latter:

> The police spies wage war against the pedlars, men who traffic in the only good books which can still be read in France, and which are therefore prohibited. These men are horribly ill-treated; all the police bloodhounds pursue the poor wretches, who are unaware of what they are selling and who would hide a copy of the Bible under their coat if the police lieutenant took it into his head to ban the Bible.[14]

In fact the pedlars' own declarations and account books bear witness to the fact that the 'persons of standing' were great lovers of prohibited literature and, like Louis-Sébastien Mercier, valued these middlemen.[15]

Because of this, those who sold books had friends amongst the village elite, friends like Louis Simon, who lived in the upper part of the Maine in the Longaunay region at La Fontaine-Saint-Martin, away from the main road which led to Angers, and who waited for a visit from Louis Boistard, the book pedlar, the contents of whose pack could satisfy Simon's thirst for novels and lure him away from the presbytery library. Without Boistard, Simon would have had to have left the local area, walked to one of the villages on the main road and waited for a day when there was a fair where news and goods circulated.[16] Thus, the pedlar's customers would wait for him and for the books which he'd talked about the last time he passed through: they even did him a few small favours, such as storing his belongings and a few bundles of merchandise in a barn until he came again.[17]

But this sympathy was won in the face of fear and shame. Priests and right-thinking people were everywhere vigilant. Parish priests never missed an opportunity to point out that not all books were worthy. In Italy, as the pedlar approached, the priest might order the bells to be rung to protect his flock:

> Non essendo raro il caso che non appena loro entravano in paese con la cassetta dei libri a tracolla, il prete suonasse le campane a martello sollevando la popolazione contro di loro.[18]

In France, the country priest would inform the bishop that some of his parishioners were numbered amongst the pedlar's customers, and that he brought them 'books which were quite immoral'.[19] Beneath the merchant's affable facade the parish priest detected the sardonic smile of a Voltaire, his Protestant origins lurking behind his false humility. He was in turn a propagandist for socialism in 1850 and for defeatism in 1870: he was evil incarnate – and didn't people also say that, as well as the immoral books, he also sold arsenic?[20] The right-thinking press did not beat about the bush in calling him a 'travelling pimp', who inflamed the baser instincts so as to corrupt young girls, who 'stopped off in all the taverns and, armed with his box with the false bottom, wormed his way into houses when the father or husband was away'. Jean-Jacques Darmon offers a fine selection of such particularly vicious diatribes from the mid-nineteenth century, when the book pedlar was painted as a member of some evil brotherhood 'having its own leaders, discipline, rules, passwords and rallying cries', whose only goal was to inflame the 'passions which endlessly exploit distress' and to leave behind him only 'darkness, hatred, turmoil and destruction'.[21] When, in 1861, the Minister of the Interior expressed astonishment that Charles Bouvier should have been banned from peddling by the prefect when 'his file contains nothing unfavourable, and the books he peddles are all authorized', the prefect told him by way of reply that Bouvier sold Protestant works and that, generally speaking, 'pedlars are more often concerned ... with preaching and spreading propaganda', that they were 'itinerants in the pay of foreign powers'.[22]

In this context, companies whose business relied on peddling had great difficulty in gaining recognition for the role played by the pedlars and the respectability of their work:

> Monsieur le Préfet, because of its size, our factory located in the Moselle producing prints and pictures takes its place amongst the major industries. We export our products to distant parts and also sell throughout France via merchants, who in their turn sell to the multitude of pedlars who cover the country. The just law which has meant that the peddling of books and prints may no longer be practised unrestrictedly, has not affected us, since we only publish religious and moral prints and pictures and others, of inoffensive nature which are intended for children. However, this law has

substantially paralysed our sales in France. We have the honour, Monsieur le Préfet, of sending our catalogues to your attention, so that you may judge them for yourself, as they have been judged in the Moselle department where all prints, images and books are registered; then, should merchant-pedlars approach you to request permission to sell our goods in your department, you may immediately be enlightened as to the nature of our publications.[23]

From the moment that there was popular involvement in politics, the government, caught between the desires of the people, an acknowledgement of the essential economic function performed by the pedlar and the fear that the intellectual influence of the texts the pedlars carried would be exploited, opted for close controls and monitoring of peddling. From the middle of the nineteenth century, the fear of immoral books being available to the common people prevailed over the convenience afforded to the elite classes (who had no real need of this any more) and the respectability which certain publishers claimed. In the end, only consumer loyalty checked the war waged by the government against the pedlars.[24] The circular of 12 June 1851, which was closely echoed by the report produced in 1858 by the Committee studying peddling, signalled that henceforth the dominant view in France – despite the hope that was entertained of using this capillary distribution network – tended towards banning the circulation of printed matter:

Eight million immoral books spread throughout our villages and our rural areas by a thousand hands . . . , such was the situation in 1847. . . . If peddling can only operate under such conditions as these, then it ought to be banned outright. But eight million decent books, presented as a way of educating oneself to a population which is impatient of its own ignorance, which would introduce them to a world of virtuous emotions and righteous ideas after the day's toil, inspiring in them an act of worship towards God, a love of their country, and gratitude toward the monarch, and make the most illustrious names in our national literature familiar in every hamlet – these are incontestable benefits which no enlightened government should relinquish lightly.

In 1869, a writer from the *Siècle* newspaper vouched for the success of the repressive measures taken:

There are two Frances today, urban France and rural France, and they are separated by a virtually impassable Customs frontier, more terrible than the interior frontiers which were swept away by the 1789 revolution. . . . This inexorable frontier is composed of a whole series of laws concerning printing, bookselling and peddling. It is there to prevent the distribution of certain goods, which it effectively does, the goods in question being books, the food of thought.[25]

They kept close tabs on the profession as a whole, right down to the Barbary organ-grinders and street-singers: the former were only allowed to play tunes which had first been heard in official operas; and the latter had to have their musical score stamped by the police and could expect to have their licence withdrawn as soon as they improvised or took any liberty with the printed text.[26]

From 1627 to 1876, the Spanish authorities enacted a long series of measures which aimed to ban or, at the very least, to circumscribe the effects of the blindmen's activity, by attempting to stop them proclaiming the headlines from the *papeles impresos* (printed pamphlets) aloud, in particular aiming to prevent them from expanding upon these headlines. Documents emphasize the outrage provoked by their *cantares*, the *expresiones malsonantes, indecencias, y chocarrerías*, and the *anuncios impropios y a veces de naturaleza alarmante* ('the offensive, indecent and shocking expressions', the 'false reports, sometimes of an alarming nature') which upset public decorum and peace. Between 1836 and 1847, successive laws and decrees aimed to regulate both the blindmen and their utterances – to force them to announce only the exact headline from the *papel* they were selling and refrain from any further commentary – or, quite simply, to ban them from publicly proclaiming their wares, as in 1839.[27]

The battle waged against the pedlars in England was much less hostile and also over much sooner. It was not until the reign of William III that the complaints against the itinerant merchants – who bankrupted urban business by evading taxes through embezzlement – were embodied in law and a system of trading licences was set up, wherein there was an obligation to register and pay four pounds. A way round the law was soon found in the form of 'lending licences', which involved getting someone to lend you a licence for the time you spent in a particular village, should the authorities prove over-fastidious. 1704 was the year which signalled the end of the policy of official regulation: although the lending of trading licences was still severely punished, the law was back-pedalling: in the same year the itinerant wool and cloth merchants were no longer required to have a trading permit, then in 1717 the lace merchants were also released from this requirement and finally, in 1785, the rule was abolished for all merchants.[28] Respectable seventeenth-century society mocked the itinerant merchants no less for putting within everyone's grasp the fine trappings which they themselves enjoyed – fine lace, smooth gloves, finely carved combs, spectacles and soap. Songs from the Elizabethan era, such as the *Cries of London* – and Pepys was later to write the same thing in his Diary – relate how the availability of current fashions in all parts of the country made inferring social rank correctly from clothes both difficult and expensive, since the lowliest of peasant women could keep up with the rapidly changing fashions and dress like a lady.

Itinerancy and identity

As he travelled through the countryside, coming up against suspicion, regulations and denunciation, the pedlar learned to turn to his own advantage the image that people had of him. His demands, and the means he had at his disposal to get what he wanted, varied, depending on whether he was destitute, a regular pedlar or a merchant.

On the one hand, the destitute pedlars were part of the culture of itinerant entertainment, on public view: like the dropouts with whom they were classed, they set themselves apart by using a particular language or expressions, which were based on an inversion of standard values; hence, on a daily basis, they imagined a topsy-turvy world, a Land of Plenty; and found a common identity in their ridicule of society and the authorities, who kept them on the fringes of the community or had them locked up.[29] On the other hand, they were able to use the negative image which the sedentary population had formed of them to commercial ends. This can be seen in documents accompanying applications for peddling permits, in which they play upon their social marginalization, the fear which the ruling classes felt towards them, their own destitution, real or implied, their infirmity, and the image of the vagabond they might become. François Botrel has shown the adroitness with which the Spanish blindmen manipulated these different registers to gain official recognition of their brotherhood and the monopoly for selling printed sheets: when confronted with the law after being caught red-handed selling illicit publications, they played on their blindness, claiming not to know, or not to have recognized, the voice of their supplier. Should the falsehood be discovered, then the guilty blindman fled, leaving no trace; if he was eventually caught, then very little changed since he was able to plead poverty so as not to pay either the expected fine or the legal costs, knowing that, if the worst came to the worst, he would only have to stay in the workhouse for a short while.[30] Their strategy hinged upon apparent submission and concealment of the infraction until arrested, then taking refuge in silence: 'El Ciego está versado en la táctica de non rebelarse contra las leyes, contentándose con eludirlas hasta que se cumple un mes desde el día en que fueron promulgadas: entonces las infringe abiertamente . . .'[31] ('The blindman is well acquainted with the strategy of apparently submitting to the law, confining himself to dodging it until, a month after it came into force, he is able to infringe it openly.') This subculture, which made use of the stereotypes which defined it, allowed the blind brotherhood – amongst whose number were to be found several respectable publishers – to go about their business (of which a significant proportion was fraudulent) without too many hindrances: over a quarter of the 'romanceros populares' in the eighteenth century – not including those in which the information was actually false – were published with no place of publication or name of publisher, and the date was systematically omitted.[32]

The regular pedlar, occupying the middle ground between the destitute pedlars and the merchants, who knew the villages that he covered as well as he knew his own, who perhaps had a shop there for part of the year, lived a life of dual loyalties. The changes in geographical location with which his seasons were punctuated informed the most basic acts of his daily life, and emigration thus gradually became a possibility. In the seventeenth century, the Protestant merchants of Mizoen in the Dauphiné, who did business in Burgundy and lived in Lyon, Paray-le-Monial, Autun or Conche, made sure that the announcements of their forthcoming marriages were published in both places: 'announcements in the church at Mizoen, and in the church at Arnay le Duc, where the church-goers from the town of Autun worship', reads an entry in the Mizoen parish registers.[33] Their wills too convey how much they had internalized their double identity, such as that left by Hugues Gasques, a Catholic, 'merchant from Auris, doing business in Moulins in Bourbonnais', who foresaw that he might die in Auris or in Moulins, and who specified his last wishes accordingly. If he died in Auris, he asked to be buried there and charged his son and heir with organizing the saying of masses, alms for the poor and bequests to both churches – even though the majority of these were intended for the mountain village; on the other hand, if he died in Moulins, his brother-in-law Nicolas d'Heu would be responsible for everything with the help of his business partners; he would then be buried at Moulins, and, in the main, masses would be said and alms distributed there.[34]

Paul Delor, who was Protestant, 'a merchant of this town [Lyon], originally from Mizoen in the Dauphiné', asked to be buried in the cemetery closest to the Protestant church and distributed alms between the three places where he had spent his life: in Mizoen, he gave 60 livres to the poor and he also donated a capital sum of 200 livres, the interest from which was to support the clergyman; in Lyon, he gave 60 livres to the needy; and in Burgundy, the region in which he conducted his campaigns, he gave 20 livres to the poor of Arnay le Duc, and the same amount to the poor in Conche.[35] Equally, his brother Thobie Delor, who was a burgher in Lyon and an influential member of the Consistory, never failed to maintain a high profile in the village through his charitable donations.[36] Once established in town, these ex-pedlars continued to stamp their influence upon their home village: their donations maintained the churches and founded schools.[37] Similarly, those who had become rich and returned to spend their final years in their home region did not then forget the land in which they had made their fortune.[38]

In the same way the migrants from the Auvergne asked to be buried where they died; but they divided their charitable gifts and requests for masses between France and Spain. Pierre Montagne, a 'travelling copper-smith' from Escorailles who had been detained by illness in an inn, distributed his gifts between the places in which he had lived his life: in his own village he arranged for 160 masses to be said for his soul's salvation, gave 30 *livres* to the church council, 50 *livres* to the almshouse, as much again to the Carmelite brotherhood on condition that they let him have a Carmelite habit in which he could be buried, and 5 *sols* to every poor person who attended his burial. In Spain the coppersmith divided his legacies between Tourente 'where he had done business for almost all his life' and Valencia, the nearest big town. To the poor of Tourente he left 50 *piastres*,[39] and 160 *écus* to the Récollet order;* he requested that three masses be sung for him in the parish church there, and released from their debts all those who had owed him money in Tourente before he went into business with his nephew Jean Bourlanges. In Valencia, he donated 10 *piastres* to the hospital, 4 *piastres* to the 'caza de Miséricorde' and endowed 12 masses which he divided between the chapel of Saint-Jean de Latran, the Lady Chapel and the church of the Saint-Sauveur.[40]

Life in these communities was thus based on a village culture of absence, of an ever-possible departure, with never a guarantee of return. Whether absence was motivated by economy or as a means of assisting the family in building up its fortune, the possibility of leaving never to return cast its shadow over daily life in every family, even in the more prosperous families. In their wills mothers would make provision for the event that their son and heir 'out of the province or the kingdom at his merchandising business should not return here to enjoy or dispose of the aforementioned property' and appointed a daughter or, failing that, a niece, as a substitute heiress.[41] This culture of absence also explains why, in the Auvergne, the continuing family line tended to be ensured by the women.

At the other end of the peddling hierarchy, how did the *Juden, Italiener und andere Stümper*, as the Frankfurt merchants called them in 1699, manage to integrate themselves politically into the bourgeoisie of the Rhine towns, so different culturally from their own class?[42] One should not forget that Frankfurt was a free city within the Empire, directly under Imperial control, and governed by a Town Council which was run by old family lines and the 'bourgeois' classes of old stock. Right up until the middle of the eighteenth century, the refusal to assimilate foreign merchants – all the more so when it was a question of Italian Catholic merchants into a Lutheran town – by denying them full polit-ical rights and granting them only reduced rights (*Beisassen*), and by refusing to allow them the *droit de bourgeoisie*, was clearly a tactic to marginalize them. This also meant that they were forbidden to take part

* A Reformed Franciscan order. [translator's note]

in retail trade, suffered tighter constraints on their business, heavier taxes and were not allowed to own property within the city.[43]

To get around the political prohibitions which bore upon them, the migratory elite, who had chosen to become integrated into the city in which they had their business, implemented an original strategy based upon a policy of cultural activity which, in return, opened the doors of urban government to them. In addition to the three ways of infiltrating a city traditionally used by Italian migrants – taking advantage of their particular status as Milanese and Catholic subjects of the Austrian Emperor; weaving a web of credit by lending money to the princes, or even to the Emperor himself; and marrying German women – they also developed a new brand of cultural sociability, which they translated into the building of magnificent residences and patronage of the arts.

Four generations after the first Brentanos were identified in Frankfurt, Peter Anton, who was born in Tremezzo in 1735 where he spent his childhood, was the first of the family to integrate himself successfully into the city. After the death of his first wife Paula Maria Brentano, who was Italian, he married again to Maximiliane La Roche, who was of cultivated bourgeois stock. Her nearest and dearest made fun of the marriage and pitied poor Maximiliane, forced to leave the pleasures of the Rhine area to be shut away in a gloomy house and subjected to 'the smell of oil and cheese, and her husband's behaviour'.[44] Through this second marriage, the Brentano family became part of the social and cultural life of the city and moved in the same circles as the Goethe family. In the wake of the Seven Years War, in exchange for substantial loans and cash payments, Peter Anton was granted the right to live in the city and, in 1776, he bought a residence there, the *Golden Knopf* which he furnished in sumptuous style and where he entertained and gave lavish banquets.[45] The Guaita, Bolongaro and Jordis families followed suit and had *palazzi* built on the banks of the Rhine. These residences were the basis of a strategy of representation which led to the merchants' effective integration into the political community of the Rhine cities. This cultural strategy was responsible for the creation of the new 'art of the interior', which Goethe had dreamt of when he returned from Italy. Expensive pieces of furniture, collections of paintings, *objets d'art* and libraries were the basis of the new social culture. The Italians extended this into patronage of the arts, thus becoming involved in all cultural events and subsidizing the theatres.[46] In 1812, Anton Maria Guaita, a descendant of Italian pedlars, became the first Catholic burgomaster of the free city of Frankfurt.[47] Integration did not occur everywhere at the same pace; the early integration of the Italians and Savoyards and the independence of the native bourgeois classes from any overlord accounts for any discrepancy. In Fribourg, as early as 1715 the patriciate consisted entirely of men of Italian origin, with names such as Perola, Belmonte, Brentano, Ribola and de Casal; in

Soleure, the patriciate was composed of men from Savoy or the Val d'Aosta.[48]

However, integration was never total, and these new Germans were always suspected, rightly or wrongly, of giving their friends preferential treatment.[49] Italian cultural references remained important for their descendants. Peter Anton Brentano's children retained both cultures: all Clemens' writings were pervaded by Italian culture; whilst Goethe was to say of his sister Bettina, 'She is the most astonishing being in the entire world, she lies unhappily between all that is Italian and all that is German, moving from one to the other without ever settling.'[50]

These strategies were not exclusive to the Italian merchant-pedlars, and all such merchant-pedlars were conspicuous by the close attention they paid to the appearance of their houses and the luxury of their interiors. In fact, as Paul Guichonnet notes, the most beautiful houses in Baden and in Bavaria were those belonging to the Alpine émigrés.[51] In France, Pierre Goubert points to the remarkable nature of the houses that the Motte family, originally from Savoy, had built in Beauvais and details the wealth that they contained – wealth that was outside the experience of the people of Beauvais of the time – the silverware; jewellery; clothes made of silk, printed calico and muslin; tapestries and wall-hangings; as well as the provisions they kept in their cellar, where spices, coffee, sugar and chocolate were to be found in place of the traditional bacon. Thus in 1714, François Motte's young widow had a bedroom which was entirely hung with 'crimson damask trimmed with gold braid'; her bed was worth 1,650 *livres*, her dressing table 1,033 *livres*, her silver vanity-case, containing her boxes for powder and beauty spots and other fancy items, was worth 616 *livres*; she owned a harpsichord and 'opera music'. Pierre Goubert concludes that 'in the houses of these cloth merchants, the atmosphere of the eighteenth century – pleasant, elegant, luxurious and slightly wild – made an early appearance'.[52] In Lyon, Jacques Bérard's inventory was in similar vein.

Material and cultural ostentation was however more than just an element of a deliberate policy of integration into the ruling classes of the town: it was a cultural trait specific to the migrant merchants and was to be found consistently in their behaviour, in the mountains as well as on the road.

In the village; urbanity and the culture of appearances

Working alongside established businesses, handling the newest goods, playing upon the expectations of merchants who would only grant credit to those who were already allowed it, and living a splintered existence between different geographical and social horizons: such were the daily aspects of the migrant merchants' lives which influenced their way of life and thought, and which opened up the mountain villages. The presence of an urban culture of materialism in mountain villages which were apparently shut off from the outside world was part of a series of wider cultural transformations: the itinerant profession had lent the migrant merchants who practised it specific cultural traits, which were not merely borrowed from the city merchants whom they frequented. These traits had been forged in the contradiction between the logic of the market, which dictated that the migrant should eventually settle in the lowlands, and the logic which dictated that, for them, profit was principally to be gleaned from their mobility and through preserving their flexibility, which alone allowed them to change their place of business rapidly. This latter way of thinking, which produced flimsy fortunes, based on bits of paper, on credit which was based on yet more credit, and on goods which had endlessly to be circulated, sold and replaced by other goods, created types of business relationships which were likely to attract and sustain confidence and to force a way into markets from which the pedlars were normally excluded.

This culture of appearances, striking in the lowlands, was also to be found in the mountain villages. Account books and inventories carried out after death bear witness to the arrival of city goods and imported urbanity: new fashions relating to the home and to food were introduced into the mountain regions, offering fresh ways of doing things to those who played no part in the merchant trade. From the seventeenth century, the houses belonging to the peddling elite stood out from those of the other villagers by their size and the number of windows and doors; in Oisans, as in Savoy, houses that were virtually small manor houses were built.[53] Later on in the villages in the Apennine valleys, *casette americane* were built, with their intricate wrought-iron balconies;[54] in the southern Alps, columns and perrons distinguished the houses of the 'American' or 'Mexican' pedlars. In Corrèze at the turn of the nineteenth and twentieth centuries, Meymac was surrounded by a ring of mansions and opulent-looking villas, owned by the last wave of successful pedlars.[55]

The interior of these houses allowed a glimpse of urban sophistication. From the seventeenth century, the houses of the important pedlars in Oisans had chairs and tables in addition to the usual bed, chest and bench. Fabrics began to appear: bed linen, sheets, curtains, tablecloths and napkins; pictures decorated the walls and carpets covered the floor. Barthélémy Rome even had a Turkish carpet on the floor and two paintings on the walls.[56] The value of this country furniture alone came to 1,500 *livres*. Claudine Liothaud, widow of *Sieur* Vincent Pic, who did business in Italy, imported some of the Italian sophistication: a bed with linen sheets, lace cushions, a carpet; vast amounts of household linen in the form of sheets, napkins, tablecloths, lengths of refined fabrics and lace (14 ells of Pragela silk, 'large pieces as well as small'); a city

wardrobe which included stockings and handkerchiefs as well as che-
mises; and, as adornment, she owned 'six pairs of plaits for her hair',
rings (one, a turquoise, another 'gold with emeralds' and a third 'gold
with rubies' as well as other, 'small and less expensive rings'), two gold
crosses; and, finally, slippers for wearing indoors.[57]

In the mountains, the incidence of crockery in merchant homes had
multiplied, but although glass had arrived, there were still no forks – a
further sign that appearances were more important than civilized manners.
Walnut and olive oils were to be found in kitchens, and the better-off
also had soap. We have already seen what sort of items Jean Bernard
of Besse had in his 'bedroom'.[58] In 1685, as he fled the kingdom for
Switzerland, Jean Giraud drew up an inventory of the goods which he
was leaving in his houses in the Haut Dauphiné, noting those which
had been stolen after his first attempt at flight and those which he had
left in the safekeeping of friends. The decor of his house in Hières had
nothing to fear from a comparison with the decor of town houses: it
was furnished with curtains, two Rouen carpets, pieces of furniture and
ten pictures (three landscapes, and seven with gilded frames representing
the Seven Wonders of the World). His daughter played with a doll
which was dressed in silk and had cost 10 *livres*. The household linen
is more difficult to determine, since he took some of it with him, and
part of the inventory certainly refers to merchandise. We will confine
ourselves to remarking that he had a separate category for 'linen and
other items for women' which came to nearly 200 *livres* in value, with
an abundance of lace in bonnets and handkerchiefs. The table linen and
dinner service included vast quantities of napkins, tablecloths, dishes,
plates and tumblers; there was even a crystal cup. Finally, his collection
of books and his tastes demonstrated that, at the highest level, pedlars
had gained entrance to the cultural universe of the important merchants. His library comprised more than 80 volumes, two-thirds of
which were religious books.[59] He hid around 50 of them, and the others
were seized and burned by the clergy.[60] Giraud gives the titles of the 32
books from the 'store room' which the priest seized: amongst them
were 'a historical dictionary, three volumes of M. Spon's Voyage of the
Levant, two volumes of the history of Geneva by M. Spon, the story of
Alexander, the history of the city of Lyon, four volumes by Dubartus
[and] over 20 curious volumes bound in *bazanne*, on different subjects,
all new'. He also owned three violins and shared the contemporary taste
for scientific curiosities by keeping an ostrich's egg.[61] By way of comparison, in Rouen at the same time more than three-quarters of the
merchants did not own a single book, and of the quarter that did,
only a quarter of them had a library comprising more than 20
volumes;[62] and a century later in Coutances in Normandy, only houses
belonging to the nobility, notaries and clergymen had curtains and
wall-hangings.[63]

These inventories allow us to appreciate just how tenuous our classifications are, since these rural houses were effectively city dwellings, belonging to families who were divided between the city and the countryside and who moved constantly from one to the other. Classifying the peddling elite among the rural merchants means losing sight of the fact that they were also an urban elite.

The movement of men went hand in hand with the movement of goods. During the year, Jean Giraud's sister took charge of supplying the villagers with fancy goods and ornaments which she ordered from her brother. He sent her taffeta, red Chartres serge, cordelat, various silks, braid, gloves, an ivory comb, gauze, watered silk, black velvet, russet-coloured cloth, painted canvas, ribbons of all colours, brocade, guipure, printed calico, thread, a box, shoes and a muff. She also asked him for groceries, soap, a sugar loaf, charms, peas, grapes, vitriol and a gold ring. All these goods were thus in circulation in the mountain villages in the seventeenth century. Anne Giraud also exchanged fabrics for leather. Throughout the year, an exchange of letters or the fleeting visits of the merchants provided opportunities for the villagers to put in their orders. Right up until the profession died out, the pedlar took the place of village trade, which only became established in the mountain villages at a much later stage (in the twentieth century). When the pedlar returned, his cart was often so weighed down that his family had to go to meet him at the bottom of the valley to help him up the sharp bends in the road leading to his home.[64]

However, although the majority of the inhabitants of the village could thus be acquainted with new fashions and consumer goods, not all villagers had access to them, as the inventory of Georges Girard's house reveals in stark terms: the house had only 'a cubbyhole serving as a kitchen', equipped with a 'dresser which held the crockery', a pail for the milk, two old saddles to hold water, an iron trammel, a small iron cauldron, an iron pot, another pot made of red pewter, two seats, a chest with no lock, a cupboard for kneading bread, a bed with two sheets, four wooden bowls, four spoons (two made of wood and two of brass), an iron lamp, a hammer, an axe, two pairs of tongs; and the stables and the barn which were equipped with the minimum of farm tools. After practically every item the notary who drew up the invoice indicated that it was 'old' or 'broken' or 'only fit for firewood'.[65]

There is a lack of research on material culture elsewhere to allow valid comparisons. However, work carried out on inventories drawn up after death in Scotland demonstrates that the merchants were great consumers[66] and the first to acquire the newest goods on the market, those which – like watches or forks – indicated new ways of life.[67]

The chains of credit and employment which linked the mountain villages to the city were also cultural chains and were a way into a wider universe of thought. Through them, new religious cults became established in the villages, like that of the cult of Saint Rosalie, the Palermo saint, which was introduced into the valleys surrounding Lake Como, and to whom prayers were addressed during the Sicilian plagues of 1575–7 and 1624–5; this was an enduring cult since, at the end of the nineteenth century, the women from the Gravedona valley still wore the grey homespun Franciscan robes, now decorated with lace, as they had sworn to do several centuries earlier in a vow made to the same Saint Rosalie *'pel ritorno in patria degli uomini di quei Communi che erano in Sicilia a negoziare, dove infieriva la peste'* ('so that those men from the valley who were in Sicily conducting business when the plague was rife may come home').[68]

The peddling elite were also the privileged intermediaries of an intellectual openness between the village and the social circles which they frequented in town for business, or perhaps even for pleasure: the correspondence they maintained with the family who managed their village property and debts, the accommodation they provided for clerks for periods of several years, and their periodic visits to their home village all meant that the highlands participated in their expanded horizons. More than other types of peddling, book-peddling was particularly suited to the diffusion of ideas: one only needs to consider the rich correspondence which Joseph Reycend maintained in the eighteenth century with the Italian elite of the Enlightenment.[69] However, they were not alone and, in Clavans around 1815, the Abbé Col chose as the theme of his Pentecostal sermon to denounce the Enlightenment thinkers and

> the irreligion of those who believe themselves to be superior to others . . . who believe themselves too learned to be Christian, too high-up to lower themselves to the practices of religion.[70]

The concern with appearances was indisputably a fundamental cultural characteristic of the migrant merchant: it represented his principal 'capital', was a reflection of his wealth and hence it vouched for the amount of credit that he could be granted. Merchants based their money-lending on appearances, and they themselves recognized this. Raymond Bellet, a bankrupt pedlar, assumed the outward appearance of success to try his luck one more time: he returned to the village in a cart, played the rich man and borrowed money on the quiet to pay back his creditors in the village, who complimented him on and teased him about his sudden wealth. In the autumn he set off in similar fashion to do business and stopped off at Lyon at his usual suppliers, who would later confess that his smart appearance had tricked them and they had agreed to supply him with more goods than was wise.[71] Similarly, Noël Gille favourably impressed Paul Malherbe, the agent of the Société typographique de Neuchâtel, with his appearance. His 'heavily loaded wagon', with its 'wide range of goods' and the clerk he had with him won Malherbe's trust: 'his affairs appear to be in order: Unless he comes unstuck with the prohibited books which he sells so many of, I don't believe he will make a loss. Moreover he has a wife in Montargis' and, in return for around 10 *louis*,* he supplied him with 300–400 *livres* worth of books.[72]

Hence the amount of attention they paid to how they were dressed was one of the specific traits of the migrant merchants. The richest among them had very expensive clothes, and their wills give us information about particular items. Paul Delor left his 'dressing gown of Spanish serge and fur', his 'boots, spurs and sword' to his appointed heirs; and offered his sister-in-law 'an outfit of Châlons serge in whichever colour she chose'.[73] André Masson took with him to Paris two outfits: either he could go around dressed entirely in red with chausses embroidered with white tulle, or, more soberly, in a grey-brown garment, embellished with two white pieces of braid.[74] Antoine Guy, from Savoy, wore only white, grey or black silk stockings, of which he had 25 pairs.[75] In contracts of employment or apprenticeship, as well as the monetary salary there was almost always the gift of a few items of clothing. In exchange for a pair of shoes, a handkerchief, a collar, a hat and 35 and 32 *livres* respectively, Jacques Roux, a merchant from Coltines, took on the brothers Pierre and Guillaume Teyssal from Ussel as boy pedlars for three successive campaigns.[76] At the end of a five-year apprenticeship, *sieur* Laurent Eytre, a merchant from Hières who was living in Piedmont, promised according to 'his discretion' and 'choice' to give Jean Baille 'an outfit';[77] and, at the lower end of the peddling hierarchy, Pierre Berthieu promised to give Antoine Arnaud 11 *livres* and 'a hat and a pair of shoes' after eight months spent on the road with him as his apprentice.[78]

These clothes which the pedlars were given or which they brought back – with great importance being placed on collars, handkerchiefs and fine shirts – created a hierarchy of appearances which reproduced the peddling hierarchy, at the same time as distinguishing the migrant merchant from the other villagers. A man's status and creditworthiness were to be gauged from the whiteness of the clothes he wore. It was not a pronounced attention to personal hygiene which was being expressed in this way; but, through the desire for white linen, a culture of appearances manifested itself. For the elite classes of the seventeenth century, in the words of Georges Vigarello, a shirt 'washed' and 'displayed'[79] (in other words, it made its wearer look cleaner and drew attention to him); in the mountains the importance of the shirt was as a status symol. The language of insults conveys the symbolic importance of clothes. There could be no worse smear for Baptiste Picart, a pedlar from the Auvergne in Spain, than the rumours which went around the village: it was said that he 'begged for charity in Spain' and that 'just

---

* A former French gold coin worth 20 francs. [translator's note]

like a beggar, he did not have a shirt to his name'.[80] Gradually other
items of clothing also came to convey social distinction: the apprentice
pedlar was offered an outfit which would distinguish him in his bearing
from a peasant, the latter stiff and starched in his costume of drugget.
This attention to their clothes was common to all temporary migrants.
Martin Nadaud explains how, when the migrant returned to the village,
his appearance had to demonstrate his success to observers.[81]

Effectively, everything about the itinerant merchant meant that he
constantly had to reassure his suppliers and potential customers, especially given the intrinsic fragility of his fortune and the fear which he
inspired in the sedentary population. Moreover, as the elite in their
home village, they were duty-bound to flaunt their rank. Hence the war
of appearances was one form of competition in the village. In this
struggle for primacy, extravagent expenditure was a privileged weapon:
the 'Spanish' pedlars from the Auvergne made themselves conspicuous
by carrying daggers illegally: 'This is a common occurrence in Haute
Auvergne where the majority of the population carry these weapons,
having picked up the habit of so doing in the kingdom of Spain, where
most of them do business.'[82]

In the Ticino region, the women flaunted finery which had been
bought in Russia or Bohemia.[83] At the very end of the nineteenth century, the pedlar-florist who went to the market in the Bourg d'Oisans
every Saturday never missed an opportunity of strutting about wearing
a red fur hat which had been brought back from Russia.[84] The desire
for distinction was also conveyed in social rituals, and merchants would
have themselves buried in the Auvergne like rich Spaniards, and in
Barcelonette like rich Mexicans. Grandeur played a part in this culture
of appearances, exemplified in the altar ornaments, paintings and stat-
ues with which the migrant presented the village church on his return;
generous gifts which attracted the attention of bishops on pastoral visits, and still strike visitors today. The culture of appearances was also
behind the importation of architectural styles from the regions which
the migrants had penetrated. On this point, I am in agreement with Paul
Guichonnet who, contradicting Arnol Van Gennep's theory, ascribes to
the region's connections with Germany the bulbous architecture found
from the eighteenth century onwards in church towers in the mountain
region of Savoy, recreating the typical High German lines to be found
in the Tyrol, in Voralberg and in the Bavarian Allgäu. Paul Guichonnet
points out that their appearance coincided with the flood of migrants
towards southern Germany, and that such lines are moreover absent
from the intra-alpine valleys on the road to Italy, thus weakening Van
Gennep's theory, which attributes northern Italian origins to these
buildings.[85] It is also difficult to ignore the architectural kinship between
Saint-Martin de Tours, Saint-Martial de Limoges and the shrine at
Santiago de Compostela.[86]

Far from being an act of severance, in their encounters with the settled populations the migrants created cultures which were able to make use of and profit from the fear inspired by mobility, and turn different ways of life to their own account, offering both lowlands and highlands new ways of existing and thinking.

9

A Civilized Business?

Is it possible to gauge the part played by the mountain dwellers, who travelled the length and breadth of the countryside bearing goods from the town, in changing social practices? The intention here is not to discuss the complex problems of popular culture, but to emphasize the importance of pedlars in the transformation of European cultural practices. As a first step, this approach demands a knowledge of the goods peddled and the chronological order in which they infiltrated different locations and social groups. This framework, difficult to establish in view of the considerable unevenness in the state of advancement of studies on material culture in Europe, can function only as a starting point, because many of the social groups who bought the pedlar's goods used them in accordance with their own customs, thus deviating from standard usage and practice.[1]

The goods that were peddled

In addition to a structure which was particularly well adapted to the weaknesses of the economic markets of the time, peddling doubtless owed its success to its ability to offer luxury goods, goods which were new and often illicit, and at a better price than that asked by sedentary businesses and shops. Of course, the pedlar had more in his pack than these new goods alone, and the variety of goods offered, like the quantity, also depended on the pedlar's range: there was a vast difference between a packman with no equipment other than a wooden box, and a pedlar travelling with horse and cart. However, descriptions written at the time always stress the novelty of the articles which the packman offered for sale at village after village and farm after farm. Through the comments of some contemporaries, let us once again emphasize this essential feature of the pedlar's selection:

The pedlar, his pack on his back or leading a pack-horse, visited all the villages and farms. Not only did he sell scissors and spectacles, coloured handkerchiefs and calendars, but stuffs, fancy leather goods and watches and blocks, in fact everything which the village wheelwright and blacksmith could not make. He went everywhere.[2]

In Germany, satirical literature seized upon the figure of the Italian *Tabulet Krämer* and portrayed him with his box open in front of him, allowing a glimpse of oranges, lemons and 'fancy goods'.[3] In Spain, Don Huarte, the sub-prior of Roncevaux, accused the petty itinerant pedlars, with 'boxes full of useless, tawdry things' slung around their necks, of taking away bona fide currency and of leaving their own counterfeit money in its place 'as false as the dice they sell';[4] and when, in the sixteenth century, Spanish edicts forbade the sale of playing cards, the authorities remarked that the people subsequently obtained them from French pedlars.[5]

In England, as in France, the selection offered by a 'Scotch Draper' or a 'Dauphinois' who had a horse at his disposal was along the same lines. Its financial basis was a vast array of fabrics (cottons, muslins, percalines, calicos and silks) which alone represented over three-quarters of the pack's value; next came a sizeable quantity of haberdashery goods and trinkets; then clothing accessories and a few articles of clothing (gloves, socks, headgear, hats, belts and cloaks) and finally, some small luxury items: spectacles, fabric collars, bracelets, spices and objects used in country ceremonies.

Let us take another look at some of these itinerant merchants. Jean Bernard, a pedlar from the Haut Dauphiné at the end of the seventeenth century, kept certain goods up in the mountains which he peddled anew should there be no takers in the villages. His inventory describes the variety of fabrics (drugget, ratine, cordillat sheets, canvases and 'sewing silks in several colours'), lace, braid, silk ribbons, haberdashery, several pairs of new shoes, walnut oil, various knives and a few spices, including ginger; the fabrics alone made up more than half the total value: 282 *livres* against 133 *livres* for the rest of the goods.[6] The inventory of goods owned by the company which had been formed by Jacques Payen and the Diaque brothers, from Clavans in the Oisans, lists fabrics, needles, thread, pins, hooks, shoe buckles, buttons, spectacles and spectacle cases, mirrors, gloves, combs, garters, stockings, jerkins, writing cases, quill pens, knives, forks, laces, ribbons, lace and flounces, handkerchiefs, rosary beads, snuffboxes, a few rings, some spices (cloves, nutmeg, pepper), and foodstuffs (sugar, anchovies, olives, as well as tobacco), wax, white wine from Spain. . . . Each article was offered in a wide variety of textures, prices and quality; gloves cost between 5 and 12 *sols* for a pair, stockings between 12 *livres* and 30 *sols* each, hand-mirrors between 15 *sols* and 6 *deniers* depending whether they were gilded or backed with card – tin ones were worth 1 *sol* and 7 *deniers*.[7] Three items were to be found in the packs of all English pedlars, offering unbelievable luxury of variety and quality: lace, handkerchiefs and scarves. William Mackerell, for example, had 16 different types of lace for sale.[8]

The poorest pedlars, who sought light goods on which they could hope to make high profits, were keener than other pedlars to offer luxury and fashionable goods. They all offered holy pictures and devotional articles as well, and in certain regions had even acquired exclusive distribution rights.[9] At the beginning of the nineteenth century, the pedlar from the Italian valleys of the southern Alps had pipes, combs, knives, buttons, small bars of soap, pencils, spectacles, spectacle cases, rosary beads, earrings, clock keys, knitting needles, garters, small chains and crosses in his pack.[10] In France, those who peddled printed matter would always add, in varying proportions, 'fancy goods', ribbons and lace to their books, prints, geographical maps, playing cards and watches.[11] The 'Chamagnons', who were known for their renditions of laments and news items, also sold small haberdashery items and knick-knacks; some called themselves 'Doctor' and others tried to sell 'miracle-drugs'.[12] The Jewish pedlars who travelled all over England in the eighteenth century confined themselves almost exclusively to small luxury items: razors, knives, buckles, buttons, cheap watches, poor-quality goods, combs, mirrors, paper, pencils, quill pens, wax, patriotic and religious prints, scarves and thimbles. In fact, some of them, in collaboration with the Jewish London jewellers, specialized in the jewellery business alone and supplied the provincial middle classes with rings, watches, watch-chains, shoe buckles, snuffboxes, hooks and tea-tongs. As early as the 1790s, the itinerant jewellery business was entirely in their hands: the Sephardi pedlars, with their links to the Eastern markets, also carried a few spices.[13] In the nineteenth century, jewellery and watches formed the bulk of the 'cheap goods' brought back across the Atlantic by the pedlars from the Dauphiné and the Auvergne.[14]

What does this dialogue between the goods for sale and the customers reveal? There were three privileged categories of goods, all of which addressed the customer intimately and spoke to the imagination: there were cures for both body and soul; finery; and games. Mixed in with the essentials, with haberdashery, cutlery or ironmongery, these items were also part of a sales technique which exploited the useful articles to show off the new and the unusual, to encourage the customer to dream. Cures, either on their own or associated with other goods, were always to be found. Citrus fruits, for example, which Italians from the valleys around Lake Como offered for sale in Switzerland and Germany, were used as a pharmaceutical product – lemons in particular – as a spice and as a perfume. Throughout the eighteenth century in England, medicines were associated with peddling catalogues: as early as 1720, the Diceys had come to an arrangement with a manufacturer of medicines, and pedlars sold 'Dr Bateman's Pectoral Drops' along with their books; other publishers adopted the same system.[15]

The scale of distribution

It is difficult to assess the market penetration within families of the goods peddled, for three reasons. Firstly because there is an absence of hard facts. Secondly, because the pedlar did not hold a monopoly over the goods he sold – how does one distinguish between a watch acquired from a pedlar and one bought in a shop? How can one know for sure that a particular print found in a rural dwelling had really been obtained from a pedlar?[16] And finally, because many items are too personal or too perishable to be recorded in archives. Looking in the inventories drawn up following a death for the items which pedlars typically sold is fraught with difficulties because of the criteria for registering items and the nature of the goods which were peddled: how can one be sure that an item's absence indicates that the family did not possess it, especially since a vital part of peddling business lay in circulating everyday objects which were intended for use in private life and which, therefore, were very likely to escape being handed down anonymously, being passed on instead to a chosen heir. Moreover, finery, games, devotional objects and even jewellery are clearly underitemized in the inventories drawn up after a death.

However, the almost exclusive role played by the pedlar in distributing certain objects is indicated in literary works, linguistic usage, and occasionally by the quantities which were sold to pedlars. For example, in England at the end of the eighteenth century, the distribution of cheap watches was so closely identified with Jewish pedlars that such watches were called Jewish watches.[17] There has been little work done on the jewellery trade; however, some of the inventories drawn up after the deaths of watch and jewellery pedlars demonstrate that they also supplied a large proportion of sedentary business.[18] Moreover, the degree of precision with which certain categories of goods were labelled within the inventories was a mark of just how common, or uncommon, the object was and how much it was worth. Thus, in contrast to French inventories, the comparative carelessness with which textiles and clothes were described in those drawn up in seventeenth-century England reveals just how much these items had already become part of everyday consumption: some inventories confined themselves to mentioning 'all the linen', which might very well include table linen and curtains; then, after 1690, cushions were henceforth only rarely mentioned, so common had they become.[19] This information alone confirms Margaret

Spufford's conclusion that the pedlars were responsible for clothing seventeenth-century England and reinforces the view put forward by English historians who refer to the existence of a consumer society and mass market as early as the beginning of the eighteenth century.[20] More recent work allows us to qualify this proposed overall picture and to demonstrate that there were pronounced regional discrepancies and, within certain regions (such as the north-west), there was a marked contrast between town and countryside. Despite its great expansion in social and geographical terms, the boundaries of consumer society fell somewhere between craftsmen and minor farm workers.[21] However, it should be emphasized that these studies were not carried out with reference to the same commodities: the market for the more specific articles which point up these inequalities is not the same market as for textiles, or more particularly the market for clothes, on which the initial studies were based. As far as the market penetration of luxury goods is concerned, the discrepancies observed raise questions about the density of the commercial network, the significance of merchant activities in general and the distance from the place of the article's manufacture.[22]

Confining herself to tracing the history of a few objects which are significant in modernist terms, Laura Weatherill shows how unevenly they were distributed. The newest, and largely decorative products such as paintings and curtains, along with those that signified new ways of eating and drinking (the figures for which are not reproduced in the table in note 23) were almost entirely confined to the towns. Spectacles were more widely distributed but were three times more likely to be found in London than in rural areas, and twice as common in provincial towns.[23] The author draws two conclusions from her analysis of this uneven distribution. In order to understand how goods were distributed, she emphasizes the essential role played by the peddling profession (for example, country merchants owned just as many books and watches as city merchants, although watches were to be found in 21 per cent of inventories drawn up in the city against 7 per cent of inventories drawn up in rural areas).[24] She also points to the efficacy which was characteristic of the cities, for, like the merchants, farm labourers in the London region owned paintings and porcelain china; and spectacles were twice as common amongst the farm labourers in provincial towns as amongst those in country villages.[25] This analysis is confirmed by evidence from 553 inventories from the Jura region between 1760 and 1790:[26] rather than being a simple opposition between city and countryside, inequalities reinforced socio-professional oppositions. In the city, as in the countryside, 23 per cent of inventories relating to merchants included books (against 19 per cent in those inventories relating to craftsmen and 6 per cent for various categories of peasants). Furthermore, objects and pictures were most often to be found in conjunction with books: 60 per cent of the inventories that referred to a devotional object also included books. Just as with books, so too the peasant classes owned the fewest devotional objects: merchants and rural craftsmen owned 70 per cent of the knick-knacks and prints inventoried. However, the peasant who met his death on the road would often have a religious book in his pocket. We must thus attempt to understand why this book, which was not included in peasant inventories, was however found in inventories relating to the wealthier social strata.

These findings bring into question once again the models which propose that cultural change spread through imitation, the lower classes imitating the patterns of behaviour emanating from the upper classes, since they demonstrate that, in England, the adoption of new forms of polite behaviour and new tastes in interior decoration were less pronounced in the inventories relating to members of the gentry than in those relating to merchants. Despite the superior wealth and status of the former, they owned fewer paintings, spectacles, porcelain china, or even pewter or earthenware crockery and saucepans than the merchants.[27] Thera Wijsenbeek-Olthius makes the same observations for Holland, from an analysis of 2,000 inventories drawn up after death in Delft in the eighteenth century.[28] This uneven distribution of goods also indicates that the pedlar's initial role was as someone who could satisfy desires even if, as with today's advertising, in bringing new products to people's attention he thus created the need for them.

Despite their shortcomings, the inventories drawn up after a death enable us to make a preliminary evaluation of the cultural influence of the travelling merchants: they introduced comfort into English homes, including those of farm workers. A home was covered in fabrics, from the bed to the windows and the table: 'No country in Europe wears or uses as much fabric, and of such good quality, as do the English', wrote Defoe in the 1720s. In fact, one had to wait until the nineteenth century and the packs of the Dauphiné pedlars before the same wealth of variety of fabrics was to be found again. Whatever the value of the inventory of an English peasant, it always included at least two pairs of sheets, and between 1580 and 1680, when a farm labourer's wealth increased by 85 per cent, the value of his household linen increased by 271 per cent. All things considered, it was the poorest who profited most from the rise in home comforts. The variety of canvas and cotton materials sold were also used to make shirts and spare sets of clothes and underclothes: babies discovered nappies and women discovered braid, ribbons and lace to embellish their outfits. However, the figures from the end of the seventeenth century were still nowhere near those which, a century later, pushed England into the consumer society.[29] However, from the seventeenth century onwards the dense network of travelling merchants introduced new fashions, which symbolized a new way of relating to oneself and to others. The enthusiasm for household linen and the emergence of underclothes overturned accepted standards of modesty and altered the way the erotic was defined; and accessories, ribbons and lace blurred the everyday distinctions of social hierarchies.

Amongst the objects inventoried in England, the most notable growth occurred amongst those which were used for completely new purposes, relating to new table manners, new culinary techniques, new beverages or to the emphasis placed on home decoration. The most marked changes dated from the decade between 1705 and 1715.[30] Fabrics, watches and books, which were some of the most important peddling articles, were to be found across the country, thus vouching for the part played by itinerant commerce; whilst paintings, porcelain china and spectacles did not yet figure largely in this particular method of distribution, or, more accurately, related to types of peddling which were more specialized, less common, or more recent. For instance, the English pedlar did not sell porcelain until the end of the seventeenth century[31] and, during the same period, spectacles were almost unknown in certain regions (in 1675, only 3 per cent of spectacles were to be found in the diocese of Carlisle, and 6 per cent in Cambridgeshire) whereas they were already extremely common in other places: 34 per cent in London and 37 per cent in Kent. Another factor which facilitated the market penetration of new products was that their prices varied considerably and all could be obtained for modest sums of money. In England, the prices of paintings and pictures varied enormously, but many were put at less than a shilling each; spectacles cost between 1 and 5 shillings; a knife and fork might come to sixpence. Evidently, better-quality versions of the same object cost a lot more, but the important thing was that they could be found cheaply, thus allowing poorer people to buy them.[32]

Rural France of the same period did not fare as well. Using 231 inventories of the seventeenth and eighteenth centuries from the Meaux region, Micheline Baulant and Stéphane Bari have drawn up a list of the 50 most frequently found objects. In this list, only four items of household linen make an appearance: bed sheets, shirts, tablecloths and napkins.[33] Although before 1665, 32 per cent of inventories made no mention of any shirts, and after 1751[34] this figure stood at 7 per cent at most, none the less shirts continued to be made primarily from hemp and were utilitarian and resilient, and were not acquired from pedlars.[35] The first signs of a change in the level of rural consumption, with the cultural changes that that implied, only appeared in the Mâconnais region after the 1780s and 1790s.[36]

Although the information was not immediately obvious from inventories, one measure of the extent of the distribution of printed materials through peddling can be glimpsed in the pre-sale stages, in the information given by those who supplied the packmen. From the seventeenth century, England was swamped with 'chap-books' (books sold by pedlars): in 1664, in his London bookshop Charles Tias had nearly 100,000 copies of such books, costing twopence or fourpence. And he was far from being the only one to specialize in this market, which emerged in the 1680s and was shared between around 15 bookshops.[37] Cyprian Blagden puts the number of almanacs sold in England in the seventeenth century at between 30 and 40 million, at prices between two and seven and a half *deniers*, depending on the category of book.[38]

In the Diceys' catalogue in England, engravings were primarily divided between 'wood royals' and 'copper royals' of 25" by 20", representing more than two-thirds of the 1764 catalogue, with 334 'wood royals' and 406 'copper royals' (the corresponding figures for the 1754 catalogues were respectively 278 and 394). The 'wood royals' were sold wholesale to the pedlars for the price of a shilling and twopence for a 'quire' of 26 plain sheets, or for a shilling and fourpence for coloured sheets. The 'copper royals' were far more expensive: 2 shillings for a quire of 26 black and white sheets; colour doubled the price to 4 shillings and varnishing and spangling took it to 6 shillings. The pedlars took a 300 per cent profit on this type of article and sold the 'wood royals' for a maximum price of twopence plain and threepence coloured, and the 'copper royals' for fourpence plain, eightpence coloured, and a shilling if they were varnished and spangled.[39]

On the continent the expansion took place in the eighteenth century, when the book became a standard component of the pedlar's pack and the peddling networks that specialized in this type of business were created. Spectacular growth was to be found at the fair at Caen, to which the packmen from Cotentin came for part of their stock: the value of the trade in chap-books and prints increased 30-fold in 60 years. At the beginning of the century, it fluctuated between 200 and 300 *livres tournois*,* increasing to between 500 and 1,000 *livres tournois* between 1710 and 1717; then rose to 7,000 *livres* in 1761 and 1762, reaching a peak of 9,000 *livres tournois* between 1765 and 1767. Sales subsequently dropped off and did not again go above 4,000 *livres tournois*. Given the modest sale price of this type of publication, the peddling chap-books and prints were traded in quantities of tens of thousands at the Caen fair.[40]

Avignon too was an important centre of production for pictures, prints and playing cards which the Alpine pedlars then distributed throughout the countryside. Here again the sales figures allow us to pinpoint the extent of trading. On 30 August 1746 (at the beginning of the period when the pedlars came down from the mountains), Jean Jouve and Jean Chaillot, booksellers who were originally from the Dauphiné mountains, entered into a contract with a merchant-printer:

---

* *livres tournois*: *livres* minted at Tours. Money minted at Tours later became the royal money. A *livre tournois* was roughly equivalent to 20 *sous*: a *sou* being equivalent to one-twentieth of a present-day French franc, in other words 5 centimes.

the printer promised to supply them with 'thirty reams of the illuminated pictures called "Domino" in return for the sum per ream of 8
livres and 15 *sols* in French money, and also to supply and send them
ten reams of the same illuminated pictures on paper of double thickness
for the sum of 3 *livres*, 7 *sols* and 6 *deniers* in the above-mentioned
currency per hundred, all bearing the Domino picture on Toulouse
card, and in the same colours'. Jouve and Chaillot could sell these
pictures to smaller merchants for 40 *sols* per hundred for the singles
and 4 *livres* per hundred for the doubles, without being able to let them
go at a lower price unless it was to someone who would take at least
three reams at a time. The printer agreed to sell at the same price.[41]

There was a further piece of evidence of the extent of the market
penetration of printed materials at the end of the century, this time
relating to forgeries, the other important aspect of the pedlar's trade. In
August 1778, so as to be able to implement with a firm hand the new
regulations concerning the privileges provided for in the rulings of 1777,
the authorities offered to set the bookshops straight by stamping all the
forged books that they had in stock. The results of their visits demonstrated the scale of the circulation of forgeries: between May 1779 and
February 1780 more than 25,000 books were stamped at Hovius'
bookshop in Saint-Malo, and a few more again at Audran's bookshop
in Rennes and at Joseph Vatar's shop in Nantes. Around 177,000 forged
books were stamped in the bookshops across Brittany.[42]

At the beginning of the nineteenth century, the Rouen bookseller
Lecrène-Labbey offered the books in the *bibliothèque bleue* series at prices
between 4 *livres*, 16 *sols* for a dozen of the most expensive to 25 *sols*
for a hundred of the cheapest.[43] For the nineteenth century, Jean-Jacques
Darmon puts the number of volumes and booklets distributed by the
Pyrenean pedlars between 1847–8 at nine million; then at one and a
half million, or perhaps two million for 1855 (this figure does not
include almanacs, songs or newssheets) and he identifies short novels
and devotional books as being the most popular. For the year 1867, he
puts the number at 1,400,000 or 1,500,000.[44]

Thanks to the dispatch records we can put a figure to the output of
the Wentzel print factory – a small but not unimportant centre of
production within the context of total French output – for the 1860s in
France: it published two million pictures a year and, on average, 100,000
pictures were peddled every year in the lower Rhine regions. Taking
into account the number of inhabitants, this means that there was one
picture a year for every six inhabitants, and two pictures for each
inhabitant over a 12-year period. From the mid-nineteenth century, 90
per cent of the pictures produced were sent to Paris, whence they were
distributed throughout France by Pyrenean pedlars.[45] Even though the
number of pictures dropped, the distribution was on such a huge scale
that at the end of the nineteenth century each home boasted at least one

picture. Damaged pictures could be replaced: 'At the end of the year the house would be given a going-over; the calendar was torn down and replaced, the torn and dirty pictures were replaced by new ones and the old ones destroyed', a doctor wrote at the beginning of the twentieth century concerning Normandy.[46] In the previous century in northern France, Zola lingered over at least one picture in each of his descriptions of the interiors of houses – in the mining cottages, in the Maheu house 'beyond the varnished sideboard, the furniture consisted of a table and chairs in the same wood. On the walls violent illuminations, portraits of the Emperor and Empress donated by the Company, soldiers and saints gaudy with gold colouring, stood out cruelly in the pale bareness of the room';[47] in Pierronne's house, the picture was engraved and framed: 'such a light room, wherein there was a certain flirtatiousness, with gilded vases on the sideboard, a mirror, three framed engravings'.[48]

The same developments occurred in Spain in the eighteenth and nineteenth centuries: the format of the *pliegos de cordel* was fixed as a booklet of one or two pages bound with string, and simultaneously its distribution increased enormously.[49] The print runs give an initial indication of the distribution. The ream was the smallest print run (500 sheets, which meant 500 copies of *pliego entero*, or 1,000 copies of a *medio pliego*), but print runs could be as high as 3,000–9,000 copies. Through resale, exchange and reproduction these printed sheets then circulated throughout Spain. In the twentieth century the pedlars had them delivered by post, depending on the timetable of fairs and religious festivals.[50] Here again the prices were very low: from the seventeenth century to the end of the nineteenth century a 4-page quarto (or sheet of paper folded four times) 'relación' or 'romance' (*medio pliego*) cost around two 'cuartos' (= six-hundredths of a peseta),[51] then went down to five-hundredths of a peseta in the twentieth century. Prices varied in relation to demand, in other words depending on the topicality or success of the *pliego*, and could well double or even triple. Moreover the blindmen (and their wives or widows in particular) set up a newspaper lending system well before reading rooms were established (and, in any case, catering for a completely different public), which the second-hand bookshops protested against in 1814, and which counted in the blindmen's favour.[52]

In addition to printed material, the speed with which watches spread throughout Europe is a clear indication of the effectiveness of peddling, since they must have been sold primarily through this channel. In Holland for example, watches were almost unknown before 1690 (almost no watches appeared in inventories between 1677 and 1686): then, 30 years later, they were to be found everywhere – between 1711 and 1750, 83 per cent of farmers owning at least ten cows had a watch, as did 58 per cent of those owning fewer than ten cows (4 per cent of this group owned watches in the previous period), and 8 per cent of those who did not own a single cow.[53] In England the market penetration was slightly different: London, Lancashire and Kent were in the top group where every other inventory mentioned a watch, but watches were five times less likely to be found in Cumbria, Hampshire, and the north-west Midlands. Around 1700, the watch began to appear in working-class Parisian inventories (13 per cent of those relating to servants and 5 per cent of those relating to employees) and spread rapidly during the eighteenth century, since just before the Revolution 70 per cent of servants' inventories mentioned a watch as did 32 per cent of the inventories of other employees.[54] On the other hand, in Normandy just before the Revolution only the elite classes possessed watches.[55] Despite professional and regional variations, from one generation to another the personalized timepiece penetrated all sections of the population.

Another source of information – the reports written after a sudden death on the road – allows us to get closer to the relationship that exists between people and certain of their possessions, and to demonstrate to what extent the inventories drawn up after death could conceal the part played by peddling in the handing-down of certain items. Two studies, one concerning the Jura mountains[56] and the other looking at Lyon and the Lyonnais and Beaujolais regions,[57] listed the items that men and women liked to have in their pockets when they left the house. The conclusions drawn for both locations were identical: along with money, handkerchiefs, snuffboxes and knives, the items which the pockets of both men and women were most likely to contain were devotional objects – rosaries or scapulars – and devotional booklets. Hence, in the Jura, a peasant who had been struck by lightning had on him 'a pocket handkerchief, a snuffbox, a spectacle case with spectacles, a farthing which had been damaged by lightning, a devotional booklet'; all of them typical peddling articles. A peasant's son had in his pocket a copy of 'Devotional hours dedicated to the King'; and a beggar found dead on the road carried with him a scapular and a book of 'Hours dedicated to the King'.

In the Lyonnais and Beaujolais regions, 65 per cent of the corpses had a scapular, a rosary or a devotional book in their pockets. A soldier enrolled in the Picardy regiment, who was originally from Nîmes, carried with him 'a prayer book in the Italian language with crosses on both front and back, a piece of white wax about the size of a 30 *sol* coin, with the paschal lamb on one side and St Carlo Borromeo on the other, with a piece of paper wrapped around it on which was a picture of the sacred shroud'.[58]

The high incidence of these everyday objects, much higher than in inventories, clearly demonstrates that the inventories under-recorded personal belongings. These were objects which were handed down to a chosen person, and they illustrate the major feature of the peddling trade which was to offer intimacy, dreams and the thousands of small things that allow the affirmation of self.

Social uses of peddled items

Was the pedlar, whose role as intermediary is undeniable, a force in the standardization of tastes?

An analysis of the distribution of engraved images would tend to indicate this. The descriptions of the interiors of peasant homes by L. Steub reveal the huge explosion in prints from Wissembourg in Catholic Bavaria in the second half of the nineteenth century: inside the houses, pictures of saints rubbed shoulders with hunting scenes, scenes of peasant life, the Siege of Sebastopol and the battles of Magenta and Solferino. In 1869, Steub described alpine chalets decorated with pictures denoting Kabyle battles.[59] The practices of the booksellers in Cracow, Brünn (now called Brno in the present-day Czech Republic) or Vienna explain this choice of subject matter: they had a fixed selection of images based around religious, secular and military themes.[60] German pedlars who were appointed by the Wentzel firm joined forces with the booksellers in spreading them throughout eastern Europe.[61] By implementing a clever linguistic strategy, the Wentzel firm conquered foreign markets on the same basis. From a pool of ten languages, it created 28 combinations of captions: four languages formed the basis of these captions – first French which was to be found in 22 out of the 28 combinations, followed by German (18 combinations), then English and Spanish which were to be found, respectively, in 12 and 9 combinations. As a secondary strategy the firm also tried to conquer the Hungarian, Dutch and Portuguese markets, as well as the Polish market through the pilgrimage centre at Czestochowa.[62]

In the face of regional and local culture, the themes of the books and pictures so widely distributed by the Wentzel, Pellerin and Remondini firms[63] contributed to the spread of a common sensibility. However, to go on to say that the consumer of these prints, so prevalent across Europe in the second half of the nineteenth century, recognized himself in the pictures with which he decorated the interior of his house, or in the tasteless and fraudulent images of religious sensibility which he hung in his home, is a big step to take, for the function of these prints – in their exaltation of the romantic city vision of the countryside, their refusal of industrialization and their views of foreign cities, in themselves world tours of the imagination – was perhaps more about escapism than identification.[64]

Thus, as did the booksellers and pedlars, the public expressed its preferences rather than its tastes, since it too could make choices within a given range.[65] However, the trade took account of the preferences expressed since the pedlars would choose their goods according to the sales patterns, in other words, according to their consumers' choice. Indeed certain pedlars, like those from the Ticino region, had pictures destined for Catholics, for Protestants and for those of Orthodox religion in their small wooden trunks (called a *cassela*): hence the same crucifixion scene would have pious women at the foot of the cross for the Catholics and an absence of such women for the Protestants.[66]

Occasional publications, in common with the *pliegos*, also changed in response to the audience they were aimed at.[67] These occasional publications appeared at the end of the fifteenth century when publishers in Paris, Rouen or Lyon published the texts of letters recounting the most important events in Charles VIII's campaign as small booklets, generally of four pages. Then, at the end of the first third of the sixteenth century, the first reports of news items were published. These increased in number after 1550, and especially after 1580 when their distribution fell into the hands of the pedlars. These texts contained the characteristic features which Shakespeare had previously mocked in *The Winter's Tale*: the oft-repeated assertion – especially in the title – that the news reported was 'true' and 'current', whereas behind the packaging, the contents revealed a preference for the timeless and symbolic aspects of events, either real or invented. Hence the same stories were published over ten years or so in different towns, with changes only in places, names and dates to bring them up to date.

In the seventeenth century, alterations to the contents, look and format of the occasional newspapers, which reported sensational news items, showed that they were in the process of losing their middle-class readership and were instead explicitly addressing a less literate readership. These changes reveal a pursuit of lower costs and a closer fit with the style of the pedlar selling the newspaper. Thus, as soon as the *Gazette* appeared in 1631, the occasional papers quickly copied its format, just as the sensational rags of the nineteenth century were to adopt that of the daily newspapers. Although, indisputably, historical events were reported less often in the occasional papers after the appearance of the *Gazette*, they did not completely disappear and every time that something out of the ordinary happened, special editions were published, initiated by the printers and also by the pedlars. Towards the end of the seventeenth century, it was noticeable that many of the occasional newspapers which reported sensational stories became cruder in appearance – printed on low-quality paper with hackneyed contents and illustrated from roughly carved woodcuts – and were written by people who were more at home with the spoken language than the written: perhaps it was already the case – as it was often to be in the nineteenth century – that they were written by the pedlars themselves.

It is difficult to prove that the pedlars played a part in the creation of the texts they sold:[68] one would have to examine the catalogues of printers who had been pedlars or who had been linked to the peddling networks; but the archives are not forthcoming with this information. However, there are a few cases which prove that some of these texts were printed in shops owned by ex-pedlars. At the end of the sixteenth century Geronimo Galleri from Pontremoli settled in Oppenheim in Germany, where he sold books and printed small booklets.[69] In the nineteenth century certain of the 'Chamagnons' had newspapers printed at their own expense, men such as Petitpoisson, amongst others, who paid Cabasse in Epinal to print 4,000 copies of a report entitled 'Extract from the judgement of the Court of Assizes in the Vosges sentencing Pierre Virion to the death penalty'.[70]

The production of *pliegos de cordel* in the nineteenth century also testifies to the vital part played by the blind pedlar in manufacturing the product: he knew what sort of news the public wanted and how they liked to hear it related. His role was a double one: first of all he created the texts around the expectations of his audience and the subjects it liked to hear about; then, through his recital, he introduced scholarly texts into the popular vernacular – Shakespeare's Autolycus did very much the same thing. Moreover, the blind pedlars often produced the printed material they sold. Although they rarely wrote the texts or put them into verse, it was often the case that they financed the operation. Caro Bajora points to the example of a blindman who, between 1855 and 1860, had a poet working for him, to whom he gave detailed instructions about exactly how he was to put into verse a particular crime of passion, or the heroic deeds of a bandit, or a theft compounded by murder. He then asked the poet to rewrite ten or so medieval texts, retaining their element of 'terrorifico'.[71] This author, and others who remained anonymous, help us to understand why a work's authorship was often attributed to the blindman himself: in a sense, they too *were* the authors of the works since they created them or chose them according to their public, whose tastes they knew well.

On the fringes of the market in printed matter, songs were indissociably linked with the pedlar, whether he sang his goods out loud to attract the customers, or whether singing was his only means of existence. The lyrics took up current topics, those being discussed in the newssheets of the time, echoing them and spreading them further:

> in Paris, everything is the subject of a song, and whoever has not been mocked in song, be he the Marshal of France or a hanged man, will remain in obscurity whatever he does.[72]

The studies carried out by Rolf Reichardt and Herbert Schneider reveal a song revival between 1762 and 1787, with 'romantic' songs on the wane and political songs becoming popular: 'satires' – which ridiculed those who were opposed to the *philosophes* and mocked the private lives of certain prelates, politicians and ladies of the court – experienced a fourfold increase in number in the 1780s; songs about legal cases tripled in the last decade of the century; and those about the most sensational stories – like the affair of the queen's necklace, or the court case won by Lally-Tollendal to clear his father's name – as well as songs recounting the current political situation, doubled in number in the 1770s.[73] A civil service clerk wrote to the Paris police lieutenant in 1788, 'one observes that the songs which are proclaimed in the street to amuse the rabble communicate the idea of freedom to them, and the vilest scoundrel sees himself as being the third estate and no longer respects his superiors. Nothing would be more useful than to censure all these Pont Neufs severely so as to snuff out this spirit of independence . . .'[74] In the final two decades of the *ancien régime*, with their memorable refrains and catchy tunes, the pedlars denounced the Court and the injustices in the system, lending support to those who, both in Paris and in the provinces, believed that things could not continue as they were.

Hence, via the city and through the goods they supplied, petty merchants brought within everyone's reach a culture which would transform ways of living and thinking. As each example demonstrates however, the relationship was neither simple nor straightforward. If watches reflected a need to synchronize one's personal time with that of others, this did not mean that time was equally valued by everyone; just as books were not always bought to be read, as is demonstrated by those found in the pockets of illiterate peasants from the Jura mountains or from the Lyonnais region. These people did not have books to hand so that they might be deciphered and read, but because they were sacred objects, invested with powers of protection, magical and reassuring. By introducing the printed and written word into the home well before illiteracy had been eliminated, by spreading – refashioned and magnified – the official news as well as information that the authorities would have preferred to conceal, the pedlars brought the population into contact with the printed word and developed a desire for access to it.

Other objects, which were essential milestones in the process of the civilization of manners, were similarly appropriated by the masses, who thus gained access to the culture which had produced them. The use of the handkerchief – like the fork – was an essential step in the 'civilization of manners', in so far as it was identified with civilized behaviour, which requires that natural functions be carried out indirectly.[75] The handkerchief – which was an obligatory item in every pedlar's stock – is proof of the distance and the discrepancies between the normal standards of civilized behaviour, the use assigned to an object, and the use to which it was put by the person who acquired it.

The invention of the handkerchief dates right back to ancient times, but until the sixteenth century, in the absence of pockets, it was customary to attach it to the left sleeve.[76] In the sixteenth century it was not very common: 'The lower classes wipe their noses without handkerchiefs, but amongst the middle classes, it is accepted behaviour to wipe one's nose on one's sleeve. As for the rich, they carry handkerchiefs in their pockets. . . .'[77] One might therefore think that its wide distribution by the pedlars in the seventeenth and eighteenth centuries attests to the advancement of good manners in the countryside.

When one looks more closely at the stocks of handkerchiefs which were peddled, one is struck by the variety. Although there are differences which can be perceived between pocket handkerchiefs and neckerchiefs,[78] an analysis of these objects blurs these distinctions. The bills kept by Auvergne merchants between 1770 and 1790 show that they played no small part in the packmen's largest purchases. A closer look at the transactions cannot fail to surprise: Espezolles, an 'itinerant merchant' from the Auvergne, filled his pack with 22 different types of handkerchief, from simple white cotton handkerchiefs to Rouen handkerchiefs (made of linen and cotton), to handkerchiefs made of silk or madras, handkerchiefs 'Cholet style', and handkerchiefs made of printed calico.[79] Similarly, the English pedlar, no matter how small his business, always carried with him a batch which varied in price and quality. In his pack, which was inventoried in York, Walter Martin carried 184 handkerchiefs of nine different types, valued between 6 *deniers* and one pound 10 *deniers* each. At the other end of the country, in his shop at Downham Market, John Mackie had handkerchiefs of Manchester cloth, of fine cloth at 6 *deniers* each, Scottish handkerchiefs for 8 *deniers*, silk and cotton handkerchiefs for 9 *deniers*, and handkerchiefs of 'good and bad quality silk' for a third of a *denier*.[80] Finally, at the beginning of the nineteenth century, between 21 October 1818 and 17 February 1819, over six visits to three different firms located in Avallon and Chalon-sur-Saône, Noël Gourand from Clavans in Oisans bought more than 230 dozen fancy handkerchiefs – printed calico handkerchiefs with red, white, deep blue and green backgrounds, handkerchiefs decorated with bunches of flowers, bordered with buttercups, carmelite handkerchiefs, at least seven types of Scottish handkerchiefs, 'Cholet style' handkerchiefs, handkerchiefs of madras silk, and several dozen handkerchiefs for mourning and for snuff – against only a few dozen 'pocket handkerchiefs'. The range of prices in each category was no less wide, and varied depending on size and quality: hence one could find handkerchiefs of printed calico for between 5.50 francs and 36 centimes – prices were usually around the 2 franc mark. The price of the Scottish handkerchiefs varied between 2.10 francs and 14 centimes; the prices for the pocket handkerchiefs varied only between singles and doubles – from 8 to 15 centimes.

The splendour and variety of handkerchiefs and, ultimately, the small proportion of pocket handkerchiefs ordered by the French packmen would lead one to believe that the peasant classes seldom used them for the purpose recommended by polite behaviour, and that they were used in other ways. In the seventeenth century, *Les lois de la galanterie* advised that one should display one's handkerchief during conversation:

After a certain amount of time has elapsed, you should pull your handkerchief from your pocket and flourish it a little, to show off its size and
the beauty of the fabric rather than to blow your nose.[81]

Around the same time Tallemant des Réaux, the self-appointed chroni-
cler of the nobility's hesitations over the correct usage of these squares
of fabric, described how Croisille, whilst listening to his contract being
read out, 'had put his handkerchief on his head and had the tassels in
his mouth'; and how Hauterive de l'Aubespine blew his nose so forcibly
with one finger that a guest, fearing an outbreak of gunfire, cried out
'Monsieur, you're not hurt?'[82] The handkerchief that Tartuffe pulled
from his pocket as he exclaimed, 'Oh, heavens, I beg you, before you
pray, cover your breast that I may not see it'[83] also demonstrates the
ambiguous uses to which it was put. Since, within the nobility, there
remained a vast discrepancy between the discourses of polite behaviour
and practice, there are grounds for thinking that the country folk did
not blow their noses in the squares of silk and printed calico which they
were so fond of buying, but continued in their old ways, although the
manuals of etiquette of the time advised that such gestures were re-
stricted to children alone.[84] In the seventeenth and eighteenth centuries,
the handkerchief was undoubtedly seen in French rural circles as part
of the lover's discourse, just as it was a century earlier by the nobility;[85]
and in the English countryside[86] it was a sure sign of social distinction,
which indicates a specific appropriation (and not a delayed usage) of an
object which was used differently by the elite classes: away from aris-
tocratic models, rural society had its own fashions.

In the *Description des arts et métiers* published in 1780, in selecting
items for a typical trousseau, only handkerchiefs made 'of half-holland'
material or 'of cambric' were recommended. On the other hand, in the
trousseau which was offered to Mademoiselle de la Briffe, handkerchiefs appeared as swathes of material: '17 ells of cambric for two
dozen handkerchiefs'.[87] Did this mean that the handkerchief intended
for blowing one's nose, or 'pocket' handkerchief, as it was politely
called, was made at home and we must thus look for it in the ells of
material that the pedlar carried with him on the road? If this was the
case, then the inventories drawn up after death should leave some trace
of this family activity. Suzanne Tardieu, who has meticulously listed
those in the Mâcon area, has found traces of this in only two out of the
88 inventories scrutinized; on 12 August 1798 there were two and a
half dozen new handkerchiefs of linen and cotton recorded at the home
of Louis J., a merchant at Guinchay – a not very conclusive example
since, next to the kitchen, he had a room which he used as a shop, and
the inventory as a whole indicates that there was no distinction made
between goods for sale and items for domestic use. Secondly, on 14 and
15 June 1799, five new handkerchiefs with red stripes were recorded at

the home of Etienne G., a shop owner in Clesse.[88] In the list of the 50 most common objects found in inventories in the Meaux region, there is no mention of handkerchiefs.[89] On the other hand around one man in four, and a little more than one woman in four, who died whilst on the road had a handkerchief in their pocket – checked, striped, made of cotton, calico, linen or even silk;[90] it is highly unlikely that it was used for purposes of hygiene. Curiously, the presence of money in the pockets of corpses almost doubled between the seventeenth and eighteenth centuries, as did the incidence of these fanciful handkerchiefs. Doubtless, like Joseph Roth's Slovenian chestnut seller who knotted the small coins he earned inside his red handkerchief, they often used it as a purse.[91]

Moreover, studies of the changing fabrics used for handkerchiefs show that, in France, hemp was consistently the most prevalent during the entire period, with linen making a diffident appearance in the seventeenth century, followed in the eighteenth century by fine linen and cotton fabrics – cretonne, cambric, lawn (but in almost as marginal a capacity as linen in the seventeenth century and replacing the uses of the latter – for certain types of men's shirts, aprons, linings for hats and collars, for instance).[92] Hence the fabrics from which the handkerchiefs which the pedlar sold were made were not widespread and were apparently not meant for this purpose. Finally, perhaps one should ask whether handkerchiefs were not excluded from inventories. We know the limits of the sources and how items were underestimated, household linen in particular,[93] but the absence of the handkerchief seems too general for it to be only the source that was at fault. One had, in fact, to wait until the nineteenth century before the pocket handkerchief gained in importance in the pedlar's pack, and was seen in terms of hygiene. From the seventeenth century the English pedlar's pack reserved the largest space for single handkerchiefs, and the inventories of the period reflect this.[94]

Before leaving the subject of the handkerchief it must be pointed out that it was also used as a medium for other branches of knowledge: in 1688 the first printed English silk handkerchiefs appeared, bearing news and information – one detailed the terms of the Treaty of Utrecht, another reproduced a road map of the country for pedlars, complete with the places and dates of the fairs. In France in the nineteenth century, soldiers bought handkerchiefs which were manuals for horse-riding, gymnastics and the proper maintenance of arms. It was also one of the vehicles responsible for the spread of popular culture.[95]

Across all of Europe, at different times, the peasant classes appropriated this object of civilized behaviour and attributed thousands of other uses to it, invested it with other needs, other ways of communicating.[96] This square of material became multiform and multipurpose: a purse, a love signal or present,[97] a mark of social distinction, more appropriate for wiping away tears than a cold. It is a fine example of the discrepancies and of the inventive uses which each group brought to bear upon the articles of urban civilization, which the pedlar supplied in abundance, with no instructions attached.

As they travelled, the pedlars offered objects and ideas which helped the recipient to consider his or her own personality and to mould it. Ultimately, whatever the manner in which these objects were used, the fact that they provided one and all with the opportunity of expressing his or her own irreducible individuality is in itself something new and radical.

Conclusion

At the end of our journey through the varieties of merchant migrations, which were simultaneously in competition with one another and interlinked, one certainty emerges: the profession of pedlar, hitherto considered as marginal, was in fact a multifaceted activity and a vital phenomenon in past communities. The history of peddling is the history of the related development of an economic phenomenon and the social structure of the village, and it recounts the double marginalization of both the profession and the communities that supported it. Effectively, between the fifteen and the twentieth centuries the influence and success of the merchant networks dwindled, signalling the impoverishment and the isolation of the regions in which peddling had its origins: as the monopolies which had been won by the migrants were demolished, the whole social hierarchy of peddling collapsed. In the end, the income from peddling dried up and the profession became an occasional refuge for the casualties of the job market.

Rediscovering the links between social and economic realities which had long been separate, and then re-establishing their development in all its complexity, was only achieved after a certain number of methodological shifts, of which I should like to underline the three principal ones. The first is a refusal to accept, a priori, the images of the profession that the societies of the time had created, or to take for granted the social and economic marginalization that these images convey. The search for the sedentary roots of the itinerants, against an urban discourse which classed them as rootless and itinerant, led to the adoption of a more oblique standpoint which looked beyond the individual figures themselves and concentrated on the social construction of which they were a part and which created them.

The second strategy was not to describe pre-categorized groups – classified in terms of their level of wealth, their geographical area (either urban or rural), or place within the business professions – but, on the contrary, to research independently the common typologies and the links which bound individuals together, and to sketch out groups on this basis, classified in terms of the pattern and nature of these links. This process allowed me to highlight two realities which are too often neglected by classical historiography: that of the wide family network which encompassed the nuclear family (in contrast to the archival sources, which naturally foreground the latter); and that of credit, which occupied a central position at all levels of the merchant structure, and was as much an economic as a social relationship.

The third methodological shift led me not to see mobility as an obligatory – and transitory – rite of passage between two states, but on the contrary to believe that it, like the sedentary way of life, could also be a way of existing and appropriating territory.

These methodological shifts, which highlight information previously concealed by the traditional frameworks of social history, are echoed in the way in which the material which is the basis of the historian's analysis is used: my reconstruction of phenomena has often been achieved in the face of – or in spite of – archival classifications and the superficial meanings of documents. The sources that discuss pedlars, which historians have naturally consulted, can be divided into four groups: administrative sources (lists of trading licences, government surveys and registry certificates of birth, death and marriage, etc.) whose aim was to keep a tally of the pedlars, so that they could be controlled and made to pay their taxes; complaints by sedentary merchants who sought to have them driven out because of the competition they posed; legal and police sources which, by definition, only dealt with the exceptional and marginal cases, whether arrests for theft, vagrancy, begging, illegal trading or the failure of a business; and, finally, the fictions. By this I mean what lives in people's memories, in the memory of words, in literature and illustrative sources. Nation states, jealous or wronged merchants, customers, spectators and descendants looking for their family roots were thus the principal authors of the documents which were immediately available. Listing them is almost sufficient to illustrate the picture of the itinerant merchant that their combined efforts painted.

In order to perceive a different reality, one must ask the archives different questions and find other documents in which the pedlars are not immediately or explicitly present. This means seizing on the traces they left of themselves as they organized their private and family lives and their web of relationships, in the family archives they kept, and in their own ways of exploiting the notarial and judicial systems.

In this game of hide-and-seek with the evidence – the pedlars' own and that of others – two separate realities have been partially revealed: the first demonstrates that peddling cannot be summed up solely in terms of the features unanimously ascribed to it by the various archival sources that relate specifically to the pedlars; the second sheds some light on the circumstances in which the texts themselves were produced, demonstrating how the traces that the pedlars left of themselves, carefully filed away in boxes, are physical proof of the battles and the issues at stake which led to them being produced at all. They thus reflect the dynamics and uncertainties of an evolving society, rather than reconstructing particular moments or situations. The sphere of activity in which these rather unusual weapons operate is primarily the sphere of imagination, in which they attempt to change the way in which things are portrayed so as to compel the adoption of a new division of power. The evidence they bring to light aims to become the framework for world views that are likely to justify or force a redefinition of the roles that each group tries to acquire in its attempts to dominate or repulse other social categories.

In this context, for the historian the silence of the archives is as eloquent as their utterances. Thus, the large numbers of pedlars taken into custody by the police would lead one to believe that they were deviants, if the police treaties did not inform us that the State used them as scapegoats to ease the tensions between divided communities. In return the pedlars exploited their marginal position which protected the freedom that was essential to their continuing wealth – or even just to their survival – and tricked their way out of all attempts to register their status, evaluate their fortunes, uncover their business connections or unravel their activities, leaving the historians battling with blank documents.

As soon as one considers these documents yielded by the archives as significant acts in an overall scheme, as being part of a battle, they lose their seeming innocence and become invaluable aids to those who are seeking to understand the dynamics and potential evolutions of a society: they reveal their essence, which is solely concerned with communicating the strategies and attempts of men to assure a future for themselves and for their social group. Because these documents are a source of information about the battles taking place, and because they have more to say about the informant than about those they are supposed to be describing, because they force the historian to ask him- or herself questions about the reasons why they were produced and about their numerous contradictions, they also compel him or her to undertake the slow and meticulous task of confrontation and of dialogue between all documents left by the groups involved. This view of the archive as being in motion, necessarily made up of conflicting realities and significant silences, allows one to grasp what were the issues at stake that produced these documents, and reveals as vital those phenomena which were previously forgotten or which, noted quantitatively, had been described as of marginal importance. The sweetest revenge for the sedentary middle classes on the migrant merchants must have been passing off as a social reality the myths which they had sought to establish concerning these groups, against whom they had long struggled in vain.

New research which allows new realities to emerge, hitherto concealed by traditional studies, also reveals social structures which are
sometimes blurred and sometimes escape the traditional categories used
by historians. It forces us to clarify certain concepts and to ask new
questions, particularly where the history of migration and trade is
concerned.

Two features distinguish the classic approaches to the question of
mobility. First of all migration is seen in dichotomous terms. The pairs
might consist of solely economic factors, like the opposition between
'pull factors' and 'push factors', which attempts to understand the reasons for departure; or they might also take into account the migrants'
culture and connect economic realities with the desire for the imaginary,
as does the sociological distinction between the membership group and
the reference group. Secondly, in applying these theories, mobility is seen
in terms of two separate geographical points (the point of departure and
the point of arrival) and two points in time (before and after).

Overall, the work done on migration in historical Europe adopts
these dichotomies and this approach, whether making the classic comparison between the point of departure and the point of arrival, or
comparing several immigrant populations in the same target location
or, alternatively, one single community in several target locations. Even
if the geographical areas are thus multiplied, it is always a question of
comparing sets of spatial pairs.

The migrant networks described in this book, however, prove that
emigration did not necessarily mean an economic and cultural break with
the home region. In the same way, the chains of credit and employment
which linked the peddling villages to the towns shattered the traditional
cultural opposition between town and country: the men who moved
between different locations, far from having to choose between conflicting systems of values, took on board and made use of the diverse
cultures they encountered. Because the desire to attain social status or
become part of the social hierarchies within the city remained foreign
to certain elements within the migrant networks, we can ask ourselves
questions about how identities are constructed: and we find that identity does not have to be built upon a defined geographical space but that
it can develop from a social space of relationships, that of a network
of relations and people from the same region as oneself, independently
of the geographical locations covered. From this we perceive the limits of
the approach to emigration which refers to two geographical points, of
departure and arrival, and to two moments in the migrant's life, before
and after.

Our analysis of the source communities teaches us that mobility can
be a way of occupying an area, and that it can support a society and,
independently of agricultural resources, create a dense human population. A settled way of life is not therefore necessarily the goal for which

all human groups are striving, any more than it is necessarily the reference point of all migratory movements. Hence one must not accept over-simplified dichotomies that see mobility in terms of attraction (pull factors) and repulsion (push factors), and the radical originality of migrant societies should be asserted.

The credit and labour which were the bases of these societies meant that the notion of solidarity was more complex, since the ties which bound the migrants to one another were not necessarily positive links (of hospitality, support and mutual aid) or neutral ones (a channel, a way into the city); they could also be negative, establishing dependencies which were likely to prevent the migrant from using the space in which he found himself for his own benefit. If, seen from an urban perspective, all the Savoyards, men from the Haut Dauphiné and other mountain dwellers discovered freedom and a means of support when they left the poor regions which were unable to provide for them, the migrant's perception and the possibilities open to him, trapped within networks of credit and dependence and compelled to work for the village's rich inhabitants, were very different. This same phenomenon was experienced completely differently by the elite classes who built their fortunes on the labour of these men, and by those who no longer had either land or labour to offer them. Rather than a natural or freely consented interdependency, it was a forced solidarity for those who had least, and a mutual dependency for all involved. Such was the foundation of these social structures, a guarantee both of their success and of their continuation.

Credit, which has been surely neglected by historians who are prone to measuring wealth solely in terms of ownership of property – especially when looking at rural societies – now appears to be a vital social link. The pedlar was at the centre of a web of credit, covering different locations and extending over different periods of time. It was the basis of 'paper' fortunes built up by the migratory elite. Thus redefined, the typical merchant – indifferent to putting down roots, always concerned with appearances, on the lookout for new items to acquire and put into circulation – loses the unconventional facet of his personality, encountered now and again, and becomes part of a merchant tradition with a secure presence in Europe from the end of the Middle Ages.

Highlighting these games of sleight of hand and hide-and-seek between the historian and his or her sources invites one to conclude by returning to the question posed at the beginning of this book: what is a pedlar? The definitions which were proposed, all inspired by the perceptions of the elite classes and the urban imagination, imprison the pedlar in over-simplified roles, in a marginality which it is no longer possible to accept. Moreover, they combine extremely diverse social realities in a single concept: what did migrants entrenched in the economy of their home village have in common with blindmen from Portugal and

Spain who exploited their disability to control the market for printed booklets; or with those who had experienced a drop in status and who were drawn to the trade in illegal books? Some pedlars remind one irresistibly of the present-day mafia organizations, others make one think of the beginnings of a wretched and lonely delinquency, yet others of the charity organizations. Commonplace definitions and categories have prevented us from seeing what links the merchant trading on a large scale in the newest goods, making only occasional appearances in the village, to the wealthy itinerant merchant with his well-stocked cart who covers the towns and the markets, the packman who adds a couple of almanacs and songs to a few haberdashery goods, and the tramp who exhibits his marmot, or tries to get by on his limited know-how.

These questions encouraged me to embark upon the indispensable task of redefining activities and men, the better to interpret the respective roles of the principal actors, and in particular that played by the State, since the history of merchant networks was initially played out in the cracks and weak links in the institutional, legal and police structures. This book attempted to follow the trails and go in search of these shopkeepers and pedlars who provided the consumers of historical Europe with precious commodities, creating new needs amongst their customers, ensuring the continued fortune of the family clan and its clients, and bringing promises of far away within the reach of one and all.

Appendix
List of Booksellers from the Briançonnais Region in Eighteenth-century Europe

Aillaud from Monêtier, bookseller in Lisbon (end of the eighteenth century – beginning of the nineteenth century).

Aillaud from Monêtier, bookseller in Coimbre (second half of the eighteenth century).

Aillaud, Daniel, from Monêtier, bookseller in the Hague (second half of the eighteenth century).

Aillaud from Monêtier, bookseller in Paris (end of the eighteenth century – beginning of the nineteenth century).

Albert, Mathieu, from La Batie des Vigneaux, bookseller in Rome (end of the eighteenth century – beginning of the nineteenth century).

Albert from Arvieux in Queyras, bookseller in Madrid (end of the eighteenth century – beginning of the nineteenth century).

Aubanel from Aspres in the Hautes Alpes, born in 1720 and, from 1746, worked for Giroud; bookseller in Avignon in 1756; in 1767, in association with J.-J. Niel and the widow Barret and sons from Lyon, he bought back the Giroud business.

Baile from Briançon, bookseller in Genoa (end of the eighteenth century – beginning of the nineteenth century).

Barthélémy, Jacques, from Monêtier-les-Bains, bookseller in Madrid in the shop facing the Puerta del Sol fountain; son of Marguerite Ourcel, he married Magdalena Bonnardel; in 1754 he went into partnership with his brother; he was an agent for the Cramer family, for Gosse and for the Société typographique de Neuchâtel; also called Don Diego Barthelemi.

The Bérard brothers, booksellers in Seville, agents to the Cramers (second half of the eighteenth century).

The Bertrand brothers from Monêtier, booksellers in Lisbon, agents for the Cramers and for the STN, recorded up until the end of the beginning of the nineteenth century; Jean-Joseph, succeeded by Joseph and then by the widow Bertrand.

Bez, Pierre, from Monêtier, bookseller in Barcelona (end of the eighteenth century – beginning of the nineteenth century).

Bez from Monêtier, bookseller in Pernambuco, Brazil (end of the eighteenth century – beginning of the nineteenth century).

Blanchon from St Chaffrey, bookseller in Parma (end of the eighteenth century – beginning of the nineteenth century).

Boeuf, Louis, from Briançon, bookseller in Turin (end of the eighteenth century – beginning of the nineteenth century).

Boeuf from Briançon, bookseller in Genoa (end of the eighteenth century – beginning of the nineteenth century).

Bompard from Villeneuve la Salle (Monêtier), bookseller in Genoa in the seventeenth century.

Bompard from Villeneuve la Salle (Monêtier), bookseller in Naples (end of the eighteenth century – beginning of the nineteenth century).

Bompard from Villeneuve la Salle (Monêtier), bookseller in Rio de Janeiro (end of the eighteenth century – beginning of the nineteenth century).

Bonnardel, Joseph & Dubeux, Jean-Joseph, booksellers in Lisbon in the mid-eighteenth century; agents for the Cramer family and to Gosse, they bought the bookshop from Reycend-Gendron in Lisbon; in 1771 Claude Dubeux, Jean-Joseph's brother, went on a business trip to Paris, giving as his address 'M. Gendron, quai des Augustins, Paris'.

Bonnardel, Louis Antoine, bookseller in Lisbon in the second half of the eighteenth century; agent for the Cramer family and for Gosse. The Bonnardels also had shops in Barcelona, in Cadiz and in all the major seaports.

Bonnardel from Briançon, bookseller in Turin (end of the eighteenth century – beginning of the nineteenth century).

Bonnardel, bookseller in Rome, eighteenth century.

Borel and Co. from Villeneuve la Salle (Monêtier), booksellers in Lisbon, agent for the Cramers, for Gosse and the STN (mid-eighteenth century – beginning of the nineteenth century).

Borel from Villeneuve la Salle (Monêtier), bookseller in Naples (end of the eighteenth century – beginning of the nineteenth century).

Bouchard, Joseph, from Monêtier, bookseller in Florence; an agent for the Cramer family and for Gosse, he was a publisher and bookseller (eighteenth century).

Bouchard from Villeneuve la Salle (Monêtier), bookseller in Bologna, cousin of Joseph Bouchard in Florence (eighteenth century).

Bouchard from Villeneuve la Salle (Monêtier), bookseller in Rome, agent for Gosse (eighteenth century).

Bouchard, Pierre Louis, bookseller in Metz, agent to the Cramer family (second half of the eighteenth century).

Bouchard, bookseller in Chambéry, to whom Jean-Jacques Rousseau went to buy books when he was at Charmettes (*Confessions*, book VI).

Bulifon, Antonio, from the Dauphiné, publisher and bookseller in Naples (eighteenth century).

Carilian-Goeury and Bousson, of Briançonnais families, booksellers in Paris (end of the eighteenth century – beginning of the nineteenth century).

Chaillot, Jean, from St Didier en Dévoluy, born in 1706; in 1735 he was a pedlar selling ironmongery and haberdashery goods and books in Avignon; in 1756, in association with his brother-in-law Jean Jouve, he was a bookseller in Avignon; he died in 1772.

Chaillot, Jean-Thomas, the oldest of Jean's sons and his successor as haberdasher, ironmonger, printer and bookseller; then a bookseller in Avignon in 1773; married the daughter of the bookseller Jean Fabre, originally from Rodez; died in 1813.

Chaillot, Jean-Etienne and Pierre, Jean-Thomas' sons; continued their father's business throughout the nineteenth century.

Collomb, Hugues Gaëtan, from Monêtier, bookseller in Lisbon, agent to the Cramer family and to Gosse (second half of the eighteenth century).

Collomb, Joseph, from Monêtier, general agent to the Cramer family in Marseille (second half of the eighteenth century).

Colomb, Jacques, from Monêtier, bookseller in Granada (second half of the eighteenth century).

Colomb, bookseller in Milan (second half of the eighteenth century).

Delorme, Jean-Baptiste & Guibert, François, from Monêtier, booksellers and printers in Avignon, agents to the Cramer family and to Gosse (eighteenth century).

The Dubeux brothers from La-Pisse-en-Vallouise, and Claude Dubeux, from Briançon, booksellers in Lisbon (end of the eighteenth century – beginning of the nineteenth century). See Joseph Bonnardel, agent for the STN. There are also references to a Du Beux, a bookseller in Lisbon.

Dubeux, Jean-Joseph, from Briançon, bookseller in Coimbra, agent to the Cramer family (second half of the eighteenth century).

Dumollard from Briançon, bookseller in Milan (end of the eighteenth century – beginning of the nineteenth century).

Eymard from Arvieux in Queyras, bookseller in Madrid (end of the eighteenth century – beginning of the nineteenth century).

Fantin and Gravier from Monêtier, booksellers in Genoa. Fantin left Genoa for Paris in 1796.

Faure and Bertrand, booksellers in Lisbon in 1755, agents to the Cramer family and to Gosse (second half of the eighteenth century).

The Faure brothers from St-Chaffrey, booksellers in Parma, agents for the Cramer family and for Gosse (second half of the eighteenth century – beginning of the nineteenth century).

Faure from St-Chaffrey, bookseller in Madrid (end of the eighteenth century – beginning of the nineteenth century).

Garnier from Briançon, bookseller in Genoa (end of the eighteenth century – beginning of the nineteenth century).

Gendron, Pierre, from Monêtier, bookseller in Lisbon, relative and associate of Joseph Reycend; Gosse's most important agent around 1740; in 1760 did virtually no business any more; settled in Paris in 1757, where he published Camoëns' work; also an agent to the Cramer family; sold his Lisbon bookshop to Bonnardel and Dubeux.

Gibert, Carlo, bookseller in Barcelona (second half of the eighteenth century).

The Ginioux brothers and nephews, booksellers in Lisbon, agents for Gosse (second half of the eighteenth century).

The Ginioux brothers, booksellers in Coimbra, agents for the Cramer family and for Gosse (second half of the eighteenth century).

Ginioux, bookseller in Porto (second half of the eighteenth century).

Giraud from Briançon, bookseller in Genoa (end of the eighteenth century – beginning of the nineteenth century).

Giraud from Briançon, bookseller in Rome (end of the eighteenth century – beginning of the nineteenth century).

Giraud, Jean's heir, bookseller in Murcia, agent to the Cramer family (second half of the eighteenth century).

Giraud, bookseller in Turin, agent to the STN (second half of the eighteenth century).

Giraud from Monêtier, bookseller in Barcelona (end of the eighteenth century – beginning of the nineteenth century).

Giraud, Laurent, from Vallouise, bookseller in Turin (end of the eighteenth century – beginning of the nineteenth century).

Giroud, (Alexandre?), bookseller in Avignon, agent for the Cramers (second half of the eighteenth century).

Giroud from Grenoble, bookseller in Grenoble, agent for the Cramers (second half of the eighteenth century).

Gravier, Martinez and Raimondo, booksellers in Malaga (second half of the eighteenth century).

Gravier, Thomas, from Villeneuve la Salle (Monêtier), bookseller in Rome (end of the eighteenth century – beginning of the nineteenth century).

Gravier, Jean, from Villeneuve la Salle (Monêtier), bookseller in Genoa 1756–60, then in Naples 1761–6; publisher and agent to the Cramers and to Gosse.

Gravier, Joseph-Antoine junior, bookseller in Genoa, one of the Cramers' bad debtors in 1762; Gravier, Yves junior, from Villeneuve la Salle (Monêtier), bookseller in Genoa and bad debtor for the Cramer family between 1765 and 1767.

Gravier, Yves and Jean-Simon, from Villeneuve la Salle (Monêtier), booksellers in Genoa. In 1870, Yves was an agent for Gosse (end of the eighteenth century – beginning of the nineteenth century).

Gravier, Jean-Simon, from Villeneuve la Salle (Monêtier), bookseller in Paris; he went into partnership with Pierre Joseph Rey and together they requested a patent to sell books in 1815 (Patent of 13 June 1816, no. 820); Jean-Simon went to Paris c. 1803 and died on 6 March 1839.

Gravier from Villeneuve la Salle (Monêtier), bookseller in Turin (end of the eighteenth century – beginning of the nineteenth century).

Gravier from Villeneuve la Salle (Monêtier), bookseller in Bologna (second half of the eighteenth century).

Guibert, Charles Michel, son of Michel Guibert of Avignon, born c. 1725. Apprenticed to F. Girard in 1743, then employed in C. Delorme's bookshop in Avignon in 1754 or 1755. There is no record of any book being published under his name and he died in 1789.

Guibert, Jean-Joseph, from Villeneuve la Salle (Monêtier), born in Turin; married Anne-Marie Josserand (widow of J. B. Delorme) in Avignon; bookseller in Lisbon with Reycend; died in Lisbon in May 1736.

Guibert, François, whose family was from Villeneuve la Salle (Monêtier); born in Lisbon in 1733, son of Jean-Joseph, brought up by Delorme in Avignon following the death of his father; in 1756 he went into business with Delorme; had a branch of the business in Cadiz; agent for Gosse.

Guibert, Joseph, from Villeneuve la Salle (Monêtier), bookseller in Bologna, agent for Joseph Bouchard of Florence (second half of the eighteenth century).

Guibert & Orgeas, booksellers in Turin, agents for Gosse (second half of the eighteenth century).

Guibert, agent in Marseille between 1783 and 1797.

The Hermil brothers, booksellers in Cadiz, amongst the Cramers' bad debtors in 1755.

Hermil, Antoine, bookseller in business with Rolland, and haberdasher in Naples; agent to Gosse (second half of the eighteenth century).

Jouve, Jean, son of Mathieu, from St Didier en Dévoluy: see Chaillot.

Mallen, Francesco, bookseller in Coimbra c. 1760–70.

Mallen, bookseller in Lisbon (second half of the eighteenth century).

The widow Mallen and sons, booksellers in Porto in 1800.

Mallen, Giacomo, bookseller in Valencia, agent for the Cramers (second half of the eighteenth century).

Mallen, Giambattista (Jean-Antoine, father and son), booksellers in Seville, agents for the Cramers (second half of the eighteenth century).

Margaillan, from Briançon, bookseller in Milan (end of the eighteenth century – beginning of the nineteenth century).

Margaillan, from Briançon, bookseller in Pavia (end of the eighteenth century – beginning of the nineteenth century).

Martin and Bertrand, Jean-Joseph, booksellers in Lisbon, agents for Gosse (second half of the eighteenth century).

Martin from Le Bez (Monêtier), bookseller in Rio de Janeiro (end of the eighteenth century – beginning of the nineteenth century).

Martin from Villeneuve la Salle (Monêtier), bookseller in Lisbon (end of the eighteenth century – beginning of the nineteenth century).

Merle from Villeneuve la Salle (Monêtier), bookseller in Rome (end of the eighteenth century – beginning of the nineteenth century).

Mounier from Villeneuve la Salle (Monêtier), bookseller in Madrid (end of the eighteenth century – beginning of the nineteenth century).

Niel, Jean-Abraham, son of Jean Gabriel, bookbinder; born in 1715 in St Didier en Dévoluy; in 1734 he was taken on by C. Delorme; in 1738 he married Anne-Marie Martin; he was a bookseller in Avignon in 1740 and died in 1750. His widow, helped by her son and her brother-in-law Balthazard Niel, continued to run his business (contract of partnership between 1754–56). She died in 1762.

Niel, Etienne Alexandre, son of Jean Gabriel, born in 1722; bookbinder with his father, and then independently after 1745; sometimes described as a bookbinder, sometimes as a printer.

Niel, Balthazard Jean, son of Jean Gabriel, born 1724, apprenticed to C. Delorme in 1737. Worked with his sister-in-law in 1761; in 1765 he married Jeanne Marie Vernet; in 1777 he was both a stockbroker and a bookseller. He went bankrupt in 1778. In 1789 he was a bookseller with his son Jean-Baptiste.

Niel, Jean-Joseph, son of Jean Abraham and Anne-Marie Martin; bookseller in 1763. In business with Aubanel and Barret from Lyon between 1767–78. Condemned to death by the *Commission d'Orange* and executed on 4 Messidor, year III (i.e. the tenth month of the Republican calendar, year 3).

Niel, Jean-Joseph, cousin to the former and son of Etienne Niel. A bookseller from 1792.

Niel, Jean-Joseph, bookseller in the Cap Français in 1786.

Orcel, Joseph, from Briançon; in the mid-eighteenth century he was a bookseller in the rue de la Montera, Madrid, and agent to the Cramers. His brother Jean-Baptiste was a bookseller in Lisbon; Joseph Orcel (of Madrid) was the favoured intermediary of the Portuguese. Jean-Baptiste had to return to Madrid before 1750 following Joseph's death; he was an agent to the STN, a cultivated letter-writer and had a shop in Coimbra.

Orcel, Jacques-Antoine, from Monêtier, bookseller in Coimbra, married into the Bertrand family who were booksellers in Lisbon (second half of the eighteenth century – beginning of the nineteenth century).

Orcel from Monêtier, bookseller in Barcelona (end of the eighteenth century – beginning of the nineteenth century).

Pic from Monêtier, bookseller in Turin (end of the eighteenth century – beginning of the nineteenth century).

Prat, François, from Val des Près, bookseller in Turin (end of the eighteenth century – beginning of the nineteenth century).

Raby, Jacques Antoine, from Monêtier; Director of the Royal Printing House in Turin; one of the Cramers' bad debtors between 1755 and 1761.

Raby, bookseller in Turin, one of Gosse's important agents (second half of the eighteenth century).

Rey, Georges and Co., Pierre Joseph, from Villeneuve la Salle (Monêtier), booksellers in Lisbon (agents for the STN), then in Paris. Pierre Joseph went back to Paris around 1800: see Jean-Simon Gravier.

Rey, Marc Michel, bookseller in Amsterdam and the bookseller who made the most inroads into the Russian market; principal agent for the Cramer family in the Netherlands; Rousseau's publisher (second half of the eighteenth century).

Reycends, Jean-Baptiste and Collomb, Jean, booksellers in Portugal, agents for the Cramers in 1758–61. Reycends, Jean-Baptiste, bookseller in Lisbon, agent for Gosse (second half of the eighteenth century).

Reycends, Joseph and Gendron, Pierre, booksellers in Lisbon, agents for Gosse sometime between 1740 and 1779; in 1747, Gendron and Co. empowered Diego Barthelemi to act for them in the matter of the estate of Pedro Simion, in getting their money back, coming to an agreement over terms and calculating how much was due to them; in particular in coming to an agreement over the small but frequent amounts he owed to the business; Joseph Reycends left Lisbon for Turin in 1756, where he went into partnership with Guibert; he was a cousin of the Barthelemy family from Madrid, and of the Bonnardel family to whom he left the Lisbon shop.

Reycends, Jean-Baptiste and Collomb, Joseph, booksellers in Lisbon, agents for the Cramers in 1758–9.

Reycends from St Chaffrey, bookseller in Parma (end of the eighteenth century – beginning of the nineteenth century).

Reycends & Colomb (from Marseille), booksellers in Milan, agents for the Cramers between 1755–8.

Reycends & Guibert & Sylvestre, from Monêtier, booksellers in Turin, agents for the Cramers between 1756–60, which then became Reycends in partnership with the Guibert brothers, who developed the bookshop business and their connections with the Cramers between 1760 and 1766 to become the biggest bookshop in Turin. Reycends and Guibert opened a branch in Cadiz in 1760; they too worked with Gosse.

Rolland, Francisco, from Saint Antoine de Vallouise, bookseller in Lisbon, then a printer in partnership with Jean Joseph Rolland and Estevao Semiond (second half of the eighteenth century).

Rolland, Gabriel and Son, booksellers and haberdashers in Naples (second half of the eighteenth century).

Sémion, from La-Pisse-en-Vallouise, bookseller in Lisbon (end of the eighteenth century – beginning of the nineteenth century).

Vallier from Monêtier, bookseller in Barcelona (end of the eighteenth century – beginning of the nineteenth century).

A Briançonnais man from Villeneuve la Salle (Monêtier), bookseller in Palma in Majorca (end of the eighteenth century – beginning of the nineteenth century).

This list was compiled from the following sources:

Gravier family private archives

Geneva State Archives, business F 61 to 63.

Albert, A., Les Briançonnais libraires, Grenoble, 1874, pp. 19–23 and Biographies bibliographie des Briançonnais, cantons de la Grave et de Monêtier-de-Briançon, Grenoble, 1877, p. 97.

Barber, G., 'The Cramers of Geneva and their Trade in Europe between 1755 and 1756', Studies on Voltaire and the 18th Century, vol. XXX, 1964, pp. 377–413.

Blanchard, R., 'Aiguilles', Revue de Géographie Alpine, 10, 1922, pp. 127–60.

Bonnant, G., 'Les libraires du Portugal au XVIIIe siècle vus à travers leurs relations d'affaires avec leurs fournisseurs de Genève, Lausanne et Neuchâtel', Arquivio de bibliographia portugesa. Ano VI, no. 23–4, Coimbra, 1961, pp. 195–200; 'La librairie genevoise dans la Péninsule ibérique au XVIIIe siècle', Genava, new series, vol. III, 1961–2, pp. 103–24; 'La librairie genevoise en Italie jusqu'à la fin du XVIIIe siècle', Genava, new series, XV, 1967, pp. 117–60.

Braida, L., Le Guide del tempo. Produzione, contenuti e forme degli almanachi piemontesi nel settecento, Deputazione subalpina di storia patria, Turin, 1989.

da Gama Caeiro, F., 'Livros e livreiros franceses em Lisboa nos fins de setecentos e no primeiro quartel do seculo XIX', *Anaia da Academia Portuguesa da Història* (Lisbon), series IIa, II (26), 1980, pp. 301–27.

Gazetta universale, vol. XIX, 1792, no. 56, p. 448.

Infelise, M., *L'editoria veneziana nel '700*, Milan, Franco Angeli, 1989.

Lay, A., 'Libro e società negli stati sardi del Settecento', in *Libri, editori e publico nell'Europa moderna. Guida storica e critica* a cura di A. Petrucci, Roma-Bari, 1977, pp. 249–82.

Lopez, F., 'Un aperçu de la librairie espagnole au milieu du XVIIIe siècle', in *De l'alphabétisation aux circuits du livre en Espagne XVIe–XXe siècle*, Editions du CNRS, Paris, 1987, pp. 387–416.

Machet, A., 'Le marché du livre français en Italie au XVIIIe siècle', *Revue des Etudes italiennes*, new series, vol. XXIX, no. 4, 1983, pp. 193–222.

Moulinas, R., *L'Imprimerie, la Librairie et la Presse à Avignon au XVIIIe siècle*, Presses Universitaires de Grenoble, 1974; 'Une famille d'imprimeurs-libraires avignonnais du XVIIIe siècle: les Delorme', *Revue française d'histoire du livre*, no. 3, 1972, pp. 45–78.

Romano, R., *Napoli dal Viceregno al regno*, Einaudi, Turin.

Piwnik, M.-H., 'Libraires français et espagnols à Lisbonne au XVIIIe siècle', in *Livres et Libraires en Espagne et au Portugal (XVIe–XXe siècles)*, Editions du CNRS, Paris, 1989, pp. 81–98.

Notes

Introduction

1   A. Furetière, *Dictionnaire universel*, The Hague, 1690: 'A merchant who sells his goods in the street. . . . *Pedlar*: Pedlars sell pictures, sheaths, scissors, laces and other small objects. The term particularly applies to those who sell newspapers, Decrees and other loose-leaf publications. . . . *To peddle*: To carry around one's neck, or on one's back, a large wicker basket or pack containing merchandise to sell on the streets and in the countryside . . .'.
   Dictionnaire de l'Académie française, Paris, 1694: '*Pedlar*: . . . more generally this term is applied to those who sell newspapers, Decrees, Judgements and other printed public documents in the streets'. There is no entry for *to peddle*. Jacques Savary des Bruslons, *Dictionnaire universel du commerce*, Geneva, 1742, vol. 1, pp. 969–71, gives a general definition relating to the city pedlar: *Pedlar*: petty merchant who shouts his various wares and produce in the streets; . . . particularly refers to the *Pauvres Maîtres du Corps de la Librairie, & de la Communauté des Relieurs* (Paupers and master craftsmen of the Bookselling Guild, and Association of Bookbinders) who were permitted to sell their goods on the street.
2   *L'Encyclopédie ou dictionnaire raisonné des sciences . . .*, Paris, vol. 3, 1753, entry for *pedlar*, pp. 659–60. *L'Encyclopédie* proposes the same definition of the city pedlar and distinguishes between the general sense of 'hawking petty, trifling objects through the streets or from door to door' and the specific usage 'in the context of bookselling', repeating the definitions contained in previous dictionaries.
3   A. Franklin, *Dictionnaire historique des Arts, métiers et professions exercées dans Paris depuis le XVIIIe siècle*, Paris, H. Walter, 1906, pp. 180–1.
4   R. B. Westerfield, *Middlemen in English Business, particularly between 1660 and 1760*, 1915, reprint New York 1968, pp. 314–15.
5   Ibid., p. 315.
6   J. Corominas, *Diccionario Crítico Etimológico de la Lengua Castellana*, Berna, Francke, 1954.
7   *Gridi nelle strade fiorentine*, G. Pecori ed., Florence, 1980.

8   I. E. Fietta, 'Con la cassetta in spalla: gli ambulanti di Tesino', *Quaderni di cultura alpina*, no. 23, 1985, pp. 4-111 (6).

9   J. Augel, *Italienische Einwanderung und Wirtschaftstätigkeit in rheinischen Städten des 17. und 18. Jahrhunderts*, Bonn, 1971, pp. 189, 191, 193. F. Braudel has brought to our attention the abundance of terms used for pedlars across Europe in order to demonstrate that this string of names refers to a group of professions which cannot be conventionally categorized: *Civilisation matérielle, économie et capitalisme, XVe-XVIIIe siècle*, Paris, 1979, II, *Les Jeux de l'Echange*, p. 58.

10   W. Shakespeare, *The Winter's Tale* (1611), Act IV, Scene 2.

11   R. Chartier, *Figures de la gueuserie*, Paris, Montalba, Bibliothèque bleue, 1982, pp. 13-30 (pp. 107-31). The book was published in 1596 in Lyon and there were several new editions published at the beginning of the seventeenth century by Nicolas Oudot, in Paris and in Troyes.

12   R. Duroux, 'L'Auvergnat de Madrid et la littérature espagnole', *Actes du colloque d'Aurillac, Le Migrant, 5-7 juin 1985*, Aurillac, 1986, pp. 63-79 (68).

13   Francisco de Quevedo, *La Hora de todos*, Scene XXXI.

14   B. Gracián, *El Criticón* (1651), Madrid, 1957, pp. 157-8. Cited by R. Duroux, 'L'Auvergnat de Madrid . . .', p. 68.

15   Lope de Vega, *El abanillo*; Tirso de Molina, *Quien no cae no se leventa* and *Por el sótano y el torno*, cited by R. Duroux, 'L'Auvergnat de Madrid . . .', p. 68.

16   As in the works of Armestro y Castro, Cáncer, Castillo Solórzano, Gracián, Lanini, Monroy y Silva, Moreto, Navarrete, Quevedo, Santos, Tirso de Molina, Vega, and many others; as cited by R. Duroux, 'L'Auvergnat de Madrid . . .', pp. 69-71.

17   G. Duval, *Littérature de colportage et imaginaire collectif en Angleterre à l'époque des Dicey (1720-v. 1800)*, Bordeaux, Presses Universitaires de Bordeaux, 1991; the original doctoral thesis was consulted (Ph.D., University of Dijon, 1986, p. 44).

18   L. Fontaine, *Le Voyage et la mémoire. Colporteurs de l'Oisans au XIXe siècle*, Presses Universitaires de Lyon, 1984, pp. 231-4. To put this in the wider context of new insights into the peasantry see R. Hubscher, 'Modèle et antimodèle paysans', in *Histoire des Français XIXe-XXe siècle*, vol. 2, *La société*, Y. Lequin ed., Armand Colin, Paris, 1983, pp. 122-44.

19   F. Braudel, *La Méditerranée et le monde méditerranéen à l'époque de Philippe II*, fourth edition, Paris, 1987, pp. 30 and 39. Translated by Siân Reynolds as *The Mediterranean and the Mediterranean World in the Age of Philip II*, London, Collins, 1973.

Chapter 1   Peddling and Major Trade between the Fifteenth and Seventeenth Centuries

1   G. Duby, 'L'état de la vallée de Barcelonnette au Moyen Age', *Sabença de la Valeia*, Barcelonnette, 1984. The Apennines became populated during the same period; R. Sarti, *Long Live the Strong: a history of rural society*

in the Apennine mountains, The University of Massachusetts Press, Amherst, 1985, p. 58.

2 A. Allix, *L'Oisans au Moyen Age. Etude de géographie historique en haute montagne d'après des documents inédits suivie de la transcription des textes*, Paris, 1929, pp. 110 and 145–53. L. C. Bollea, 'Il mercado di Pinerolo nel sec. XIV', *Bolletino Storico–Bibliografico Subalpino*, 1929, pp. 237–246 (239).

3 P. Guichonnet 'L'émigration alpine vers les pays de langue allemande', *Revue de géographie alpine*, 1948, pp. 553–76 (540 and 543). P. Aebischer, 'Voyageurs, artisans et marchands valdôtains à Fribourg au XVe siècle, et brigands fribourgeois dans la vallée d'Aoste', *Augusta Pretoria. Revue valdôtaine de pensée et d'action régionaliste*, 1926, pp. 58–65. (This document brings to light the existence of a combined trade in leather and in woollen sheets, centred on a colony of men from the Valle d'Aosta in Fribourg, who imported dyes from Italy for the Fribourg textile industry and employed others from the Valle d'Aosta in the factories making the sheets.)

4 I. Guy, 'The Scottish Export Trade, 1460–1599', *Scotland and Europe, 1200–1850*, T. C. Smout ed., Edinburgh, 1986, pp. 62–9.

5 J. Heers, 'Gênes, Lyon et Genève: les origines des foires de change', *Cahiers d'Histoire*, V, 1, 1960, pp. 7–15 (8–9). Jean-François Bergier, 'Genève et la Suisse dans la vie économique de Lyon aux XVe–XVIe siècles', *Cahiers d'Histoire*, V, 1, 1960, pp. 33–44.

6 A. Allix, *L'Oisans au Moyen Age*, pp. 138–9. All the routes were described – along with how difficult they were and the length of time they took – by Jacques Signot, in 1515. His descriptions were published as 'Description des passaignes des Alpes en 1515', *Bulletin de la Société des Études des Hautes Alpes*, Gap, 1887, pp. 225–34. See also C. F. Capello, 'La "Descrizione degli itinerari alpini" di Jacques Signot (o Sigault) (*Codici e stampe dei secoli XV–XVI*)', *Revista Geografica italiana*, 1980, pp. 223–42. For more information on the 'lofty trade route', the succession of mountain passes taken by men from Faucigny and the Valle d'Aosta on their way to Germany, see P. Guichonnet, 'L'émigration alpine...' pp. 548–9.

7 Trip to Spain made by Barthélemy Joly, 1603–4, mentioned by A. Poitrineau in *Les Espagnols de l'Auvergne et du Limousin du XVIIe au XIXe siècle*, Mazel-Malroux, Aurillac, 1985.

8 Again, in the middle of the thirteenth century, the Savoyard Alps experienced a real growth in population. The population figures demonstrate this: the important towns were now in the highlands. Barcelonnette in the Ubaye valley was one of the large towns in Provence, with 3–4,000 people at the beginning of the fourteenth century, in other words half the population of Nice, and two-thirds of that of Toulon (G. Duby, *art. cit.*). In the Dauphiné, La Grave at the foot of the Lautaret mountain pass, with 320 families recorded in 1339, was out in front, way ahead of the Bourg d'Oisans, situated where the valleys opened out onto the plain, which had 271 families and was second – and second with a population scarcely higher than any of the other mountain valleys with pasture-land located near the mountain passes (A. Allix, *L'Oisans au Moyen Age...*, pp. 150–1).

9 In the sixteenth century, the geographers were already referring to certain Alpine valleys as 'peddling valleys'; 'Krämerthal', or 'Kremertal': Tschudy in his *Die Uralt Warhaftig Rhetica* (Basel, 1538), or Sébastien Münster in *Cosmographie* (Basel, 1538), thus designated the Challant valley; and a century later, Scheuchzer, in his *Alpenreise*, called the eastern part of the Valle d'Aosta 'Pedlar's valley'. These documents are cited by H. Helmerking in *Zwei Augstaler Krämerfamilien im Kanton Zürich, Separatabdruck aus Zürcher Monatschronik*, Winterthurseen, 1937, quoted by P. Guichonnet, 'L'émigration alpine ...' p. 550 and note 57. From the Blenio valley in Lombardy, there is a record of long-distance migration dating back to the fourteenth century, which makes particular mention of the highland villages: F. C. Farra and Don G. Gallizia, 'L'emigrazione dalla Val Blenio a Milano attraverso i secoli', *Archivio Storico Lombardo*, 9th series, vol. 1, 1961, pp. 117–30 (118).

10 J. Augel, *Italienische Einwanderung und Wirtschaftstätigkeit in rheinischen Städten des 17. und 18. Jahrhunderts*, Bonn, 1971, pp. 42–58. M. Aymard, 'La Sicile, terre d'immigration', *Les Migrations dans les pays méditerranéens au XVIIIe et au début du XIXe*, Centre de la Méditerranée moderne et contemporaine, Université de Nice, Nice, 1973, pp. 134–57 (150).

11 Upper Faucigny in the Savoy region, including Cluses, Nancy-sur-Cluses, Bonneville, Scionzier, Magland, Sallanche, Passy Arâches; the Valle d'Aosta, including Gressoney, Antey, Valtournanche, Ayas, Challant, Issime. P. Guichonnet, 'L'émigration alpine ...', pp. 542–3, describes this progression, using work done by Hektor Ammann, *Neue Beiträge zur Geschichte der Zurzacher Messen*, Aarau, Sauerländer, 1930; by Adolf Birkenmaier, 'Die fremden Krämer zu Freiburg in Breisgau und Zürich', *Zeitschrift der Gesellschaft für Beförderung der Geschichte-Altertums und Volkskunde von Freiburg*, 1913, vol. XXIX; by K. Martin, 'Die Savoyische Einwanderung in das alemannische Süddeutschland', *Deutsches Archiv für Landes und Volksforschung*, vol. VI, fasc. 4, 1942, pp. 647–58; and by A. Schulte, *Geschichte des mittelalterlichen Handels und Verkehrs zwischen Westdeutschland und Italien, mit Ausschluss von Venedig*, Leipzig, Duncker and Humblot, 2 vols, 1900.

12 A. Dietz, *Frankfurter Handelgeschichte*, Frankfurt, 4 vols, 1921, vol. 2, pp. 414–15.

13 M. Aymard, 'La Sicile, terre d'immigration', in *Les migrations dans les pays méditerranéens au XVIIIe et au début du XIXe*, Centre de la Méditerranée moderne et contemporaine, Université de Nice, 1973, pp. 134–57 (147–52). R Merzario, 'Una fabbrica di uomini. L'emigrazione dalla montagna comasca (1650–1750)', *Mélanges de l'Ecole française de Rome*, 96, 1984, 1, pp. 153–75.

14 From 1700, a small community of grocery and haberdashery merchants, originally from Lommel in Brabant, established itself in the region of Bitche in Lorraine. In three-quarters of a century they had developed a network of shops and stalls across the area, and pedlars of lesser means revolved around those who had succeeded in setting up business there. Today Lommel is situated in Limburg in Belgium. D. Hemmert, 'Quelques aspects de l'immigration dans le comté de Bitche, fin du XVIIe siècle, début XVIIIe',

Actes du 103e Congrès national des Sociétés savantes, Nancy–Metz, 1978,
Histoire moderne et contemporaine, Paris, 1979, pp. 41–56.

15 K. Martin, 'Die Savoyische Einwanderung in das alemannische Süddeutschland', *Deutsches Archiv für Landes und Volksforschung,* vol. VI, fasc. 4,
1942, pp. 647–58 (656). E. Gothein, *Wirtschaftsgeschichte des Schwarzwaldes*
und der angrenzenden Landschaften, Strasbourg, 1892, pp. 406–7 and
433.

16 P. Guichonnet, 'L'émigration alpine . . .', p. 567, where he gives numerous
examples.

17 D. Hemmert, 'Quelques aspects . . .', pp. 44–5.

18 T. Riis, *Should Auld Acquaintance Be Forgot . . . Scottish–Danish relations*
c. 1450–1707, 2 vols, Odense University Press, 1988, pp. 8–40.

19 Their total numbers were more modest, however. A Biegansa, 'A note
on the Scots in Poland, 1550–1800', in *Scotland and Europe, 1200–1850,*
T. C. Smout ed., Edinburgh, 1986, pp. 157–65 (157).

20 M. Spufford, *The Great Reclothing of Rural England, Petty Chapmen and*
their Wares in the Seventeenth Century, London, The Hambledon Press,
1984, p. 26.

21 F. Braudel, *La Méditerranée et le monde méditerranéen à l'époque de*
Philippe II, fourth edition, Paris, 1987. Trans. Siân Reynolds as *The*
Mediterranean and the Mediterranean World in the Age of Philip II (London,
Collins, 1973). See p. 45 on the importance of Armenian pedlars in eastern
trade. A. Bieganska, 'A note on the Scots in Poland . . .', pp. 158–9. In
contrast, emigration from Italy was a Court emigration of intellectuals and
artists in the King's service; the Saxon emigration was primarily military
in nature and the English emigration was confined to a few firms of rich
merchants.

22 T. Riis, 'Scottish–Danish relations in the sixteenth century', *Scotland and*
Europe 1200–1850, T. C. Smout ed., Edinburgh, 1986, pp. 82–96 (88–91).

23 J. Augel, *Italienische Einwanderung . . .*, ends his book with a note on each
of these men, as does K. Martin, 'Die Savoyische Einwanderung . . .'. Wilhem
Mauer, in his 'Piemonteser und Savoyer in Süddeutschland', taken from *50*
Jahre Familienforschung in Südwest-Deutschland, Gustav Hahn ed., Stutt-
gart, 1970, pp. 117–27 continued the task of enumeration undertaken by
K. Martin and J. Rumpf-Fleck in *Italienische Kultur in Frankfurt am Main*
im 18. Jahrhundert, Petrarca-Haus, Cologne, 1936, which gives an account
of the Italian merchants established in Frankfurt in the eighteenth century
on pp. 130–9. For a list of Savoyard émigrés in Vienna, Bavaria and in the
Empire, see C. and G. Maistre, G. Heintz, *Colporteurs et marchands*
savoyards dans l'Europe des XVIIe et XVIIIe siècles, reports and documents published by the Academy of Saint François de Sales, vol. 98, Annecy,
1992, pp. 217–41.

24 A. Bieganska, 'A note on the Scots in Poland . . .', p. 158; T. Riis, *Should*
Auld . . ., p. 39.

25 F. Braudel, *La Méditerranée . . .*, p. 46.

26 Strasbourg Municipal Archives, Vth series, 121/20. I am here taking my
lead from J.-P. Kintz, 'Savoyards et grand commerce à l'aube du XVIIe
siècle, l'exemple de la Compagnie des Trois Frères', *L'Europe, l'Alsace et*

la France. Problèmes intérieurs et relations internationales à l'époque moderne. Etudes réunies en l'honneur du doyen Georges Livet pour son 70e anniversaire, Colmar, éditions d'Alsace, 1986, pp. 32–8.

27 G. Livet, 'Une page d'histoire sociale: les Savoyards à Strasbourg au début du XVIIIe siècle', *Cahiers d'Histoire*, vol. 4, 1959, pp. 131–45. See also C. Wolff, 'Un type de marchands sous Louis XIV: Les Savoyards de Barr', *Annuaire de la Société d'histoire et d'archéologie de Dambach-la-Ville*, Barr, Obernai, vol. 3, 1969, pp. 122–7.

28 Departmental archives of the Isère 1J 1102. *Livre de raizon apartenant à Moy Jean Giraud de Lagrave où est contenu mais affaires emparticulier. Comancé le 17 janvier 1670 à Lion.* His Account Book is unfortunately far from complete: he only noted down a certain amount of his business dealings, which were usually recorded in five separate books, which have not been preserved: the 'ledger' which dealt with official business dealings; the 'daybook'; his 'secret book' in which he noted down everything related to the structure, changes, and accounts between the partners of the successive commercial firms he set up; his 'travel notebook' and his 'La Grave notebook', which was reserved for his business dealings with the highlands. Thus Geneva is not mentioned as a place in which he did business and had a temporary residence, except in the chronicle which closes his Account Book which tells of the persecution suffered by the Protestant community and by his family in the summer of 1685.

29 Departmental archives of the Rhône, B series, 8 May 1690.

30 For more information on merchant-migrants and links with the home village, see O. Martin, *La Conversion protestante à Lyon (1659–1687)*, Geneva, Paris, Droz, 1986, pp. 50–65.

31 E. Arnaud, *Histoire des protestants du Dauphiné aux XVIe, XVIIe et XVIIIe siècles*, 3 vols, Paris, 1875, vol. 1, pp. 499–510.

32 J. Augel, *Italienische Einwanderung . . .*, pp. 62–105, 193.

33 J. Augel's index in *Italienische Einwanderung . . .* mentions 77 members of the Brentano family who were established in the Rhine area between the end of the seventeenth century and the end of the eighteenth century. See also A. Dietz, *Frankfurter Handelgeschichte*, Frankfurt, 1921, pp. 240–59 and J. Rumpf-Fleck, *Italienische Kultur . . .*, p. 18, which also looks at the different branches of the Brentano family in Frankfurt (pp. 25–8), and lists on pp. 133–5 the members of the four branches of the family in Frankfurt in the seventeenth and eighteenth centuries.

34 H. Onde, 'L'émigration en Maurienne et en Tarentaise', *Bulletin de la Société scientifique de Dauphiné*, 1942, pp. 41–99 (43). There are numerous examples in Chanoine Dechavassine's 'L'émigration savoyarde dans les pays de langue allemande', *Congrès des Sociétés savantes de la Province de Savoie, Actes du Congrés de Moûtiers, 5 et 6 septembre 1964*, pp. 86–97.

35 T. Riis, 'Scotttish–Danish . . .', p. 90.

36 T. A. Fischer, *The Scots in Sweden*, Edinburgh, 1907, pp. 10–17. See also *The Scots in Germany*, Edinburgh, 1902, and *The Scots in Eastern and Western Prussia*, Edinburgh, 1903, both from the same author.

37 E.-B. Grage, 'Scottish merchants in Gothenburg, 1621–1850', *Scotland and Europe, 1200–1850*, T. C. Smout ed., Edinburgh, 1986, p. 113.

38 T. C. Smout, 'The Glasgow merchant community in the seventeenth cen-
    tury', *Scottish Historical Review*, 47, 1968, pp. 53–71 (64–5). In the 1680s,
    one-eighth of Glasgow merchants peddled fabrics in England.
39 D. Hemmert, 'Quelques aspects de l'immigration ...', pp. 43–4. Italian
    immigration was obviously not confined to the peddling movement, and
    all European countries had their 'Court Italians'; Victor-Louis Tapié,
    Baroque et classicisme, Paris, 1972, book 3; Jean-Michel Thiriet,
    'L'immigration italienne dans la Vienne baroque (1620–1750)', *Revue
    d'Histoire économique et sociale*, 52, 1974, pp. 339–49.
40 Departmental archives of the Isère, 1J 1102.
41 E. Gothein, *Wirtgeschaftsgeschichte ...*, p. 578. E.-B. Grage, 'Scottish
    merchants in Gothenburg ...', pp. 112–27 (112).
42 Departmental archives of the Hautes Alpes, 4E 4839, 6 August 1686.
43 J. Augel, *Italienische Einwanderung ...*, pp. 201–2.
44 M. Aymard, 'La Sicile, terre d'immigration', pp. 150–1.
45 R. Merzario, *Il Capitalismo nelle montagne. Strategie famigliari nella prima
    fase di industrializzazione nel Comasco*, Il Mulino, Bologna, 1989, pp. 139–
    40. At the beginning of the eighteenth century, a handful of men headed
    towards Russia.
46 Departmental archives of the Isère, 1J 1102.
47 National Archives: MC, et/LXXXVI/213.
48 Departmental archives of the Isère, 4G 271/283.
49 J. Augel, *Italienische Einwanderung ...*, p. 164.
50 E. Gothein, *Wirtschaftsgeschichte ...*, pp. 740–1 and 849.
51 J. Augel, *Italienische Einwanderung ...*, p. 192.
52 J. Augel, *Italienische Einwanderung ...*, p. 198. In 1708, a Frankfurt
    ruling tried to resolve this problem.
53 J. Augel, *Italienische Einwanderung ...*, p. 195.
54 National Archives: MC, et/LXXXVI/213.
55 L. Fontaine, 'Family Cycles, Peddling and Society in Upper Alpine Valleys
    in the Eighteenth Century', in *Domestic Strategies: Work and Family in
    France and Italy, 17–18th Century*, S. Woolf ed., Editions de la Maison
    des Sciences de l'Homme/Cambridge University Press, 1991, pp. 43–68.
56 H. Ammann, *Freiburg und Bern und die Genfer Messen* (dissertation),
    Langensalza, Beyer, 1921, pp. 35, 41, 51, cited by P. Guichonnet in
    'L'émigration alpine ...', pp. 551, 559–60 concerning the temporary ware-
    houses established by men from the Savoy and the Valle d'Aosta, where
    the pedlars from each network came to stock up with goods.
57 Departmental archives of the Creuse, E 511, 11 April 1591, as cited by
    André Thomas in 'Gaspar le Loup, ligueur et chef de brigands en 1595',
    Mémoire de la Société des Sciences naturelles et archéologiques de la Creuse,
    vol. XXIV, pp. 363–73 (368–72). I should like to thank Michel Cassan
    who was kind enough to send me this document from the archive.
58 J. B. Kälin, 'Alte Klagen gegen fremde Hausierer und Krämer', *Mitteilungen
    des historischen Vereins des Kantons Schwyz*, 1885, fasc. 4, pp. 69–72.
    Cited by P. Guichonnet, 'L'émigration alpine ...', p. 555.
59 Rulings from 1628, 1632, 1671, 1692. J. Augel, *Italienische Einwanderung
    ...*, pp. 193–4.

226 NOTES TO PAGES 20–24

60 Complaint from the Frankfurt merchants in 1772. J. Augel, *Italienische Einwanderung* ..., p. 203.

61 J. Augel, *Italienische Einwanderung* ... p. 189. G. Levi demonstrates this in his study of immigration in Turin in the seventeenth century, *Centro e periferia di uno stato assoluto*, Turin, 1985, pp. 11–27.

62 A. Bieganska, 'A note on the Scots in Poland ...', *art. cit.* p. 156.

63 T. Riis, 'Scottish–Danish ...', p. 88.

64 E.-B. Grage, 'Scottish merchants in Gothenburg ...', p. 114.

65 T. Riis, 'Scottish–Danish ...', p. 87. It should one day be possible to study the links between artisan and merchant networks. Until fuller and more complex studies on occupational migration have been undertaken, we should merely highlight the common village origins of craftsmen and pedlars.

66 Departmental archives of the Hautes Alpes, 1E 4839, 10 July 1684.

67 Departmental archives of the Hautes Alpes, 1E 7218, 19 October 1680.

68 Departmental archives of the Hautes Alpes, 1E 7215, 10 August 1684.

69 Departmental archives of the Hautes Alpes, 1E 7218, 14 February 1690.

70 E. Gothein, *Wirtschaftsgeschichte* ..., p. 849.

71 Departmental archives of the Hautes Alpes, 1E 4839, 2 December 1685.

72 Departmental archives of the Hautes Alpes, 1E 4839, 6 August 1686. Vincent Albert was to have his son with him for six months of the year, in winter for the first three years; the firm would pay him 20 *livres* in wages, would look after him for a month were he to fall ill, and would provide him with 'silk stockings, shoes and gaiters'.

73 G. Livet, 'Une page ...', pp. 134–5.

74 P. Guichonnet, 'L'émigration alpine ...', pp. 555–6 and 559. There remain numerous exchanges of letters between towns on this subject. The same complaints arose in Strasbourg from the 1620s onwards. G. Livet, 'Une page ...', p. 138.

75 A Birkenmaier, 'Die fremden Krämer ...', pp. 93–110, describes the regulations in Fribourg between the mid-fifteenth century and the end of the sixteenth century which aimed at restricting the Italian pedlars.

76 K. Martin has shown that, out of a group of 384 wives of immigrants, only 60 came from the Savoy or were born of Savoyard parents who had settled in Germany, and all the others were German.

77 D. Hemmert makes the same observation concerning the Savoyards' entry into the bourgeois class of Bitche, 'Quelques aspects de l'immigration ...', p. 51; P. Guichonnet, 'L'émigration alpine ...', p. 565.

78 The native merchants of Frankfurt obtained repeated rulings (1707, 1722, 1734) forbidding the establishment of these 'mixed' ventures. J. Augel, *Italienische Einwanderung* ..., p. 202.

79 D. Ozanam, 'La colonie française de Cadix au XVIIIe siècle, d'après un document inédit (1777)', *Mélanges de la Casa de Vélasquez*, IV, 1968, pp. 259–349 (287). To trace the development of the legislation, see A. Dominguez Ortiz, *Los Extranjeros en la vida española durante el siglo XVII*, Madrid, 1960, pp. 59–64; and also D. Ozanam, *ibid.*, pp. 261–4. This distinction complicates research into the French community in Spain, since a certain number of them were counted as Spanish.

80 J. Nadal and E. Giralt, *La Population catalane de 1553 à 1717. L'immigration française et les autres facteurs de son développement*, Paris, SEVPEN, 1960, p. 51.
81 G. Livet, 'Une page ...', pp. 133–4.
82 P. Guichonnet, 'L'émigration alpine ...', p. 559.
83 *Ibid.*, pp. 556–7.
84 A. Poitrineau, *Les Espagnols*, p. 223.
85 P. Guichonnet, 'L'émigration alpine ...', p. 557.
86 E. Gothein, *Wirtschaftsgeschichte* ..., p. 578.
87 J. Augel, *Italienische Einwanderung* ..., gives numerous examples on pp. 160–6.
88 H. Kellenbenz, *art. cit.*, pp. 159–60.
89 P. Guichonnet, 'L'émigration alpine ...', gives numerous examples for Switzerland and southern Germany on p. 555.
90 E. Gothein, *Wirtschaftsgeschichte* ..., p. 434.
91 A. Bieganska, 'A note on the Scots in Poland ...', *art. cit.*, p. 158.
92 A. Dominguez Ortiz, *Los Extranjeros* ..., pp. 64–5.
93 J. Augel, *Italienische Einwanderung* ..., p. 197. T. Riis, *Should Auld* ..., p. 196.
94 D. Ozanam, 'La colonie française de Cadix ...', p. 266. M. Aymard, 'La Sicile, terre d'immigration', p. 148.
95 S. Cerutti, 'Du corps au métier: la corporation des tailleurs à Turin entre XVIIe et XVIIIe siècle', *Annales ESC*, 1988, no. 2, pp. 323–52. *La Ville et les métiers. Naissance d'un langage corporatif (Turin, XVIIe–XVIIIe siècles)*, Ecole des Hautes Etudes en Sciences sociales, Paris, 1990.
96 E. Gothein, *Wirtschaftsgeschichte* ..., p. 433.
97 Ruling of 1531. K. Martin, 'Die savoyische Einwanderung ...', pp. 647–58.
98 T. Riis, *Should Auld* ..., pp. 75–6.
99 A. Bieganska, 'A note on the Scots in Poland ...', *art. cit.*, p. 158.
100 T. A. Fischer, *The Scots in Sweden*, pp. 5–7. There was the same indignation on the part of the Stockholm burghers in 1635 (p. 7).
101 The pragmatic ordinance of 1623 forbade goods that had been produced elsewhere being brought into the country. In 1625, the Frenchmen who had set up business in the ports had a certain amount of their property seized, and some of them were even imprisoned. In 1635, there was a further confiscation of goods. In 1647, Philippe IV laid down strict limits on the amount of currency that could be taken out of the country. The treaty of 1659 asserted freedom of movement and trade, and the French were given solemn guarantees. The war over devolution and Holland provoked a further reaction which went beyond policies involving customs and prohibition to include inspections of houses and shops, and further confiscation of goods. At the end of the century, a more normal situation was re-established and lasted for the better part of the eighteenth century, despite rulings concerning bans and higher tariffs (notably in 1778). J. Perrel, 'Introduction à une étude sur l'émigration corrézienne vers l'Espagne sous l'Ancien Régime', *Bulletin de la Société des Lettres, sciences et arts de la Corrèze*, LXVII, 1963, pp. 92–101 (95).

In 1593 the French pedlars found themselves banned from selling a number of products; in 1626 Spain refused to allow fancy goods, ironmongery, and numerous items produced in France into the country; the only articles allowed in were sails, rigging and items of haberdashery indispensable to the shippers of the fleet in Seville, destined for the Indies. A. Poitrineau, Les 'Espagnols' de l'Auvergne et du Limousin du XVIIe au XIXe siècle, Aurillac, Mazel-Malroux, 1985, pp. 221–2. A further example: in 1657, a royal proclamation forbade the French pedlars from going into the street, from door to door, selling their rubbish and buying gold and silver braid, and scraps of precious metal; a proclamation which was revoked some 20 years later. [A. Poitrineau, Les Espagnols . . . , p. 225.]

102 E. Gothein, Wirtschaftsgeschichte . . . , p. 466.
103 T. A. Fischer, The Scots in Sweden, pp. 29–32.
104 E.-B. Grage, 'Scottish merchants in Gothenburg. . . .', p. 114.
105 J. Augel, Italienische Einwanderung . . . , p. 196.
106 A. Dietz, Frankfurter . . . , pp. 243–4.
107 K. Martin, 'Die Savoyische Einwanderung . . .', p. 8; and P. Guichonnet, 'L'émigration alpine . . .', pp. 555–6.
108 P. Guichonnet, 'L'émigration alpine . . .', p. 558.
109 P. Guichonnet, 'L'émigration alpine . . .', pp. 554–8.
110 J. Augel, Italienische Einwanderung . . . , p. 194.
111 A. Bieganska, 'A note on the Scots in Poland . . .', pp. 157–8.
112 T. A. Fischer, The Scots in Sweden, pp. 5–7.
113 Frankfurt ruling, 1628. J. Augel, Italienische Einwanderung . . . , p. 192.
114 The first rulings date back to 1632, and reached their maximum force in Frankfurt and Mainz in 1671. J. Augel, Italienische Einwanderung . . . , pp. 160 and 193.
115 A. Dietz, Frankfurter . . . , p. 601.
116 G. Livet, 'Une page . . .', pp. 142–5.
117 National Archives: MC, et/LXXXVI/213; Departmental archives of the Isère, 1J 1102.
118 The record book for debts owed to the Compagnie des Trois Frères concerns 507 people and, apart from a few debts which are a decade or so old, all the others were contracted between 1608 and 1611.
119 Complaint from the Society of Swabia in 1582; K. Martin, 'Die Savoyische Einwanderung . . .', p. 7.
120 E. Gothein, Wirtschaftsgeschichte . . . , p. 741.
121 H. Kellenbenz, 'Le déclin de Venise et les relations économiques de Venise avec les marchés au nord des Alpes (fin XVIe siècle – commencement du XVIIIe siècle', Aspetti e cause della decadenza economica veneziana nel secolo XVII, Atti del convegno 27 giugno – 2 luglio 1957, Venice 1961, pp. 107–83 (145–9).
122 P. Guichonnet, 'L'émigration alpine . . .', pp. 559–60 gives numerous examples of these Savoy and Piedmont families.
123 B. Caizza, Industria e commercio della repubblica veneta nel XVIIIe secolo, Banca Commerciale Italiana, Milan, 1965, pp. 13–15 and pp. 160–70.
124 G. Livet, 'Une page . . .', p. 138.
125 Savoyards (from Sallanche) established themselves in the Bitche area right in the middle of a period of unrest (1672); from 1700 these 'mercatores

Sabaudii' made up the elite of the merchant bourgeoisie. D. Hemmert, 'Quelques aspects de l'immigration...', p. 45; and P. Guichonnet, 'L'émigration alpine...', p. 559.
126 G. Livet, 'Une page...', p. 132; C. and G. Maistre, *L'Emigration marchande savoyarde aux XVIIe–XVIIIe siècles: l'exemple de Nancy-sur-Cluses*. Academy of Saint François de Sales, Annecy, 1986, pp. 21–2.
127 M. Virieux, 'Les migrations en Dauphiné d'après les passeports délivrés par le commandement de la province (1740–1743)', *Evocations*, 1973, pp. 97–116 (112), emphasizes the influx of merchants and carters from the dioceses of Die, Gap and Embrun heading for the Savoy which was at war.
128 G. Livet, 'Une page...', pp. 135–8.
129 J. Augel, *Italienische Einwanderung...*, pp. 197–8.
130 J. Augel, *Italienische Einwanderung...*, p. 199.
131 Departmental archives of the Rhône, 3E 4781B, notary Antoine Favard.
132 M. Balard, *La Romanie génoise...*, J. Le Goff, *Marchands et banquiers du Moyen Age*, Paris, Presses Universitaires de France, 1980. Peddling also played an essential part in Asiatic trade; see *The Cambridge Economic History of Europe*, vol. V, *The Economic Organisation of Early Modern Europe*, p. 279.
133 F. Braudel, *Civilisation matérielle, économie et capitalisme, XVe–XVIIIe siècles*, vol. 2, *Les Jeux de l'Echange*, Paris, 1979 edition, p. 129.

Chapter 2 The Eighteenth Century: a Return to the Regional Areas

1 A. Allix, *L'Oisans au Moyen Age. Étude de géographie historique en haute montagne d'après des documents inédits suivie de la transcription des textes*, Paris, 1929, pp. 150–1.
2 Thus, in 1713, there was the handing over of the valleys to the King of Sardinia; the tax that he imposed on fabrics which came from the Dauphiné, and the subsequent ban on importing such fabrics; followed in 1745 by the French ban on exporting wool and hides from France. A. Albert, 'Le pays briançonnais: les Queyrassins négociants', *Bulletin de la Société d'étude des Hautes-Alpes*, first series, vol. 8, 1889, pp. 313–31 (316–17).
3 R. Bornecque, 'La vie dans le Briançonnais au XVIIIe siècle d'après les mémoires des ingénieurs militaires', *Cahiers d'Histoire*, XV, 1, 1970, pp. 15–42 (28–31).
4 E. Gothein, *Wirtschaftsgeschichte des Schwarzwaldes und der angrenzenden Landschaften*, Strasbourg, 1892, p. 741.
5 See chapter 6: Credit and social relationships.
6 J.-P. Poussou, *Bordeaux et le Sud-Ouest au XVIIIe siècle. Croissance économique et attraction urbaine*, Paris, Editions de l'E.H.E.S.S, 1983.
7 T. A. Fischer, *The Scots in Sweden*, Edinburgh, 1907, p. 17.
8 T. Riis, 'Scottish–Danish relations in the sixteenth century', *Scotland and Europe, 1200–1850*, T. C. Smout (ed.), Edinburgh, 1986, pp. 82–96 (88–91). J. J. Israel, *Dutch Trade Hegemony*, Oxford, 1989.
9 A. Bieganska, 'A note on the Scots in Poland, 1500–1800', *Scotland and Europe...*, pp. 157–65 (p. 159).

10 T. C. Smout, 'The Glasgow Merchant Community in the Seventeenth Century', *Scottish Historical Review*, 47, 1968, pp. 53–71 (66).

11 T. A. Fischer, *The Scots in Sweden* . . . , p. 37.

12 E.-B. Grage, 'Scottish merchants in Gothenburg, 1621–1850', *Scotland and Europe* . . . , p. 117.

13 D. R. Ringrose, *Madrid and the Spanish Economy* (1560–1850), University of Carolina Press, 1983, pp. 164–92.

14 My apologies for placing so little emphasis in this book on the merchant migration of the Jewish communities. The work involved in putting the structure of these networks in some sort of perspective vis-à-vis the home communities is beyond the proposed scope of this volume. However, I should like to draw attention to three meticulously researched and interesting studies, covering Holland, England and France: B. W. de Vries, *From Pedlars to Textile Barons: The Economic Development of a Jewish Minority Group in the Netherlands*, Amsterdam, 1989; T. Endelman, 'L'activité économique des juifs anglais', *Dix-huitième siècle*, no. 13, 1981, pp. 113–26; R. Moulinas, 'Le Conseil du Roi et le commerce des Juifs d'Avignon en France', *Dix-huitième siècle*, no. 13, 1981, pp. 169–79; and the beautiful book by Elias Canetti which describes how, at the beginning of the twentieth century, his Rumanian grandfather travelled through Europe just like any seventeenth-century merchant, *Histoire d'une jeunesse, la langue sauvée*, Munich, 1977, Paris, 1987, p. 127.

15 D. Albera, M. Dossetti, S. Ottonelli, 'Società ed emigrazioni nell'alta valle Varaita in eta moderna', *Bollettino storico-bibliografico subalpino*, LXXXVI, 1988, 1, pp. 117–69 (132–3). In the Savoy, P. Guichonnet noted 'the progressive reduction of the distance covered', and the end of large-scale successes for the merchants who came from the Val de Montjoie and were established in Vienna, Bavaria, or even Poland; 'L'émigration saisonnière en Faucigny pendant la première moitié du XIXe siècle (1783–1860)', *Revue de Géographie alpine*, 1945, vol. XXXIII, fasc. 3, pp. 465–534 (489 and 501).

16 L. Zanzi and T. Rizzi, *I walser nella storia delle Alpi, un modello di civilizzazione ei suoi problemi metodologici*, Edizioni universizari Jaca, Milan, 1988; P. P. Viazzo, *Upland Communities: Environment, Population and Social Structure in the Alps since the Sixteenth Century*, Cambridge, Cambridge University Press, 1989.

17 N. Daupias d'Alcochete, 'Bourgeoisie pombaline et noblesse libérale au Portugal', *Mémorias e documentos para a historia luso–francesca. IV*, Fundaçao Calouste Gubenkian, Paris, 1969, pp. 15–39.

18 For more information on the education of merchants' sons, see D. Julia, 'L'éducation des négociants en France au XVIIIe siècle', *Colloque Négoce et Culture à l'époque moderne*, European University Institute of Florence, 3 and 4 December 1987.

19 P. Guichonnet, 'L'émigration alpine vers les pays de langue allemande', *Revue de Géographie alpine*, 1948, pp. 553–76 (567).

20 C. and G. Maistre, *L'Émigration marchande savoyarde aux XVIIe–XVIIIe siècles: L'exemple de Nancy-sur-Cluses*, Academy of Saint François de Sales, Annecy, 1986, p. 185.

21 See Ulrich Pfister's analyses of the activities of the Brentano and Curti families in the Zurich region, *Die Zürcher Fabriques, Protoindustrielles*

Wachstum vom 16. zum 18. Jahrhundert, Editions Chronos, Zurich, 1992, pp. 141–4 and 258–70.

22 French National Archives, MC, et/CXXII/1552, 30 August 1604. My thanks to Robert Descimon who shared with me his knowledge of Paris merchants and his experience of the handwriting of notaries of the period, which was not easy to read.

23 French National Archives, MC, et/XXI/69, 2 July 1605 and 6 July 1605. Henry Bompart, a merchant haberdasher of Bagnoles, originally from Monêtier, was also involved in this traffic of mulberry bush seeds, *idem*, 17 May 1605.

24 A. Chatelain, *Les Migrants temporaires en France de 1800 à 1914: Histoire économique et sociale des migrants temporaires des campagnes françaises du XIXe au début du XXe siècle*, Lille, 1976; A. Poitrineau, *Remues d'hommes: Les migrations montagnardes en France XVIIe–XVIIIe siècles*, Paris, 1983; J.-J. Darmon, *Le Colportage de librairie en France sous le Second Empire*, Paris, 1972.

25 M. Spufford, *The Great Reclothing of Rural England: Petty Chapmen and their Wares in the Seventeenth Century*, London, The Hambledon Press, 1984, p. 27.

26 S. Jaumain, 'Les colporteurs Hainuyers du XIXe siècle', *Annales du Cercle royal d'Histoire et d'Archéologie d'Ath et Musées athois*, 1984, pp. 282–340 (298) – the villages of Quevaucamps and Stambruges in particular. Unfortunately the study is too late to allow any valuable comparisons to be made.

27 However, the research currently being pursued by J. Torras i Elias from the (autonomous) Barcelona University leads one to believe that certain Catalan villages in the Pyrenees had developed peddling societies.

28 N. McKendrick is unable to provide accurate figures for the itinerant pedlars, since, given their reluctance to buy trading licences or register themselves, they are very difficult to pin down; however, he gives the number from the Census of 1851 (right in the middle of a period of decline) which was around 30,000: N. McKendrick, J. Brewer and J. H. Plumb, *The Birth of Consumer Society: The Commercialization of Eighteenth Century England*, Bloomington, Indiana University Press, 1982, pp. 87–8. In 1676, when the question of peddling was troubling Parliament, it was estimated that there were 10,000 of them, and in 1696–7 they were compelled to buy trading licences: the first register recorded around 2,500; M. Spufford, *The Great Reclothing . . .*, pp. 14–15. A. Chatelain gives national and regional figures for France for all migrants at the beginning of the nineteenth century but is unable to isolate the peddling component: *Les Migrants temporaires en France de 1800 à 1914 . . .*, pp. 41–7. There is also an upsurge in the numbers certified for the Savoy in H. Onde, 'L'émigration en Maurienne et en Tarentaise', *Bulletin de la Société scientifique du Dauphiné*, 1942, pp. 41–99 (68). There is a lack of comprehensive information in A. Poitrineau's *Remues d'hommes . . .*, pp. 26–7, where he only gives certain regional numbers: 6,000 coppersmiths, tinsmiths and pedlars out of a total resident population of 57,000 in Murat, in the Cantal in year II. In Oisans, according to the register of trading licences, there were 270 pedlars in year VI, and at the height of the profession in 1850, there was a maximum number of

700: L. Fontaine, *Le Voyage et la Mémoire, colporteurs de l'Oisans au XIXe siècle*, Presses Universitaires de Lyon, 1984, pp. 34–5.

29 M. Spufford, *The Great Reclothing* ..., p. 21.

30 For more information on the Auvergne, see A. Poitrineau, 'Petits marchands colporteurs de la haute Planèze d'Auvergne à la fin de l'Ancien Régime', *Annales du Midi*, vol. 88, 1976, pp. 423–36 (434); for Oisans, see L. Fontaine, 'Family Cycles, Peddling and Society in Upper Alpine valleys in the Eighteenth Century', in *Domestic Strategies, Work and Family in France and Italy, 17th–18th Century*, Stuart Woolf (ed.), Editions de la Maison des Sciences de l'Homme/Cambridge University Press, 1991, pp. 43–68.

31 M. Virieux, 'Les migrations en Dauphiné d'après les passeports délivrés par le commandement de la province (1740–1743)', *Evocations*, 1973, pp. 97–116 (104 and 109).

32 R. Blanchard, 'Aiguilles', *Revue de Géographie alpine*, 10, 1922, pp. 127–60 (141).

33 P. Guichonnet, 'L'émigration saisonnière en Faucigny ...', pp. 507–10.

34 R. Chartier, 'Livres bleus et lectures populaires', *Histoire de l'édition française*, vol. 2, *Le Livre triomphant 1660–1830*, Paris, Promodis, 1984, pp. 498–511.

35 Quoted by R. Mandrou in *De la culture populaire aux XVIIe et XVIIIe siècles*, La Bibliothèque bleue de Troyes, Paris, Stock, 1964, new edition 1975, pp. 40–2. For more information on the regulation of peddling and on the role of pedlars in the illicit business of books, see J. Queniart, *L'Imprimerie et la librairie à Rouen au XVIIIe siècle*, Paris, Klincksieck, 1969, pp. 189–206. M. Marsol, 'Un oublié: Pierre Héron, "marchand libraire" à Langres en Bassigny (1756–1776)', *Bulletin d'histoire moderne et contemporaine du Comité des travaux historiques et philologiques*, no. 11, 1978, pp. 33–74 shows that his business was based on the sale of tens of thousands of almanacs, Books of Hours and devotional books, and thus proves that his was a shop where the pedlars came to stock up.

36 Letter from Paul Malherbe (the elder) to the Société typographique de Neuchâtel, 13 August 1774, quoted by R. Darnton, 'Un colporteur sous l'Ancien Régime', *Censures, de la Bible aux larmes d'Eros*, Centre Georges Pompidou, Paris, 1987, pp. 130–9 (133–4).

37 J. Queniart, *L'imprimerie et la librairie à Rouen* ..., p. 205.

38 C. Berkvens-Stevelink, 'L'édition française en Hollande', *Histoire de l'édition française*, vol. 2, p. 324.

39 R. Mandrou, *De la culture populaire* ..., p. 32.

40 As well as men from the Pyrenees, mention is also made of men from the Vosges, originally from the village of Chamagne, hence the name 'Chamagnons' which was applied as a general term for all pedlars from the East. Mention should also be made of men from the Savoy, the Jura, from Cantal in the Auvergne and certain groups from outside France: Italians, especially those from Piedmont and Parma; Swiss from the Ticino region now living in Lorraine; and Germans from the Bavarian Rhine regions who came to Alsace to stock up. J.-J. Darmon, *Le colportage de librairie* ..., p. 61.

41 The ridge of granite plateaux between the Corrèze and the Dordogne was the route taken by those emigrating to Spain. Many men from the cantons of Brive, Tulle, Corrèze, Egletons, Lapleau, La Roche-Canillac, Beynat,

Meyssac, Beaulieu, Argentat, Mercoeur and Saint-Privat took part in this emigration. This region was linked to the Cantal cantons by Xaintie: Pleaux, Mauriac, Salers. . . . J. Perrel, 'Introduction à une étude sur l'émigration corrézienne vers l'Espagne sous l'Ancien Régime', *Bulletin de la Société des Lettres, Sciences et Arts de la Corrèze*, LXVII, 1963, pp. 92–101 (34).

42 J. Perrel, 'Les Limousins en Espagne aux XVIe, XVIIe et XVIIIe siècles: les émigrants', *Bulletin de la Société des Lettres, Sciences et Arts de la Corrèze*, LXVIII, 1964, pp. 31–40 (31).

43 J. Perrel, 'L'émigration bas-limousine en Espagne aux XVIIe et XVIIIe siècles', *Actes du 88e Congrès national des Sociétés Savantes, section d'histoire moderne et contemporaine, Clermont-Ferrand, 1963*, Paris, 1964, pp. 709–29; for more information on religious links see pp. 712–15; map on p. 717.

44 J. Bodin, *Livres de la République*, V, 1576, p. 471.

45 A. Girard, *Le commerce français à Séville et Cadix au temps des Habsbourg. Contribution à l'étude du commerce étranger en Espagne aux XVIe et XVIIe siècles*, Paris, 1932, p. 566. J. Nadal, *La población española, siglo XVI à XX*, revised and expanded edition, Barcelona, 1984, pp. 64–72. N. Castells i Calzada, 'Els moviments migratoris en la Catalunya moderna: el cas de la immigració envers la ciutat de Girona (1473–1576)', *Primer Congrés d'historia moderna de Catalunya*, Barcelona, 1984, pp. 65–74 (70–71).

46 E. Giralt y Raventos, 'La colonia mercantil francesca de Barcelona a mediados del siglo XVII', *Estudios de historia moderna*, vol. 6, 1960, pp. 216–78.

47 As quoted by J. Perrel, 'Introduction . . .', p. 93. Throughout the seventeenth century, estimates as to their number varied: according to Montchrétien, there were 200,000 Frenchmen who had settled in Spain in 1596. In 1626, the French ambassador referred to the same numbers as did Thomas Le Fèvre in 1650 and Brunelet Van Aerssen in 1655. In the same year, Martina de la Mata put the number of foreigners settled in the Kingdom at 120,000, most of whom were French. In 1680, the Marquis de Villars hesitated between 65,000 and 70,000; and, in 1682, La Vauguyon talked of their being between 80,000–100,000. In 1700 the Gremios from Seville thought that Spain had 160,000 foreigners. See p. 93, *ibid.*

48 Trip undertaken by Père Labat, from the Dominican order, into Spain and Italy, vol. 1, p. 285 and following, quoted by A. Girard, *Le Commerce français . . .*, pp. 561–2.

49 J. Perrel, 'Les Limousins . . .', pp. 36–7.

50 A. Girard, *Le commerce français . . .*, p. 555.

51 A. Poitrineau, *Les 'Espagnols' de l'Auvergne et du Limousin du XVIIe au XIXe siècle*, Aurillac, Mazel-Malroux, 1985, pp. 20–2, 150 and 233.

52 A. Girard, 'Saisie des biens français en Espagne', *Revue d'Histoire économique et sociale*, 1931, pp. 297–315.

53 D. Ozanam, 'La colonie française de Cadix au XVIIIe siècle, d'après un document inédit (1777)', *Mélanges de la Casa de Vélasquez*, IV, 1968, pp. 259–349.

54 Archives Nationales, Affaires Etrangères, B1 294, Mongelas to Castries, 1 August 1786: 'From time immemorial, men from the province of Limousin who travel round Spain have been able to peddle their wares in the streets of Cadiz and sell oil, vinegar and coal. The value of their activities has always been recognised: these commodities were good value, and beyond

that, individuals had the advantage of being furnished with goods at their home by these men . . . / . . . Spain, especially Cadiz, is a real source of wealth for this province. None of these men who came to Spain settled here. After three or four years spent in Cadiz, the pedlar goes back to his own country, returns to Spain, undertakes four or five campaigns in Spain, then goes back to his homeland with the fruits of his labour, gets married there and settles down surrounded by his family. When they leave Spain, those such as the oil-sellers, who have their own occupation, as it were, hand it on to their children or nephews, or sell it – what they call 'passing on the pitcher' [*passer le jarròn*]. Each group in the same line of trade combines forces and has a common fund to finance their expenditure . . .'; quoted by D. Ozanam, 'La colonie française de Cadix . . .', pp. 300–1.

55 R. Duroux, 'L'Auvergnat de Madrid et la littérature espagnole', *Actes du colloque d'Aurillac, Le Migrant, 5–7 juin, 1985*, Aurillac, 1986, pp. 63–79 (72). In Castile, the Valencia region and Andalusia, according to research done by Hamilton, there was an additional 20–30 per cent drop in the purchasing power of the average wage-earner – see J. Nadal, *La población . . .*, p. 67. For an overview of the erosion of trading terms between the price of pasture-land and the price of wool, and for the tension between the number of men and the yield from the land in the eighteenth century, see D. R. Ringrose, *Madrid . . .*, pp. 169–71.

56 R. Duroux, 'Les boutiquiers cantaliens de Nouvelle-Castille au XIXe siècle', *Mélanges de la Casa de Vélasquez*, 1985, vol. XXI, pp. 281–307 (284–5).

57 A. Girard, *Le Commerce français . . .*, pp. 554–8.

58 A. Girard, *Le Commerce français . . .*, pp. 553–4. In 1680, the Marquis de Villars put the number of Frenchmen in Andalusia at 16,000 (*ibid.*, p. 567). For contemporary estimates, see R. Duroux, 'L'Auvergnat de Madrid . . .', pp. 63–4.

59 A. E. Paris, *Reports and documents*, Spain, 133, p. 19, dated 1770, quoted by A. Poitrineau in *Les 'Espagnols' . . .*, p. 33.

60 D. Ozanam, 'La colonie française de Cadix . . .', p. 287. On the changes in legislation, see A. Dominguez Ortiz, *Los extranjeros en la vida española durante el siglo XVII*, Madrid, 1960, pp. 59–64; and D. Ozanam, 'La colonie française de Cadix . . .', pp. 261–4. This distinction makes research into the French community in Spain difficult, since a proportion of this community was counted as being Spanish.

61 A. Poitrineau, *Les 'Espagnols' . . .*, p. 161.

62 R. Duroux, 'Les boutiquiers cantaliens . . .', p. 286.

63 National archives, F20/434, quoted by R. Duroux, 'Les boutiquiers cantaliens . . .', p. 287.

64 National archives, F20/434, quoted by R. Duroux, 'Les boutiquiers cantaliens . . .', p. 287.

65 A Spanish baker looks back fondly to the days before the War of Independence, when French men married Spanish women, 'which they no longer do today'. Quoted by R. Duroux, 'Les boutiquiers cantaliens', p. 290. A. Poitrineau, *Les 'Espagnols' . . .*, p. 160.

66 R. Duroux, 'Les deux centres d'attraction des cantaliens de Castille (XIXe siècle)', *Centres et périphéries. Actes du 21e congrès de la société des Hispanistes français*, Clermont-Ferrand, Adosa, 1987, pp. 193–212 (201).

67 National archives, F20/434, quoted by R. Duroux, 'Les boutiquiers cantaliens', p. 287.
68 One such merchant wrote to his cousin to ask him to bring some 'razo' from the Auvergne (a type of woollen material), rather than cotton fabrics. A. Poitrineau, Les 'Espagnols' . . . , p. 94.
69 D. R. Ringrose, Madrid . . . , pp. 165–7.
70 A. Poitrineau, Les 'Espagnols' . . . , p. 86 counts the servants amongst the casualties of the Spanish adventure.
71 A. Poitrineau, Les 'Espagnols' . . . , pp. 40–4.
72 See chapter 7.
73 A. Poitrineau, Les 'Espagnols' . . . , pp. 238–40.

Chapter 3 The Eighteenth Century: the Networks of Booksellers and Book Pedlars in Southern Europe

1 Bibliothèque Nationale, Ms. fr. 22130, fo. 37, November 1754.
2 G. Bonnant, 'La librairie genevoise dans la Péninsule ibérique au XVIIIe siècle', Genava, new series, vol. III, pp. 103–24. P.-J. Guinard, 'Le livre dans la péninsule ibérique au XVIIIe siècle; témoignage d'un libraire français', Bulletin hispanique, vol. LIX, 1957, pp. 176–98.
3 M. Infelise, L'editora veneziana nel '700, Milan, Franco Angeli, 1989. A. Machet, 'Le marché du livre français en Italie au XVIIIe siècle', Revue des Etudes italiennes, new series, vol. XXIX, no. 4, 1983, pp. 193–222 and 'Librairie et commerce du livre en Italie dans la deuxième moitié du XVIIIe siècle', Studies on Voltaire and the Eighteenth Century, vol. CLIII, Oxford, 1976, pp. 1347–80.
4 F. Lopez, 'Un aperçu de la librairie espagnole au milieu du XVIIIe siècle', in De l'alphabétisation aux circuits du livre en Espagne XVIe–XXe siècle, CNRS, Paris, 1987, pp. 387–416.
5 C. Berkvens-Stevelink, 'L'édition et le commerce du livre français en Europe', Histoire de l'édition française, vol. II: Le Livre triomphant 1660–1830, Paris, Promodis, 1984, pp. 305–13 (309).
6 In particular in Barcelona, Madrid and towns in Andalusia; 79 French firms were recorded in Cadiz in 1772; 8,734 foreigners (of which 2,701 were French) in 1791; and, out of the 20 or so booksellers in Cadiz between 1770 and 1790, a fair number were French. C. Péligry, 'Le marché espagnol', Histoire de l'édition française, vol. II: Le Livre triomphant 1660–1830, pp. 370–7.
7 The syndic of Lyon booksellers is quite clear on this point: in 1783, books came from 'all over Germany, from Holland, Switzerland, and Italy; primarily from Geneva, Lausanne, Berne, Yverdon, Basle, Neuchâtel, The Hague, Brussels, Liège, Avignon, Rome, Venice, Turin, Milan, etc. . . .'; and, he added, were intended both for the Lyon trade and also for the southern provinces of France, as well as being in transit for Italy and Spain. R. Chartier: 'Livre et espace: circuits commerciaux et géographie culturelle de la librairie lyonnaise au XVIIIe siècle', Revue française d'histoire

du livre, 1–2, 1971, pp. 77–108. For more information on the circulation of the book see H. J. Martin, *Livre, pouvoir et société à Paris au XVIIe siècle, 1598–1701*, Paris, 1969, 2 vols, pp. 296–330.

8 G. Barber, 'The Cramers of Geneva and their trade in Europe between 1755 and 1766', *Studies on Voltaire and the Eighteenth Century*, vol. XXX, 1964, pp. 377–413; 'Who were the booksellers of the Enlightenment?', *Buch und Buchhandel im 18 Jahrhundert*, ed. G. Barber and B. Fabian, Hamburg, 1981, pp. 211–24. G. Barber, 'Pendred abroad: a view of the late eighteenth century book trade in Europe', *Studies in the Book Trade in Honour of Graham Pollard*, Oxford, 1975, pp. 231–77. 'Books from the old world and for the new: the British international trade in books in the eighteenth century', *Studies on Voltaire and the Eighteenth Century*, CLI–CLV, 1976, pp. 185–224.

9 *Annales des Alpes*, XII, 1908–1909, pp. 219–25.

10 A. Albert, *Les Briançonnais libraires*, Grenoble, 1874, pp. 19–23; and *Biographie, bibliographie des Briançonnais, cantons de La Grave et de Monêtier-de-Briançon*, Grenoble, 1877, 97 pp.

11 This network which, unlike the mountain networks, make use of temporary migration was however bound by family ties. For more information, see D. Ozanam, 'La colonie française de Cadix au XVIIIe siècle, d'après un document inédit (1777)', *Mélanges de la Casa de Vélasquez*, IV, 1968, pp. 259–349 (281–8).

12 M.-H. Piwnik, 'Libraires français et espagnols à Lisbonne au XVIIIe siècle', in *Livres et Libraires en Espagne et au Portugal (XVIe–XXe siècles)*, CNRS publications, Paris, 1989, pp. 81–98 (85). The author also demonstrates the important role played by Spaniards such as Mena from Madrid, who was one of the Cramers' most important correspondents.

13 R. Pasta, 'Prima della Rivoluzione: aspetti e vicendi del mercato librario italiano nelle carte della Société typographique de Neuchâtel', *Mélanges de l'Ecole Française de Rome*, 2, 1990, pp. 5–43.

14 *Ibid.*, pp. 19–20.

15 H.-J. Martin, M. Lecocq, H. Carrier, A. Sauvy, *Livres et lecteurs à Grenoble, Les registres du Libraire Nicolas (1654–1668)*, 2 vols, Geneva, 1977; and E. Maignien, 'Les Nicolas, libraires à Grenoble (1608–1681)', *Petite revue des bibliophiles dauphinois*, vol. IV, 1913, pp. 220–24; and 'L'imprimerie, les imprimeurs et les libraires à Grenoble du XVe au XVIIIe siècle', *Bulletin de l'Academie Delphinale*, third series, vol. 18, 1883, part 2, Grenoble, 1884. Departmental Archives, Isère, H 963 to 968, account book belonging to Jean Nicolas, father and son, 1647–1677; IJ 1102, account book belonging to Jean Giraud, merchant from La Grave; and the Gravier family private archives. I should also like to thank Mlle Geneviève Juillard who lent me precious documents from her family archives.

16 Departmental archives of Isère, IJ 1102.

17 For example, the case of Miquel Albert is intriguing; he was a Spanish lawyer whose surname was extremely common in La Grave and in the Villard d'Arène. He launched into publishing in Valencia in 1493. His editorial style, as much in the choice of subject matter as in his business practices, sat uneasily with the cultural background of a Spanish lawyer in

the fifteenth century and were in sharp contrast to those of other publishers in Valencia. P. Berger, *Libro y lectura en la Valencia del Renacimiento*, 2 vols, Valencia, 1987, pp. 156–7. Right at the beginning of the seventeenth century, at the very least between 1603 and 1609, Simon Graffart, a print-seller and printer of story books, sold his prints into the Spanish market. He had business dealings with some of the Dauphiné merchants who traded in Spain, such as Jean Ramband and Jacques Bertrant who were very probably part of the same network. M. Préand, P. Casselle, M. Grirel, C. Le Bizouné, *Dictionnaire des éditeurs d'estampes à Paris sous l'Ancien Régime*, Paris, Promodis, 1987, entry on Graffart, Simon.

18 The Rigaud family were numbered amongst the most important Lyon booksellers in the seventeenth century. They specialized in the production of literary and spiritual works and made a significant contribution to the introduction of Spanish and Italian spiritual works into France. H.-J. Martin, *Livre, pouvoir et société à Paris au XVIIe siècle, 1598–1701*, Paris, 1969, 2 vols, pp. 324–5. On 12 November, 1587, Mathieu Thomas Guesse [Guerre] and Pierre Nicolas, merchants from La Grave, jointly declared the sum of 4 gold ecus owed to B. Rigaud, for the sale and delivery of books', Baudrier, *Bibliographie lyonnaise*, third series, Paris, 1964, pp. 178–83.

19 Baudrier, *Bibliographie lyonnaise* . . . , devotes a large part of volume 3 to the printer Benoît Rigaud. J. P. Seguin, *L'Information en France avant le périodique: 517 canards imprimés entre 1529 et 1631*, Maisonneuve et Larose, Paris, 1964, p. 14.

20 Departmental archives of Isère, 5E 238/1, 5E 580, Protestant registers from Mizoen kept between 1669 and 1681.

21 H.-J. Martin, M. Lecocq, *Livres et lecteurs à Grenoble* . . . , pp. 55–9.

22 Departmental archives of Isère, H963.

23 Furthermore, Nicolas was clerk to the extraordinary war effort in the tax district of Grenoble and general treasurer to the Duke of Lesdiguières; E. Maignien, 'Les Nicolas . . .', p. 224.

24 On 15 October 1578, Didier Mathourel (Mathonnet), Jean Gravier and Claude Juge, merchants from La Grave, acknowledged jointly owing 3 gold ecus to Benoît Rigaud, for goods from his bookshop, the debt being repayable at the next fair. Baudrier, *Bibliographie lyonnaise* . . . , pp. 178–83.

25 Departmental archives of the Hautes Alpes, archives from the commune of La Grave, unclassified, tallage register of 1671.

26 Departmental archives of the Hautes Alpes, 1E 7214, 12 June 1680; and departmental archives of the Isère, IJ 1102.

27 Departmental archives of Isère, IJ 1102.

28 Departmental archives of the Rhône, B series, 8 May 1690. See appendix.

29 H. Lüthy, *La banque protestante en France de la Révocation de l'Edit de Nantes à la Révolution*, Paris, 2 vols, 1959, pp. 36–7. Until the eighteenth century, Lyon was the main stop-off point for men and goods from Geneva on their way into France.

30 E. Arnaud, *Histoire des protestants du Dauphiné aux XVIe, XVIIe et XVIIIe siècles*, 3 vols, Paris, 1875, vol. 1, pp. 499–510. A chronological

list of those admitted into the bourgeois class has been published in A. L. Covelle, *Le livre des bourgeois de l'ancienne République de Genève, publié d'après les registres officiels*, Geneva, J. Jullien, 1897.

31 H.-J. Martin, M. Lecocq, *Livres et lecteurs à Grenoble* . . . , pp. 58, 64, 270 and 282. In the seventeenth century, the Chouet and de Tournes families were the only significant Genevan booksellers in the French market, and the only ones to sustain important networks of correspondents, which primarily comprised Calvinist booksellers.

32 Departmental archives of the Isère, IJ 1102.

33 H.-J. Martin, *Livre, pouvoir et société* . . . , p. 323. On the de Tournes, by the same author, see also 'Stratégies éditoriales dans la France d'Ancien Régime et du dix-neuvième siècle', *Livre et lecture en Espagne et en France sous l'Ancien Régime*, Paris, 1981, pp. 63–77 (71 and 72); and P.-F. Geisendorf, 'Lyon et Genève du XVIe au XVIIIe siècle: les foires et l'imprimerie', *Cahiers d'Histoire*, V, 1, 1960, pp. 65–76.

34 Around 1730, the bookselling trade in Geneva had no further use for the Lyon stopover: 'The printing presses in our country have run for twenty to thirty years for Spain and Portugal', wrote François Grasset to Malesherbes in 1754. Bibliothèque Nationale, Paris, Ms fr. 22130/37, quoted by G. Bonnant, 'Les libraires du Portugal au XVIIIe siècle vus à travers leurs relations d'affaires avec leurs fournisseurs de Genève, Lausanne et Neuchâtel', *Arquivio de bibliographia portuguesa*, Ano VI, no. 23–24, Coimbra, 1961.

35 The output from Lyon came to an abrupt halt when the Revocation was announced; a very real collapse took place in subsequent years. H.-J. Martin, *Livre, pouvoir et société* . . . , p. 324. From their ledger, Giles Barber has analysed the Cramers' business activities from 1755. Between 1755 and 1766, they did half their business with France, and a quarter with the Iberian peninsula. Italy and the German states represented 12 per cent and 8 per cent of their business respectively; as for the northern European states, their share of business was negligible – 3 per cent was done with England and 2 per cent with the Netherlands. They continued to trade in books in Latin and prayer books, aimed at the southern European market. G. Barber, 'The Cramers . . .', pp. 394–5.

36 Private Gravier family archives.

37 G. Barber, 'The Cramers . . .', p. 392.

38 Private Gravier family archives; R. Blanchard, 'Aiguilles', p. 144. In 1786, Jean-Joseph Niel was a creditor to a bookseller in the Cap Français. R. Moulinas, *L'Imprimerie, la Librairie et la Presse à Avignon au XVIIIe siècle*, Grenoble, Presses Universitaires, 1974, p. 139.

39 R. Moulinas, *L'Imprimerie* . . . , pp. 180–1. In Paris, the law demanded a minimum of four printing presses; figures were similar in Lyon (p. 182, *ibid.*).

40 R. Moulinas, *L'Imprimerie* . . . , pp. 192–3.

41 J. Queniart, *L'Imprimerie et la librairie à Rouen au XVIIIe siècle*, Paris, Klincksieck, 1969, p. 192.

42 The Parisian bookseller Antoine Boudet, a capable man and one little given to bias, on returning from Spain in 1763 put the volume of trade in books with Spain at 800,000 *livres tournois* (currency originally minted at Tours,

which later became the royal money); and at 50,000 *livres tournois* the proportion of book imports into Spain for which Avignon was responsible, very much below Venice's share (350,000 *livres tournois*) and Antwerp (200,000), but well above that of Paris which, added to that of Lausanne, Geneva and Lyon, constituted only 100,000 *livres tournois*. In the case of Portugal, the same source indicates that Switzerland, Avignon, Antwerp and Italy together accounted for 200,000 *livres*, whereas France only sold 50,000 *livres* worth there. From one of Boudet's letters, an extract from the Bibliothèque Nationale Française, 22 130, no. 44, printed at the end of the article by P. J. Guinard, 'Le livre dans la péninsule ibérique...'.

43 R. Moulinas, *L'Imprimerie* ..., p. 136.

44 The account book belonging to the Cramer brothers indicates that they had Garrigan print a book in Portuguese for them. R. Moulinas, *L'Imprimerie* ..., p. 140. State Archives of Geneva, business, F57, p. 96.

45 G. Bonnant, 'La Librairie genevoise en Italie jusqu'à la fin du XVIIIe siècle', *Genava*, new series, volume XV, 1967, p. 140.

46 Here I am following in the footsteps of R. Moulinas, 'Une famille d'imprimeurs-libraires avignonnais du XVIIIe siècle: les Delorme', *Révue française d'histoire du livre*, no. 3, 1972, pp. 45–78; A. Albert, *Le maître d'école briançonnais. Les Briançonnais libraires*, Grenoble, 1874, 23 pages.

47 G. Barber, 'The Cramers...' *art. cit.* The book trade also operated directly between Italy and Spain. G. Bonnant, 'La librairie genevoise en Italie...', p. 149.

48 A. Lay, 'Libro e società negli stati sardi del Settecento', in *Libri, editori e pubblico nell'Europa moderna. Guida storica e critica*, a cura di A. Petrucci, Roma-Bari, 1977, pp. 249–82.

49 R. Moulinas, *L'Imprimerie* ..., pp. 145 and the note on page 58.

50 P. Pironti, *Bulifon – Raillard – Gravier. Editori francesi in Napoli*, Naples, 1982.

51 F. da Gama Caeiro, 'Livros e livreiros franceses em Lisboa nos fins de setecentos e no primeiro quartel do seculo XIX', *Anais da Academia Portuguesa da História* (Lisbon), series IIa, II (26), 1980, pp. 301–27 (313).

52 R. Moulinas, 'Une famille...', p. 68.

53 R. Moulinas, 'Une famille...', pp. 72–3.

54 Letter from Thomas Gravier in Rome to his father Simon Gravier in Bez, parish of La Salle, 1762, Gravier family archives.

55 Contract of apprenticeship with the merchants Bérard and Tardieu, 22 September 1769, Gravier family archives.

56 Letter from Thomas Gravier in Rome to his father Simon Gravier in Bez, parish of La Salle, 1762, Gravier family archives.

57 This information was gleaned from the payment of a debt owed to Joseph Antoine Raby, Gravier family archives.

58 Borel, who was to be the people's representative at the *Convention Nationale*, was sent away at a very young age to be a clerk in the Gravier bookshop. A. Albert, *Biographie, Bibliographie du Briançonnais, Cantons de la Grave et de Monêtier-de-Briançon*, Grenoble, 1877, p. 29.

59 In his memoirs, Jean-Simon explained that his departure was motivated by the approach of the revolutionary army and by the fact that he had been

threatened with arrest for undertaking to print the *Mémoires pour servir à l'Histoire de la Révolution française* by the Abbé d'Auribeau, who had emigrated to Rome.

60 From the Gravier family archives.

61 M.-H. Piwnik, 'Libraires français et espagnols à Lisbonne...', p. 87.

62 M.-H. Piwnik, 'Libraires français et espagnols à Lisbonne...', pp. 87–8.

63 Geneva State Archives, business, F62, letter of 31 March 1780 to Yves Gravier in Genoa.

64 G. Barber, 'The Cramers...', *art. cit.* The book trade also operated directly from Italy to Spain.

65 A. Machet, 'Librairie et commerce du livre en Italie...', pp. 1365–6.

66 M.-H. Piwnik, 'Libraires français et espagnols à Lisbonne...', p. 88.

67 A. Machet, 'Le marché du livre...', p. 200.

68 H.-J. Martin, *Livre, pouvoir et société*..., pp. 324–5. The business that the de Tournes family did with the Jesuits and the Catholic Mediterranean regions was always considerable, whether they were in Geneva or Lyon. P.-F. Geisendorf, 'Lyon et Genève du XVIe au XVIIIe siècle: les foires et l'imprimerie', *Cahiers d'Histoire*, V, 1, 1960, pp. 65–76 (73).

69 G. Bonnant, 'Les libraires du Portugal au XVIIIe siècle...'. See also M.-H. Piwnik, 'Libraires français et espagnols à Lisbonne...', pp. 88–9.

70 G. Bonnant, 'La librairie genevoise en Italie jusqu'à la fin du XVIIIe siècle', *Genava*, new series, vol. XV, 1967, pp. 117–60 (131–2). On numerous occasions Yves Gravier from Genoa was accused of distributing banned literature: see E. Parodi, 'Yves Gravier libraio-editore in Genova nel sec. XVIII', *La Berio*, XXIII, 1983, pp. 38–47. See also Renato Pata's work on the distribution in Italy of work by the Enlightenment thinkers, in particular 'Venezia e la Svizzera: tracce di un commercio librario' (a paper given at the conference *L'editoria del Settecento e i Remondini*, Bassano, 28–29 September 1990), and 'Produzione, commercio e circolazione del libro nel Settecento' (a paper given at the conference *Un decennio di storiografia italiana sul secolo XVIII*, Vico Equense, 25–28 October 1990).

71 L.-M. Enciso Recio, 'Actividades de los Franceses de Cadiz 1789–1790', *Hispania XIX*, 1959, pp. 250–89, quoted by A. Poitrineau, *Les 'Espagnols' de l'Auvergne et du Limousin du XVIIe au XIXe siècle*, Aurillac, Mazel-Malroux, 1985, p. 238.

72 L. Braida, *Le Guide del Tempo. Produzione, contenuti e forme degli almanachi piemontesi nel settecento*. Deputazione subalpina di storia patria, Turin, 1989, pp. 232–3. A. Lay, 'Libro e società negli stati sardi del Settecento', in *Libri, editori e pubblico nell'Europa moderna. Guida storica e critica* a cura di A. Petrucci, Roma-Bari, 1977, pp. 249–82 (274–81). The author also provides a letter from Giraud to the Société typographique de Neuchâtel, asking them to mix those books which were banned in with the others, or even to conceal them in the paper in which the books were wrapped: p. 273.

73 R. Pasta, 'Prima della Rivoluzione...', pp. 16–17.

74 N. Dallai Belgrano, 'Gravier et Beuf librai-editori e le guide illustrate di Genova fra '700 e '800', *La Berio*, XXVI, 1986, pp. 43–86.

75 Letter from Thomas Gravier to Jean-Simon Gravier, 21 July 1798.

76 A. Lay, 'Libro e società...', pp. 249–82 (261).

77 Letter from Thomas Gravier to Jean-Simon Gravier, 16 August 1789. A letter from 1802 stated that Thomas had bought the contents of several convent libraries and that he had stored – or, in other words, hidden – the valuable titles with private individuals. These letters have reached us in fragmentary fashion, quoted in the legal proceedings taken out by Thomas' heirs against Jean-Simon. Bibliothèque Municipale de Grenoble, 8/3220.

78 Bibliothèque municipale de Grenoble, R. 7451.

79 The account between *sieur* Cormontaigne from Rome and Thomas Gravier reveals that coffee and chocolate changed hands, as well as books. In Lisbon, Rolland received large quantities of coffee, sugar and rice; F. da Gama Caeiro, 'Livros e livreiros franceses em Lisboa . . .', p. 314.

80 M.-H. Piwnik, 'Libraires français et espagnols à Lisbonne . . .', p. 87.

81 R. Moulinas, 'Une famille . . .', p. 65, note 55.

82 Bibliothèque Municipale de Grenoble, R 7451.

83 For more information on the Raby family, see P. Léon, *Marchands et spéculateurs dauphinois dans le monde antillais du XVIIIe siècle. Les Dolle et les Raby*, Paris, 1963.

84 Quoted by R. Moulinas in *L'Imprimerie . . .*, pp. 148–9.

85 Malesherbes, quoted by A. Sauvy, 'Le livre aux champs', *Historie de l'Edition française*, vol. II: *Le Livre triomphant 1660–1830*, Paris, Promodis, 1984, pp. 430–43 (431).

86 F. Lopez, 'Un aperçu de la librairie espagnole . . .', pp. 406–7.

87 F. Lopez, 'Un aperçu de la librairie espagnole . . .', p. 408.

88 His Spanish first name does not necessarily mean that he was born in Spain. François Lopez has himself seen the death certificate of Don Diego Barthélémi, born in 'Monastier de Brianzon'. To make integration easier, such pedlars might assume Spanish first names for the time they spent in Spain. In Italy too, first names were Italianized in registers. Elsewhere, parish registers in Alpine villages gave us the name 'Scolastique'. . . .

89 C. Lamoignon de Malesherbes, *Mémoires sur la librairie*, p. 155, quoted by Anne Sauvy in 'Le livre aux champs . . .', p. 431: 'By chance I have learnt that there is a significant trade in books printed in France being done with Spain, Portugal and Italy. This is perhaps the only active business which the French booksellers do: for in Germany, Holland, Switzerland and elsewhere, they prefer to forge our books than buy them from us because our bookshops charge too much for them. The trade being done with Italy and Spain concerns books intended for these two Nations, which are printed in Lyon and in other Southern towns and it is then the itinerant merchants or pedlars, who are called *Bisoards* and who live in the area around Briançon, who come down from the mountains every year to put together a selection of books from Lyon and elsewhere and then take them themselves as far as Cadiz or Sicily.'

90 Through the debts owed, the inventories drawn up after a death refer indirectly to these essential links: the inventory drawn up in 1750 of Jean-Abraham Niel's goods also mentions the debts owed by two 'ironmongers'. R. Moulinas, *L'Imprimerie . . .*, p. 136.

91 Bibliothèque nationale de France, Fr 22 124, fo. 285, quoted by R. Moulinas in *L'Imprimerie . . .*, p. 147.

92 Report by the Parisian bookseller David after his visit to the fair at Beaucaire

in 1754, quoted by R. Moulinas in *L'Imprimerie* ... , p. 147. For more information on the Beaucaire fair and its prosperous period between 1730 and 1789, see P. Léon, 'Vie et mort d'un grand marché international, la Foire de Beaucaire (XVIIIe–XIXe siècle)', *Revue de géographie de Lyon*, vol. XXVIII, no. 4, 1953, pp. 309–28.

93 Bibliothèque nationale de France, Fr 22 075, fo. 214, quoted by R. Moulinas in *L'Imprimerie* ... , p. 146.

94 BNF, Ms Fr 22127, fo. 46–9, De La Porte, *Mémoire au sujet du commerce des livres que font les colporteurs qui descendent des montagnes de Provence et de Dauphiné*, 15 October 1754. I should like to thank René Favier who passed on this reference to me.

95 M. Infelise, *L'editoria veneziana nel '700*, Milan, Franco Angeli, 1989, p. 237; M. Infelise, *I Remondini di Bassano, Stampa e industria nel Veneto del Settecento*, Bassano, 1980. L. Braida, *Le guide del Tempo* ... , pp. 102–5 refer to the part played by book pedlars from the Tyrol valleys to Turin.

96 J. De Lalande, *Voyage d'un François en Italie dans les années 1765 and 1766*, II, Paris, 1769.

97 M. Infelise, *L'editoria veneziana* ... , p. 260.

98 *Stampe per via. L'incisione dei secoli XVII–XIX nel commercio ambulante dei tesini*, exhibition catalogue by B. Passamani, Pieve Tesino-Trento-Bassano del Grappa, 1972, Calliano, Arti grafiche R. Manfredi, 1972. See in particular the article by E. Fietta on 'Il commercio tesino nel mondo', pp. 31–42 (32); and by the same author: 'Con la cassetta in spalla: gli ambulanti di tessino', *Quaderni di cultura alpina*, no. 23, 1985, pp. 4–111.

99 M. Infelise, *L'editoria veneziana* ... , p. 260.

100 *Stampe per via* ... , p. 25.

101 *Stampe per via* ... , pp. 37–8 and the individual notes on pp. 79–98.

102 M. Infelise, *L'editoria veneziana* ... , p. 259.

103 A. Machet, 'Le marché du livre ...', p. 200.

104 P. Casselle, 'Recherche sur les marchands d'estampes parisiens d'origine cotentinoise à la fin de l'Ancien Régime', *Comité des travaux historiques et scientifiques. Bulletin d'histoire moderne et contemporaine*, 11, 1978, pp. 74–93. A. Sauvy, 'Noël Gille dit La Pistole, marchand forain libraire roulant par la France', *Bulletin des bibliothèques de France*, May 1967, pp. 177–90. R. Darnton, 'Un colporteur sous l'Ancien Régime', *Censures, de la Bible aux larmes d'Eros*, Centre Georges Pompidou, Paris, 1987, pp. 130–9. J. Queniart, *L'Imprimerie et la librairie à Rouen au XVIIIe siècle* Paris, Klincksieck, 1969, pp. 56–9 and 198–206 and *Culture et sociétés urbaines dans la France de l'Ouest au XVIIIe siècle*, Paris, Klincksieck, 1978, pp. 387 and 402–12.

105 D. Ozanam, 'La colonie française de Cadiz au XVIIIe siècle ...', p. 328.

106 P. Casselle, 'Recherche sur les marchands d'estampes ...', p. 89.

107 A. Sauvy, 'Noël Gille ...', p. 185 and R. Moulinas, *L'Imprimerie* ... , p. 136.

108 F. Lopez, 'Un aperçu de la librairie espagnole ...', p. 395. A. Gutierrez, *La France et les Français dans la littérature espagnole. Un aspect de la xénophobie en Espagne (1598–1665)*, Lille, Atelier national de reproduction des thèses, Université de Lille, 1982, part II, chapter 3.

109 J.-J. Darmon, *Le Colportage de librairie en France sous le Second Empire*, Paris, 1972.
110 G. B. Martinelli, *Origine e sviluppo dell attività dei librai pontremolesi*, Pontremoli, 1973, pp. 15–16.
111 R. Moulinas, *L'Imprimerie* . . . , pp. 399–401.
112 G. Bonnant, 'La librairie genevoise dans la Péninsule ibérique . . .', p. 112. Bernard Lescaze, 'Commerce d'assortiment et livres interdits: Genève', *Histoire de l'Edition française*, vol. II: *Le Livre triomphant 1660–1830*, Paris, Promodis, 1984, pp. 326–33 (333).
113 G. Bonnant, 'La librairie genevoise dans la Péninsule ibérique . . .', pp. 114–16. P.-F. Geisendorf, 'Lyon et Genève du XVIe au XVIIIe siècle: les foires et l'imprimerie', *Cahiers d'Histoire*, V, 1, 1960, pp. 65–76 (see p. 73 for the importance of this religious literature to the de Tournes business).
114 G. Bonnant, 'Les libraires du Portugal au XVIIIe siècle . . .'.
115 Except in Navarre which enjoyed special status. F. Lopez, 'Un aperçu de la librairie espagnole . . .', pp. 399–400.
116 Bibliothèque municipale de Grenoble, 8/3220.
117 M. Infelise, *L'editoria veneziana* . . . , p. 249.

Chapter 4 A Flexible Typology

1 Cited by A. Sauvy in 'Noël Gille dit La Pistole, marchand forain libraire roulant par la France', *Bulletin des bibliothèques de France*, May 1967, pp. 177–190 (178). Montsurvent, Boisroger, Gouville and Montcarville were the parishes where peddling was most prevalent. To which one can add Ancteville, Vaudrimesnil, Gouvelle-sur-mer, La Rondehaye, Geffosses and especially Muneville-le-Bingard, which was a real breeding ground for fairground bookstalls, according to J.-D. Mellot, in his article 'Rouen et les "libraires forains" à la fin du XVIIIe siècle: la veuve Machuel et ses correspondants (1768–1773)', in the *Bibliothèque de l'Ecole des chartes*, vol. 147, 1989, pp. 503–48 (511). Savary des Bruslons' *Dictionnaire* mentions the sale of light-coloured fabrics called *rapatelle* as being a traditional specialization of the Coutances pedlars.
2 A. Sauvy 'Noël Gille . . .', p. 178 and R. Darnton, 'Un colporteur sous l'Ancien Régime', *Censures, de la Bible aux larmes d'Eros*, Centre Georges Pompidou, Paris, 1987, pp. 130–9 (131). J.-D. Mellot, 'Rouen et les "libraires forains" . . .', p. 511. The same career path can be observed in the Ticino region: I. E. Fietta: 'Con la cassetta in spalla: gli ambulanti di Tessino, *Quaderni di cultura alpina*, no. 23, 1985, pp. 4–111 (46–50).
3 J.-J. Darmon, *Le colportage de librairie en France sous le Second Empire* Paris, 1972, pp. 28–9.
4 Letter from Orléans, 6 July 1772, J.-D. Mellot, 'Rouen et les "libraires forains" . . .', p. 513.
5 A. Sauvy, 'Noël Gille . . .', p. 182 and J.-D. Mellot, 'Rouen et les "libraires forains" . . .', pp. 532–5.
6 1755 Report on pedlars, J.-D. Mellot, 'Rouen et les "libraires forains" . . .', pp. 516–7.

7 A. Sauvy, 'Noël Gille...', pp. 180–90. There are also numerous examples of this pattern in J.-D. Mellot, 'Rouen et les "libraires forains"...', pp. 519–20.

8 J.-D. Mellot, 'Rouen et les "libraires forains"...', p. 530.

9 H.-J. Martin, 'La préeminence de la librairie parisienne', *Histoire de l'Edition française*, vol. II: *Le Livre triomphant 1660–1830*, Paris, Promodis, 1984, pp. 263–81.

10 P. Casselle, 'Recherches sur les marchands d'estampes parisiens d'origine cotentinoise à la fin de l'Ancien Régime', *Comité des travaux historiques et scientifiques. Bulletin d'histoire moderne et contemporaine*, 11, 1978, pp. 74–93 (84–85).

11 J.-J. Darmon, *Le colportage de librairie...*, pp. 32 and 48–50; L. Fontaine, 'I reti del credito', *Quaderni Storici*, no. 68, 1988, pp. 573–93. For the Auvergne region, A Poitrineau has recorded the terms of certain contracts of employment, 'Aspects de l'émigration temporaire et saisonnière en Auvergne à la fin du XVIIIe siècle', *Revue d'Histoire Moderne et Contemporaine*, 1962, pp. 5–50 (426–7).

12 M. Spufford, *The Great Reclothing of Rural England, Petty Chapmen and their Wares in the Seventeenth Century*, London, The Hambledon Press, 1984, pp. 61 and 82–3; R. B. Westerfield, *Middlemen in English Business, particularly between 1660 and 1760*, 1915, reprint New York 1968, p. 376. Generally speaking, the economic life of modern England was in the grip of interdependent regional credit networks, so that every man, even the poorest, was trapped in a 'spider's web of credit'. N. McKendrick, J. Brewer and J. H. Plumb, *The Birth of Consumer Society. The Commercialization of Eighteenth century England*, Bloomington, Indiana University Press, 1982, pp. 205–10.

13 S. Jaumain, 'Les colporteurs Hainuyers du XIXe siècle', *Annales du Cercle royal d'Histoire at d'Archéologie d'Ath et Musées athois*, 1984, pp. 282–340 (315).

14 C. Niermann, 'Gewebe im Umherzien – Hausierer und Wanderlager in Bremen vor 1914', *Geschäfte der Bremer Kleinhandel um 1900, Beiträge zur Sozialgeschischte Bremens*, Heft 4, Teil 1, p. 212.

15 J.-D. Mellot, 'Rouen et les "libraires forains"...', p. 511. However, it is still not known where the widow Machuel was originally from.

16 *Ibid.*, p. 525.

17 A. Sauvy, 'Noël Gille...', p. 185. J. Quéniart, *Cultures et sociétés urbaines dans la France de l'Ouest au XVIIIe siècle*, Paris, Klincksieck, 1978, pp. 387–412 provides numerous insights into the role played by this Cotentin network.

18 A. Sauvy, 'Noël Gille...', p. 189. For a comparison with England, see the list drawn up by Richard Trendall of Norfolk in M. Spufford, *The Great Reclothing...*, pp. 53 and 69, and the study by R. B. Westerfield, *Middlemen in English Business...*, p. 383.

19 P. Casselle, 'Recherche sur les marchands d'estampes...', pp. 82–3.

20 *Ibid.*, p. 83.

21 19 May 1765, Bibliothèque nationale, mss. fr. 22096 (118) as cited by P. Casselle in his 'Recherche sur les marchands d'estampes...', p. 77.

22 J. Queniart, *L'imprimerie et la librairies à Rouen au XVIIIe siècle*, Paris, Klincksieck, 1969, pp. 402–12.

23 A. Sauvy, 'Noël Gille . . .', *art. cit.* p. 185; and R. Moulinas, *L'Imprimerie, la Librairie et la Presse à Avignon au XVIIIe siècle*, Grenoble, Presses Universitaires, 1974, p. 136.

24 For more on the establishment of book pedlars in Paris, and the changing policies concerning them, see H.-J. Martin, *Livre, pouvoir et société à Paris au XVIIe siècle, 1598–1701*, Paris, 1969, vol. 2, pp. 357–8.

25 Victor Hugo, *Quatre-vingt-treize*, ed. Garnier-Flammarion, Paris, 1965, p. 111.

26 D. Roche, 'La Police du livre'. *Histoire de l'Edition française*, vol. 2, *le Livre triomphant 1660–1830*, Paris, Promodis, 1984, pp. 84–91 (90–91); A. Sauvy, 'Livres contrefaits et livres interdits', *Histoire de l'Edition française*, vol. 2, *Le Livre triomphant 1660–1830*, Paris, Promodis, 1984, pp. 104–19.

27 M. Trifoni, 'I "santari". Venditori itineranti di immagini devozionali a Campli e nel teramano', *La Ricera Folklorica*, 19, 1989, pp. 113–20. Nizard: *Essai sur le colportage de librairie*, 1855, pp. 41–2, quoted by J.-J. Darmon in *Le colportage de librairie . . .*, p. 74.

28 There are examples of such existences, never far from that of beggar, in A. Poitrineau, 'Aspects de l'émigration . . .', pp. 36–7; or, on temporary work see R. Sarti, *Long Live the Strong: a history of rural society in the Apennine Mountains*, The University of Massachusetts Press, Amherst, 1985, pp. 88–9.

29 J.-F. Botrel, 'Les aveugles colporteurs d'imprimés en Espagne', *Mélanges de la Casa de Vélasquez*, 9, 1973, pp. 417–82 and 10, 1974, pp. 233–71. J. Marco, *Literatura popular en España en los siglos XVIII y XIX. Una aproximación a los pliegos de cordel*, Madrid, Taurus, 1977, pp. 103–9.

30 J.-F. Botrel, 'Les aveugles colporteurs . . .', pp. 253–4.

31 J. Caro Bajora, *Ensayo sobre la literatura de cordel*, Revista de occidente, Madrid, 1969, p. 61. Blindmen who travelled from fair to fair, singing to the accompaniment of a guitar or violin, then selling the printed text of their song, were to be found all over Europe; but were not organized in the same way as the Spanish blindmen. With regard to Italy, Gabriella Solari has discovered various references to this in the archives, and the Università degli studi di Siena has brought together a certain number of such songs in its *Archiveiodelle fonti orali*.

32 D. Curto, 'Littératures de large circulation au Portugal (XVIe–XVIIe siècles), Colloque *Les imprimés de large circulation et la littérature de colportage dans l'Europe des XVIe–XIXe siècles*, Herzog August Bibliothek Wolfenbutel, April 1991, to be published.

33 W. Shakespeare, *The Winter's Tale*, Act 4, Scene 3.

34 D. Diderot, *Jacques le Fataliste et son maître*, edited with an introduction and notes by Yvon Belaval, Paris, 1973, p. 60: '. . . garters, belts, watch straps, snuff-boxes in the latest style [real *jaback*], rings, watch cases'. The name Jaback was taken from the Jaback Hotel in the rue Saint-Merre in Paris. Jewellery and novelty goods of all types were sold there for a time. It was fashionable then only to buy 'real *jaback*' articles.

35 J. Taylor, *Prologue to A Very Merry Wherry-Ferry Voyage: or Yorke for My Money*, quoted by V. E. Neuberg in *Popular Literature: a history and guide from the beginning of printing to the year 1897*, London, 1977, p. 56.

36 *Le Mercier Inventif*, from the Bibliothèque bleue, Troyes, 1632. My thanks to Daniel Roche for having brought this text to my attention.

37 N. McKendrick, J. Brewer and J. H. Plumb, *The Birth of Consumer Society* ... p. 93.
38 T. Endelman, 'L'activité économique des juifs anglais', *Dix-huitième siècle*, no. 13, 1981, pp. 113–126 (123).
39 B. Geremek, *Truands et misérables dans l'Europe moderne (1350–1600)*, Gallimard/Julliard, 1980.
40 S. Ferrone, 'La vendita del teatro: tipologie europee tra cinque e seicento', Institut Universitaire Européen, Florence, Symposium: *Négoce et culture à l'époque moderne*, 327/88 (col. 76) 41 pp.
41 'Comici, Ciarlatini, Montainbanco, Erborari', as cited by A. Paglicci-Brozzi in *Contributo alla storia del teatro italiano. Il teatro a Milano nel secolo XVII*, Milan, 1891, cited by S. Ferrone, 'La vendita del teatro ...', p. 28.
42 For more on the world of street theatre, see P. Burke, *Popular Culture in Early Modern Europe*, Cambridge, 1978. I have consulted the Italian translation, *Cultura popolare nell'Europa moderna*, Milan, 1980, pp. 92–9.
43 As cited by V. E. Neuberg, *Popular Literature* ... , p. 76.
44 22 July 1732, cited by V. E. Neuberg in *Popular Literature* ... , p. 117.
45 G. Pitrè, *Usi e costumi, credenze e pregiudizi del popolo siciliano*, Palermo, 1978, vol. 1, pp. 177–216. O. Niccoli, *Profeti e popolo nell'Italia del Rinascimento*, Rome-Bari, Laterza, 1987, pp. 27–37. *Il libro dei vagabondi*, Piero Camporesi ed., Turin, 1973.
46 *Stampe per via. L'incisione dei secoli XVII–XIX nel commercio ambulante dei tesini*, the catalogue of the exhibition put on by Bruno Passamani, Pieve Tesino-Trento-Bassano del Grappa, 1972, Calliano, Arti grafiche R. Manfredi, 1972, p. 33.
47 G. Duval, *Littérature de colportage et imaginaire collectif en Angleterre à l'époque des Dicey (1720–1800)*, Presses Universitaires de Bordeaux, Talence, 1991 (I consulted the Ph.D. thesis deposited in the University of Dijon, 1986, p. 85.) [author's note]
48 In France, those who chanted hymns and laments were recruited from the Chamagne region in the Jura, according to Nisard. Nisard, *Essai sur le colportage de librairie*, 1855, pp. 41–2, as cited by J.-J. Darmon, *Le colportage de librairie* ... , p. 74; and B. Maradan, 'Chamagne et les Chamagnons, colporteurs en livres', *Les Intermédiaires culturels*, Aix-en-Provence, 1981, pp. 277–89. J. Lesueur, 'Une figure populaire en Lorraine au siècle dernier, le colporteur ou chamagnon', *Bulletin de la Société lorraine des Etudes locales de l'enseignement public*, 1969, 3, pp. 29–39.
49 J. Lesueur, 'Une figure populaire en Lorraine ...', p. 32.
50 D. Roche, *Le Peuple de Paris*, Paris, 1981, p. 225.
51 L. S. Mercier, *Tableaux de Paris*, Amsterdam, 1783–88, vol. 1, pp. 285–7; cited in D. Roche, *Le Peuple de Paris*, pp. 225–6.
52 T. Endelman, 'L'activité ...', p. 123.
53 R. Sarti, *Long Live the Strong* ... , p. 66.
54 A. B. 11 923, in the year 1756, cited by A. Farge, *Le Goût de l'archive*, Paris, Seuil, 1989, p. 111.
55 J.-F. Botrel, 'Les aveugles colporteurs ...', p. 255.
56 On at least three occasions – in 1666, 1674 and 1721 – the brotherhood had their status confirmed as professionals who earned a living from their labour and not from begging; J.-F. Botrel, 'Les aveugles colporteurs ...', p. 425–7.

57 Also known as *pliego suelto* [loose sheets], this was a notebook of a few pages, formed from one sheet of paper folded twice to constitute 8 pages. The idea gradually spread and booklets of 32 pages or more were termed *pliegos*. J. Marco, *Literatura popular* . . . , p. 33.

58 J. Marco, *Literatura popular* . . .

59 J.-F. Botrel, 'Les aveugles colporteurs . . .', pp. 251–2.

60 J. Marco, *Literatura popular* . . . , pp. 33–50. The following is an example of the length of the titles: 'Aquí se contiene un dulce tratato, / de como une mujer natural de Valladolid, / siendo cautiva desde Bugia nególa ley de Nuestro Señor, y se casócon un rico moro, do estuvo veinte y tres años en la secta de Mahoma, y fue Dios servido, que al cabo de este tiempo cautivaron un clérigo hermano suyo, el cual sirvió a su hermanas tres años de su esclavo sin conocerle y cómo fue Dios servido que al cabo de tres años se conocieron por ciertas preguntas, y el arrepentimiento de la Renegata, y las sentidas lamentaciones quebizo, / y como tuvieron lugar de venir a Roma y reconsiliarse con el Santo Padre.'

61 J. Marco, *Literatura popular* . . . , pp. 33–50 and 194. J.-F. Botrel, 'Les aveugles colporteurs . . .', pp. 259–60. Also *infra*, chapter 8: The Culture of Itinerancy.

62 J.-F. Botrel, 'Les aveugles colporteurs . . .', pp. 253–4. There is a description of the iconography of Goya's paintings of blindmen in J. Caro Bajora, *Ensayo* . . . , chapter 1.

63 J.-F. Botrel, *La diffusion du livre en Espagne (1848–1914)*, Madrid, 1988.

64 J. Caro Bajora, *Ensayo* . . . , p. 60. The art of the Sicilian *cantastorie* was similarly codified in the diction, gestures and expressions which accompanied the narration: see G. Pitrè, *Usi e costumi*, . . . , pp. 178–9 and S. Burgaretta, ' "Cuntu" e contastorie nella Sicilia di oggi', *La Ricerca Folklorica*, 19, 1989, pp. 121–5.

65 R. Schenda, *Folklore e letteratura popolare: Italia–Germania–Francia*, translated by Maria Chiara Figliozzi and Ingeborg Walter, Bibliotheca Biographica, Istituto della Enciclopedia Italiana fondata da Giovanni Treccani, Rome, 1986, p. 279. *L'Information en France avant le périodique. 517 canards imprimés entre 1529 et 1631*, Maisonneuve et Larose, Paris, 1964, p. 16.

66 O. Niccoli, *Profeti e popolo nell'Italia* . . . , p. 29.

67 However, in the Auvergne in the nineteenth century, the women took care of the sale of livestock. R. Duroux, 'Femme seule, Femme paysanne, Femme de migrant', *Colloque d'Histoire d'Aurillac, le Paysan*, 1988, pp. 145–68 (160); the situation was similar in the Val Varaita: D. Albera, M. Dossetti, S. Ottonelli, 'Società' ed emigrazioni . . .', p. 129.

68 Jean Eymard's account book in the Musée Dauphinois.

69 A. D. Rhône, 7B 21, 21 July 1734. Archive discovered by Renaud Ferrand for his Master's dissertation *Sacrilèges et blasphèmes en Lyonnais et Beaujolais*, Lyon II, 1989.

70 J.-D. Mellot, 'Rouen et les "libraires forains" . . .', p. 524; M. Trifoni, 'I "santari". Venditori itineranti di immagini devozionali . . .', p. 117; F. Barbier, 'Un exemple d'émigration temporaire: Les colporteurs de librairie pyrénéens (1840–1880)', *Annales du Midi*, vol. 95, 1983, pp. 289–307. B. Maradan, 'Chamagne et les Chamagnons, colporteurs en livres', *Les Intermédiares culturels*, Publication de l'Université d'Aix-en-Provence, 1978, pp. 277–89, and J.-J. Darmon's book *Le colportage de librairie*. . . .

71 I. E. Fietta, 'Con la cassetta in spalla . . . , pp. 4–111.
72 There are examples given for the Auvergne at the end of the eighteenth century in A. Poitrineau: 'Aspects de l'émigration . . .', p. 427; for Savoy in C. and G. Maistre's *L'émigration marchande savoyarde aux XVIIe–XVIIIe siècles. L'exemple de Nancy-sur-Cluses*, Académie Salésienne, Annecy, 1986, pp. 70–80.
73 London's overwhelming domination was also a reflection of the importance of the city, in which, in 1800, one English person in ten lived: in 1801 the total population was estimated at 9 million, with 900,000 in London.
74 L. Weatherill, *The Growth of the Pottery Industry in England 1660–1815*, New York, London, 1986, p. 123.
75 M. Spufford, *The Great Reclothing* . . . , pp. 79–80.
76 B. Amouretti, 'La tournée d'un colporteur dans les monts du Beaujolais sous le Second Empire, 1864–1868', *Cahiers d'Histoire*, vol. XXXII, nos 3–4, 1987, pp. 341–58 (343).
77 M. Spufford, *The Great Reclothing* . . . , pp. 43 and 69.
78 S. Jaumain, 'Les colporteurs Hainuyers . . .', pp. 310 and 313.
79 Charles Nizard, *Essai sur le colportage de librairie*, p. 48, as cited by J.-J. Darmon, *Le colportage de librairie* . . . , p. 37.
80 A. Sauvy, 'Noël Gille. . . .', pp. 180–2.
81 *Mémoire au sujet des colporteurs dans diverses provinces, fait pour M. Anisson*, 1755, Bibliothèque nationale, ms. fr. 22 128, document 92, as cited by A. Sauvy, 'Le livre aux champs', p. 432.
82 A. Sauvy, 'Noël Gille . . .', pp. 184–5.
83 J.-D. Mellot, 'Rouen et les "libraires forains" . . .', p. 529.
84 5 March 1765, Bibliothèque nationale, mss. fr. 22096 (120), as cited by P. Casselle, 'Recherche sur les marchands d'estampes . . .', p. 76.
85 Notice of 15 December 1764 'concerning those merchants selling prints who trade in immoral books'; Bibliothèque nationale, mss. fr. 22096 (113), as cited by P. Casselle, 'Recherche sur les marchands d'estampes . . .', p. 76.
86 P. Casselle, 'Recherche sur les marchands d'estampes . . .', pp. 76–8.
87 M. Spufford, *The Great Reclothing* . . . , pp. 88–9; A Poitrineau, 'Aspects de l'émigration . . .', p. 308.
88 L. Fontaine, *Le Voyage et la Mémoire, colporteurs de l'Oisans au XIXe siècle*, Lyon, Presses Universitaires de Lyon, 1984, p. 126; B. Amouretti, 'La tournée . . .', p. 349. Gravier family archives.
89 *Ibid.*, pp. 113–40. P. Martin-Charpenel, 'Les colporteurs de l'Ubaye en basse Provence', *Annale de Haute Provence*, no. 291, 1981, pp. 3–57. B. Amouretti, 'La tournée . . .', pp. 350–2.
90 R. Duroux, 'Les boutiquiers cantaliens de Nouvelle-Castille au XIXe siècle', *Mélanges de la casa de Vélasquez*, 1985, vol. XXI, pp. 281–307 (295).
91 *La vie pénible et laborieuse de Jean-Joseph Esmieu, Annales de Haute Provence*, no. 255, 1969, pp. 329–41; no. 256, 1969, pp. 414–27; nos 257–8, 1969, pp. 453–75; no. 259, 1970, pp. 33–49; no. 260, pp. 100–21; nos 261–2, pp. 161–87 (no. 259).
92 P. Martin-Charpenel, 'Les colporteurs de l'Ubaye . . .', p. 13.
93 F. da Gama Caeiro, 'Livros e livreiros franceses em Lisboa nos fins de setecentos e no primeiro quartel do seculo XIX', *Anais de Academia Portuguesa da História* (Lisbon), Series IIa, II (26), 1980, pp. 301–27 (312). See chapter 7.

94 N. McKendrick, J. Brewer and J. H. Plumb, *The Birth of Consumer Society* ..., pp. 88–9.
95 R. B. Westerfield, *Middlemen in English Business*..., pp. 313–14.
96 N. McKendrick, J. Brewer and J. H. Plumb, *The Birth of Consumer Society* ..., pp. 77–81.

Chapter 5 In the Village: Reasons for Itinerancy and the Structures Supporting It

1 R. Blanchard, 'Le haut Dauphiné à la fin du XVIIe siècle, d'après les procès-verbaux de la Révision des feux de 1700', *Revue de Géographie alpine*, vol. 3, 1915, pp. 317–419. A. Allix, *L'Oisans au Moyen Age, étude de géographie historique en haute montagne d'après des documents inédits suivie de la transcription des textes*, Paris, 1929, p. 157. J. Augel, *Italienische Einwanderung und Wirtschaftstätigkeit in rheinischen Städten des 17. und 18. Jahrhunderts*, Bonn, 1971, p. 56. A Poitrineau, *Remues d'hommes. Les migrations montagnardes en France 17e–18e siècles*, Paris, 1983, pp. 5–24. D. Sella, 'Au dossier des migrations montagnardes: l'exemple de la Lombardie au XVIIe siècle', *Mélanges en l'honneur de Fernand Braudel. Histoire économique du monde méditerranéen*, Toulouse, 1973, pp. 547–54. C. and G. Maistre, *L'émigration marchande savoyarde aux XVIIe–XVIIIe siècles. L'exemple de Nancy-sur-Cluses*, Académie Salésienne, Annecy, 1986, pp. 24–31.
2 R. Blanchard, 'Le haut Dauphiné ...', p. 402. For these men, migration was also a response to the winter which left them unemployed for more than half the year, when the isolation of the villages, cut off from one another by snow and avalanches, made enforced idleness even more difficult to bear. R. Blanchard, *Les Alpes Occidentales*, vol. III, *Les Grandes Alpes françaises du nord*, Arthaud, 1943, 2 vols, vol. II, p. 324. P. Guichonnet, 'L'émigration saisonnière pendant la première moitié du XIXe siècle (1783–1860)', *Revue de Géographie alpine*, vol. XXXIII, fasc. 3, pp. 465–534 (468–70).
3 B. Bonnin, *La terre et les paysans en Dauphiné au XVIIe siècle (1580–1730)*, doctoral thesis, University of Lyon II, 1982. A Poitrineau, *Remues d'hommes*..., pp. 6–24. H. G. Rosenberg, *A Negotiated World, Three Centuries of Change in a French Alpine Community*, University of Toronto Press, 1988 adopts the same line of argument for the modern period in the history of the Queyras valleys.
4 Tallage register for La Grave 1671: 'register to which we have not added an estimation of the price of assets, nor of personal property or business, not knowing how to go about this, never having yet seen it practised in any community under this Mandate'.
5 1 *sétérée* = c 38 *ares*. L. Cortes, *L'Oisans, recherches historiques, tourisme*, Grenoble, 1926, p. 122.
6 L. Fontaine, 'Family Cycles, Peddling and Society in Upper Alpine Valleys in the Eighteenth Century', in *Domestic Strategies. Work and Family in France and Italy 17–18th Century*, Stuart Woolf ed., Editions de la Maison des Sciences de l'Homme and Cambridge University Press, 1991, pp. 43–68.
7 It should be noted that the tables of those registered repeat the figures given in the wills.

250 NOTES TO PAGES 99-105

8 César Eustache formed a business partnership with Jacques Blattier 'in Paris, as elsewhere . . . and takes up residence in the house of *sieur* Olivier Picque, merchant, residing in the city of Paris, 6 rue Saint Denis, where they agree that all writs, summons and other legal acts be carried out'. French National Archives, M.C. et/CXXII/ 1552, 30 August 1604.
9 French National Archives, MC, et/XXX/18, 30 August 1635.
10 G. Denière, *La Juridiction consulaire de Paris 1563-1792*, Paris, 1872.
11 Departmental archives of the Hautes Alpes, 1E 7214, 1 April 1680.
12 Departmental archives of the Hautes Alpes, 1E 7214, 9 June 1680.
13 French National Archives, MC, et/LXXXVI/213. I should like to thank Robert Descimon who found this inventory, helped me to decipher it and supplied me with a wealth of information on the merchants – mostly concerning well-established silk merchants – with whom André Masson did business. In particular, I owe all information concerning the Picque family to him.
14 Bibliothèque Municipale, Lyon, manuscript no. 1161, p. 13, quoted by L. Cortes, *L'Oisans . . .*, p. 269.
15 Departmental archives of the Hautes Alpes, 1E 7214, 1 March 1680.
16 Departmental archives of the Isère, 3E 846, Master Bard's legal records. Besse had 230 householders in 1685, and 132 in 1695: Departmental archives of the Isère 4E 25 1G 36 and 1G 39.
17 Information imparted to me by Gérard Béaur, to whom I extend my thanks for the discussion we had on this subject. G. Béaur, *Le Marché foncier à la veille de la Révolution. Les mouvements de propriété beaucerons dans les régions de Maintenon et de Janville de 1761 à 1790*, Paris, Editions de l'EHESS, 1984.
18 The family archives of the tax collector of Clavans demonstrate the extraordinary extent of his network of village debtors: he had bills, promises and obligations relating to 83 families, in a village where the number of landowning householders dropped from 171 in 1676 to 64 in 1695. Ribot family archives, Maison du Patrimoine d'Huez in Oisans.
19 L. Fontaine, 'Family Cycle . . .'.
20 The sale of land prompted by tax debts accounted for 15 out of the 53 sales; in other cases the money lent to pay taxes was not distinct from other loans.
21 L. Fontaine, 'L'Oisans au pluriel. Perceptions de la montagne uissane 1750–1900', *Imaginaires de la haute montagne*, Documents d'Ethnologie Régionale, no. 9, C.A.R.E., Grenoble, 1987, pp. 85–96.
22 Departmental archives of the Rhône, B series, 8 May 1690.
23 Departmental archives of the Hautes Alpes, 1E 4839, 8 and 30 June 1684.
24 Departmental archives of the Isère, 4 G 277, pastoral visit by Monseigneur Le Camus.
25 Departmental archives of the Isère, 4E 25 S3.
26 Departmental archives of the Isère, 4E 31 1D2.
27 Departmental archives of the Isère, 1J 1102.
28 M. Sauvan-Michou, 'La Révocation de l'Edit de Nantes à Grenoble, 1685–1700', *Cahiers d'Histoire*, 1956, pp. 147–71 (166–7). B. Diefendorf, 'Les divisions religieuses dans les familles parisiennes avant la Saint-Barthélémy', *Histoire, Economie et Société*, 7, 1, 1988, pp. 57–77 (71–3).
29 See G. Levi's analyses of recent approaches to the family, and his study of

family groups in Piedmont: *L'Eredità immateriale. Carriera di un esorcista nel Piemonte del seicento*, Einaudi, Turin, 1985.

30 Departmental archives of the Hautes Alpes, 1E 4939, 8 and 30 June 1684.

31 Departmental archives of the Hautes Alpes, 1E 7215, 4 and 6 July 1684.

32 P. Goubert, *Familles marchandes sous l'Ancien Régime: les Danse et les Motte de Beauvais*, Paris, SEVPEN, 1959, pp. 27–30.

33 *Ibid.*, p. 176.

34 Departmental archives of the Isère, 3E 846, 9 June 1684.

35 L. Fontaine, 'Family cycle . . .', p. 64.

36 Departmental archives of the Hautes Alpes, 1E 4839, 18 May 1684.

37 Departmental archives of the Hautes Alpes, 1E 16 October 1684 and 19 March 1685.

38 L. Fontaine 'Affare di Stato, affari di famiglie: politica anti-protestante, strategie private et vita communitaria in una valle alpina del XVIIe secolo', *Quaderni Storici*, 72, 1989, pp. 849–82. C. and G. Maistre, *L'Emigration marchande savoyarde aux XVIIe–XVIIIe siècles. L'exemple de Nancy-sur-Cluses*. Académie Salesienne, Annecy, 1986, pp. 128–36.

39 Departmental archives of the Hautes Alpes, 1E 7214, 4 April 1680.

40 Departmental archives of the Hautes Alpes, 1E 7214, 5 January 1689. The debtor agreed to mow his merchant creditor's pasture-land for 20 *sols* per *setier*. See footnote p. 17.

41 In 1679, *sieur* Raphael Rome paid 20 *livres* for the upkeep of two cows and a calf. Departmental archives of the Hautes Alpes, 1E 7214, 27 April 1679.

42 Departmental archives of the Hautes Alpes, 1E 4839, 18 September 1684.

43 Departmental archives of the Hautes Alpes, 1E 4839, 20 August, 1684.

44 Departmental archives of the Isère, 4E 26 GG9, 13 March 1668.

45 L. Fontaine, 'Solidarités familiales et logiques migratoires en pays de montagne à l'époque moderne', *Annales ESC*, 6, 1990, pp. 1433–50. In the Varaita valley, the beggars recorded in the nineteenth century were children, widows and old people. D. Albera, M. Dossetti, S. Ottonelli, 'Società ed emigrazioni nell'alta valle Varaita in età moderna', *Bollettino storico-bibliografico subalpino*, LXXXVI, 1988, 1, pp. 117–69 (126).

46 H. Onde, 'L'emigration en Maurienne et en Tarentaise', *Bulletin de la Société Scientifique du Dauphiné*, 1942, pp. 41–99 (79–84).

47 A. Allix, *L'oisans au Moyen Age*. As early as the population censuses of 1434 and 1459 in Queyras, temporary migrations were already in evidence, as were the settling elsewhere of the richest members of the community and the mass departures of the poorest. 59 empty houses were recorded, against 57 which remained occupied. R. Blanchard estimated that the population fell by between 600 and 700 people in the first part of the fifteenth century. The census of 1700 recorded the same phenomenon. R. Blanchard, 'Aiguilles', *Revue de Géographie Alpine*, 10, 1922, pp. 127–60 (138–9). For comparable information for the Dauphiné in the seventeenth century, see R. Blanchard, 'Le haut Dauphiné . . .', pp. 409–10. Departmental archives of the Isère, 4E 25 S 10, 'Report on those who have left the area, leaving behind their assets because they could not pay the rates'. This report draws up a list of 56 families in the 16th century and makes a note of the destination for which they were heading.

48 Bibliothèque municipale, Grenoble R. 30 f. 130–2 and departmental archives of the Isère, B. 2153, 22 June 1686.

49 J. Nicolas, 'L'émigration des Mauriennais en Espagne en 1767', *Congrès des Sociétés Savantes de la Province de Savoie*, new series, 1, 1964, pp. 72–80.

50 The people of the Auvergne profited from this imagined fear right up until the end of the eighteenth century. A. Poitrineau, *Les 'Espagnols' de l'Auvergne et du Limousin du XVIIe au XIXe siècles*, Aurillac, Mazel-Malroux, 1985, p. 198.

51 A. Poitrineau, 'Aspects de l'émigration temporaire et saisonnière en Auvergne à la fin du XVIIIe siècle', *Revue d'Histoire Moderne et Contemporaine*, 1962, pp. 5–50 (38).

52 R. Blanchard, 'Le haut Dauphiné...', p. 401.

53 Departmental archives of the Isère, 4G 271/283.

54 In 1746, 82 inherited estates out of 366 were not even worth 5 *sols*; in 1773 this was the case for 65 out of 360 and in 1814 for 64 out of 341. D. Albera, M. Dossetti, S. Ottonelli, 'Società' ed emigrazioni...', pp. 26–127. The tallage registers are likely to be misrepresentative in the same way as those in the Upper Dauphiné, and to be similarly distorted by the fact that members of the families represented on them were often spread over several tax bandings. In 1860 in the Lucques mountains, the average land surface area owned was less than 3 hectares; R. Sarti, *Long Live the Strong. A History of Rural Society in the Apennine Mountains*, The University of Massachusetts Press, Amherst, 1985, p. 101.

55 D. Albera, M. Dossetti, S. Ottonelli, 'Società' ed emigrazioni...', p. 125.

56 D. Albera *et al.*, 'Società' ed emigrazioni...', pp. 128–36. In the eighteenth century, according to the priest in Chianale, the poor would go to Spain bearing certificates given them by Capuchin monks to the effect that they were newly converted to Catholicism: they used them to beg for alms 'and since the country is extremely wealthy, they returned much laden down with money...', p. 138.

57 A. Dietz, *Frankfurter Handelgeschichte*, Frankfurt, 4 vols, 1921, vol. 2, pp. 240–59.

58 Even though certain villages in the Auvergne were renowned for their fertile soil. A. Poitrineau, *Les 'Espagnols'*..., p. 67.

59 Quoted by Jean Perrel, 'Introduction à une étude sur l'émigration corrézienne vers l'Espagne sous l'Ancien Régime', *Bulletin de la Société des Lettres, Sciences et Arts de la Corrèze*, LXX, 1966, pp. 183–98 (191–2).

60 J. Perrel, 'Les Limousins en Espagne aux XVIe, XVIIe et XVIIIe siècles: les émigrants', *Bulletin de la Société des Lettres, Sciences et Arts de la Corrèze*, LXVIII, 1964, pp. 31–40 (38).

61 *Ibid.*, p. 37.

62 J. Perrel, 'Une région d'émigration vers l'Espagne aux XVIIe–XVIIIe siècle: le plateau de Roche-de-Vic (Corrèze)', *Bulletin de la Société des Lettres, Sciences et Arts de la Corrèze*, LXX, 1966, pp. 183–98 (191–2).

63 A. Poitrineau, *Les 'Espagnols'*..., p. 140 and pp. 55–6.

64 L. Fontaine, *Le Voyage et la Mémoire, colporteurs de l'Oisans au XIXe siècle*, Presses Universitaires de Lyon, 1984, p. 193; J. Perrel, 'Une région d'émigration...', p. 193.

65 A. Poitrineau, *Les 'Espagnols'*..., pp. 141–2. J. Perrel, 'Une région

d'émigration. . . .', p. 192 gives examples of fortunes bequeathed in Spain in 1793. One man left a bakery worth more than 12,000 *livres*; the fortunes of the others were more modest – between 1,800 and 600 *livres*.

66 A. Poitrineau, *Les 'Espagnols'* . . . , pp. 55–7.

67 J.-F. Soulet, *La Vie quotidienne dans les Pyrénées sous l'Ancien Régime (du XVIe au XVIIIe siècle)*, Paris, 1974, pp. 50–1.

68 J.-P. Zuniga, 'La mobilité sociale dans une sociéte coloniale: le cas du Chili au XVIIe siècle', *Bulletin du Centre Pierre Léon d'histoire économique et sociale*, nos 2–4, 1992, pp. 41–51.

69 M. Spufford, *The Great Reclothing of Rural England. Petty Chapmen and their Wares in the Seventeenth Century*, London, The Hambledon Press, 1984, p. 44.

70 T. C. Smout, 'The Glasgow Merchant Community in the Seventeenth Century', *Scottish Historical Review*, 47, 1968, pp. 53–71 (55).

71 *Ibid.*, pp. 59–62. The author puts the merchant population of Glasgow between 400 and 500 in the seventeenth century. The customs registers between November 1683 and November 1686 allow one to put the number of those who traded on a more or less regular basis with England at 50 or 60; whereas there were between 35 and 45 trading with Ireland, and between 55 and 65 with Europe or America, some of whom were involved in several markets. McUre puts the number of those trading with England at 67: J. McUre, *A View of Glasgow*, 1736, edited by J. F. S Gordon, *Glasghu fancies*, Glasgow, 1872.

72 R. A. Dodgson, *Land and Society in Early Scotland*, Oxford, 1981, pp. 205–70. See also T. C. Smout, *Scottish Trade on the Eve of the Union, 1660–1707*, Edinburgh, 1963. For more information on the workings of tenant farming, see I. D. Whyte, *Agriculture and Society in Seventeenth Century Scotland*, Oxford, 1981, pp. 33–6.

73 R. A. Dodgson, *Land and Society* . . . , pp. 205–70.

74 U. Pfister, *Die Zürcher fabriques, Protoindustrielles Wachstum vom 16. zum 18. Jahrhundert*, Editions Chronos, Zurich, 1992, p. 258.

75 R. A. Dodgson, *Land and Society* . . . , pp. 271–5.

76 R. A. Dodgson, *Land and Society* . . . , pp. 314–20.

77 I. D. Whyte, *Agriculture and Society* . . . , pp. 39–41.

Chapter 6 Credit and Social Relationships

1 A. Poitrineau, 'Petits marchands colporteurs de la haute Planèze d'Auvergne à la fin de l'Ancien Régime', *Annales du Midi*, vol. 88, 1976, pp. 423–36 (429); L. Fontaine, *Le Voyage et la Mémoire, colporteurs de l'Oisans au XIXe siècle*, Presses Universitaires de Lyon, 1984, pp. 129–39; and N. McKendrick, J. Brewer and J. H. Plumb, *The Birth of Consumer Society: The Commercialization of Eighteenth Century England*, Bloomington, Indiana University Press, 1982, pp. 208–9.

2 D. J. Ormorod, *Anglo-Dutch commerce, 1700–1760*, Cambridge Ph.D., 1973, p. 110, quoted by M. Spufford, *The Great Reclothing of Rural England: Petty Chapmen and their Wares in the Seventeenth Century*, London, The

Hambledon Press, 1984, p. 80, note 28; L. Fontaine, 'Le reti del credito. La montagna, la città, la pianura: mercanti dell'Oisans tra XVII e XIX secolo', *Quaderni Storici*, 68, 1988, pp. 573–93; A. Poitrineau, 'Petits marchands colporteurs . . .', pp. 427–8 and 432–3. In international markets, the usual credit time allowed was 3–6 months, *The Cambridge Economy of Europe*, vol. V, *The Economic Organisation of Early Modern Europe*, p. 307.

3 R. B. Westerfield, *Middlemen in English Business, particularly between 1660 and 1760*, 1915, New York, 1968, pp. 313–4 (385).

4 R. Moulinas, *L'Imprimerie, la Librairie et la Presse à Avignon au XVIIIe siècle*, Grenoble, Presses Universitaires, 1974, p. 148.

5 A. Poitrineau, *Les 'Espagnols' de l'Auvergne et du Limousin du XVIIe au XIXe siècle*, Aurillac, Mazel-Malroux, 1985, pp. 143 and 146.

6 J.-D. Mellot, 'Rouen et les "libraires forains" à la fin du XVIIIe siècle: la veuve Machuel et ses correspondants (1768–1773)', *Bibliothèque de l'Ecole des chartes*, vol. 147, 1989, pp. 503–38 (511).

7 R. Moulinas, 'Une famille d'imprimeurs-libraires avignonnais du XVIIIe siècle: les Delorme', *Revue française d'histoire du livre*, no. 3, 1972, pp. 45–78 (47).

8 In such cases, it was the financial guarantee which was more important than a business association. J. Augel, *Italienische Einwanderung and Wirtschaftstätigkeit in rheinischen Städten des 17. und 18. Jahrhunderts*, Bonn, 1971, p. 199.

9 Departmental archives of the Isère, 4E 24, S11, statement of 24 December 1654 of the merchandise belonging to Jehan Hostache and Jacques Garden, Auris en Dauphiné.

10 J.-D. Mellot, 'Rouen et les "libraires forains" . . .', pp. 512–13. Departmental archives of the Isère, 1J 829, register of copies of letters sent by Victor Nicolet, glove manufacturer, from the rue Saint-Jacques in Grenoble, to various merchant pedlars in the Oisans region (7 January 1828–10 April 1842).

11 Exercise book belonging to Jean-Baptiste Bompard, Villeneuve la Salle, completed 28 January 1788. Gravier family private archives.

12 Departmental archives of the Isère, 1J 829, letter of 2 August 1834.

13 From the memoirs of Jean-Pierre Magne of Mont-de-Lans, 1804–98, Musée Dauphinois, Grenoble.

14 Departmental archives of the Isère, 1J, 927, from the papers of Jean Gourand of Clavans in the Dauphiné, a pedlar in the Yonne and Nievre *départements* (1834–59).

15 Departmental archives of the Isère, 1J 829. A detailed analysis is given in L. Fontaine, *Le Voyage et la Mémoire, colporteurs de l'Oisans au XIXe siècle*, Presses Universitaires de Lyon, 1984, pp. 45–103.

16 This is a minimum figure, given the shortcomings of the source documents. One can compare it with the number of trading licences taken out in year V (of the Revolutionary Calendar), and with the number given in the labour survey of 1848 – 269 and 594 respectively, bearing in mind that these records also include shopkeepers. L. Cortes, *L'Oisans, recherches historiques, tourisme*, Grenoble, 1926, pp. 226; and the departmental archives of the Isère, 162 Mi.

17 Departmental archives of the Isère, 1J 829.

18 Departmental archives of the Isère, 1J 829; and A. Poitrineau, 'Aspects de l'émigration temporaire et saisonnière en Auvergne à la fin du XVIIIe siècle', *Revue d'Histoire moderne et contemporaine*, 1962, p. 32.

19 L. Fontaine, *Le Voyage*..., pp. 88–94.

20 A. Sauvy, 'Noël Gille dit La Pistole, marchand forain libraire roulant par la France', *Bulletin des bibliothèques de France*, May 1967, pp. 177–90 (189–90) and R. Darnton, 'Un colporteur sous l'Ancien Régime', *Censures, de la Bible aux larmes d'Eros*, Centre Georges Pompidou, Paris, 1987, pp. 130–9 (137–8).

21 Departmental archives of the Isère, 4U 376, legal proceedings against André Reymond, 1861–2.

22 R. Darnton, 'Le colporteur...', p. 134.

23 G. Duval, *Littérature de colportage et imaginatif collectif en Angleterre à l'époque des Dicey (1720–v. 1800)*, doctoral thesis, University of Dijon, 1986, p. 120.

24 R. B. Westerfield, *Middlemen in English Business*..., p. 316.

25 Departmental archives of the Isère, 1J 829, May 1830.

26 Bibliothèque nationale de France, mss. fr. 22099 (150), February 1769, quoted by P. Casselle in 'Recherche sur les marchands d'estampes parisiens d'origine cotentinoise à la fin de l'Ancien Régime', *Comité des travaux historiques et scientifiques. Bulletin d'histoire moderne et contemporaine*, 11, 1978, pp. 74–93 (77).

27 Departmental archives of the Isère, 1 Mi 218, 1863–1914.

28 Letter from Gustave Ratié of Castille, one of the last survivors of the migrants from the Auvergne, to Rose Duroux, 11 November 1980, quoted in R. Duroux's 'Monographie d'une famille d' "Espagnols". La Saga des Ratié', *Revue d'Auvergne*, vol. 99, no. 3, 1985, pp. 271–310 (276).

29 See the court case which surrounded the dissolution of firms in Chinchon and Navalcarnero in A. Poitrineau, *Les 'Espagnols'*..., pp. 172–4.

30 For information on the ways in which the economic and human structures of the merchant-migrant villages changed, see P. Vigier, *Essai sur la répartition de la propriété foncière dans la région alpine*, Paris, SEVPEN, 1963 for the Alps; R. Blanchard, 'Aiguilles', *Revue de Géographie Alpine*, 10, 1922, pp. 127–60 (153–61). For the Apennines, see R. Sarti, *Long Live The Strong. A History of Rural Society in the Apennine Mountains*, The University of Massachusetts Press, Amherst, 1985, pp. 100–1, 106–7, 129 and 216. For the Pyrenees see J.-J. Darmon, *Le Colportage de librairie en France sous le Second Empire*, Paris, 1972, p. 32. For the Massif Central region, see J. Perrel, 'Une région d'émigration vers l'Espagne aux XVIIe–XVIIIe siècle: Le plateau de Roche-de-Vic (Corrèze)', *Bulletin de la Société des Lettres, Sciences et Arts de la Corrèze*, vol. 70, 1966, pp. 183–98 (194–7).

Chapter 7 The Demise of the Profession

1 R. B. Westerfield, *Middlemen in English Business, particularly between 1660 and 1760*, 1915, New York, 1968, p. 316.

2 D. R. Ringrose, *Madrid and the Spanish Economy (1560–1850)*, University of California Press, 1983, pp. 185–92.

3 R. Duroux, 'Les boutiquiers cantaliens de Nouvelle-Castille au XIXe siècle', *Mélanges de la Casa de Vélasquez*, 1985, vol. XXI, pp. 281–307 (289–91).

4 *Ibid.*, pp. 292–3. A. Poitrineau, *Les 'Espagnols' de l'Auvergne et du Limousin du XVIIe au XIXe siècle*, Aurillac, Mazel-Malroux, 1985, p. 176.

5 R. Duroux, 'Les boutiquiers cantaliens . . .', pp. 297–8. See the correspondence studied by A. Poitrineau (*Les 'Espagnols' . . .*, pp. 95–6) which shows the tensions between the credit networks and, in particular, the difficulties experienced by the migrant merchants in recovering the debts agreed during their campaign; and, as an indirect consequence, their determination to get back what was owed to them in the highlands.

6 A. Poitrineau: *Les 'Espagnols' . . .*, p. 242.

7 In this vein was the following announcement which appeared in the *Boletín oficial* of the province of León on 8 September 1876, inviting 'pedlars and all those selling the same type of goods (school books) to come and stock up with books for boys' and girls' schools' from Raphael Garzo and Sons, printers. J.-F. Botrel, *La Diffusion du livre en Espagne (1848–1914)*, Madrid, 1988, p. 15.

8 C. Robert-Muller and A. Allix, *Les colporteurs de l'Oisans*, Grenoble, 1925, republished 1979 by the Presses Universitaires de Grenoble.

9 Departmental archives of the Isère, 1Mi 155, canton of Bourg d'Oisans.

10 Departmental archives of the Isère, série R, the Bureau de Recrutement, which existed from 1867.

11 L. Fontaine, *Le Voyage et la Mémoire, colporteurs de l'Oisans au XIXe siècle*, Presses Universitaires de Lyon, 1984, pp. 205–29. P. Guichonnet 'L'émigration saisonnière en Faucigny pendant la première moitié du XIXe siècle (1783–1860), *Revue de Géographie alpine*, 1945, vol. XXXIII, fasc. 3, pp. 465–534 (495–6) demonstrates how these men alternated between employment in the watch-making workshops and time spent as a pedlar when there was no work to be had.

12 R. Schenda, *Folklore e letteratura popolare: Italia–Germania–Francia* [translated from the German into Italian by Maria Chiara Figliozzi and Ingeborg Walter], Bibliotheca Biographica, Istituto della Enciclopedia Italiana fondata da Giovanni Treccani, Rome, 1986, pp. 212–14.

13 D. Lerch, *Imagerie et Société, l'Imagerie Wentzel de Wissembourg au XIXe siècle*, Strasbourg, Librairie Istra, 1982 (the page numbers quoted are those of the typed thesis, Strasbourg, 1978), p. 240. A more detailed analysis of the applications for permits appears in D. Lerch, 'Du colportage à l'errance, Réflexions sur le colportage en Alsace au XIXe siècle', *Revue d'Alsace*, published by the Fédération des sociétés d'histoire et d'archéologie d'Alsace, no. 113, 1987, pp. 163–89.

14 S. Jaumain, 'Les colporteurs Hainuyers du XIXe siècle', *Annales du Cercle royal d'Histoire et d'Archéologie d'Ath at Musées athois*, 1984, pp. 282–340 (314–15).

15 J.-J. Darmon, *Le colportage de librairie en France sous le Second Empire*, Paris, 1972, p. 71.

16 Departmental archives of the Isère, 9T 78.

17 In his *Notas cordobesas* Ricardo de Montes y Romero recalls Torrezno, the beggar who turned pedlar at the end of the year to go and sell calendars and

almanacs in Cordoba and in the farms and hamlets of both the near and the more distant rural areas, 'advertising them with a peculiar, almost unintelligible shout', *Recuerdos del Passado*, vol. II, 1914, p. 112, quoted by J.-F. Botrel in *La Diffusion du livre en Espagne* ... , p. 16.

18 G. B. Martinelli, *Origine e sviluppo dell'attività dei librai pontremolesi*, Pontremoli, 1973, pp. 74–5; the child was doubtless put up for sale again in Parma and taken by a man with a bear from the village of Bedonia in the Parma mountains.

19 *Ibid.*, pp. 77–82.

20 C. T. Genoino, 'Suonatori ambulanti nelle province meridionali. Archivi della polizia borbonica e postunitaria nell'Ottocento', *La Ricerca Folklorica*, 19, 1989, pp. 69–75.

21 L. Fontaine, 'Solidarités familiales et logiques migratoires en pays de montagne à l'époque moderne', *Annales ESC*, 6, 1990, pp. 1433–1450. Examples for the Apennine region are given in R. Sarti, *Long Live the Strong. A History of Rural Society in the Apennine Mountains*, University of Massachusetts Press, Amherst, 1985, p. 86.

22 L. Fontaine, 'Solidarités familiales ...'; examples for the Apennine region in R. Sarti, *Long Live the Strong* ... , p. 120. G. B. Martinelli, *Origine e sviluppo* ... , pp. 85–8 gives details of the legislation drawn up to prevent these children being abandoned. C. T. Genoino, 'Suonatori ambulanti ...', pp. 73–4.

23 G. B. Martinelli, *Origine e sviluppo* ... , pp. 82–90.

24 J.-J. Darmon, *Le colportage de librairie* ... , p. 88. See also A. Dubuc, 'Un colporteur évangéliste rouennais de 1877 à 1891', *Actes du 109e Congrès national des Sociétés savantes, Dijon, 1984, Section d'histoire moderne et contemporaine*, vol. 1, Paris, 1984, pp. 245–57.

25 J.-F. Botrel, *La Diffusion du livre en Espagne* ... , p. 14.

26 O. Niccoli, *Profeti e popolo nell'Italia del Rinascimento*, Rome-Bari, Laterza, 1987, pp. 125–32. A. Della Portella, 'La parabola della memoria: racconti di servitori di Dio nell'Italia del secolo corso', *Bollettino Storico-Bibliografico Subalpino*, 1991, pp. 91–113.

27 R. Schenda, *Folklore e letteratura popolare* ... , p. 213.

28 F. G. Frutaz, 'Anciennes familles valdôtaines à l'étranger', *Bulletin de la Société Académique, Scientifique et religieuse du Duché d'Aoste*, no. 20, 1913, pp. 191–4.

29 D. Lerch, *Imagerie et Société* ... , p. 243, uses the inhabitants of Obermorschwihr as an example.

30 R. Sarti, *Long Live the Strong* ... , p. 84.

31 F. C. Farra and Don G. Galliza, 'L'emigrazione dalla Val blenio a Milano attraverso i secoli', *Archivio Storico Lombardo*, 9th series, vol. 1, 1961, pp. 117–30 (126–7). G. Levi, *Centro e periferia di uno stato assoluto*, Turin, 1985.

32 *Stampe per via. L'incisione dei secoli XVII–XIX nel commercio ambulante dei tesini*, exhibition catalogue by B. Passamani, Pieve Tesino-Trento-Bassano del Grappa, 1972, Calliano, Arti grafichi R Manfredi, 1972, pp. 39–40.

33 R. Sarti, *Long Live the Strong* ... , pp. 84–5.

34 J.-J. Darmon, *Le Colportage de librairie* ... , pp. 30–1.

35 J.-J. Darmon, *Le Colportage de librairie* ... , pp. 37–41.

36 J.-J. Darmon, *Le Colportage de librairie* . . . , p. 91. Moreover, the prefects' reports show that in peddling regions such as the Alps, the Isère and the Massif Central, the *Gascons* were not as active (p. 55).

37 Charles Noblet, Chronique du Journal général de l'Imprimerie et de la Librairie, 25 December 1869, quoted by J.-J. Darmon in *Le colportage de librairie* . . . , p. 41.

38 J.-J. Darmon, *Le Colportage de librairie* . . . , pp. 72–3.

39 Charles Nisard, *Essai sur le colportage de librairie*, 1855, quoted by J.-J. Darmon, *Le Colportage de librairie* . . . , p. 41.

40 J.-J. Darmon, *Le Colportage de librairie* . . . , pp. 48–50.

41 J.-J. Darmon, *Le Colportage de librairie* . . . , pp. 50–4.

42 R. Schenda, *Folklore e letteratura popolare* . . . , p. 182.

43 J. Lesueur, 'Une figure populaire en Lorraine au siècle dernier, le colporteur ou chamagnon', *Bulletin de la Société lorraine des Etudes locales de l'enseignement public*, 1969, 3, pp. 29–39 (38).

44 J.-J. Darmon, *Le Colportage de librairie* . . . , pp. 71 and 123–4.

45 V. E. Neuberg, *Popular Literature, a History and Guide from the Beginning of Printing to the Year 1897*, London, 1977, p. 212, quoted by G. Duval in his doctoral thesis *Littérature de colportage et imaginaire collectif en Angleterre à l'époque des Dicey (1720–v. 1800)* (University of Dijon, 1986, p. 41), Bordeaux, Presses Universitaires de Bordeaux, 1991.

46 J.-F. Botrel, *La Diffusion du livre en Espagne* . . . , pp. 18–20.

47 J.-F. Botrel, *La Diffusion du livre en Espagne* . . . , pp. 11–33.

48 G. B. Martinelli, *Origine e sviluppo* . . . , pp. 19–59.

49 G. B. Martinelli, *Origine e sviluppo* . . . , pp. 60–1 and 65, 68, 107. Many travelled to Corsica without a passport.

50 G. B. Martinelli, *Origine e sviluppo* . . . , p. 123, and the list of books declared on p. 124.

51 G. B. Martinelli, *Origine e sviluppo* . . . , pp. 118–21.

52 G. B. Martinelli, *Origine e sviluppo* . . . , pp. 69 and 115. In the examples, the amount of merchandise borrowed this way ranged from 55 to 325 *livres*-worth.

53 G. B. Martinelli, *Origine e sviluppo* . . . , pp. 117–8.

54 G. B. Martinelli, *Origine e sviluppo* . . . , pp. 69–72.

55 E. Gothein, *Wirtschaftsgeschichte des Schwarzwaldes und der angrenzenden Landschaften*, Strasbourg, 1892, p. 849.

56 P. Luès, 'L'émigration des "marchands de vin de Meymac" (Corrèze)', *Révue de Géographie alpine*, 1936, pp. 925–42. The first branch was opened in Egletons around 1909 and a short time afterwards, three others were established in Meymac.

57 C. Robert-Muller and A. Allix, *Les Colporteurs de l'Oisans* . . . , p. 37.

58 Departmental archives of the Isère, 1J 829, letter of 1 February 1839.

59 D. Ozanam, 'La colonie française de Cadiz au XVIIIe siècle, d'après un document inédit (1777)', *Mélanges de la Casa de Vélasquez*, IV, 1968, pp. 259–349 shows how (pp. 271–2), following the war of Succession in Austria, the French merchants seized upon the chance to do business with the Spanish Indies which had been cut off from Europe for several years: there followed a series of individual ventures in which several amateur merchants foundered, having thought to make their fortunes in a short space of time,

as well as a few supposedly stable firms. The tradition was none the less an old one.

60 As Nicolas Barker so rightly pointed out to me, for which my thanks.

61 Departmental archives of the Isère, 1J 829 and 11U 29, 10 November 1837, a 'firm dealing in plants, bulbs, flowers and gloves' linked the pedlars Arnol, Oddoux, Guille and Magne. From the memoirs of Jean-Pierre Magne of Mont-de-Lans, Musée Dauphinois, Grenoble.

62 Departmental archives of the Isère, 11U 29 (10 November 1837).

63 At the beginning of the twentieth century, the migrants from the Auvergne also began to use the banking system to finance their attempts at changing the focus of their business. Hence the Andrieux brothers became involved in the hydroelectric industry in Spain so as to supply their flour-mill. R. Duroux, 'Monographie d'une famille d'"Espagnols". La saga des Ratié', Revue d'Auvergne, 99, 3, pp. 271–310 (302).

64 Departmental archives of the Isère, 1J 829.

65 L. Fontaine, Le Voyage . . . , pp. 147–92.

66 R. Duroux, 'Monographie d'une famille d'"Espagnols" . . .', pp. 281–4 and 291. In fact, after the collapse of the large firms, the predominant type of specialization in Spain remained the bakery.

67 R. Becquevort, Les Colporteurs d'Arconsat au XIXe siècle, Cercle occitain d'Auvergne, Clermont-Ferrand, 1973.

68 Letter from Antoine Thérias, written in Santa-Cruz in Tenerife and addressed to his friends Beauvoir and Griffon in Messina, quoted by R. Becquevort in Les Colporteurs d'Arconsat . . . , p. 17.

69 Recent work done by Béatrice Veyrassat demonstrates that the old merchant-pedlar regions such as le Valais, St Gall, Schaffouse and Winthertour (where many from the Dauphiné emigrated after the Revocation of the Edict of Nantes) had also developed vast business networks with Latin America in the nineteenth century. B. Veyrassat, Réseaux d'affaires internationaux, émigrations et exportations en Amérique Latine au XIXe siècle. Le commerce suisse aux Amériques, Librairie Droz, Geneva, 1993.

70 R. Blanchard, 'Aiguilles', Revue de Géographie Alpine, 10, 1922, pp. 127–60 (145–8).

71 P. Gouy, Pérégrinations des 'Barcelonettes' au Mexique, Presses Universitaires de Grenoble, 1980, p. 52.

72 Ibid., pp. 56–7.

73 Ibid., p. 60.

74 Ibid., pp. 93–101.

75 A. Albert, 'Le pays briançonnais: les Queyrassins négociants', Bulletin de la Société d'Etude des Hautes-Alpes, 1st series, vol. 8, 1889, pp. 313–31 (326–7).

76 E. Charpenel, L'Epopée des Barcelonettes, Imprimerie petites affiches B. Vial, Digne, 1978, pp. 15–16.

77 P. Gouy, Pérégrinations . . . , p. 80.

78 P. Gouy, Pérégrinations . . . , pp. 83–5.

79 A. Genin, Les Français au Mexique du XVIe à nos jours, new edition published by Argos, Paris 1933, p. 407, quoted by P. Gouy in Pérégrinations . . . , p. 90: for more information on these associations, see also pp. 86–92.

80 Quoted by E. Charpenel, L'Epopée des Barcelonnettes . . . , pp. 21–2.

81 P. Gouy, *Pérégrinations* ..., pp. 110–11.
82 F. Arnaud, *L'Emigration et le commerce français au Mexique*, E. Prayer, Paris, 1902, p. 164; quoted by P. Gouy in *Pérégrinations* ..., p. 85.
83 R. Blanchard, 'Aiguilles ...', p. 147.
84 L. Fontaine, *Le Voyage* ..., pp. 140–3.
85 E. Borruso and R. Bossaglia, *E. Frette & C.*, Milan, 1989.
86 S. Serra, *Travail et travailleurs de l'albâtre à Volterra*, thesis written at the Ecole des Hautes Etudes en Sciences Sociales, 1983, pp. 344–63.
87 For an analysis of the desire of those concerned to find new terms for describing their activities see P. Retureau, *Une forme méconnue de vente à domicile, les négociants-voyageurs*, Ph.D. dissertation, Lille, 1971.
88 L. Fontaine, *Le Voyage* ..., pp. 140–92.
89 J.-D. Mellot, 'Rouen et les "libraires forains"', p. 514.
90 P. Retureau, *Une forme méconnue* ..., pp. 18 and 36.

Chapter 8 The Culture of Itinerancy

1 M. Spufford, *The Great Reclothing of Rural England, Petty Chapmen and their Wares in the Seventeenth Century*, London, The Hambledon Press, 1984, pp. 13–14; and N. McKendrick, J. Brewer and J. H. Plumb, *The Birth of Consumer Society. The Commercialization of Eighteenth Century England*, Bloomington, Indiana University Press, 1982, p. 87.
2 P. Guichonnet, 'L'émigration alpine vers les pays de langue allemande', *Revue de Géographie alpine*, 1948, pp. 553–76 (550).
3 K. Martin, 'Die Savoyische Einwanderung in das alemannische Süddeutschland', *Deutsches Archiv für Landes und Volkforschung*, vol. VI, fasc. 4, 1942, pp. 647–58 (650).
4 J. Augel, *Italienische Einwanderung und Wirtschaftstätigkeit in rheinischen Städten des 17. und 18. Jahrhunderts*, Bonn, 1971, p. 252.
5 *Ibid.*, p. 194.
6 K. Martin, 'Die Savoyische Einwanderung ...', pp. 647–58, quoted by P. Guichonnet in 'L'émigration alpine ...', p. 555.
7 P. Guichonnet, 'L'émigration alpine ...', p. 553 and the bibliography contained in note 65.
8 M. Baulant, 'Groupes mobiles dans une société sédentaire: la société autour de Meaux aux XVIIe et XVIIIe siècle', *Les Marginaux et les exclus dans l'histoire*, Cahiers Jussieu, no. 5, Paris, U.G.E, 10/18, 1979, pp. 78–121.
9 Alletz, 'Traité de la police moderne', Paris, 1823, quoted by R. Cobb in *La protestation populaire en France (1789–1820)*, Paris, 1975, p. 36 and all of chapter 1 on police practices.
10 S.P.O.I Rebellion Papers 620/35/87 used by N. O'Ciosàin of the University of Galway, to whom I should like to extend my thanks for having lent me his then unpublished work on the circulation of printed matter in Ireland.
11 Departmental archives of the Isère, 4U 321 and 4U 376; the trial of Auguste Bellet and André Reymond.
12 Quoted by M. Ventre in *L'imprimerie et la librairie en Languedoc au dernier siècle de l'Ancien Régime*, 1700–1789, Paris, The Hague, 1958, p. 280.

13 R. Lick, 'Les intérieurs domestiques dans la seconde moitié du XVIIIe siècle, d'après les inventaires après décès de Coutances', *Annales de Normandie*, no. 4, 1970, pp. 293–316 (309).

14 Louis-Sebastien Mercier, quoted by D. Roche in *Le Peuple de Paris*, Paris, 1981, p. 223.

15 J. Queniart, *L'Imprimerie et la librairie à Rouen au XVIIIe siècle*, Paris, Klincksieck, 1969, p. 204.

16 D. Roche, *Les Républicains des lettres, Gens de culture et Lumières au XVIIIe siècle*, Paris, Fayard, 1988, pp. 375–7. A. Fillon, *Louis Simon: étaminier, 1741–1820 dans son village du Haut Marne au siècle des Lumières*, Le Mans, 2 vols, 1983.

17 Departmental archives of the Isère, 4U 376 and 4U 321. Bankruptcy trial of André Reymond and Auguste Bellet.

18 9 October 1859, extract from the correspondence between the civil criminal court of Pontremoli and the mayor of Mulazzo: 'It is not unusual that, scarcely is the pedlar within the village, with his basket of books around his neck, than the priest orders the bells to be rung loudly so as to stir the population up against him'. Quoted by G. B. Martinelli, *Origine e sviluppo dell attività dei librai pontremolesi*, Pontremoli, sup. Artigianelli, 1973, p. 53.

19 C. Marcilhacy, *Le Diocèse d'Orléans au milieu du XIXe siècle*, Paris, 1964, p. 281.

20 J.-J. Darmon, *Le Colportage de librairie en France sous le Second Empire*, Paris, 1972, pp. 26–7 develops this idea in some admirable passages and provides numerous references. For more information on legislation between the Revolution and the Third Republic, see M. J. Hefferman, 'Rogues, rascals and rude books: policing the popular book trade in early nineteenth-century France', *Journal of Historical Geography*, 16, 1, 1990, pp. 90–107.

21 J.-J. Darmon, *Le Colportage de librairie . . .*, pp. 26–7.

22 F. Barbier, 'Un exemple d'émigration temporaire: les colporteurs de librairie pyrénéens (1840–1880)', *Annales du Midi*, vol. 95, no. 163, 1983, pp. 289–307.

23 Departmental archives of the Bas-Rhin, T.39, quoted by R. Schenda in *Folklore e letteratura popolare: Italia–Germanica–Francia*, translation by Maria Chiara Figliozzi and Ingeborg Walter, Bibliotheca Biographica, Istituto della Enciclopedia Italiana fondata da Giovanni Treccani, Rome, 1986, p. 182.

24 See J.-J. Darmon, *Le Colportage de librairie . . .*, pp. 97–128, for more on the attitude adopted and the legislation implemented throughout the nineteenth century in France.

25 Quoted by J.-J. Darmon, *Le Colportage de librairie . . .*, p. 106.

26 R. Cobb, *La Protestation . . .*, p. 45.

27 J.-F. Botrel, 'Les aveugles colporteurs d'imprimés en Espagne', *Mélanges de la casa de Vélasquez*, 9, 1973, pp. 417–82; and 10, 1974, pp. 233–71 (238); and 'Des professionnels de la clandestinité: les aveugles colporteurs dans l'Espagne contemporaine', *Histoire et clandestinité . . .*, Revue du Vivarais, 1979, pp. 301–16; see also, in the appendix, the list of edicts concerning the peddling and selling of printed material between 1627 and 1867.

28 R. B. Westerfield, *Middlemen in English Business, particularly between 1660 and 1760*, 1915, New York, 1968, pp. 315–6.

29 O. Lurati, 'I marginali e la loro mentalità attraverso il gergo', Glauco Sanga, 'Estetica del gergo. Coma una cultura si fa forma linguistica', *La Ricerca Folklorica*, 19, 1989, pp. 7–16, 17–26. B. Geremek, *Truands et misérables dans l'Europe moderne (1350–1600)*, Gallimard/Julliard, 1980. The chimney-sweeps also created their own language: C. Favre, 'Le patois des ramoneurs ou "terasu" (alias "térafué")', *Travaux de la Société d'Histoire et d'Archéologie de Maurienne*, vol. XII, 1955, pp. 29–38.

30 J.-F. Botrel, 'Les aveugles colporteurs . . .', pp. 428–9, 438, 449. In 1835, Salustiano de Olózaga in his *Informe sobre las ordenanzas de la Hermandad de Ciegos de Madrid* was well aware of this when he wrote that the blind could commit crimes 'a sabiendas, en la confianza de que no podrá probárseles legalmente, y aunque se les pruebe pueden estar seguros de que no se les castigará con mucho rigor, ya por la compasión que naturalmente excitan, ya porque en realidad hay en ellos menos materia punible que en los demás hombres'; quoted by J.-F. Botrel, 'Les aveugles colporteurs . . .', p. 235 'knowing exactly what they were doing and confident that no official proof could be produced, and that even if what they had done could be proved, they were certain not to be punished too harshly, either because of the pity that they naturally aroused, or because in real terms, they had fewer possessions which could be seized than other men.'

31 A. Ferrer del Rio and J. Pères Calvo, *Los Españoles pintados por su mismos*, Madrid, 1844, p. 471, quoted by J.-F. Botrel, 'Les aveugles colporteurs . . .', p. 235. For more on the legislation concerning the printing of pamphlets, see J. Marco, *Literatura popular en España en los siglos XVIII y XIX. Una aproximacion a los pliegos de cordel*, Madrid, Taurus, 1977, pp. 173–82.

32 J. Marco, *Literatura popular . . .*, pp. 119–21. J.-F. Botrel, 'Les aveugles colporteurs . . .', p. 236.

33 Departmental archives of the Isère, 5E 238/1 (example from 1676).

34 Departmental archives of the Isère, 27J 3/67, 'the testament of Hugues Gasques, son of Pierre, a merchant from Auris conducting his business in Moulin in Bourbonnais' drawn up in 1682.

35 Departmental archives of the Rhône, 3E 4781B, 15 May 1656.

36 O. Martin, *La Conversion protestante à Lyon (1659–1687)*, Geneva, Paris, Droz, 1986, pp. 50–65. Odile Martin quotes Thobie Delor's will and the donations it includes for Mizoen (1658). A. Poitrineau, *Les 'Espagnols' de l'Auvergne et du Limousin du XVIIe au XIXe siècle*, Aurillac, Mazel-Malroux, 1985, pp. 209–10.

37 J. Augel, *Italienische Einwanderung . . .*, p. 292.

38 P. Guichonnet, 'L'émigration saisonnière en Faucigny pendant la première moitié du XIXe siècle (1783–1860)', *Revue de Géographie alpine*, vol. XXXIII, fasc. 3, pp. 465–534 (510) takes as an example an inhabitant of Taninges in Faucigny who, at the end of the nineteenth century, left 25,000 francs to the town of Lima in recognition of the friendship he had been shown. There are other examples concerning the Savoy region in Ch. Wolff. 'Un type de marchands sous Louis XIV: Les Savoyards de Barr', *Annuaire de la Société d'histoire et d'archéologie de Dambach-la-Ville*, Barr, Obernai, vol. 3, 1969, pp. 122–7; and C. and G. Maistre, G. Heitz, *Colporteurs et*

marchands savoyards dans l'Europe des XVIIe et XVIIIe siècles. Papers and documents published by the Académie Salésienne, vol. 98, Annecy, 1992, p. 120.

39 There were two types of *piastres*: the ordinary *piastre*, or *peso sencillo*, which was worth between 15 and 16 *réaux* (around 4 French *livres*); and the 'strong' or 'real' *piastre*, *peso fuerte*, which was equivalent to 20 *réaux* (or 5 French *livres*). Since this concerned rates within Spain, in this case it is probably the ordinary *piastre* which is meant. D. Ozanam, 'La colonie française de Cadix au XVIIIe siècle, d'après un document inédit (1777)', *Mélanges de la Casa de Vélasquez*, IV, 1968, pp. 259–349 (esp. 277, note 1).

40 A. Poitrineau, *Les 'Espagnols'* . . . , pp. 83–4 and 208.

41 Departmental archives of the Hautes Alpes, 1E 4839, 5 March 1686.

42 Complaint from the Frankfurt merchants to the town council, 16 February 1699, quoted by M.-C. Hoock-Demarle, 'Etre Brentano à Franckfort à la fin du XVIIIe siècle', *E.U.I. Florence*, November 1988, p. 4.

43 J. Augel, *Italienische Einwanderung* . . . , p. 109.

44 Merck, the Darmstadt scholar, quoted by M.-C. Hoock-Demarle in 'Etre Brentano à Francfort . . .'.

45 J. Rumpf-Fleck, *Italienische Kultur in Frankfurt am Main im 18. Jahrhundert* . . . , Petrarca-Haus, Cologne, 1936, pp. 20–2.

46 *Ibid.*, p. 38. Here again they were acting within the tradition of patronage established by the merchants of the Middle Ages. Jacques le Goff, *Marchands et banquiers du Moyen Age*, Paris, PUF, 1980, pp. 106–16.

47 M.-C. Hoock-Demarle, 'Etre Brentano à Franckfort . . .'.

48 B. Amiet and H. Sigrist, *Solothurnische Geschichte*, vol. 2, Soleure, 1976. G. von Vivis, 'Les Besenval de Brunnstatt', *Bulletin de la Société Académique religieuse et scientifique du Duché d'Aoste*, 1913, pp. 206ff.

49 E. Gothein, *Wirtschaftsgeschichte des Schwarzwaldes und der angrenzenden Landschaften*, Strasbourg, 1892, p. 740.

50 Quoted by J. Rumpf-Fleck, *Italienische Kultur* . . . , p. 24.

51 P. Guichonnet, 'L'émigration alpine . . .', p. 567.

52 P. Goubert, *Familles marchandes sous l'Ancien Régime: les Danse et les Motte, de Beauvais*, Paris, SEVPEN, 1959, p. 149.

53 C. and G. Maistre, *L'émigration marchande savoyarde aux XVIIe–XVIIIe siècles. L'exemple de Nancy-sur-Cluses*, Académie Salésienne, Annecy, 1986, pp. 161–3.

54 R. Sarti, *Long Live the Strong. A History of Rural Society in the Apennine Mountains*, The University of Massachusetts Press, Amherst, 1985, pp. 66 and 129. The same phenomenon was observed in the Ticino region where the elegant houses belonging to the émigrés contrasted strongly with those belonging to the settled population; *Stampe per via. L'incisione dei secoli XVII–XIX nel commercio ambulante dei tesini*, exhibition catalogue by Bruno Passamani, Pieve Tesino-Trento-Bassano del Grappa, 1972, Calliano, Arti grafiche R. Manfredi, 1972, p. 14.

55 P. Luès, 'L'émigration des "marchands de vins de Meymac" (Corrèze)', *Revue de Géographie alpine*, 1936, pp. 925–42 (941).

56 Departmental archives of the Hautes Alpes, 1E 7217, summary inventory carried out by honest Cecile Clot, widow of *Sieur* Barthélémy Rome from La Grave, 25 September 1688.

57 Departmental archives of the Hautes Alpes, 1E 7218, general inventory of each and every piece of furniture, gold, silver, debts, papers, deeds and documents left by the aforementioned late Claudine Liothaud, wife when alive of *Sieur* Vincent Pic, begun on the 1 December 1691 at the aforementioned location of Terrasse in La Grave. The inventories relating to merchants in Nancy-sur-Cluses examined by Chantal and Gilbert Maistre share the same features: C. and G. Maistre, *L'émigration marchande savoyarde aux XVIIe–XVIIIe siècles...*, pp. 166–7.

58 Departmental archives of the Isère, 3E 846, 9 June 1684, noted in the records of Maître Bard, Besse notary.

59 By way of comparison, see Ph. Benedict, 'Bibliothèques protestantes et catholiques à Metz au XVIIe siècle', *Annales ESC*, 2, 1985, pp. 343–70.

60 He left in a chest in Louis Aymon's house 40 books 'on our religion and on the history of the Reformed Church' and prayer books 'which hold no memories, apart from the monotony of the mass'; 'behind a beam on the wall' in the pavilion in his garden he hid another six books 'concerning our religion', and yet more in the stairways of his house.

61 Departmental archives of the Isère, 1J 1102, 'Livre de raizon a Moi Jean Giraud de Lagrave, où est contenu mais affaires emparticulier, commencé le 17 janvier 1670 à Lion' [daybook belonging to me, Jean Giraud, containing my private affairs, begun in Lyon on 17 January 1670].

62 J. Queniart, *L'imprimerie et la librairie à Rouen...*, p. 286.

63 R. Lick, 'Les intérieurs domestiques...', p. 301. For information on Lyon, see M. Garden, *Lyon et les Lyonnais au XVIIIe siècle*, Paris, 1970, p. 459. For Paris, see D. Roche, *Le peuple de Paris, essai sur la culture populaire au XVIIIe siècle*, Paris, 1981, p. 217 and illustration p. 218. For Grenoble, see G. Berger, 'Littérature et lecteurs à Grenoble aux XVIIe et XVIIIe siècles. Le public littéraire dans une capitale provinciale', *Revue d'histoire moderne et contemporaine*, 1984, pp. 114–32.

64 L. Fontaine, 'Le colporteur familier: un commerce de la sociabilité', *Bulletin du Centre d'historie économique et sociale de la région lyonnaise*, no. 3–4, 1984, pp. 85–102 (96–9).

65 Departmental archives of the Hautes Alpes, 4E 4839, 4 September 1685.

66 J. G. Fyfe (ed.), *Scottish Diaries and Memoirs. 1746–1843*, Stirling, 1942, pp. 257–88 and L. Weatherill, *Consumer Behaviour and Material Culture in Britain, 1660–1760*, Routledge, London and New York, 1988, p. 171.

67 L. Weatherill, *Consumer Behaviour...*, p. 180.

68 M. Zecchinelli, 'Arte e folclore siciliani sui monti dell'Alto Lario nei secoli XVI–XVIII', *Rivista Archeologica Comense*, 1950–1, pp. 65–119; quoted by M. Aymard in 'La Sicile, terre d'immigration', in *Les migrations dans les pays méditerranéens au XVIIIe et au début du XIXe*, Centre de la Méditerranée moderne et contemporaine, Université de Nice, 1973, pp. 149–50.

69 A. Lay, 'Libro e società negli stati sardi del Settecento', in *Libri, editori e publico nell'Europa moderna, Guida storica e critica* a cura di A. Petrucci, Roma-Bari, 1977, pp. 249–82 (268).

70 Departmental archives of the Isère, 27/j 3/46, Sermons by the Abbé Col.

71 Departmental archives of the Isère, 4U 321, the trial of Auguste Bellet, 1862.

72 R. Darnton, 'Un colporteur sous l'Ancien Régime', *Censures, de la Bible aux larmes d'Eros*, Centre Georges Pompidou, Paris, 1987, pp. 130–9 (134).

73 Departmental archives of the Rhône, 3E 4781B, 15 May 1656.

74 French National Archives, MC, et/LXXXVI/213, 7 December 1610.

75 C. and G. Maistre, *L'émigration marchande savoyarde aux XVIIe–XVIIIe siècles . . .*, p. 167.

76 A. Poitrineau, 'Petits marchands colporteurs de la haute Planèze d'Auvergne à la fin de l'Ancien Régime', *Annales du Midi*, vol. 88, 1976, pp. 423–36 (426).

77 Departmental archives of the Hautes Alpes, 1E 4839, contract of apprenticeship between Pierre Baille, son of Jean, on behalf of his son Jean, and *sieur* Laurent Eytre of Hières, 10 July 1684.

78 Departmental archives of the Hautes Alpes, 1E 3839, 2 October 1685.

79 G. Vigarello, *Le Propre et le Sale, l'hygiène du corps depuis le Moyen Age*, Paris, 1985, p. 82. The author demonstrates (pp. 68–89) that the word 'clean' changed its connotations during the course of the seventeenth century; cleanliness became a criteria of social distinction, and the whiteness of one's shirt a fundamental indication of this.

80 A. Poitrineau, *Les 'Espagnols' . . .*, p. 99.

81 M. Nadaud, *Mémoires de Léonard ancien garçon maçon*, text edited and with notes by M. Agulhon, Paris, Hachette, 1977, pp. 118–19.

82 A. Poitrineau, 'Aspects de l'émigration . . .', p. 42.

83 I. E. Fietta, 'Con la cassetta in spalla: gli ambulanti di Tesino', *Quaderni di cultura alpina*, no. 23, 1985, pp. 4–111 (100–1).

84 L. Fontaine, *Le Voyage et la Mémoire, colporteurs de l'Oisans au XIXe siècle*, Presses Universitaires de Lyon, 1984, p. 193. Martin Nadaud also talks of how the Auvergne emigrants stopped wearing drugget: M. Nadaud, *Mémoires de Léonard . . .*, pp. 118–19.

85 P. Guichonnet, 'L'émigration alpine . . .', p. 564.

86 J. Perrel, 'L'émigration bas-limousine en Espagne aux XVIIe et XVIIIe siècles', *Actes du 88e Congrès national des Sociétés Savantes, section d'histoire moderne et contemporaine, Clermont-Ferrand, 1963*, Paris, 1964, pp. 709–29 (717–21).

Chapter 9 A Civilized Business?

1 M. de Certeau, *L'Invention du quotidien*, Paris, 1974 (*The Practice of Everyday Life*, translated by Steven Rendall, University of California Press, 1985). Hogarth, *La culture du pauvre*, Paris, 1976. P. Bourdieu, *La Distinction, critique sociale du jugement*, Paris, 1979.

2 P. Mantoux, *The Industrial Revolution in the Eighteenth Century*, quoted by V. E. Neuberg in *Popular Education . . .*, pp. 122–3.

3 E. Gothein, *Wirtschaftsgeschichte des Schwarzwaldes und der angrenzenden Landschaften*, Strasbourg, 1892, p. 432.

4 Quoted by A. Poitrineau, *Les 'Espagnols' de l'Auvergne et du Limousin du XVIIe au XIXe siècle*, Aurillac, Mazel-Malroux, 1985, p. 36.

5 C. Douais, Letters from Charles IX to M. de Fourquevaux, the ambassador to Spain, 1565–72, Paris, 1897, p. 263, quoted by A. Poitrineau, *Les 'Espagnols' . . .*, p. 27.

6 Departmental Archives of the Isère, 3E 846, 9 June 1684, from the records of Maître Bard, a notary of Besse.

7 Departmental archives of the Isère, 3E 846, 5 April 1684 from the records of Maître Bard, notary of Besse. See also the inventory of Joseph Ducret, a Savoyard in Barr, in Ch. Wolff, 'Un type de marchands sous Louis XIV: Les Savoyards de Barr', *Annuaire de la Société d'histoire et d'archéologie de Dambach-la-Ville*, Barr, Obernai, vol. 3, 1969, pp. 122–7 (125).

8 There are examples for seventeenth-century England in M. Spufford, *The Great Reclothing of Rural England, Petty Chapmen and their Wares in the Seventeenth Century*, London, The Hambledon Press, 1984, pp. 85–106. The author notes how accurate the description of Autolycus' pack is. For France, A. Poitrineau has published an inventory of the pack belonging to a Dauphiné pedlar in 1623, 'Petits marchands colporteurs de la haute Planèze d'Auvergne à la fin de l'Ancien Régime, *Annales du Midi*, vol. 88, 1976, pp. 423–36 (311).

9 M. Vernus, 'La diffusion du petit livre de piété et de la bimbeloterie religieuse dans le Jura (au XVIIIe siècle)', *Actes du 105e Congrès national des Sociétés savantes, Caen, 1980*, Paris, 1983, pp. 135–6.

10 D. Albera, M. Dossetti, S. Ottonelli, 'Società' ed emigrazioni nell'alta valle Varaita in eta moderna', *Bollettino storico-bibliografico subalpino*, LXXXVI, 1988, 1, pp. 117–69 (135).

11 A. Sauvy, 'Noël Gille dit La Pistole, marchand forain libraire roulant par la France', *Bulletin des bibliothèques de France*, May, 1967, pp. 177–90 (184).

12 J. Lesueur, 'Une figure populaire en Lorraine au siècle dernier, le colporteur ou chamagnon', *Bulletin de la Société lorraine des Etudes locales de l'enseignement public*, 1969, 3, pp. 29–39 (34).

13 T. Endelman, 'L'activité économique des juifs anglais', *Dix-huitième siècle*, no. 13, 1981, pp. 113–26 (121–2).

14 Letter from Augustin Jauriac to his sister, written from Mexico on 23 August 1852; R. Duroux, 'Monographie d'une famille d'"Espagnols". La Saga des Ratié', *Revue d'Auvergne*, vol. 99, no. 3, 1985, pp. 271–310 (282).

15 J. Feather, *The Provincial Book Trade in Eighteenth-Century England*, Cambridge University Press, 1985, p. 83; and V. E. Neuberg, *Popular Literature, a History and Guide from the Beginning of Printing to the Year 1897*, London, 1977, p. 113.

16 A. Sauvy, 'Le livre aux champs', *Histoire de l'Edition française*, vol. 2, Paris, 1984, pp. 430–43 (431), for example, reveals that the pedlar was not the only one to sell books in the countryside.

17 T. Endelman, 'L'activité . . .', p. 121–2.

18 See, for example, the account book belonging to the pedlar Pierre Rullier from Le Chatelard in the Tarentaise (Savoy), who in the 1770s supplied numerous businesses in northern and eastern France with watches, gold chains, clocks, snuffboxes etc. He himself obtained the goods by mail order from Geneva and London, and received the Genevan merchandise through another Savoyard who had a business in Dijon. Paris archives, D5 B6 3611.

19 L. Weatherill, *Consumer Behaviour and Material Culture in Britain, 1660–1760*, Routledge, London and New York, 1988 p. 3 and appendix 1, pp. 206–7.

NOTES TO PAGES 187–189

20 M. Spufford, *The Great Reclothing* ...; J. Thirsk, *Economic Policy and Projects: the Development of a Consumer Society in Early Modern England*, Oxford, 1978; N. McKendrick, J. Brewer and J. H. Plumb, *The Birth of Consumer Society. The Commercialization of Eighteenth Century England*, Bloomington, Indiana University Press, 1982. For a discussion of the concepts, see J. Styles, 'Manufacturing, Consumption and Design in Eighteenth-Century England' in *Consumption and the World of Goods*, J. Brewer and R. Porter, eds, Routledge, London and New York, 1993, pp. 527–54.
21 L. Weatherill, *Consumer Behaviour* ..., pp. 192–3.
22 L. Weatherill, *Consumer Behaviour* ...; see pp. 43–61 for an analysis of regional contrasts.
23 L. Weatherill, *Consumer Behaviour* ..., p. 77.

Table 6 **Frequency (in %) of certain goods in a sample of English inventories, 1675–1725**

	Books	Watches	Painting	Spectacles	Curtains
London	31	29	41	77	43
Large towns	21	18	41	58	27
Medium-sized towns	23	20	23	50	15
Villages and rural areas	17	17	5	21	6

Source: L. Weatherill, *Consumer Behaviour* ..., p. 76. For a discussion of the sample chosen, see chapter 1 and appendix 1 of *Consumer Behaviour*. ... There were only 40 or 50 towns in England with a population of between 2,000 and 5,000 inhabitants; 24 towns had a population of above 5,000 and 7 towns had more than 10,000 inhabitants. London dominated the urban network with around 500,000 inhabitants in 1700 (which was 19 times more than Norwich, the second largest town in the country); one tenth of the population of England was concentrated in London (pp. 72–3, ibid.).

24 L. Weatherill, *Consumer Behaviour* ..., p. 52.
25 L. Weatherill, *Consumer Behaviour* ..., p. 79.
26 M. Vernus, 'La diffusion du petit livre de piété et de la bimbeloterie religieuse dans le Jura (au XVIIIe siècle)', *Actes du 105e Congrès national des Sociétés savantes, Caen, 1980*, Paris, 1983, pp. 127–41.
27 L. Weatherill, *Consumer Behaviour* ..., p. 169. See table 8.2 on the ownership of goods according to status (1675–1725), p. 184; as far as crockery and receptacles used for the new beverages were concerned, the merchant classes were well ahead of the gentry and the artisan classes, despite the fact that members of the gentry had been amongst the first to introduce such things. The merchants were on equal footing with the gentry where paintings, spectacles, table linen, curtains, and knives and forks were concerned. On the other hand, they had fewer books and watches than the gentry. See pp. 184–5 and 194–6.
28 T. Wijsenbeek, *Achter de gevels van Delft*, Hilversum, 1987.
29 M. Spufford, *The Great Reclothing* ..., pp. 107–46.
30 L. Weatherill, *Consumer Behaviour* ..., pp. 25–42.

31 L. Weatherill, *The Growth of the Pottery Industry in England 1660–1815*, New York and London, 1986, p. 121.
32 L. Weatherill, *Consumer Behaviour* . . . , table on p. 108.
33 M. Baulant and S. Bari, 'Du fil à l'armoire, production et consommation du linge à Meaux et dans ses campagnes 17e–18e siècle', *Ethnologie française*, vol. 16, 1986, pp. 273–80 (273).
34 *Ibid.*, p. 274, note 7.
35 S. Tardieu, *La Vie domestique dans le Mâconnais rural préindustriel*, Travaux et Mémoires de l'Institut d'Ethnologie, Paris, 1964; the author notes the same increase in the numbers of sheets and shirts.
36 Analysed by century, S. Tardieu, *La Vie domestique* . . . , pp. 167–76 describes in five sections the different furniture inventoried in terms of the material from which it was constructed.
37 M. Spufford, *Small Books and Pleasant Histories. Popular Fiction and its Readership in Seventeenth-Century England*, London, Methuen, 1981.
38 C. Blagden, 'The distribution of Almanacs in the second half of the seventeenth century' in *Papers of the Bibliographical Society of the University of Virginia*, vol. II, 1958. In the author's opinion, Bosanquet's estimations – which he considers relate only to the decade 1663–73 – should be multiplied by 10.
39 G. Duval, *Littérature de colportage et imaginaire collectif en Angleterre à l'époque des Dicey (1720–1800)* (doctoral thesis, University of Dijon, 1986, pp. 711–2. For an analysis of the subject, see pp. 714–52), Bordeaux, Presses Universitaires de Bordeaux, 1991.
40 J. Queniart, *Cultures et sociétés urbaines dans la France de l'Ouest au XVIIIe siècle*, Paris, Klincksieck, 1978, pp. 384–5. In 1749, Oursel from Rouen supplied the Chalopin bookshop in Caen with 1,035 books of this type for the sum of 161 *livres tournois* (p. 385).
41 R. Moulinas, *L'Imprimerie, la Librairie et la Presse à Avignon au XVIIIe siècle*, Grenoble, Presses Universitaires de Grenoble, 1974, p. 148, note 73.
42 J. Queniart, *Culture et sociétés urbaines* . . . , pp. 399–400.
43 J. Queniart, *Culture et sociétés urbaines* . . . , p. 385.
44 J.-J. Darmon, *Le Colportage de librairie en France sous le Second Empire*, Paris, 1972, pp. 84–90.
45 D. Lerch, *Imagerie et Société. L'Imagerie Wentzel de Wissembourg au XIXe siècle*, Strasbourg, Librairie Istra, 1982, pp. 104–6 and 250.
46 Dr R. Hélot, *Notes sur l'imagerie populaire en Normandie*, Lille, 1908, p. 5, quoted by D. Lerch in *Imagerie et Société* . . . , p. 252.
47 E. Zola, *Germinal*, part 1, chapter 2.
48 *Ibid.*, part 2, chapter 3.
49 J. Marco, *Literatura popular en España en los siglos XVIII y XIX. Una aproximación a los pliegos de cordel*, Madrid, Taurus, 1977.
50 J.-F. Botrel, 'Les aveugles colporteurs d'imprimés en Espagne', *Mélanges de la casa de Vélasquez*, 9, 1973, pp. 417–82; and 10, 1974, pp. 233–71 and pp. 247–8.
51 J. Marco, *Literatura popular.* . . . , p. 146.
52 'Los pobres y ciegos y mujeres . . . que de tiempo inmemorial tuvieron sus puestos arrimados a la tapia de Correos de la Puerta del sol para dar a leer Gacetas a aquellas personas que por sus pocos posibles no puedan comprarlas', quoted by J.-F. Botrel, 'Les aveugles colporteurs . . .', p. 285.

53 J. de Vries, 'Peasant Demand Patterns and Economic Development in Friesland, 1550–1750', *European Peasants and their Markets*, W. N. Parker and E. L. Jones (eds), Princeton, 1975, pp. 205–68 (221) and tables 6.8, 6.9 and 6.10. The study was carried out from 512 inventories.

54 D. Roche, *Le Peuple de Paris*, Paris, 1981, p. 226.

55 R. Lick, 'Les intérieurs domestiques dans la seconde moitié du XVIIIe siècle, d'après les inventaires après décès de Coutances', *Annales de Normandie*, no. 4, 1970, pp. 293–316 (308).

56 M. Vernus, 'La diffusion du petit livre de piété et de la bimbeloterie religieuse dans le Jura (au XVIIIe siècle)', *Actes du 105e Congrès national des Sociétés savantes, Caen, 1980*, Paris, 1983, pp. 127–41.

57 F. Bayard, 'Au coeur de l'intime: les poches des cadavres. Lyon, Lyonnais, Beaujolais (XVIIe–XVIIIe siècles)', *Bulletin du Centre d'histoire économique et sociale de la région lyonnaise*, no. 2, 1989, pp. 5–41.

58 F. Bayard, 'Au coeur de l'intime . . .', p. 21.

59 L. Steub, *Wanderungen im bayerischen Gebirge*, Munich, 1862, p. 171; and *Drei Sommer in Tyrol*, Munich, 1895, vol. 1, p. 10, quoted by D. Lerch, *Imagerie et Société . . .*, p. 212.

60 D. Lerch, *Imagerie et Société . . .*, pp. 212–3.

61 D. Lerch (*Imagerie et Société . . .*, p. 216) has drawn a map of the commercial territory.

62 D. Lerch, *Imagerie et Société . . .*, pp. 179–81 and 263.

63 Who had the same policy of diversifying their goods depending on the country they were selling to. I. E. Fietta, 'Con la cassetta in spalla: gli ambulanti di Tessino', *Quaderni di cultura alpina*, no. 23, 1985, pp. 4–111 (19).

64 D. Lerch, *Imagerie et Société . . .*, p. 171.

65 R. Schenda, *Folklore e letteratura popolare: Italia–Germania–Francia*. Translated from the German by Maria Chiara Figliozzi and Ingeborg Walter, Bibliotheca Biographica, Istituto della Enciclopedia Italiana fondata da Giovanni Treccani, Rome, 1986, pp. 467–9.

66 *Stampe per via. L'incisione dei secoli XVII–XIX nel commercio ambulante dei tesini*, exhibition catalogue by B. Passamani, Pieve Tesino-Trento-Bassano del Grappa, 1972, Calliano, Arti grafiche R. Manfredi, 1972, p. 34.

67 J.-P. Seguin, 'Les occasionnels au XVIIIe siècle et en particulier après l'apparition de La Gazette. Une source d'information pour l'histoire des mentalités et de la littérature "populaire"', *L'Informazione in Francia nel Seicento, Quaderni del Seicento francese*, 5, Bari, Adriatica and Paris, Nizet, 1983, pp. 33–59.

68 J.-P. Seguin believes that they composed a number of texts: *L'information en France avant le périodique. 517 canards imprimés entre 1529 et 1631*, Maissoneuve et Larose, Paris, 1964, p. 16.

69 G. B. Martinelli, *Origine e sviluppo dell actività dei librai pontremolesi*, Pontremoli, sup. Artigianelli, pp. 17–18.

70 J. Lesueur, 'Une figure populaire en Lorraine au siècle dernier, le colporteur ou chamagnon', *Bulletin de la Société lorraine des Etudes locales de l'enseignement public*, 1969, 3, pp. 29–39 (34).

71 Don Julio Nombela y Tabares, quoted by J. Caro Bajora, *Ensayo sobre la literatura de cordel*, Revista de occidente, Madrid, 1969, pp. 55–6, which also cites the few well-known blind poets.

72 L.-S. Mercier, *Tableaux de Paris*, new corrected and expanded edition, Amsterdam, 1783, vol. 6, chapter CCCCLXIII, p. 37.

73 R. Reichardt and H. Schneider, 'Chanson et musique populaires devant l'histoire à la fin de l'Ancien régime', *Dix-huitième siècle*, no. 18, 1986, pp. 117–36.

74 P. Manuel, *La Police de Paris dévoilée*, Paris, Year II, 2nd vol, part 1, pp. 66–7, quoted by D. Roche, *Le Peuple de Paris*, Paris 1981, p. 228.

75 N. Elias, *La Civilisation des Moeurs* (1st edition, in German 1939), Paris, 1973, pp. 204–17.

76 A. Franklin, *Les Magasins de Nouveautés, La vie privée d'autrefois, arts et métiers: mode, moeurs, usages des parisiens du XIIe au XVIIIe siècle, d'après des documents originaux ou inédits*, Paris, 1898, vol. 4, p. 26.

77 Monteil, quoted by N. Elias in *La Civilisation des Moeurs*, p. 208.

78 Nicole Pellegrin, *Les Vêtements de la liberté, Abécédaire des pratiques vestimentaires françaises de 1780 à 1800*, Editions Alinea, Aix-en-Provence, 1989.

79 A. Poitrineau, 'Petits marchands colporteurs . . .', pp. 428–9.

80 M. Spufford, *The Great Reclothing . . .*, pp. 103–4.

81 *Les Lois de la galanterie*, p. 83, quoted by A. Franklin in *Les Magasins . . .*, p. 114.

82 Tallemant des Réaux, *op. cit.*, vol. III, p. 31 and vol. I, p. 493, quoted by A. Franklin in *Les Magasins . . .*, pp. 114–16.

83 Molière, *Tartuffe*, 1664.

84 'Be very careful not to blow your nose with your fingers or on your sleeve as children do, but use your handkerchief and do not look into it after you have finished': extract from *Civilité française*, an anonymous work, Liège, 1714, p. 41, quoted by N. Elias in *La Civilisation des Moeurs*, p. 209. Exactly the same text appears in *La Civilité puérile et honneste*, drawn up by a missionary in 1749; and Jean Baptiste de la Salle's 1782 edition of *Les Règles de la bienséance et de la civilité chrétienne* reminds us that 'it is unattractive to wipe one's nose with one's bare hand by rubbing it under the nose, or blow one's nose on one's sleeve or in one's clothes', quoted by A. Franklin, *Les Magasins . . .*, pp. 117–8.

85 There are examples of this in A. Franklin, *Les Magasins . . .*, pp. 71–2.

86 M. Spufford, *The Great Reclothing . . .*, p. 103.

87 A. Franklin, *Les Magasins . . .*, pp. 126–30.

88 S. Tardieu, *La vie domestique . . .*, pp. 267, 450–2.

89 M. Baulant and S. Bari, 'Du fil à l'armoire . . .', p. 273.

90 F. Bayard, 'Au coeur de l'intime . . .', p. 22.

91 Joseph Roth, *La Crypte des capucins*, p. 24.

92 M. Baulant and S. Bari, 'Du fil à l'armoire . . .', p. 277.

93 D. Roche, 'L'invention du linge au XVIIIe siècle', *Ethnologie Française*, vol. 16, no. 3, 1986, pp. 227–38 (228–9); M. Baulant and S. Bari, 'Du fil à l'armoire . . .', p. 274, note 6, and p. 278.

94 H. Best, *Rural Economy in Yorkshire in 1641, being the Farming and Account Books of Henry Best of Elmeswell in the East Riding*, C. B. Robinson (ed.), Surtees Society XXXIII, 1857, pp. 105–6, quoted by M. Spufford in *The Great Reclothing . . .*, p. 107, note 1.

95 I was given this information by Daniel Roche, whom I should like to thank. See D. Roche, *La culture des apparences. Une histoire du vêtement XVIIe–XVIIIe siècle*, Paris, 1989.

96 Hence the significance of the gesture of dropping one's handkerchief, which Voltaire mocked when Candide rushed forward to pick up the handkerchief belonging to Cunégonde.

97 At the beginning of the twentieth century in Sicily it was still a gift symbolizing love, as Luchino Visconti shows in *La Terra Trema*.

Index

Bold entries denote major section/chapter devoted to subject.